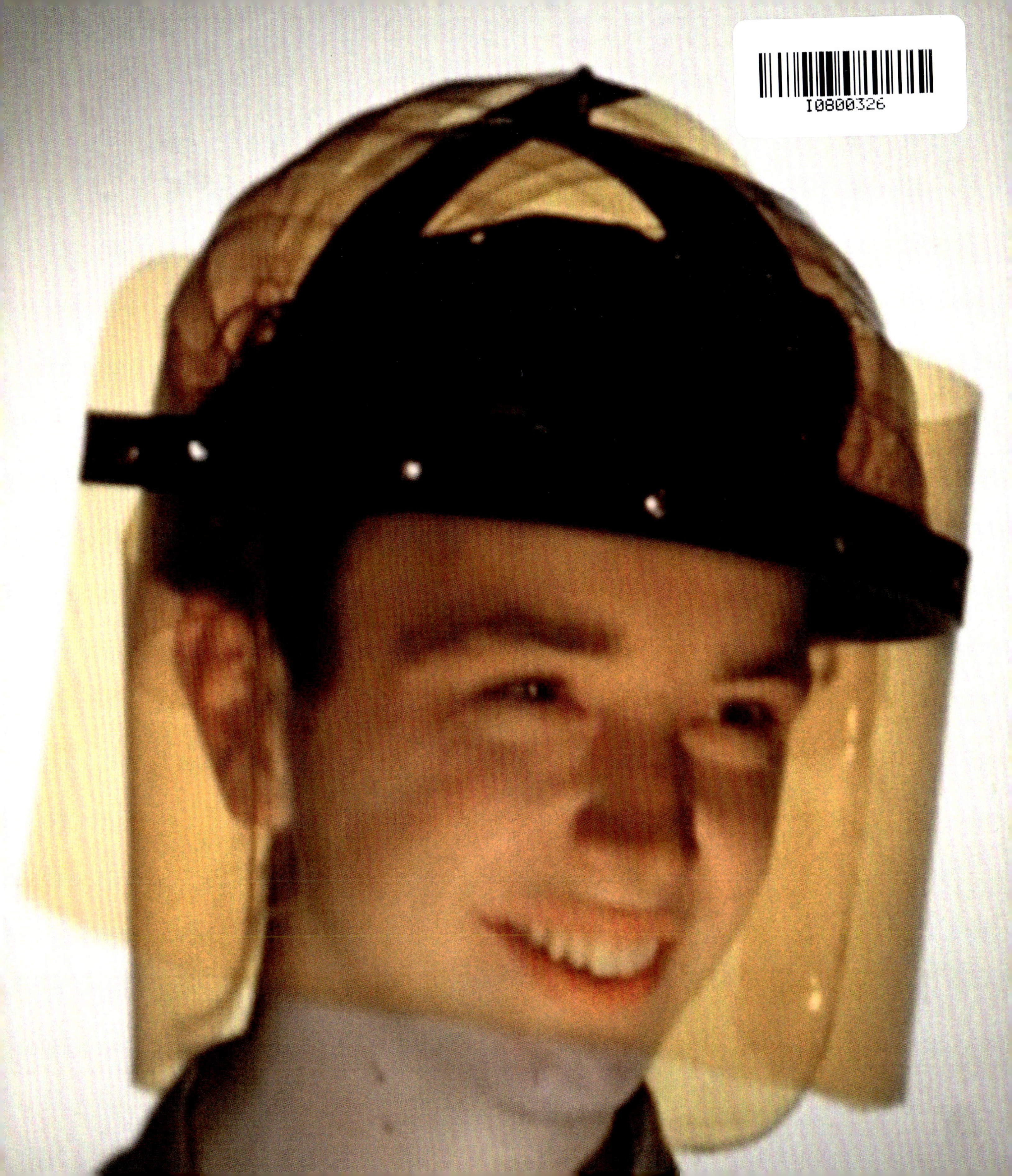

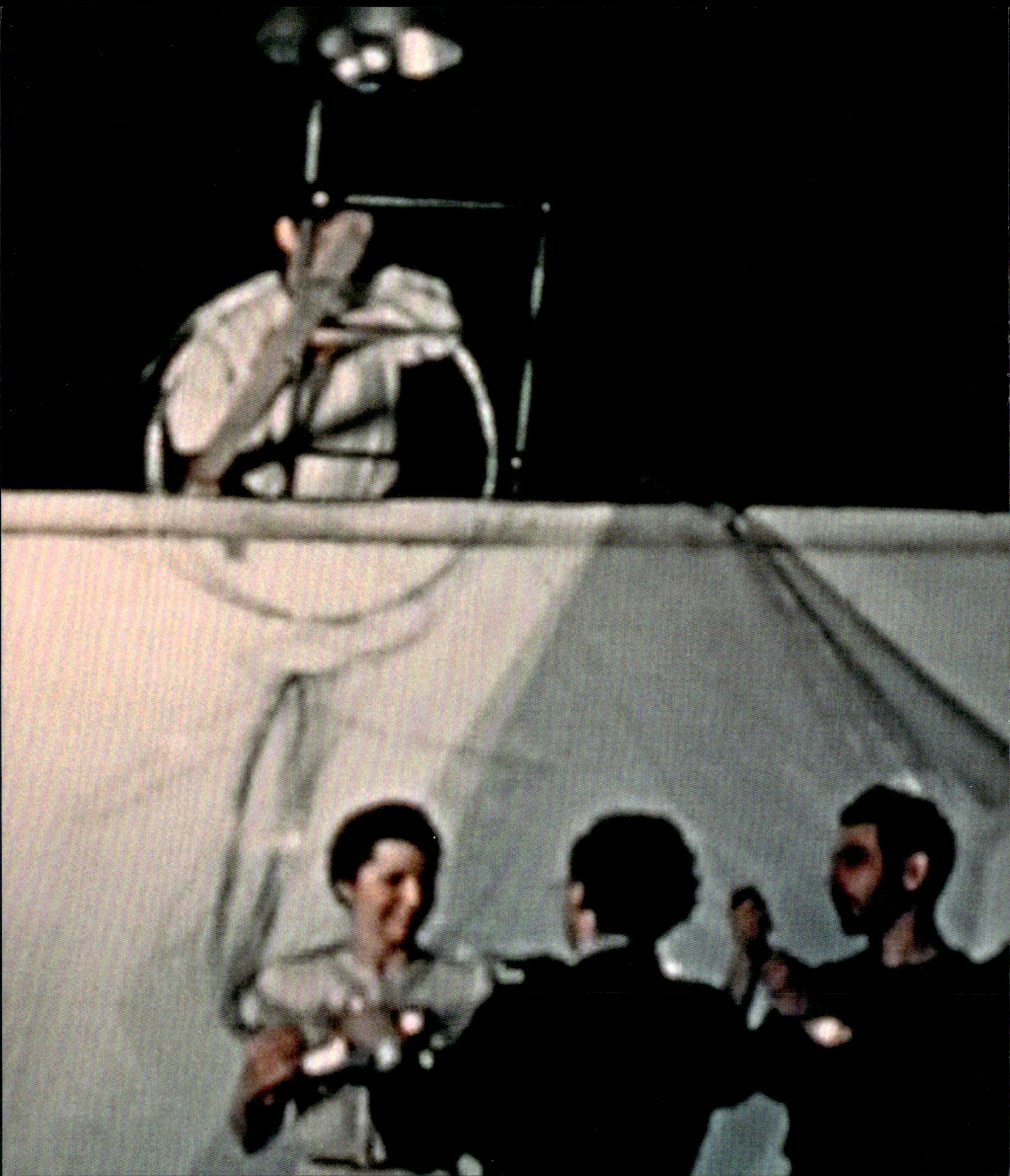

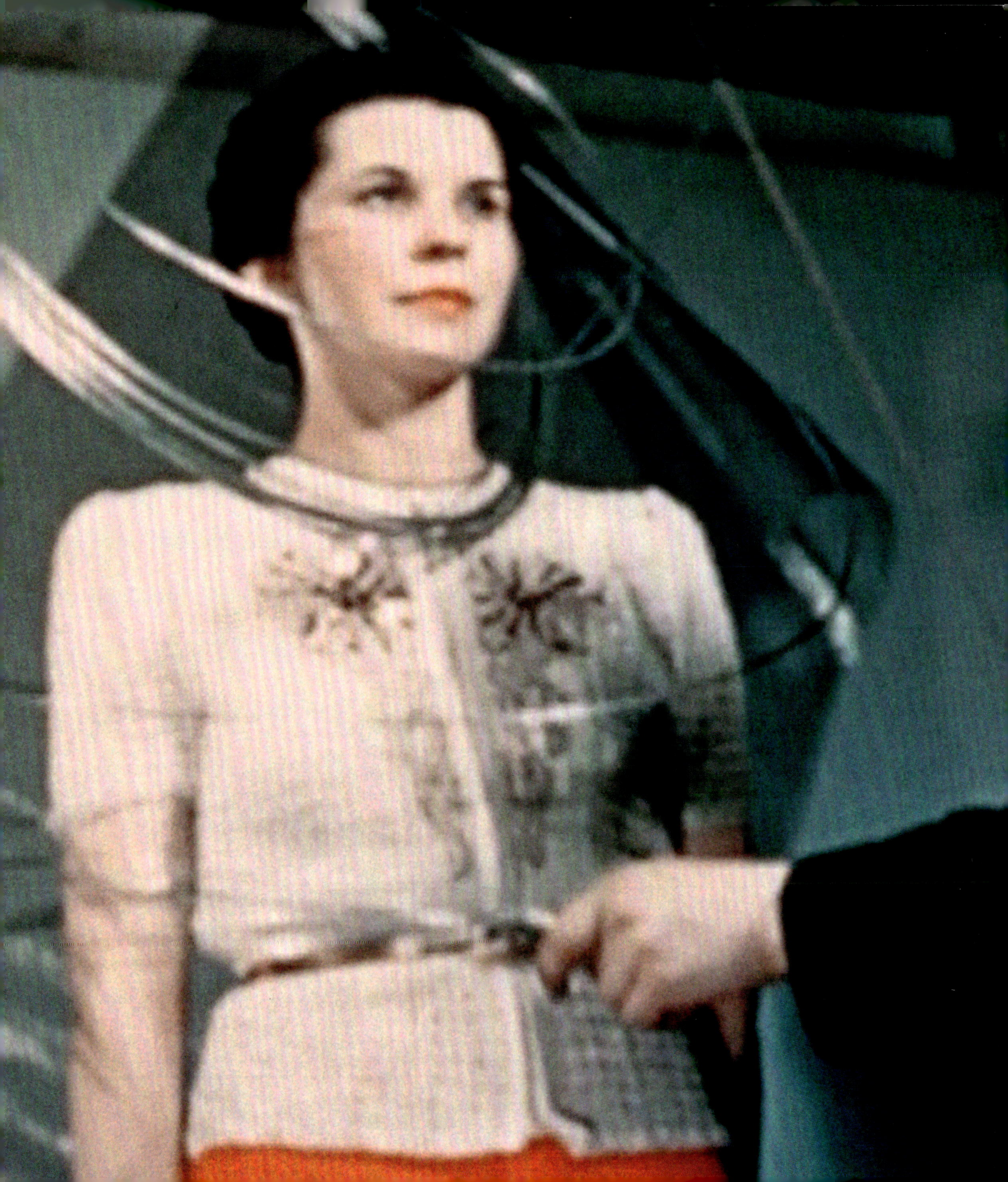

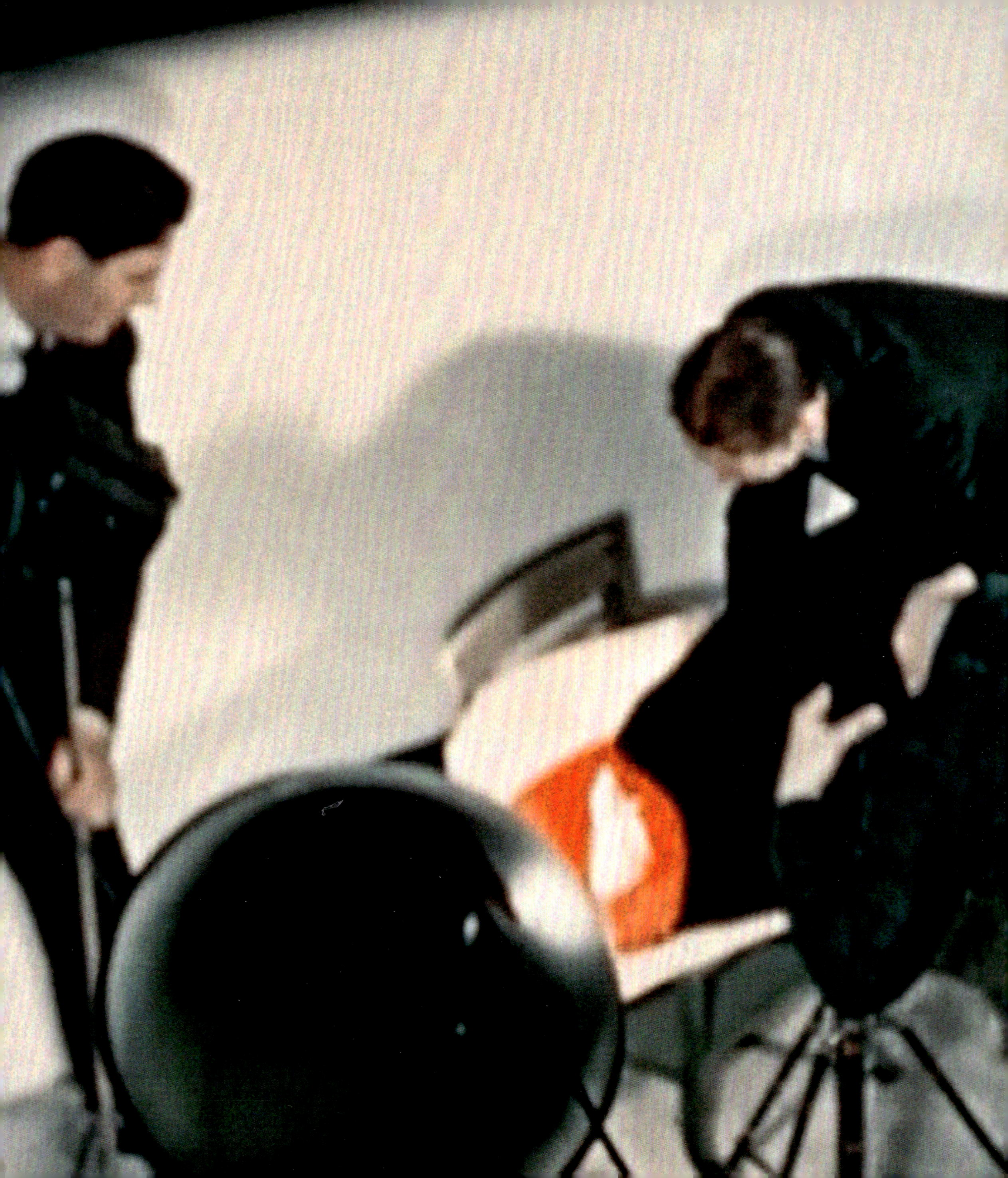

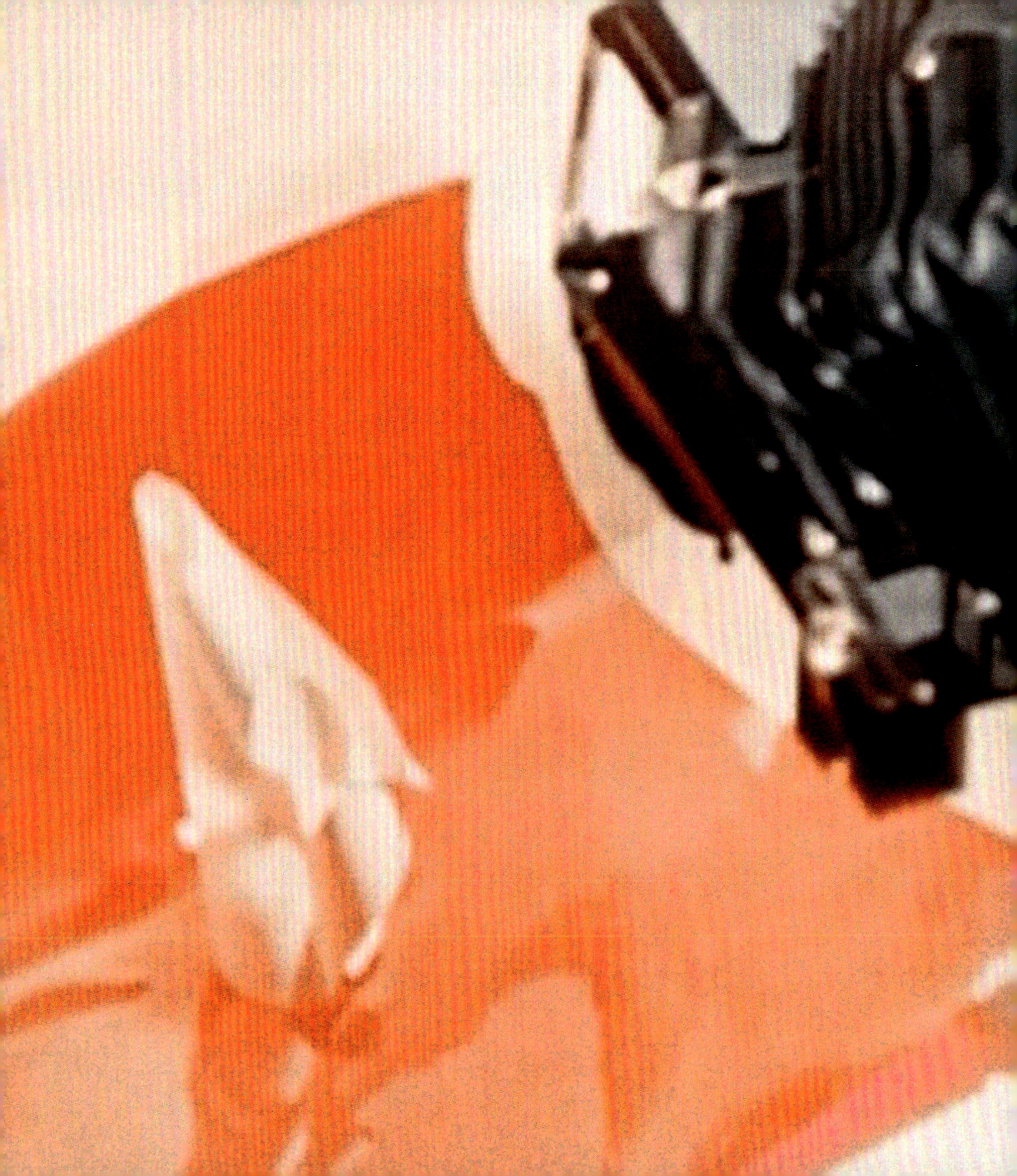

(→ 1–5)
László Moholy-Nagy with students of the ID
Design Workshops, 1944
images from the digitized film

New Bauhaus Chicago

EXPERIMENT

Photography

edited by Kristina Lowis for the
Bauhaus-Archiv / Museum für Gestaltung
Berlin

bauhaus-archiv
museum für gestaltung

HIRMER

CONTENTS

Contents

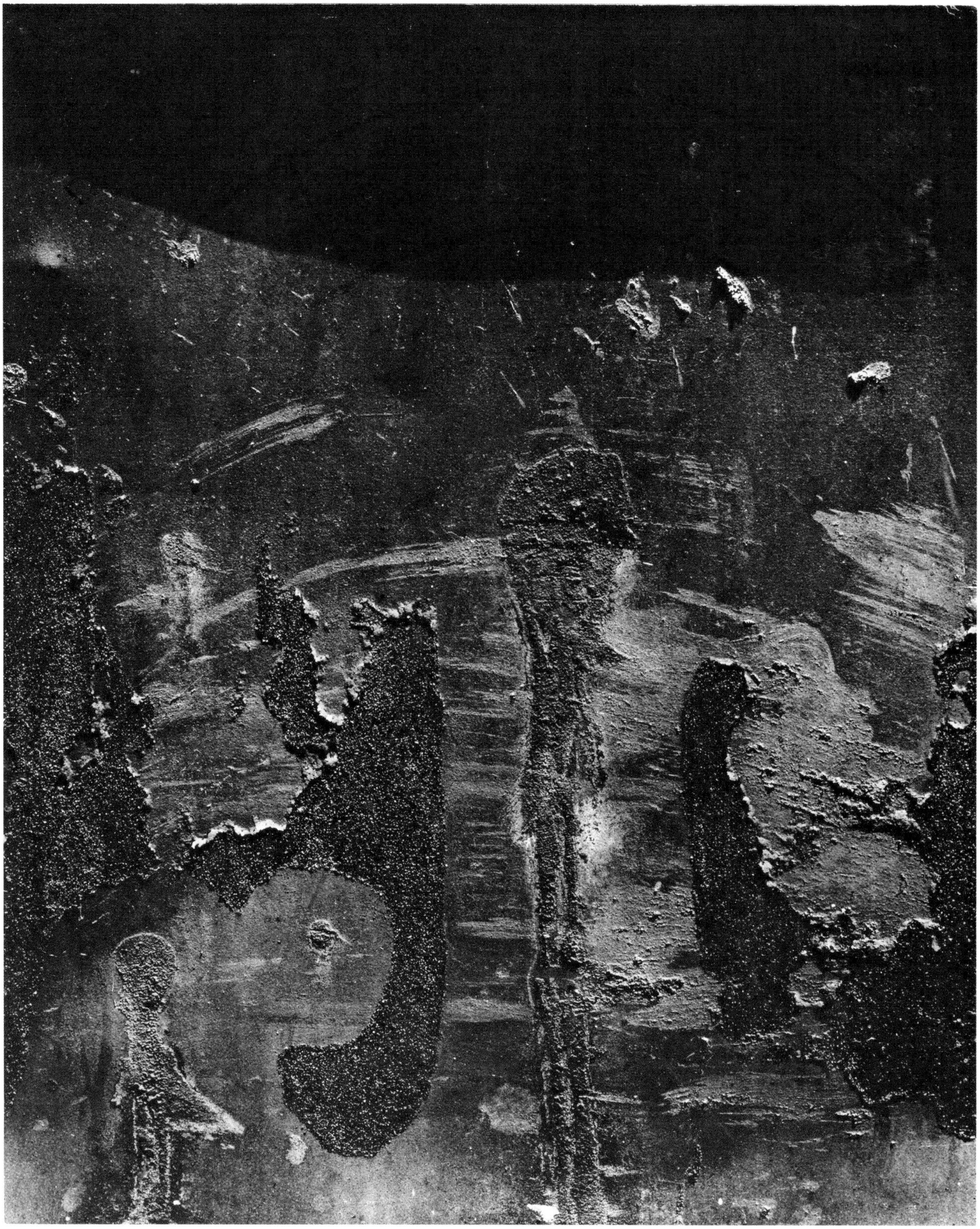

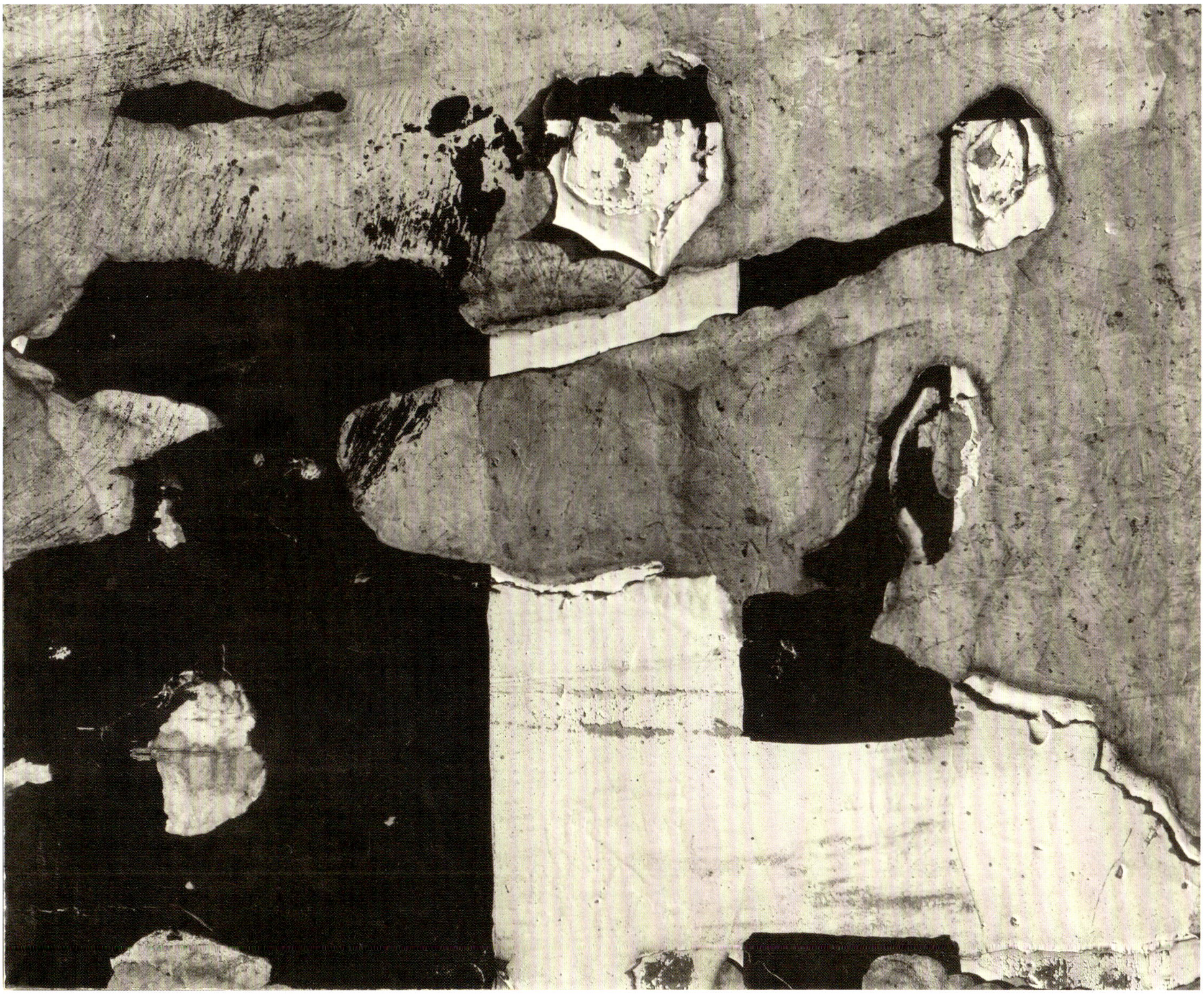

Aaron Siskind
Untitled, 1947
gelatin silver, 41.5 x 34.1 cm

Aaron Siskind
Untitled, 1952
gelatin silver, 33.5 x 41.7 cm

FOREWORDS

In 1937, when László Moholy-Nagy assumed responsibility for the refounded New Bauhaus in Chicago, he based his teaching on the proven practice of the Bauhaus in Weimar and Dessau. It was not just the preliminary course and workshop principle as well as the idea of experimentation that found their way into the curriculum in Chicago: Moholy-Nagy also provided these maxims with a space of their own. This is how the Light Workshop emerged: a center for the forging of experimental photography and multimedia design, which still plays a defining role today in the international standing of the Institute of Design that grew out of the New Bauhaus in Illinois.

This exhibition opens up an extensive view onto the experimental field of photography and film and presents the seminal influence of the Chicago photo school on subsequent generations of artists. The exhibition project showcases not just historical positions of representatives of the New Bauhaus Chicago—from László Moholy-Nagy, a multimedia artist *avant la lettre*, to Barbara Crane, Charles Swedlund, and Joe Jachna—but also selected works from young artists like Sonja Thomsen in unprecedented abundance.

The exhibition *New Bauhaus Chicago: Experiment Photography and Film* forms the Berlin prologue to the Bauhaus's centennial celebration in 2019. In Berlin, Dessau, Weimar and beyond, the German Federal Cultural Foundation is providing support for numerous initiatives testifying to the extraordinary influence the Bauhaus has had and still continues to have today on how we practice design and how we think about photography, art, architecture, and urban planning. The German Federal Cultural Foundation thanks Dr. Annemarie Jaeggi, Director of the Bauhaus Archiv/Museum für Gestaltung, and the curators Dr. Kristina Lowis and Dr. Sibylle Hoiman as well as everyone else involved in this project for realizing an exhibition that impressively demonstrates how the ideas and methods of the Bauhaus—old and new—set an example for the design of the world.

Hortensia Völckers
Executive Board/Artistic Director
German Federal Cultural Foundation

Alexander Farenholtz
Executive Board/Administrative Director
German Federal Cultural Foundation

Bauhaus: For many enthusiasts of art and culture, merely mentioning this word opens up a broad panorama of images, names, and links leading to the present. This is also true in my case. The first keywords that occur to me are Weimar, Dessau, functionalism, design revolution, Wagenfeld, and Gropius.

Berlin—the city where the Bauhaus-Archiv, which features the largest holdings of Bauhaus art, is now located—played only a relatively small role in the history of the Bauhaus. After Weimar and Dessau, Berlin became the home of the avant-garde school from 1932 to 1933: until the Nazis forced it to close.

Lászlo Moholy-Nagy, the man who added the art of photography to the Bauhaus canon, was among those who had to emigrate. He understood light in terms of an independent working material, thus seeing to it that photography could achieve its breakthrough at the Bauhaus. Moholy-Nagy then carried on the Bauhaus concept in Chicago as the New Bauhaus.

This was very fortunate, because the importance of the New Bauhaus in Chicago was so great that it has resonated far into the contemporary period. It is a pleasure and a privilege to have this exhibition here to enrich Berlin and show us a facet of the Bauhaus's creativity that can still provide inspiration to Berlin's wide-ranging art scene today.

This exhibition begins the festivities marking the 100th anniversary of the Bauhaus in 2019. The state of Berlin's Senate Department for Culture and Europe was very pleased to advance and support the exhibition.

Klaus Lederer
Senator for Culture and Europe
State of Berlin

FOREWORD

On the occasion of the 80th anniversary of the New Bauhaus in Chicago, the Bauhaus-Archiv/Museum für Gestaltung is looking at the circumstances under which the methods and training developed at the Bauhaus were adopted and adapted in the US. The Bauhaus-Archiv's rich collection, which encompasses a substantial portion of the legacy left behind by both the Bauhaus as well as the New Bauhaus has provided the material basis for this project. The holdings were established under its first director, Hans Maria Wingler. A team gathered around his successor, Peter Hahn, and Lloyd C. Engelbrecht carried out extensive research that culminated in a 1987 exhibition and its accompanying catalogue. For the first time ever outside the US, they examined the activities and influence (covering the period from its founding in 1937 to 1951) of what was presumably the Bauhaus's most important institutional successor. The catalogue is to be seen as a standard work on this topic.

By contrast, the present exhibition concentrates on photography at the New Bauhaus and extends all the way to the present. There is probably no other discipline that displays the school's great potential based on its experimental approach as clearly as the Light Workshop and the photography department that emerged from it. Photographs form the focus of our archive's collection related to the New Bauhaus, which is

Annemarie Jaeggi

among the largest and most important outside the US. This is not least due to the numerous generous gifts received from New Bauhaus teachers and students that still continue to reach us today: We consider ourselves extremely fortunate for the new materials that Charles Swedlund, Joseph D. Jachna's widow Virginia Jachna, and Else Tholstrup have donated to us in preparation for this exhibition. Nathan Lerner's widow Kiyoko Lerner had already repeatedly and generously provided us with groups of his photographs. They all deserve our great gratitude, as do Stephen Daiter and Agathe Cancellieri, who have established numerous contacts for us in Chicago. The Stephen Daiter Gallery, the Museum of Contemporary Photography at Columbia College Chicago, the archive of the Paul V. Galvin Library at the Illinois Institute of Technology, the Chicago History Museum, the Chicago Film Archives, the archive of the Richard J. Daley Library at the University of Illinois at Chicago and the Bauhaus Chicago Foundation—in the person of Paul T. Young, whom we owe our sincere gratitude for his extraordinary dedication—and as well as the Art Institute of Chicago and the Kunstbibliothek Berlin have provided us with important loans that ideally complement our own holdings. We warmly thank everyone who has lent us works for the faith they have placed in us! The Goethe-Institut's focused support additionally enabled us to carry out extensive research into contemporary photographers working in Chicago, who have also placed their work at our disposal for the exhibition.

Without the financial support generously provided by Berlin's Senate Department for Culture and Europe and by Germany's Federal Cultural Foundation in connection with the 100th anniversary of the Bauhaus's founding, this ambitious project would have been impossible. I would like to express my special gratitude for this.

Kristina Lowis, a proven expert in the history of photography and guest curator at the Bauhaus-Archiv, designed the concept for both the exhibition and the catalogue. She developed them with consistency and dedication and realized this project together with Sibylle Hoiman, collection curator at our museum. I extend my heartfelt thanks to them for their excellent work. gewerkdesign was responsible for designing the exhibition and catalogue; we thank Birgit Schlegel, Jens Imig, Bianca Mohr and Marie Uhle for their trustful and creative collaboration. Michael Wetzel and Sonja Knecht have taken care of the translations in their accustomed manner and done outstanding work. I thank the authors for their contributions and Hirmer Verlag for the successful catalogue.

Annemarie Jaeggi
Director Bauhaus-Archiv Berlin

THE MOST IMPORTANT DATES AT A GLANCE

1933 Closing of the Bauhaus in Berlin

1937 Opening of The New Bauhaus: American School of Design in Chicago (exists for one year)

1939 Reopening as School of Design

1944 Renamed Institute of Design (ID)

1946 Six-week summer seminar *New Vision* and independent photography department established

1949 Institute of Design (ID) becomes part of Illinois Institute of Technology (IIT)

1951 Harry Callahan, Aaron Siskind, and Arthur Siegel teach at Black Mountain College in the summer

1955 School moves into Crown Hall on the IIT campus

2001 Last independent thesis projects in photography at ID; the school still exists as part of the IIT in Chicago

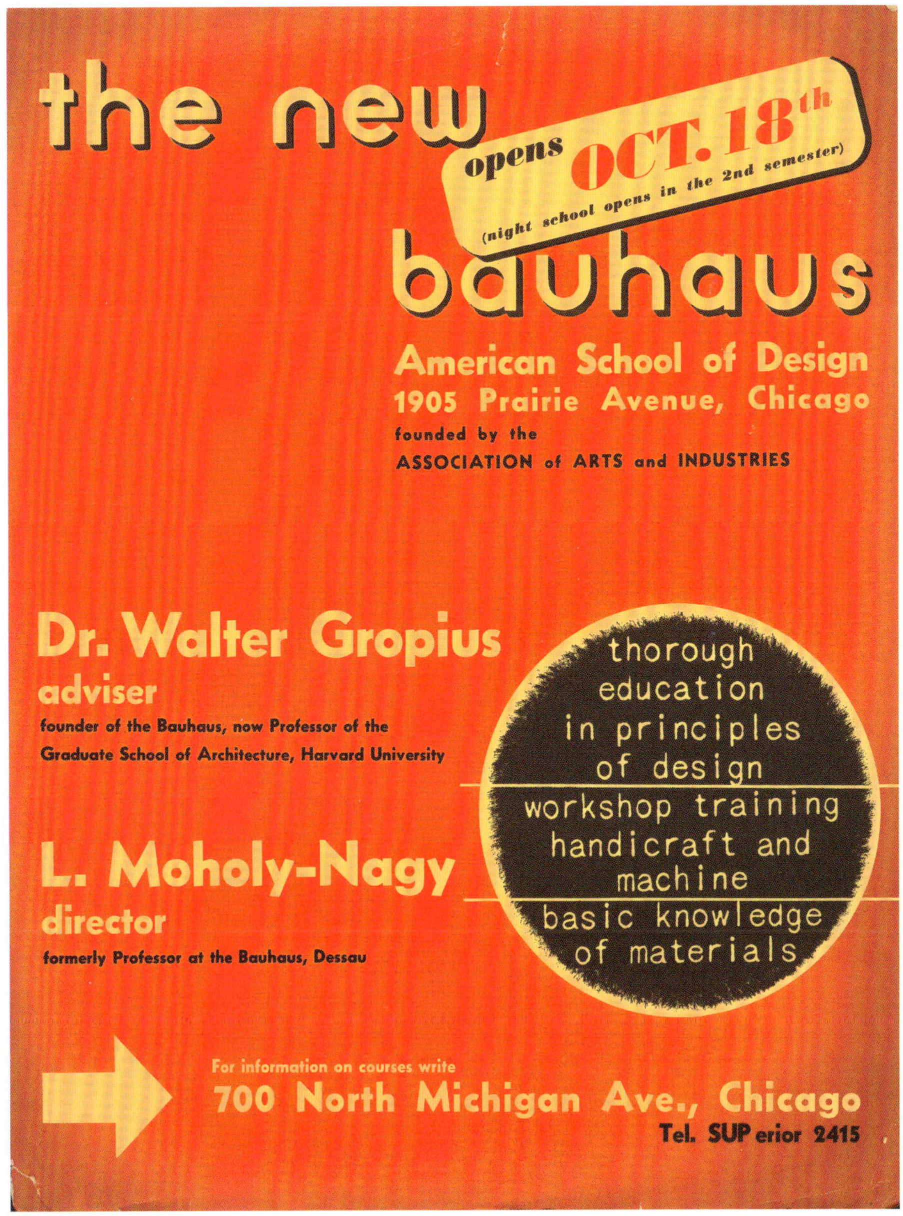

Anonymous
the new bauhaus: American School of Design opens Oct. 18th, 1937
poster, 31.7 x 24.1 cm

We know that art itself cannot be taught, only the way to it. We have in the past given the function of art a formal importance, which segregates it from our daily existence, whereas art is always present where healthy and unaffected people live. Our task is, therefore, to contrive a new system of education which, along with a specialized training in science and technique leads to a thorough awareness of fundamental human needs and a universal outlook. Thus, our concern is to develop a new type of designer, able to face all kinds of requirements, not because he is a prodigy but because he has the right method of approach. We wish to make him conscious of his own creative power, not afraid of new facts, working independently of recipes.

Upon this premise we have built our program.

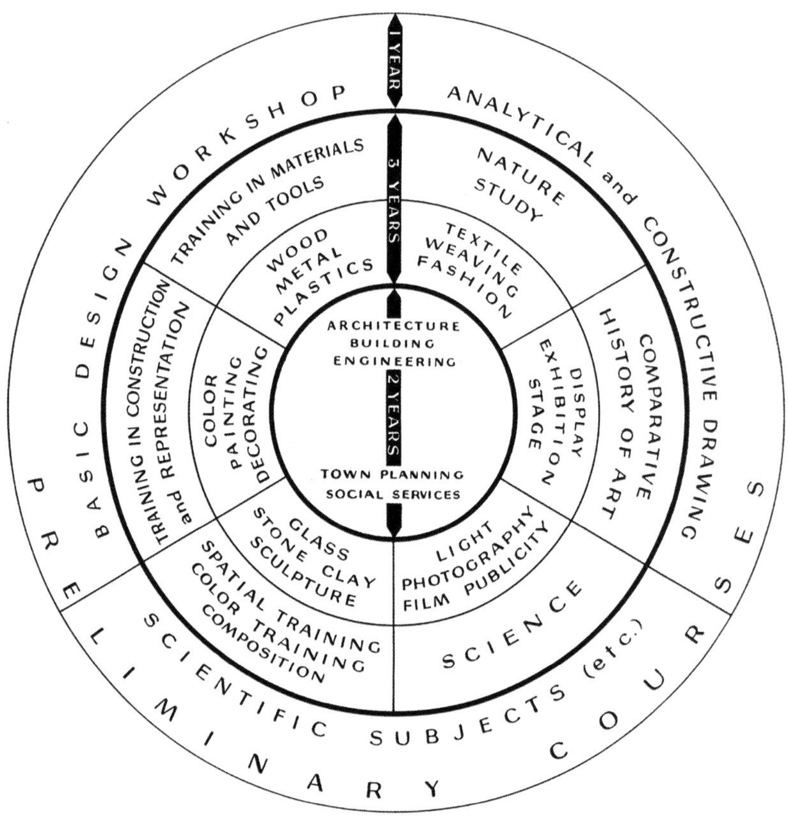

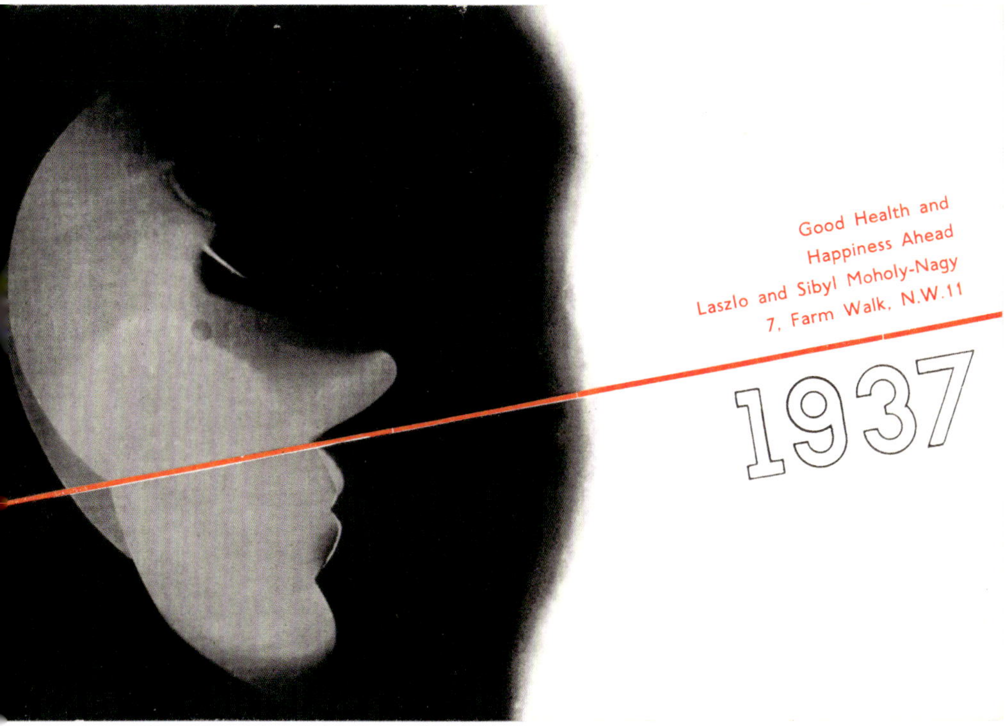

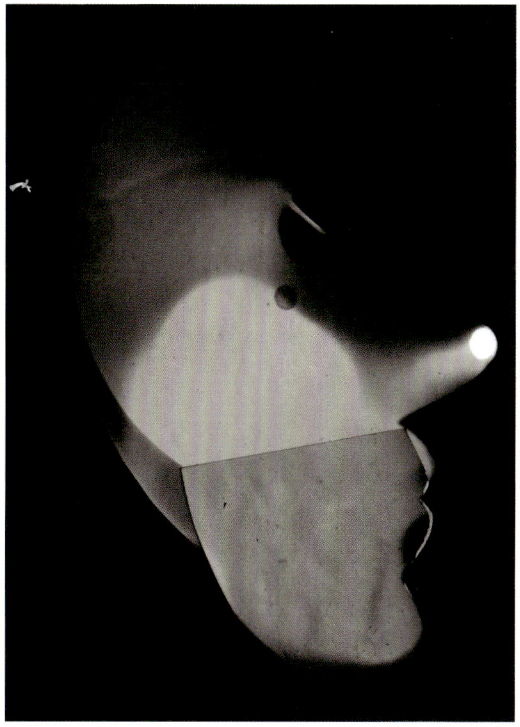

The New Bauhaus: American School of Design, Chicago, 1937
school brochure, interior page with logo and curriculum

László Moholy-Nagy
Good Health and Happiness Ahead: László and Sibyl Moholy-Nagy, 1937
greeting card, 12.5 x 19.1 cm

László Moholy-Nagy
Untitled, 1926, print of 1928
photogram, gelatin silver, 30.2 x 23.6 cm

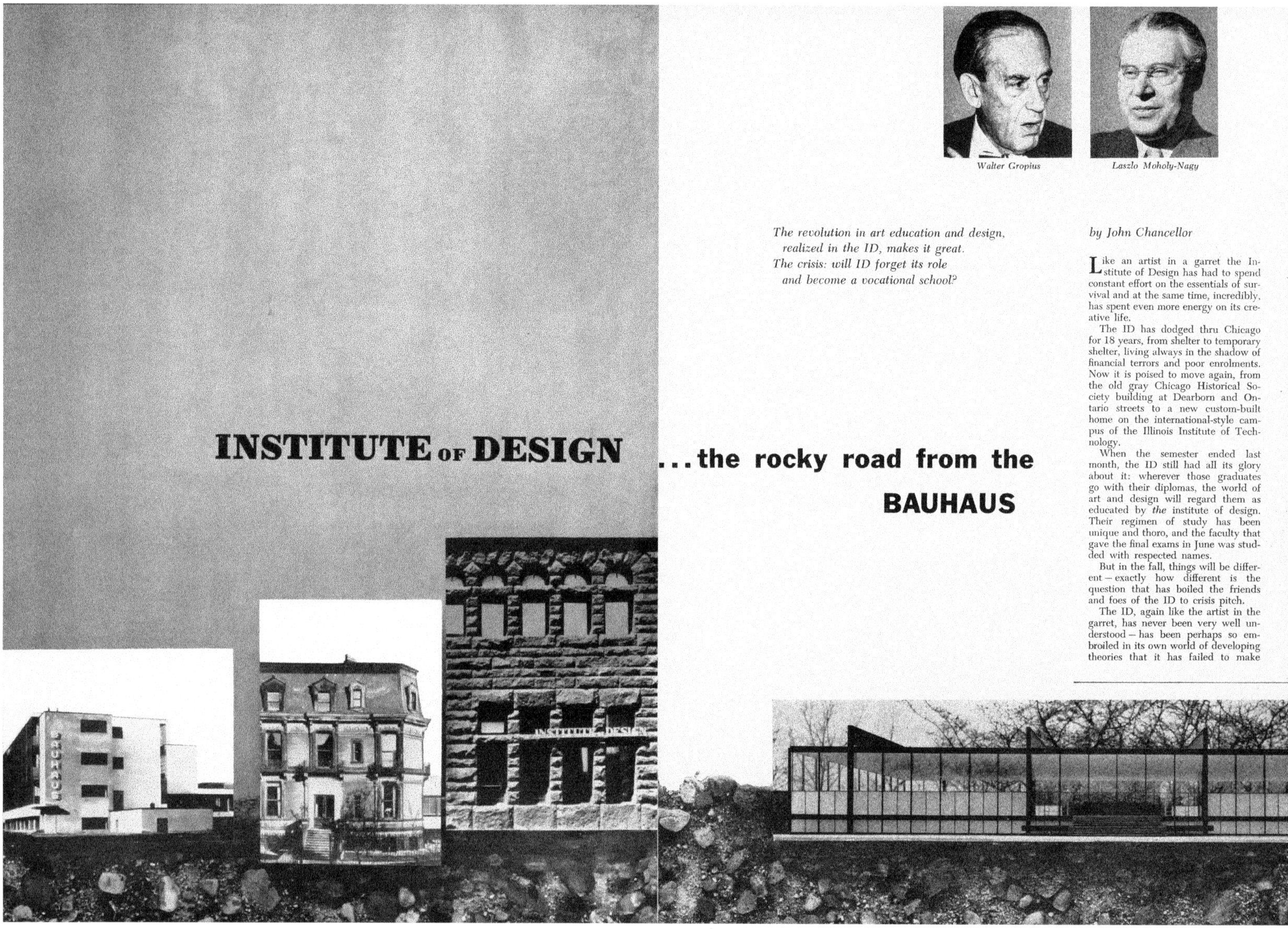

INSTITUTE OF DESIGN ...the rocky road from the BAUHAUS

Walter Gropius

Laszlo Moholy-Nagy

The revolution in art education and design, realized in the ID, makes it great. The crisis: will ID forget its role and become a vocational school?

by John Chancellor

Like an artist in a garret the Institute of Design has had to spend constant effort on the essentials of survival and at the same time, incredibly, has spent even more energy on its creative life.

The ID has dodged thru Chicago for 18 years, from shelter to temporary shelter, living always in the shadow of financial terrors and poor enrolments. Now it is poised to move again, from the old gray Chicago Historical Society building at Dearborn and Ontario streets to a new custom-built home on the international-style campus of the Illinois Institute of Technology.

When the semester ended last month, the ID still had all its glory about it: wherever those graduates go with their diplomas, the world of art and design will regard them as educated by *the* institute of design. Their regimen of study has been unique and thoro, and the faculty that gave the final exams in June was studded with respected names.

But in the fall, things will be different – exactly how different is the question that has boiled the friends and foes of the ID to crisis pitch.

The ID, again like the artist in the garret, has never been very well understood – has been perhaps so embroiled in its own world of developing theories that it has failed to make

Institute of Design ... the rocky road from the Bauhaus, in: *Chicago Magazine*, July 1955, pp. 28–31

much effort to be understood.

For example, it is possible to arouse hostility on the part of intense ID personnel (they are all intense) by calling the place an art school. It is *not* an art school; it is a school of design. Before the Bauhaus, there were no schools of design; and the ID is the lineal heir of the great German Bauhaus of the 1920s, the organization that broke the visual barrier to make way for the design of all things we call modern.

These days, it's called the Institute of Design of the Illinois Institute of Technology, but that is its married name. In its vagabond youth, it was known as the School of Design, the New Bauhaus or just the Bauhaus. In 36 years of gypsy life, thru a succession of harrowing crises, it has made its influence felt in most schools of architecture in the world, in many millions of products, in the advertising aeries of Madison and Michigan avenues, in print shops and furniture showrooms, and in all things touched by mid-twentieth century design.

It has turned out some 1,500 teachers, designers and architects, as well as a relatively good percentage of first class artists.

To get the full flavor of the Perils-of-Pauline history of the ID, one must reach back to the first toddling days of the Weimar Republic in Germany. The war had ruined relics of the artistic past and produced technologies for the artistic future, and in 1918 Berlin, Paris and London were filled with young artists, seeking the new art forms and a merging of art with the war-born industrial techniques and products.

They produced first those tubular monstrosities that were the elder cousins of today's design. And they matured quickly. For the Barcelona exhibition of 1927, Mies van der Rohe designed, in addition to a beautiful, startling pavilion, a chair. The same chair perches gracefully today in the lobby of his glass houses at 880 Lake Shore drive: as fluid and functional a design as it was 28 years ago.

Those were the days of Constructivism, the Suprematists, of Piet Mondrian's first experiments in black line and primary-colored rectangles on white canvas; of the settings designed by Picasso and Leger for the Diaghilev ballet; the Eisenstein films; Le Corbusier's *City of Three Million People;* Marcel Duchamp's staircase; of Walter Gropius' *Total Theater.*

The decade after 1920 was a visual renaissance: out of it flowered a single, altho international, community of designers and experimenters.

Thus, in 1919, at Weimar, the *Staatliche Bauhaus* was organized. The original program promised "intellectual, manual and technological education of creative people for design work." Wassily Kandinsky, Lyonel Feininger, Paul Klee and Walter Gropius were on the faculty. They were joined in 1923 by an intense young Hungarian named Laszlo Moholy-Nagy, the man destined to inherit the Bauhaus and all its future problems.

MOHOLY BECAME a philosopher and a great teacher. Gropius has written of him: "His greatest effort as an artist was devoted to the conquest of space. His genius ventured into all realms of science and art to unravel the phenomena of space and light. In painting, sculpture and architecture, in theater and industrial design, in photography and film, in advertising and typography, he strove incessantly to interpret space in its relation to time, that is, motion in space."

The interpretation of space in its relation to time admittedly is not a course of inquiry for the amateur or the faint of heart. But an appreciation of the art of the 1920s may throw some light of this subject: the painters of immovable objects had been replaced by artists like Duchamp with his famous *Nude Descending the Stairs*. Film, both in the still photograph and motion pictures, was achieving status as an art form. The cubists had broken objects up into their fundamental shapes. And Moholy was interested in *moving* lines, rather than static forms.

The charting of these frontiers at the Bauhaus led directly to the clean, sculptured lines of today's design, found in objects as dissimilar as hospitals and the Parker '51 pen – as a Saarinen chair and an airplane hangar.

Within a few fast-moving years, the Bauhaus drew an international audience. Fourteen Bauhaus Books, which were to become the books of the bible of modern design, had been published, and the Bauhaus itself had moved to Dessau.

Then came Hitler and the Bauhaus fell. It fell because the German nation became an impossible place for Moholy and Gropius and their kind of theorist.

Moholy and his wife, Sibyl, a woman of exceptional intelligence and patience, went to Holland, then England, where he worked at such varied tasks as window-dressing and the production of experimental films. Sibyl was to accompany Moholy to America and, after his death, write a perceptive biography: *Moholy-Nagy – Experiment in Totality*.

By 1937, most of the old Bauhaus men were scattered around the world. Gropius had come to America, where he was teaching, building houses of notable architectural interest and boosting Moholy.

In June of 1937 a cable arrived at the Moholy-Nagy home in London:

PLAN DESIGN SCHOOL ON BAUHAUS LINES TO OPEN IN FALL. MARSHALL FIELD OF-

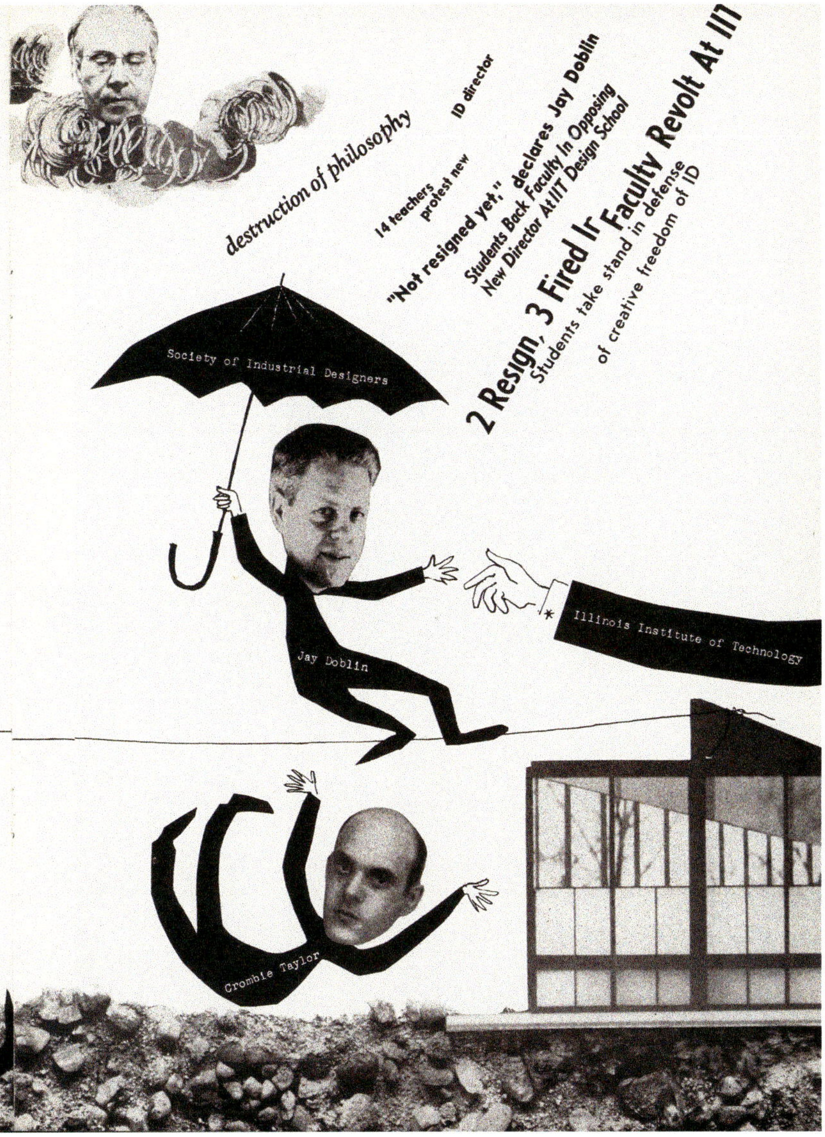

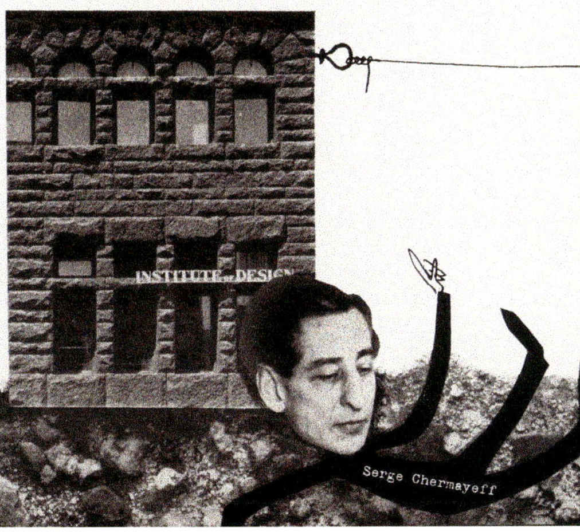

INTRODUCTION

Both the Bauhaus located in Germany and the conceptually related New Bauhaus (later the Institute of Design [ID]) in Chicago were exceptional places of artistic education. They shaped how whole generations of students (many of whom later became teachers themselves) approached creative work. In spite of all the obvious differences between the continents and systems, mental and institutional divergences, and their individual characters, we feel it is worthwhile to inquire into the overarching value and significance of both schools within the context of their time and in terms of their reception. In our project, we have shed more light on the "experiment photography" at the eighty-year-old New Bauhaus (now ID) in an effort to find out how the composition of light was taught there and how this Chicago photo school has been perceived ever since.

Our perspective is that of a later generation, born at the halfway point, the moment when the historiography of the New Bauhaus was just beginning: for example, Hans Maria Wingler began to occupy himself more intensely with this topic during the 1970s at Berlin's Bauhaus-Archiv. Thus, our knowledge and our documentary material are substantially based on prior work done by people who were personally involved or who knew active participants. Here, we particularly want to mention Lloyd C. Engelbrecht, who passed away in 2016, as well as Peter Hahn and Jeannine Fiedler, Charles Traub and John Grimes, David Travis and Elizabeth Siegel, and also Stephen Daiter. We consider ourselves fortunate to have gained three of these experts as authors for this catalogue, which considers external factors affecting the production and presentation of New Bauhaus photography more intensely than earlier publications. Therefore, in spite of our enthusiasm for the works of individuals, this volume accompanying the exhibition concentrates on the teaching principles behind the institutional photographic education provided at this school of design as well as the context in which work was created and shown. It additionally thematizes the diverse prerequisites as well as consequences for photography's production and reception. In her introductory essay, Kristina Lowis deals with distinctive features and permanent aspects of photographic practice at the school and, in doing so, shows how experiment became a system. John Grimes, former instructor at the ID and pioneer of the school's historiography, depicts the development of the ID's photo curriculum from a deliberately subjective perspective. Stephen Daiter, who has been a connoisseur of the New Bauhaus and a photo gallerist in Chicago for many years, provides unaccustomed insights into his work with graduates of the ID, and he traces the images' paths from the school to the market and into collections. From her perspective as curator of photography at the Art Institute of Chicago, Elizabeth Siegel clarifies how the photography of the ID has made its way from the school into the museum. Sibylle Hoiman complements this by revealing how the New Bauhaus collection at Berlin's Bauhaus-Archiv is to be evaluated in the context of collection strategy and historiography, while Astrid Bähr uses the school brochures from this collection to take an in-depth look at the school's self-presentation and the history of its reception.

Kristina Lowis and Sibylle Hoiman

In the exhibition *New Bauhaus Chicago: Experiment Photography and Film*, which allots more space to film than the catalogue, we have assigned ourselves the task—and permitted ourselves the luxury—of exploring the photographic visual work of Chicago's institutional successor to the Bauhaus less monographically and more phenomenologically. Thus—entirely in keeping with the notions of the American school, whose ancestry was made explicit only in its original name, "The New Bauhaus," although it always also emphasized this heritage in its publications and teaching under its later names, "School of Design" and "Institute of Design"—we have opened up plenty of room for experimentation and delved into the abundance of our own collections to show the creative range of former teachers and students. We present examples of typical exercises and assignments in the area of photography, and these lead us into the two broad realms of abstraction and figuration. An entire room is devoted to the many facets of urban photography.

Commemorating an anniversary only makes sense when what we are celebrating is relevant to the present. Within the overarching context of the Bauhaus's successors, it would surely be worthwhile to apply historical scrutiny to the didactic impact of subjective, generative, concrete, or experimental photography at some point. However, within the specific context of Chicago, we have pursued the question of whether there are photographic approaches today that display parallels to, elaborations upon, connections with—in short, a kinship with—the teaching done at the New Bauhaus/Institute of Design. Selected contemporary photographic positions from Chicago have therefore been used to round off the exhibition and the catalogue.

Both would have been inconceivable without the knowledgeable, dedicated, and stimulating support of numerous individuals and institutions, to whom we would like to express our great personal gratitude here:

Roland Angst, Kerstin Bartels, Linda Blackwell, James Blair, Clarissa Bonet, Wayne Boyer, Agathe Cancellieri, Barbara Diener, Lynne Brown, Barbara Crane, Stephen Daiter, Ludger Derenthal, Catherine Edelman, Assaf Evron, Anita Eylmann, Doug Fogelson, John Grimes, Valerie A. Harris, Karen Irvine, Mary Jane Jacob, Kenneth Josephson, Anne Jüster, Lewis and Ann Neri Kostiner, Christine Kühn, Raquel Ladensack Voakes, Kiyoko Lerner, Ashley Lumb, Julie Katz, Irmi Maunu-Kocian, Jeffery Mau, Jonathan Miller, Hattula Moholy-Nagy, Matthias Noell, Ralph Pugh, Betty Rivard, Petra Roggel, Sabine Schnakenberg, Ulrich Schwarz, Elizabeth Siegel, Julie Siegel, Charles and Frances Swedlund, Kristin Taylor, Else Tholstrup, Sonja Thomsen, Julien Trillat, Charles Traub, Mathilde Weh, Hedwig Wingler, Amy Yoes, T. Paul Young, Marilyn Zimmerman and Maxi Zimmermann. Last but not least, we wish to warmly thank all our colleagues at the Bauhaus-Archiv in Berlin for their magnificent support!

July 2017
Kristina Lowis and Sibylle Hoiman

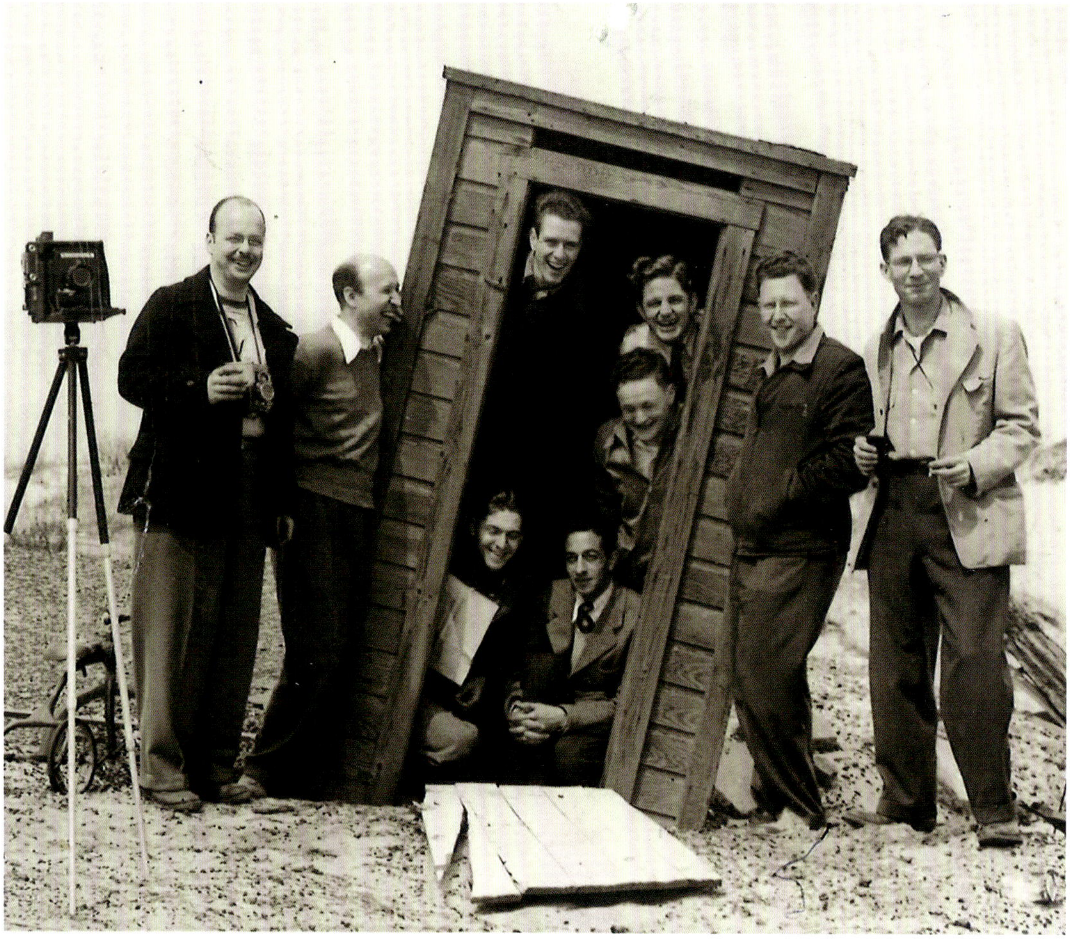

Anonymous
Photography class excursion to Indiana Dunes with Harry Callahan (2nd from l.) April 30, 1948
gelatin silver, 9.6 x 11.8 cm

Anonymous
Excursion of Aaron Siskind's (4th from l.) photography class with Else Tholstrup (3rd from l.) to Iowa, in: Else Tholstrup's album *Chicago–1952*, 1952
gelatin silver, 19.3 x 24 cm

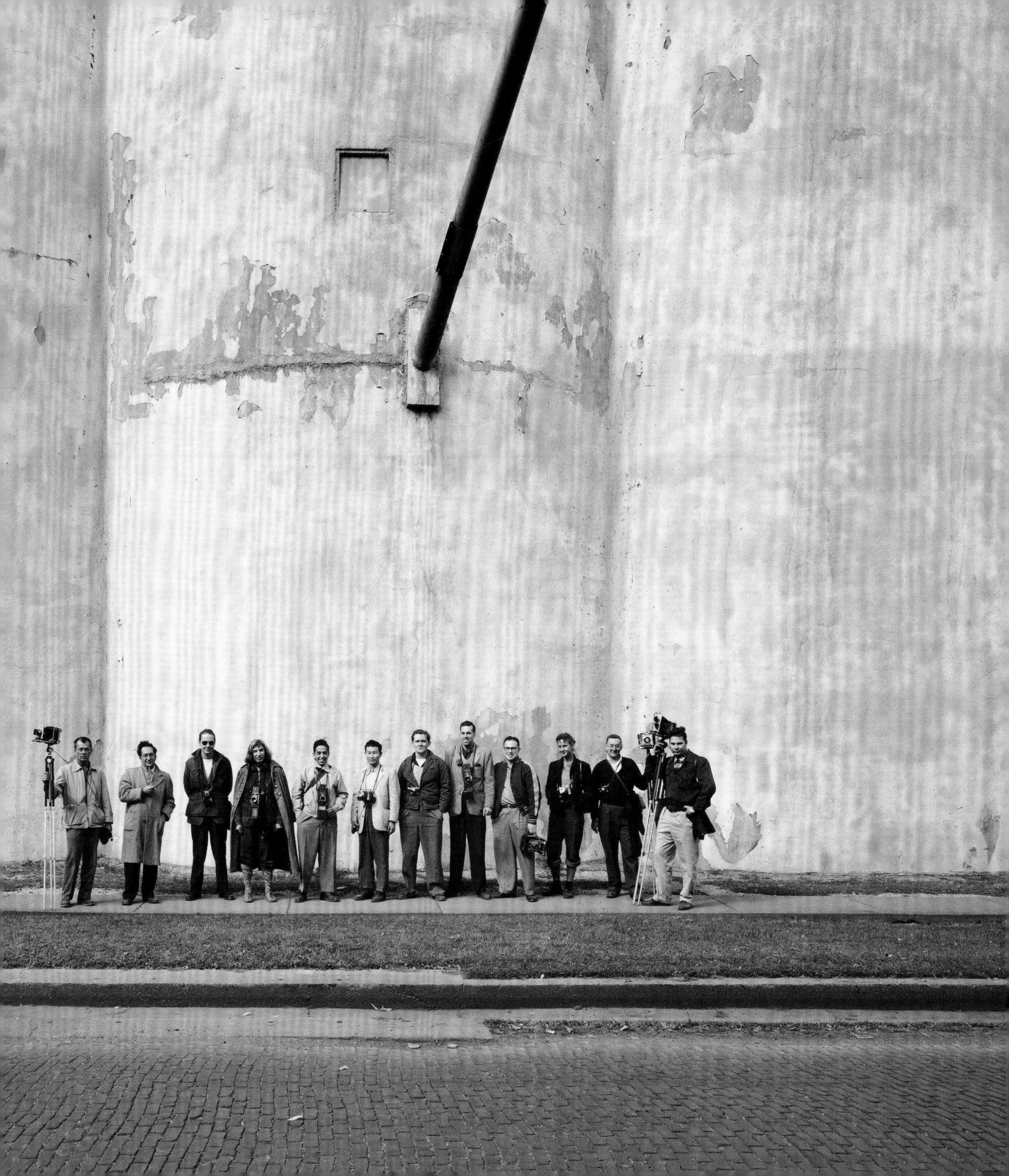

Anonymous
Documentation of the children's course by R. D. Erickson (middle), in: Robert Donald Erickson, *A Child Sees*, 1945/46
master's thesis at the ID, ring binder with grid paper, photographs, and drawings, 29 x 24 cm

19

THE ART LABORATORY

The art room becomes a laboratory. Here the child experiments -- the teacher experiments. As life is concerned with problems involving the use of our senses and our intellect, so too are we in the art laboratory concerned with problems involving the use of senses and intellect. No longer do we set up a flower and say, "Today we will draw this flower as it is." For how can we draw its odor -- its motion in the wind -- its structure -- its growth -- its color -- its shape -- its form? Problems must be simple, involving but one aspect of life yet allowing room for the hundreds of different interpretations of just that one aspect. Why in problem form? Because all creative activity must of necessity be concerned with problems. Without problems there would be no inventions, writing, composing, painting, sculpture, architecture -- in fact, no creative activities.

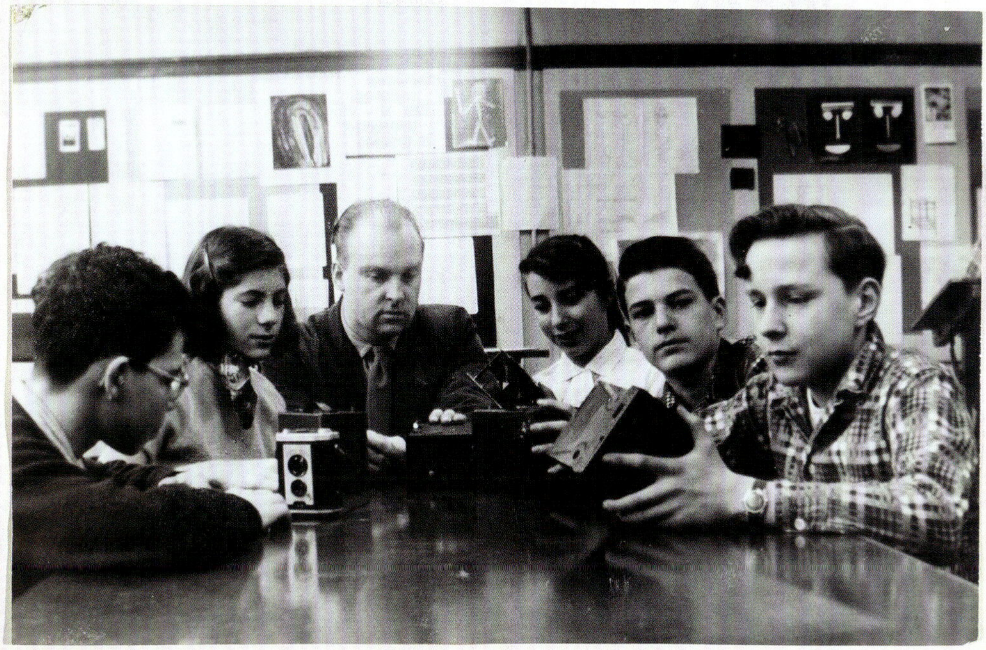

Author leads Box camera instruction session
High School Students with author

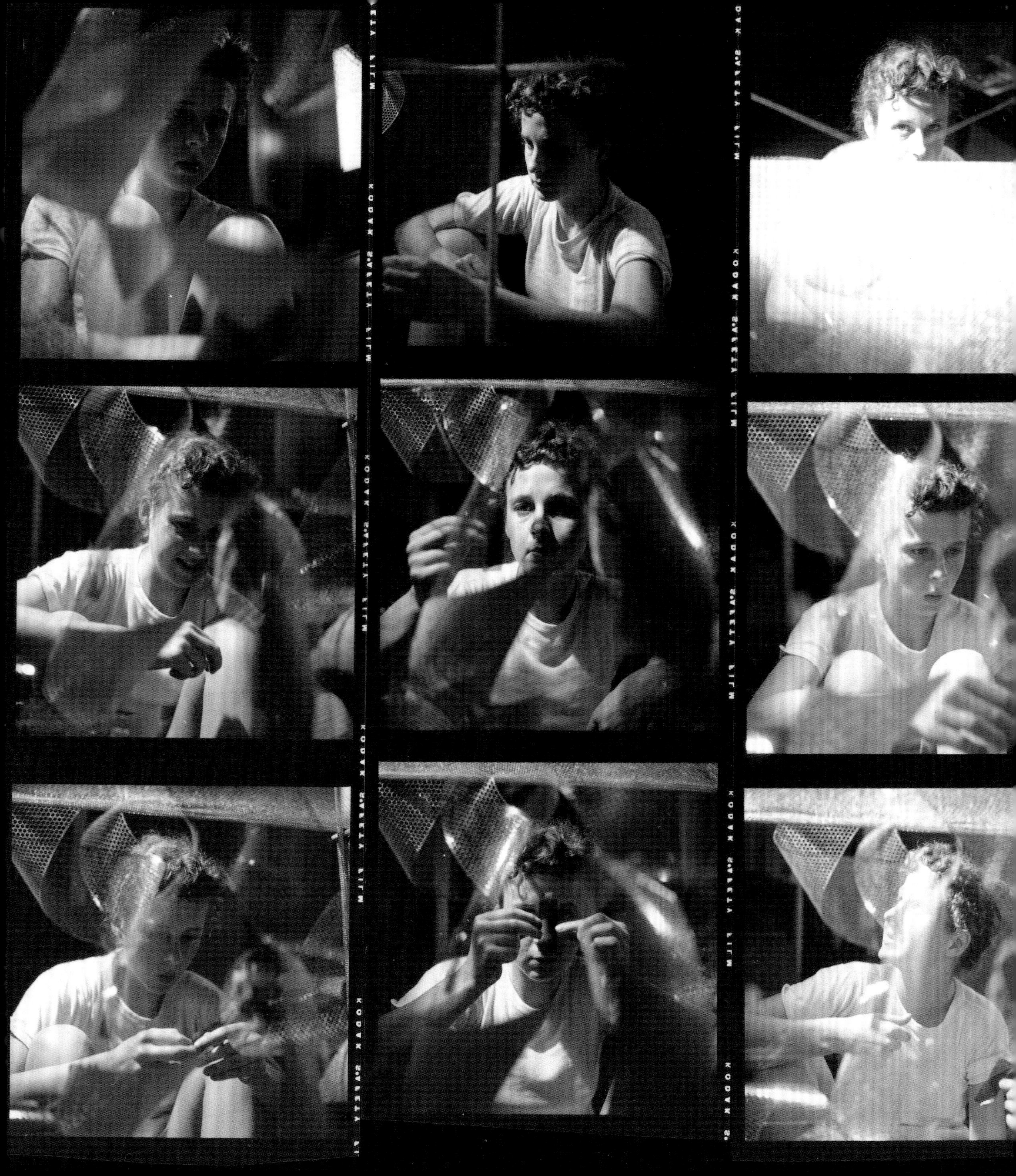

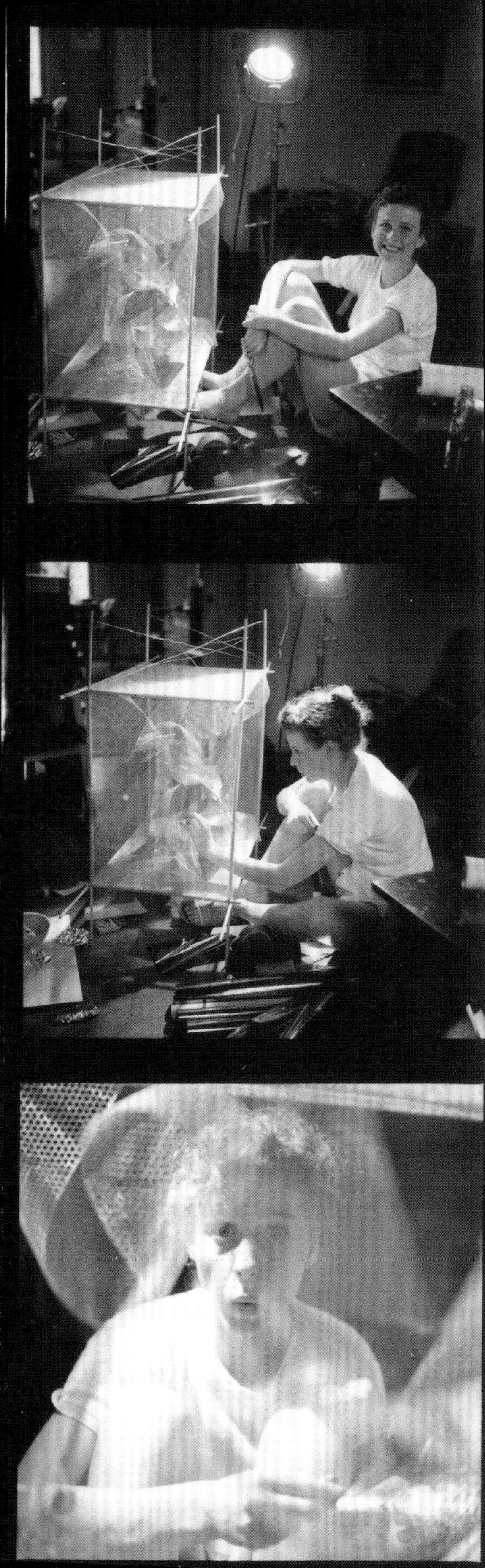

Anonymous
Else Tholstrup constructing an installation, 1952
contact sheet with 12 images
gelatin silver, 20.2 x 25.2 cm

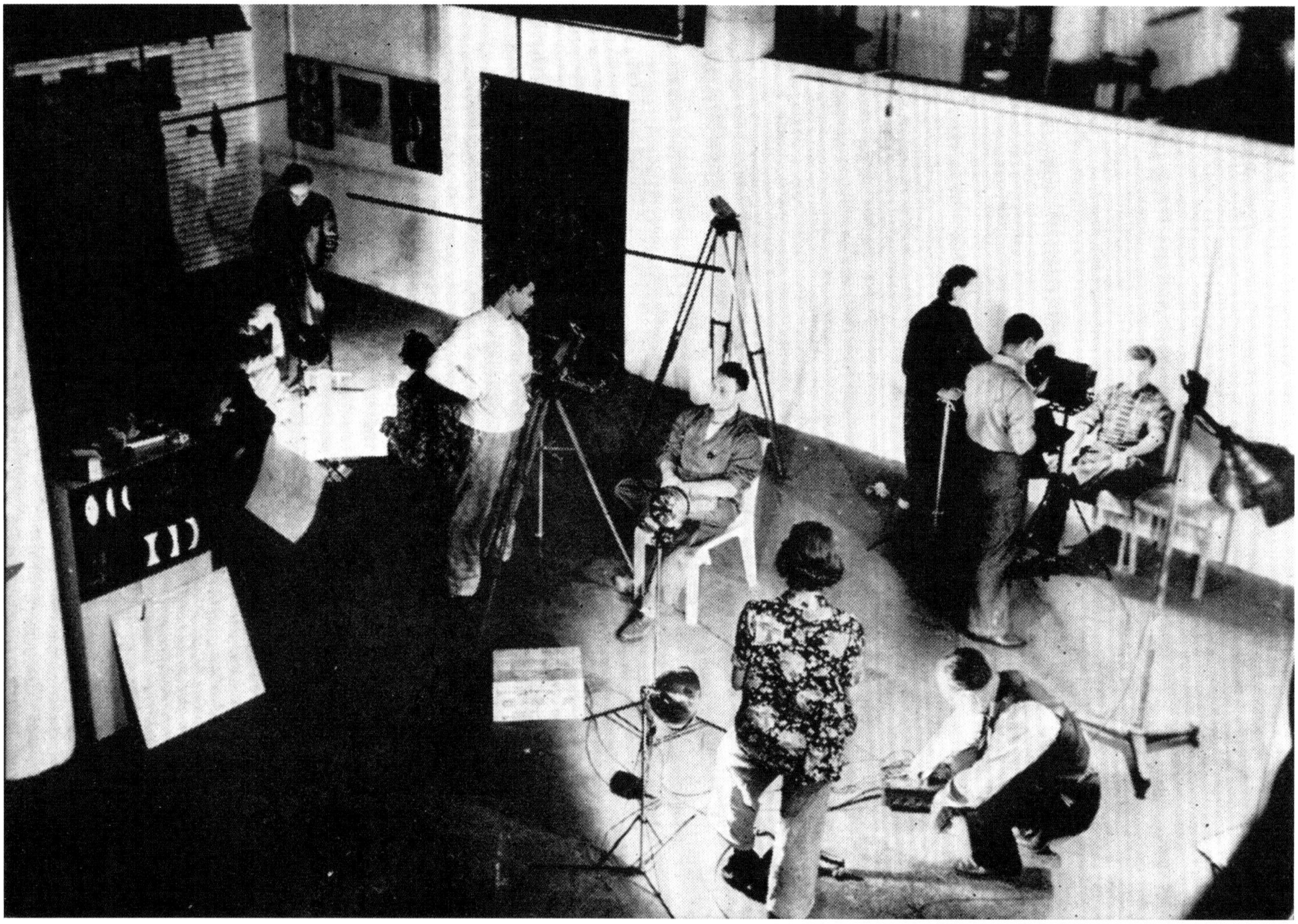

Nathan Lerner
The photo studio at the ID, in: *Institute of Design formerly School of Design*, Chicago, 1944
school brochure

Anonymous
Erwin Blumenfeld at the *New Vision* seminar, 1946
gelatin silver, 19 x 24 cm

Anonymous
Greeting card of the ID photography faculty, 1957
gelatin silver, 20.3 x 25.5 cm

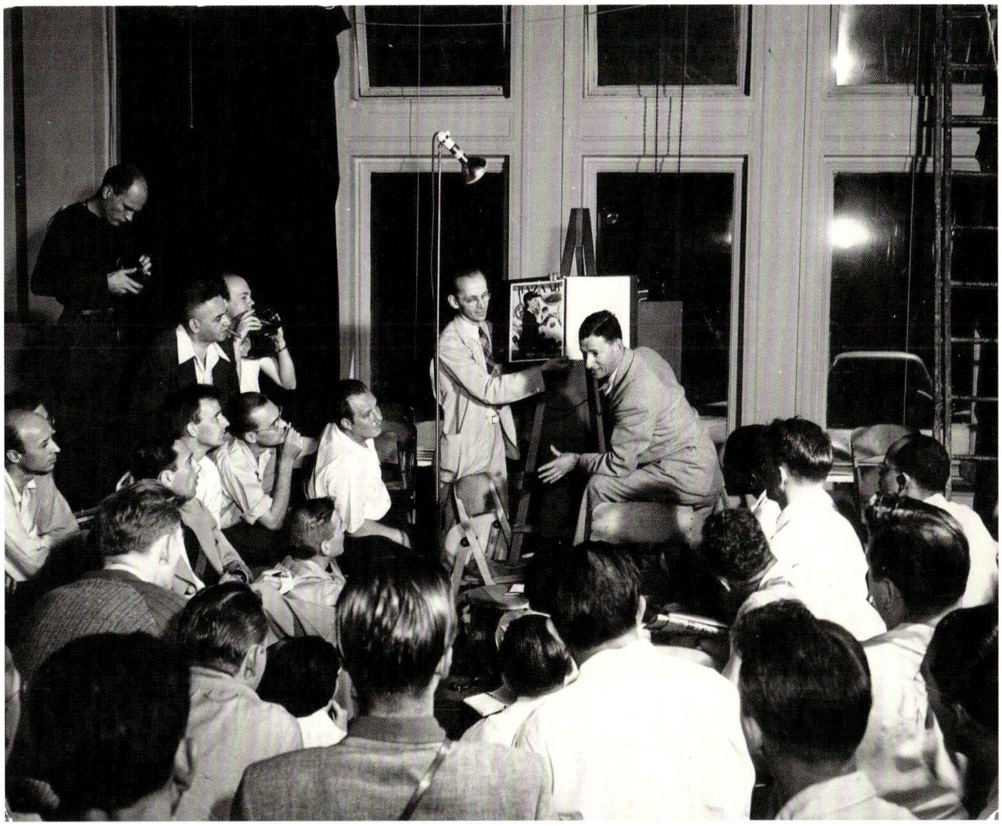

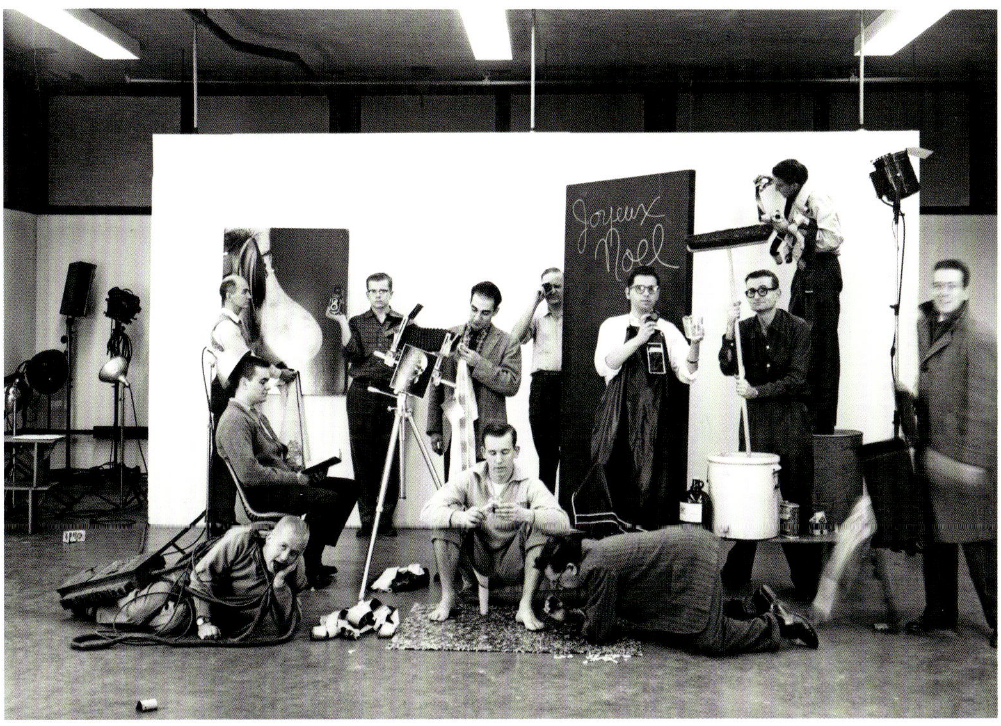

1st row: Ray K. Metzker, Joseph D. Jachna, Aaron Siskind
2nd row on the right: Arthur Sinsabaugh

ELEMENT, EXPERIMENT, SYSTEM, PROCESS: PHOTOGRAPHY AT THE NEW BAUHAUS AND INSTITUTE OF DESIGN

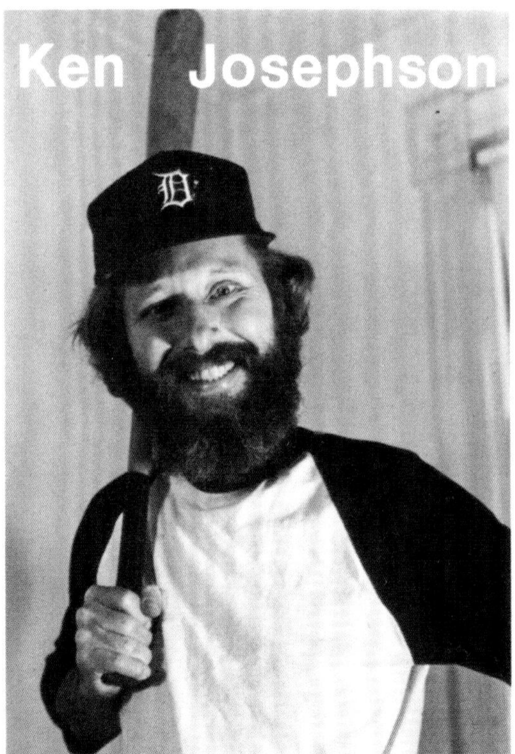

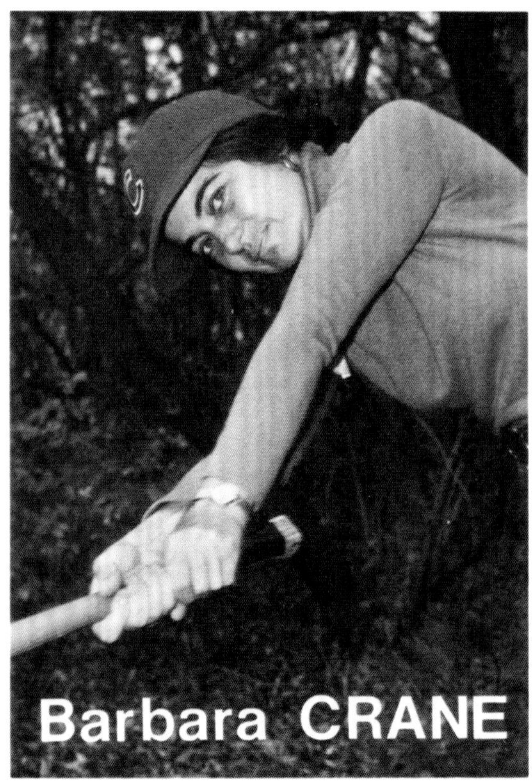

Mike Mandel
Baseball Photographer Trading Cards: Kenneth Josephson, Barbara Crane, 1975
2 playing cards, 9 x 6.3 cm each

Kristina Lowis

The photographers looking out at us from Mike Mandel's *Baseball Photographer Trading Cards* seem unusually athletic for their profession. Barbara Crane and Kenneth Josephson are two of the graduates and instructors from the photography program at Chicago's Institute of Design who were deemed worthy of inclusion in the 1975 collection of well-known players in the field of US photography (→ 32).[1] Who was throwing the pitches—and where did they hit them?

"The difference comes when the ball is hit. Then nothing is the same."[2] To draw loosely on an elegant and no less athletic narrative thread by Don DeLillo: It has now been 80 years since a ball was hit that would expand the field of the Bauhaus all the way to Chicago. All eyes were fixed on László Moholy-Nagy: The director of the New Bauhaus, who had been hired by Walter Gropius, was getting ready for the next pitch in Chicago in 1937. A new school of design was created, and initially—for just one decisive year—it bore the name New Bauhaus. In 1939 it was renamed the School of Design and then, in 1944, it finally became the Institute of Design (ID); it continues to exist under this name today and has been a part of the Illinois Institute of Technology (IIT) since 1949.

The school achieved fame through a photography program shaped by its remarkable teachers; its influence on American photography's development in the second half of the 20th century is considered formative. Aside from Moholy-Nagy, György Kepes was there from 1937 to 1943, Arthur Siegel between 1946 and 1978 (with interruptions), Harry Callahan from 1946 to 1961, and Aaron Siskind from 1951 to 1971, and they were presumably the best-known instructors in their field. The school and, particularly, its photography teachers and teaching have already been the subject of various research and exhibition projects.[3] More than anything else, dealing with photography in the context of this school means acknowledging the breadth of its teachers and students' photographic work. However, the school's infrastructure—that is, its curriculum, attitude, networking, and public image at the level of the institution and its personnel—is also relevant.

1 The photographer has offered the following explanation regarding his ironic series of 134 figures active in American photography, which were originally sold in a package that included a stick of gum: "[...] a strange thing happened about that time: the art world discovered photography [...]. Competitions for [...] grants and university jobs began to revolve around the hierarchy of art world professionals." Cited in Schuman 2010, p. 60.

2 DeLillo 1998, p. 27. *Underworld* uses the stations of a baseball's trajectory and subsequent travels to tell the history of the second half of the 20th century.

3 See Introduction. Jeannine Fiedler carried out fundamental work on the New Bauhaus in 1987. Agathe Cancellieri is currently writing her dissertation on *An American New Vision: The department of photography at the Institute of Design in Chicago from 1946 to 1971* at the University Paris I Panthéon.

Drawing a photographic line to the present leading straight through the period considered here (from 1937 to the contemporary) would mean failing to recognize the transformation in the framework of surrounding circumstances and, particularly, the paradigm shift that took place in terms of how photography is dealt with. The homogenization of stylistic history in order to construct a line of succession leading from the Bauhaus in Weimar to the contemporary Institute of Design in Chicago was already being criticized in the early 1980s: "rituals consist of the establishment of a suitable ancestry."[4] And with regard to political and economic changes, personal motives, social factors, and photographic developments, this attempt really would miss the point. To provide just one example: After teaching for five years at the publicly funded Bauhaus in Germany, Moholy-Nagy was a freelancer for ten years, working in various places and on diverse projects, including the major travelling exhibition *Film und Foto* (Film and Photo; 1929). Authorized by Gropius to represent "the" Bauhaus, the 42-year-old then took over the task of developing a concept for "The New Bauhaus: American School of Design" with funding from businesses and the proactive acquisition of additional private funding.[5] Subsequently, individuals with very different approaches to photography, professional life, politics, and art would play a decisive role in shaping the program for photography (and film), which had not existed in this form at the Bauhaus. Interpretive models restricted to European influence on American culture or the watering down of a politicized avant-garde in a commercial environment are too limited here. Instead, the school, which underwent major changes, formed a space in which and out of which emerged a thoroughly heterogeneous photography. Thus, the primary intention here is to shed light not on this or that monographically significant individual but on the practice of the many: How did students learn about photography at the New Bauhaus? What kinds of images were created as a result? How did the photography department present itself? What did its continuities and discontinuities look like? (And what does "bauhausy" actually mean for photography today?)

TRAINING: BACK TO BASICS

Together with György Kepes and Henry Holmes Smith (instructor in 1937/38), Moholy-Nagy developed a concept for teaching photography within the framework of a curriculum that was originally formally based on the Bauhaus and covered diverse types of design. Its fundamental features would be applied at the school for around four decades. The photography program's core was twofold: The foundation course initiated in 1937 was based on experimentation and an interdisciplinary concept and was designed to introduce all students to photography. The master's thesis was introduced in the early 1950s and remained in place until 2001, when photography ceased to exist as an independent program at the school.

- "Like the other workshops, photography and motion picture start out with experimentation."[6]
- "… it was back to kindergarten!"[7]

When the New Bauhaus was founded, photography was made a part of the Light Workshop. This provided a terminological signal that, from then on, light was to be handled as an independent material that students had to be learn to deal with: "The

4 Solomon-Godeau 1983, p. 83.
5 A letter from January 10, 1945, written by the management of Sears, Roebuck & Co. to Walter Paepcke, who financed the school and owned the Container Corporation of America conveys the effect made by this offensive: "I haven't made up my mind whether you have on your hands a school or just a one-man show," copy in BHA, Archiv NB 16, W. Paepcke II.
6 School brochure 1944
7 James Blair in a conversation with Annemarie Jaeggi, 2 June 2016.

problem is to find an approach to photography which breaks down the complex tasks into their fundamental elements, mastering them one by one yet pointing through each function to the wholeness of the solution."[8] During students' education as designers, fundamental elements of photography were to be identified that would enable all of them to develop answers to holistically framed questions.

The ID archive contains an inventory listing the contents of a collection of examples: These were presumably used for reference from the early 1940s until the 1970s, and the list illustrates the deliberate reduction of design photography into learnable elements (→ 36).[9] It is remarkable how assignments and corresponding learning objectives are intertwined: Questions related to technical and material aspects, perceptual phenomenology, composition, and content merge together. Remembering that the school's recommended reading list included Moholy-Nagy's *Vision in Motion* and Kepes's *Language of Vision*, which both cover various epochs, it becomes apparent that the approach presented as socially revolutionary was certainly not based on a technological fetishism. Instead, it was intended in a clearly psychological sense and was aimed at the individual's subjective perception and aesthetically stimulating experience in addition to the creation of a modern visual idiom. While all of the school's students were taught the fundamental principles, the photo program continued to expand the experiment based on these assignments during the semesters that followed. The introduction of a bachelor's degree in 1946 and a master of science in photography in 1950 additionally created room for students to work intensively on their own projects.

Just under twenty years after the school's founding, an article written jointly by Harry Callahan and Aaron Siskind—an instructor duo who would go down in the history of the ID—presented their teaching practice and explained their intention of uncovering individual paths by way of a broadly conceived professional education.[10] These paths could lead in various directions, not just in terms of careers but also in terms of personal development. It is essential not to overlook the fact that the subjects of sociology and economics also formed fixed elements in the curriculum. This concept of photography extending beyond purely artistic aspirations is conveyed by a poetic and simultaneously refreshingly realistic list by Siegel, by which he introduces a passionate statement: "Photography is [...] science, system, process, technique, tool, documentation, pages from life, creative treatment of actuality, archives of memory, mirrors of memory, extension of the eye, enlargement of vision, hobby, business, profession, means of expression, way of life, poor man's Rorschach, language, art, etc., etc., etc."[11]

The photogram was the programmatic key to photography. All students became acquainted with the equally simple and impressive experience of this concentration on light and objects' direct influence on photosensitive materials (initially printing-out paper), which was far more than a "kindergarten" exercise (→ 46, 55). In 1957 the photogram achieved a unique quality in the work of Charles Swedlund, who laid his newborn child on the light-sensitive material in a gesture that was no less radical than it was symbolic—placing photography back at the beginning, so to speak (→ 121).[12] Photograms in motion were also created by means of cameraless filming, a technique that was also practiced systematically. For example, Larry Janiak explores a line's existence and disappearance in *Disintegration Line* (1960),[13] and Art Wise also

8 Moholy-Nagy 1947, p. 187.

9 "A photograms, B light modulators, C virtual volume, D lighting, E negative techniques, F refraction, G reflection, H viewpoint, I microphotography, J multiple exposure, K form, L related forms, M series, N portraits, O documentary/sociological studies, P children, Q people without people, R texture, S collages, T macro."

10 "[...] from within the framework of a broad professional education to open an individual way.", in: Aperture Magazine Anthology 2012, p. 217. See the contribution by Grimes.

11 Arthur Siegel: "Photography Is," in: *ID* 5, 1961, unpag.

12 This act found successors in the work of Floris Neusüss in the 1960s and Adam Fuss in the 1990s.

13 Looking back at his subsequent activity as an instructor (1968–1980) at the ID in his documentary work *Animation Film Making*, Larry Janiak explains how natural it was to work directly on the film. Precursors for this included Norman McLaren and Stan Brakhage, who came to Chicago in 1969.

PHOTOGRAPHY

A photograms

B light modulators

C virtual volume

D lighting

E negative techniques

F refraction

G reflection

H viewpoint

I microphotography

J multiple exposure

K form

L related forms

M series
see also EXHIBITIONS F-G

N portraits

O documentary
sociological studies

P children

Q people without people

R texture

S collages

T macro

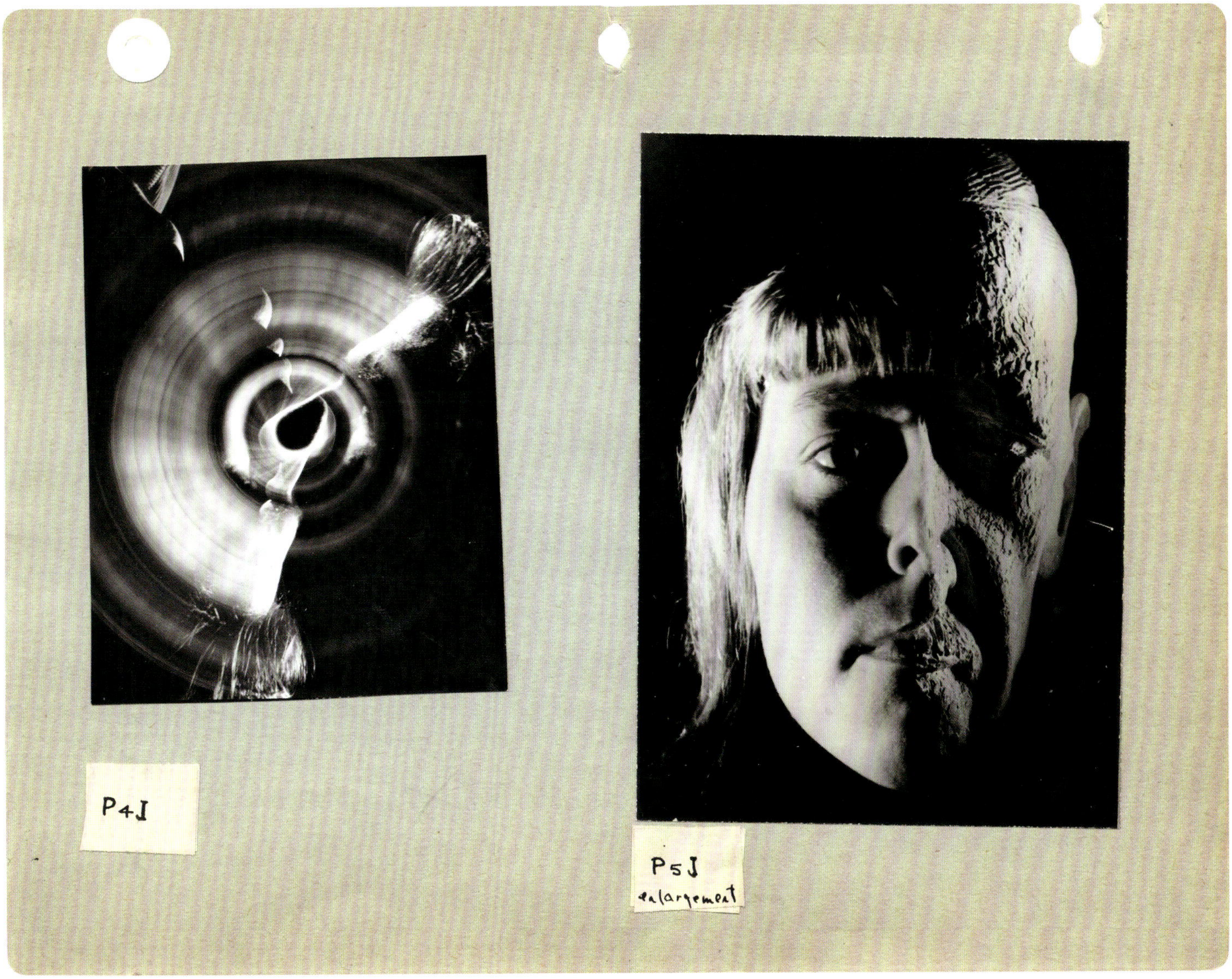

Typewritten list of standard exercises from the photo department at the ID
1940s–1970s
28 x 21.5 cm

Page from the collection of standard exercises from the photo department at the ID
1940s–1970s
28 x 21.5 cm

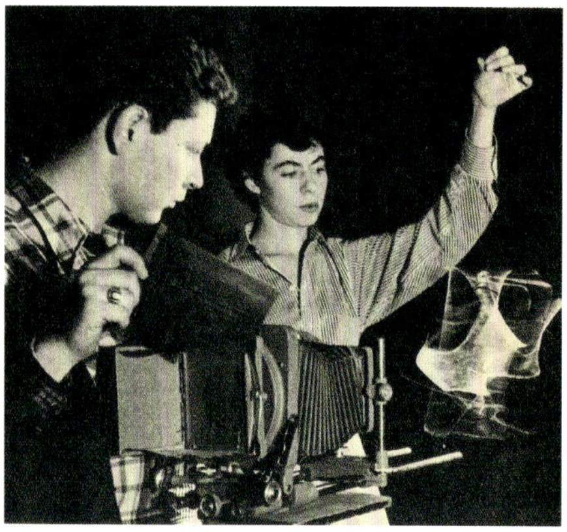

renounced the use of a lens while using Letraset patterns to create the forms and rhythms of his image-and-tone composition *Zippatatta*, his 1973 thesis work.
Experiments with light-sensitive material incorporating diverse substances and tools proceeded in a manner that was just as direct, but was even more emphatically experimental. Eugene Whitehorne's image of a tactile chart features various materials that are to be explored haptically, as is illustrated by the two hands lying on the object, and it represents the school's groping path forward and the investigation of materials there (→ 58). In 1938 Myron Kozman explored the alchemy of the medium with oil or paint on photosensitive material (→ 54), thus creating "chemigrams."[14] This approach was still being practiced in the classroom in the 1960s, as demonstrated by the work of an unknown student from the collection of the Bauhaus Chicago Foundation.[15]
Kepes worked with cliché verre, a technique in which the negative is scratched; in the 1970s the daguerreotype process was experimentally resurrected—with puzzlingly anachronistic-looking images that feature cars instead of carriages.[16]
When studying the effect of light on pieces of paper formed specifically for this purpose (so-called light modulators) or on other objects, the focus was on active composition. The repeated trials not only provided experience to serve as a reference point: They also made it possible to produce photographs independently, from the motif to the print, and they made this seem natural as a creative process. The works created in this way range aesthetically from seemingly timeless crumpled pieces of paper by Jerome Sharff (→ 56) to Rick Fucik's 1975 thesis work *In No Strange Land*, which was created under the supervision of Siegel and in which the moving light renders the objective character of the abstract form entirely abstract and spherical.
Light notations always imply a temporal component. Thus, solarization directly on the photographic material requires the factor of time during development. Or photos can be varied, for example, through differences in exposure time, thus creating light paintings and traces of movement of varying origin: The gesture can be the movement of the light source or camera, but also of an object in front of it. To illustrate the latter, an object rotating around its axis—sometimes the course instructor spinning around on a swiveling chair—was photographed as a "virtual volume" (→ 38, 60, 69). Multiple exposures, like other possibilities for combining photographs, merge a corresponding number of moments together. The moving image is not the only logical elaboration upon compositional principles of this kind. Composite images, series, and experiments with film demonstrate the deliberate exploration of the temporal aspect of photography.
A three-dimensional miniature stage, a kind of concentrated studio space with adjustable lighting, was also employed as an aid in the classroom: Nathan Lerner presented this *Light Box* as his invention. The most interesting studies created at this "shooting location" make us forget the concrete material: In order to point toward the macrocosm from within this microcosm, they are accordingly given titles like *Planets* (→ 38).

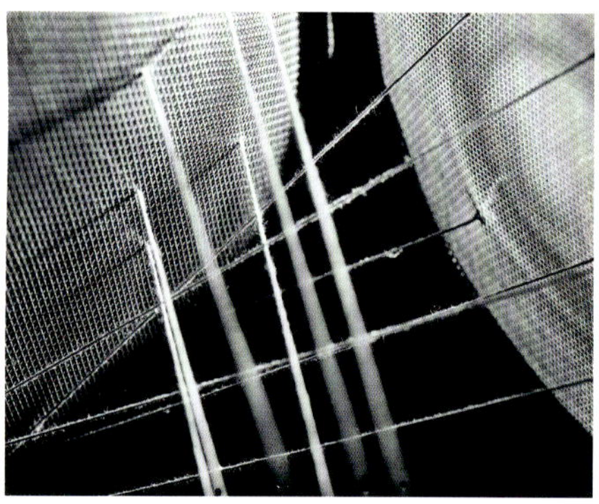

Anonymous
"... students Leonard Gittleman and Ati Forberg team up in a virtual volume exercise," in: *Saint Louis Post Dispatch – Pictures*, January 28, 1951
10 x 11.6 cm

Nathan Lerner
Planets, 1939, later print
gelatin silver, 40.4 x 50.8 cm

Out of the microcosm of the school, photography moved into the macrocosm of the city of Chicago. The title *City Light Box* (→ 90) is representative of this transfer. Patterns and textures as well as forms and the effects of light on objects could also be found in the urban working space, and these were joined by new themes, processes,

14 Pierre Cordier called his invention the "chimigramme." Others, such as Chargesheimer in the late 1940s, had already experimented with emulsions on photo paper before him.
15 Thanks to T. Paul Young for providing this information.
16 Chicago History Museum, Research Center, Arthur Siegel Photograph Collection, G1980.024, Box 62, student works by Larry Foster and Paul Weidrich.

and conceptual possibilities. Assignments like "The next 36 people," "All that glitters is not gold," "Near and far," "Numbers" and "Letters of the alphabet," "Natural and man-made environment," "People without people," and "90% white" or "90% black" as well as "Multiple exposure" and "Reflection" revealed a thematically and formally rich visual world, which we also repeatedly seem to find in later works by graduates and instructors. In the 1970s Barbara Crane focused on people's movements as a phenomenon and on individual forms isolated out of the urban space, systematically creating new configurations of photography's encounter with the biotope of the city. Along with the primarily abstract works from the Light Workshop, these are the photographs that can be most readily classified in terms of an "ID aesthetic," which mainly manifested itself in black and white (→ 162–169). Although color had aroused photographic desires from the beginning, the realization of qualitatively satisfying and durable paper prints remained as difficult as it was expensive: Like Moholy-Nagy, Callahan had already experimented with color in the 1940s. In the 1950s Siegel invested a great deal of money in high-quality dye-transfer prints;[17] color photographs (Ektachrome) were also shot parallel to the black-and-white images during the many years spent documenting the architecture of Dankmar Adler and Louis Sullivan.[18] Thus, for a long time, it was primarily material for projection (that is, color slides and films) that demonstrated a very intense occupation with color. Together with students, Moholy-Nagy created *Do Not Disturb* (1944), a drama based on a love triangle, featuring a somewhat psychedelic atmosphere. Morton and Millie Goldsholl's *Night Drive* (1957) shows Chicago's nocturnal rhythm of colored light as seen from a moving car. *Adam's Film* (1963), by Larry Janiak, meanders through the filmmaker's perceptions and is painted over with lines and shapes. All three films provide exemplary illustrations of the desire for color from the 1940s to the 1960s (→ 180–183). Callahan gave his students the following recommendation for their final year: "Spend the first semester just photographing, trying to figure out who you are, and the second semester do a project on that!"[19] The thesis projects represent a concentrated body of work often decisive for students' later practice. Many are based on the principle of the series and, beginning in 1967, films could also be submitted as theses.

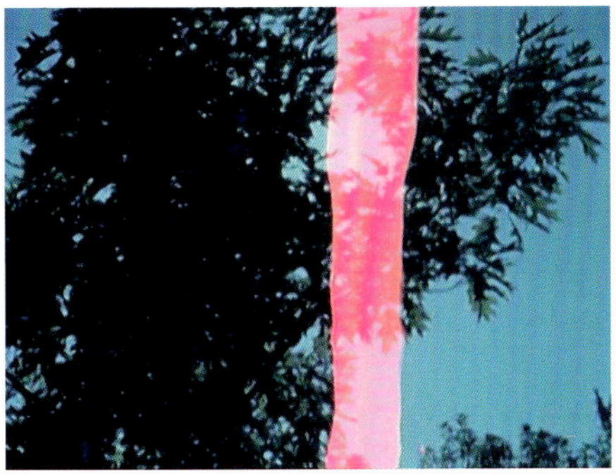

Larry Janiak
Adam's Film, 1963
image from the digitized film

While the assigned technical exercises were developed largely out of the existing vocabulary of photography, the programmatic freedom in approaching them and the invitation to experimentation coupled with a systematic structure was remarkable for that period. Although photographic strategies bear the risk of remaining soulless, at the ID, they nonetheless also provided impulses for very personal works and inspirational repertoires (such as water and landscape for Joseph Jachna) as well as a processual working principle. Here and there in the works or within the images, the "stream of consciousness" creative principle recommended by Moholy-Nagy is unmistakable: in the urban encounters, the attentively aesthetic capturing of forms and structures, the immersion in the material and ideas. In each case, the Chicago school used photography to unearth individual themes, questions, and fascinations, and this education formed the foundation for an associative creative approach based on photographers' own visual experiences as well as the development of conceptual forms of working. In a series of images, Kenneth Josephson deals with the theme of the photographer's own role by incorporating into the photograph his own shadow above his son's crib or his own hand holding a photograph (→ 122, 123).

17 Dye transfer is a laborious process that usually begins with a color slide: Separate matrices for the primary colors are transferred in three layers to create an image with adjustable, light-resistant, and very intense color.
18 The project, begun in 1952, was not concluded until the comprehensive publication nearly 60 years later: Nickel/Siskind 2010.
19 Davis 2002, p. 81.

While the substantially European influence of the New Vision and Surrealism can still be noted in the 1940s, more existential attitudes questioning individuals' own view of the world emerged after the war. The repressive politics of Joseph McCarthy and Richard Nixon may have contributed to this, favoring quiet and generally introverted positions among those who did not identify with a *Family of Man* fulfilled through humanistic "documentary" photography.[20] One of the school's clearest societal contributions lay in the critical examination of a city that was highly stratified racially, socially, and culturally: In the 1960s and 1970s Chicago was one of the most segregated cities in the US, and it simultaneously saw an economic boom and central protests. In 1960 Yasuhiro Ishimoto symbolically photographed white businessmen in front of commercial high-rises and Martin Luther King Jr., as spokesman of the marginalized African-American population, surrounded by demonstrators (→ 179). Photographs and films draw attention to the constant demolition of buildings and to architectural heritage worthy of preservation, but also to forms of living and life in the city (→ 156–159).[21] Some of these projects related to the city were created in collectives. It was not just in the interdisciplinary foundation course that students were encouraged to work together: This was also practiced in the advanced courses for future professionals.

The explicit goal that presumably dominated an ID mindset extending across the generations consisted in training the free compositional gaze: "It is intended that these become means for expressive ends, not just so many technical gimmicks."[22] Until the mid-1970s, pure technique and theory remained subordinate to "making pictures." Although the history of photography and film were an established component in the curriculum and charismatic teachers made an impression through their work, imitation was looked down upon—a situation often emphasized as a liberation from the traditional art-academy training long dominant in the US. Thus, in spite of many discontinuities, photographic education at the ID pursued a thought structure leading from material to content and simultaneously to technique; from the cameraless photograph to patterns of vision in individual photographs, photographic sequences, and the moving image; and from systematic experimentation to a process and finally a concept. For those who continued to occupy themselves with the photographic image, their experience at the school equipped them for the rest of their lives: "The ID was a place of discipline and craziness. I have kept the tradition resolutely."[23]

THE BIG WIN

The import of the Bauhaus "brand"—whose value had been established in the US since the 1938 MoMA exhibition, at the latest—stirred expectations among the school's private funders[24] as well as its potential students.[25] The institution addressed these simultaneous artistic and economic interests by pursuing two parallel lines of communication from the very beginning: One invoked the Bauhaus to articulate an innovative, polyvalent education under a new and unfettered approach (even or precisely for those who had already completed their education). The other sought to highlight the economic advantage or, alternatively, the broad applicability of creative production. One defining characteristic of the New Bauhaus's influence and public image was the school's fundamental openness in general and, specifically, its teaching design with photography to the greatest possible number of interested individuals. On the

20 The title of an exhibition that was developed by Edward Steichen and was sent around the world with public funding.
21 See Otti 2014.
22 In: Aperture Magazine Anthology 2012, p. 219. Siskind had come to photography by way of the social activism of the New York Photo League; the emphasis on technique and technology, as in the zone system of Ansel Adams or the Group f/64's identification with an aperture setting, was foreign to him.
23 Patty Carroll, in: *A Lasting Vision* 2015, p. 57.
24 See the research in Llyod C. Engelbrecht's lifework as well as Allen 1983 and Jones 2009.
25 "Today I am a photographer, a progressive, modern and I hope a good photographer. Tomorrow, I want to be a designer, but not second rate, not 1 of 10,000, as photographers are. […] I am willing to quit my present job and devote four years of intensive study for a glimpse of the goal I have dreamed of—but I would like to arrive at a fair and logical solution," letter from LaMont Benah [?] to Walter Paepcke, 1 March 1950, University of Illinois at Chicago, Special Collections, Institute of Design Papers II, Folder 36.

one hand, this was motivated by the worldly search for sources of income, but it also derived from a fundamental intellectual conviction regarding the positive effect of creative (in this case, photographic) activity. Occupational therapy courses were launched under the striking motto "Better than before."[26] From the very beginning, in addition to the classes held during the day, the school offered courses in the evening, on Saturdays, and in the summer for people who worked in the daytime and for children,[27] handicapped people, and veterans as well as art teachers.[28] Many of the regular students, mostly aged 18 to 30, were already trained photographers or professional designers, and they provided their work with a new impulse at the ID.
In addition to early guest appearances by the school (for example, in the summer at its own country estate or at Mills College, a California liberal arts college for women [1940]) the six-week seminar on the *New Vision*,[29] which was organized in 1946, represents a remarkable event. This seminar "established the tenor of all subsequent teaching at the ID. Henceforth, learning photography there would be collaborative, practical, professional, intellectual and have strong components of film and photohistory."[30] This was the first event to which the school invited a substantial number of representatives from the field of photography, including Erwin Blumenfeld (fashion), Berenice Abbott and Paul Strand (documentary tradition), Weegee (press), Roy Stryker (public client), and Beaumont Newhall (museum). In this way, it positioned itself as the representative of a new vision and as an essential player in the field of American photography—specifically as a school whose network linked it with the different areas in which photography is used.

In the sense of this networking, Siegel and Callahan—together with Siskind, who would also be won for the ID soon afterward—spent the summer of 1951 teaching at Black Mountain College, which had been founded by Josef Albers. Else Tholstrup and Keld Helmer-Petersen came from Scandinavia and greedily soaked up the town and the joy of experimentation with their cameras (→ 84, 162).[32] Photographers like Frederick Sommer, who filled Callahan's position while he spent time in France in 1957, and Garry Winogrand, who took over for Siskind for a year in 1971, also brought their own approaches to the school. Alongside their connections with art institutions, the teaching staff additionally maintained contacts in the commercial market for photography, that is, patrons or clients from the press and businesses.
The New Bauhaus's promise of an education focused on producing highly marketable designers was not fulfilled by the photography department. Nonetheless, numerous works document the applied use of photography. Once again, things began with a photogram: Around 1940 Kepes utilized this form of image for graphic designs, and in 1955 Siegel placed a photogram on the cover of the annual report released by a company with the appealing slogan "Finer products through imagination."[32] A particularly coherent example for the use of visual strategies that were originally developed in the school's early period was commissioned by the Kodak company: In 1968 Morton and Millie Goldsholl produced the advertising film *How Many Words*, a hymn of praise to photography in which large portions were composed using the "fundamental elements" presented at the outset.[33] Marvin Newman and James Blair worked for the press after graduating. It is worth recalling that the question of photography's status as art brings less insight than inquiries into individual images' creation, presenta-

26 In her 1985 film *The Color Bunch*, Judith Rothschild documents the integration of cameraless film experiments into therapeutic work.
27 Especially the works of Robert Donald Erickson, who was responsible for the children's courses.
28 In the evening program for 1955, the orientation of the art education course is described as "Photography as means of self-expression"; in the school program of 1960, it is described as "Analysis of light as expressive force" and "the camera as artist's tool."
29 See Pohlad 2000 and Cancellieri 2015.
30 Pohlad 2000, p. 148.
31 This led to the photobook Helmer-Petersen 1960.
32 Annual Report of Bell & Howell 1955, Chicago History Museum, Research Center, Arthur Siegel Files, G1980.024.
33 See Beste 2012.

tion, and reception. These works were meant to circulate. Accordingly, students and teachers published their works in the context of the school. Thus, five thesis works were presented in a special edition of *Aperture*, and the first publication of the ID Press was *The Multiple Image: Photographs by Harry Callahan*. A self-standing series of portfolios published at irregular intervals, the so-called *Student Independents*, provided an overview of current developments. The works' diversity is not the only remarkable thing about them: Siskind, who was surely the most established artist among the teaching staff, did not set his work apart and simply mixed his prints in among the students'.

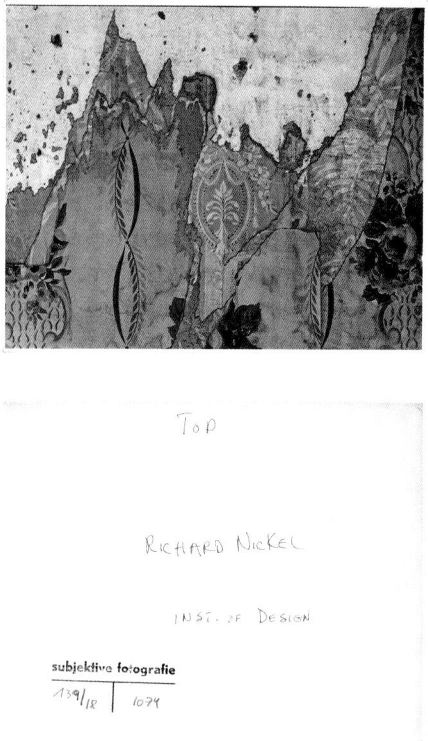

Richard Nickel
Wallpaper, ca. 1952–53
gelatin silver, 20.2 x 25.2 cm
stamp on verso: "subjektive fotografie"

The medium of the exhibition was used from the very beginning and was also dealt with as part of the students' education. Exhibition venues ranged from the institute itself to self-organized gallery spaces to museums.[34] The exhibition series *Subjektive Fotografie* provided a point of contact with Germany; in 1953 the travelling show was also presented at the George Eastman House in Rochester, New York. Photos created by and bearing the stamp of Richard Nickel (→ 42) provide an exemplary testament to this intersection: Along with his teachers Callahan and Siskind, he was among those chosen to represent his country.[35]

Since the 1970s, when the photo program at the ID gradually ceased to be significantly distinct, a large number of alumni—now instructors at other schools around the country—have carried on its principles in their own individually adapted form. They have been supported in this by the presumably equally great number of art teachers who came into contact with the ID's approach to photography through its Art Education program.[36]
Parallel to this outward movement, the school began to be considered in historical terms.[37] From that point on, certain photographers took a look back at their own work: After thirty years in the design industry, Lerner reflected on his own photographic beginnings and photographed Japan in color. Kepes reinterpreted early works on reflective foil and Callahan had earlier images printed using the dye-transfer process.[38] For these artists, market-based concepts like vintage prints or limited editions initially played no role: They were less interested in the "original" than in the entirely uncomplicated reproducibility of images—sometimes in other forms for new purposes.

EVERY ENDING IS A NEW BEGINNING

The teachers who worked at the New Bauhaus/Institute of Design were often charismatic. In their own way, each of them also stimulated a free, unfettered, open-minded, and simultaneously critical and continuous photographic practice distinguished by a constantly renewed approach and systematic experimentation with visual concepts and photographic questions. Basic fundamentals, assignments, serial working processes, and critiques took on a life of their own as a creative way of thinking in which empowerment and discussion were essential.[39] The qualitative impulse is always provided by the individual—on whom the achievement of a convincing body of work depends—and by his or her fascination with the medium, which is what maintains that oeuvre's vitality. Most of the ID photography department's graduates

34 See the contributions by Bähr, Siegel, and Daiter.
35 Otto Steinert, who organized this exhibition, taught photography in Saarbrücken and later in Essen. As an instructor, his American colleagues' principle of accessibility was probably just as foreign to him as their undogmatic and collegial attitude. See Breuer 2012. Regarding the context of German photography training, see Kaufhold in: *Bielefelder Schule* 2014.
36 See Selz/Koppe 1954.
37 See Introduction.
38 *Harry Callahan* 2013.
39 Crane 2014, p. 69: "They need to know that someone believes in them. […] It's all about light […] It's also all about practice."

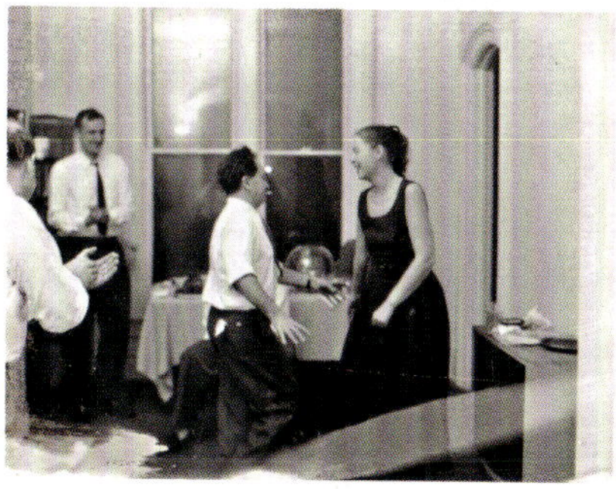

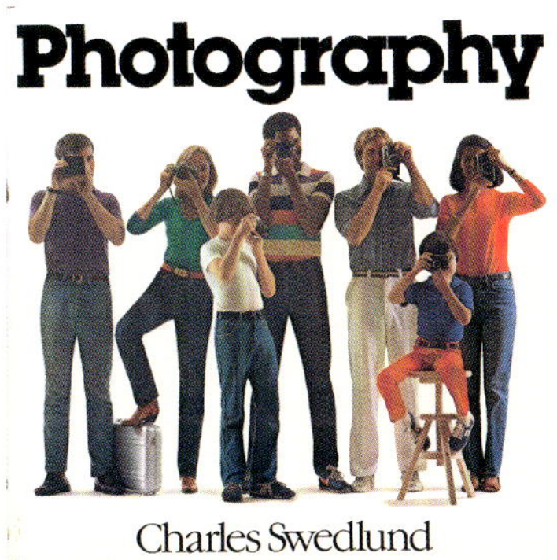

Anonymous
Aaron Siskind dancing, ca. 1952
black-and-white Polaroid, 8.5 x 10.5 cm

Charles Swedlund
Photography Handbook 1974

strongly identified with it and, later on, they have often continued to speak enthusiastically about the program as a formative period,[40] an inspiring atmosphere, its team spirit,[41] and of course (like anyone looking back at college) about the parties (→ 43). For the relatively few female students,[42] this male-dominated world was also a formative experience with regard to other aspects: "[...] what I really learned at the ID was how to speak up for myself as an artist and as a woman."[43]

Regarding the question of the present status of New Bauhaus/Institute of Design alumni's photographic work beyond the perspective of art institutions,[44] it is important to inquire into an attitude defined more by personal preferences and curiosity than by a need for recognition and also to examine the well-reasoned considerations that can provide the basis for an active decision to teach. The Society for Photographic Education was established in 1962 and, along with Minor White and Beaumont Newhall, its founders also included Aaron Siskind, Arthur Sinsabaugh, and Henry Holmes Smith. Now a nationwide professional association, it supports the professionalization and recognition of photography education.[45] Perhaps the following notion can be attributed to one or another of these photographers, just as it was to the founder of the New Bauhaus: "Not even exhibitions are enough. [...] it reaches so few and it reaches them in such a completed, rarefied form that the living problem gets obscured by the finish. There are very few people who can look at a picture and take its basic problem home to work on it. No money one makes in the industry and no satisfaction of shows and public recognition can equal teaching."[46] Even if others went into teaching for less idealistic reasons and thus remained active figures in the field of photography, all of them have taught future photographers how to work with the medium and opened up a wide range of creative possibilities to their students. Seen in this light, the two baseball photographers presented at the outset seem like prototypes. Both of them already had the skills of solid practitioners of photography at their disposal, but it was only their education at the ID that launched their personal oeuvres and their teaching careers spanning many years. This essay concludes with an expression of hope that the intellectual openness and supportive attitude of their teacher Siskind will live on: "A yippee and a hip-hip-hooray to you young photographers—unselfconscious about means, curious about life, perplexed by meaning and devoted to the picture-object [...] you are changing the face and the heart of photography."[47]

40 Lewis Kostiner, a graduate of 1974, summarized this in a conversation with the author in September of 2016: "It was psychotherapy!"
41 Personally confirmed by Barbara Crane, Kenneth Josephson, Charles Swedlund, and Wayne Boyer in the spring of 2017.
42 Including Barbara Crane, Barbara Blondeau, Linda Connor, Patty Carroll, and Eileen Cowin.
43 Eileen Cowin, in: *A Lasting Vision* 2015, p. 59.
44 See the contributions by Daiter and Siegel.
45 Josephson and Crane are among those who have received awards.
46 László Moholy-Nagy, posthumously cited by his widow Sibyl Moholy-Nagy, in: *Experiment in Totality* 1969 (1950), p. 137.
47 From Siskind's introductory speech at the George Eastman House in Rochester, New York, in 1965, cited in: Chiarenza 1982, p. 167.

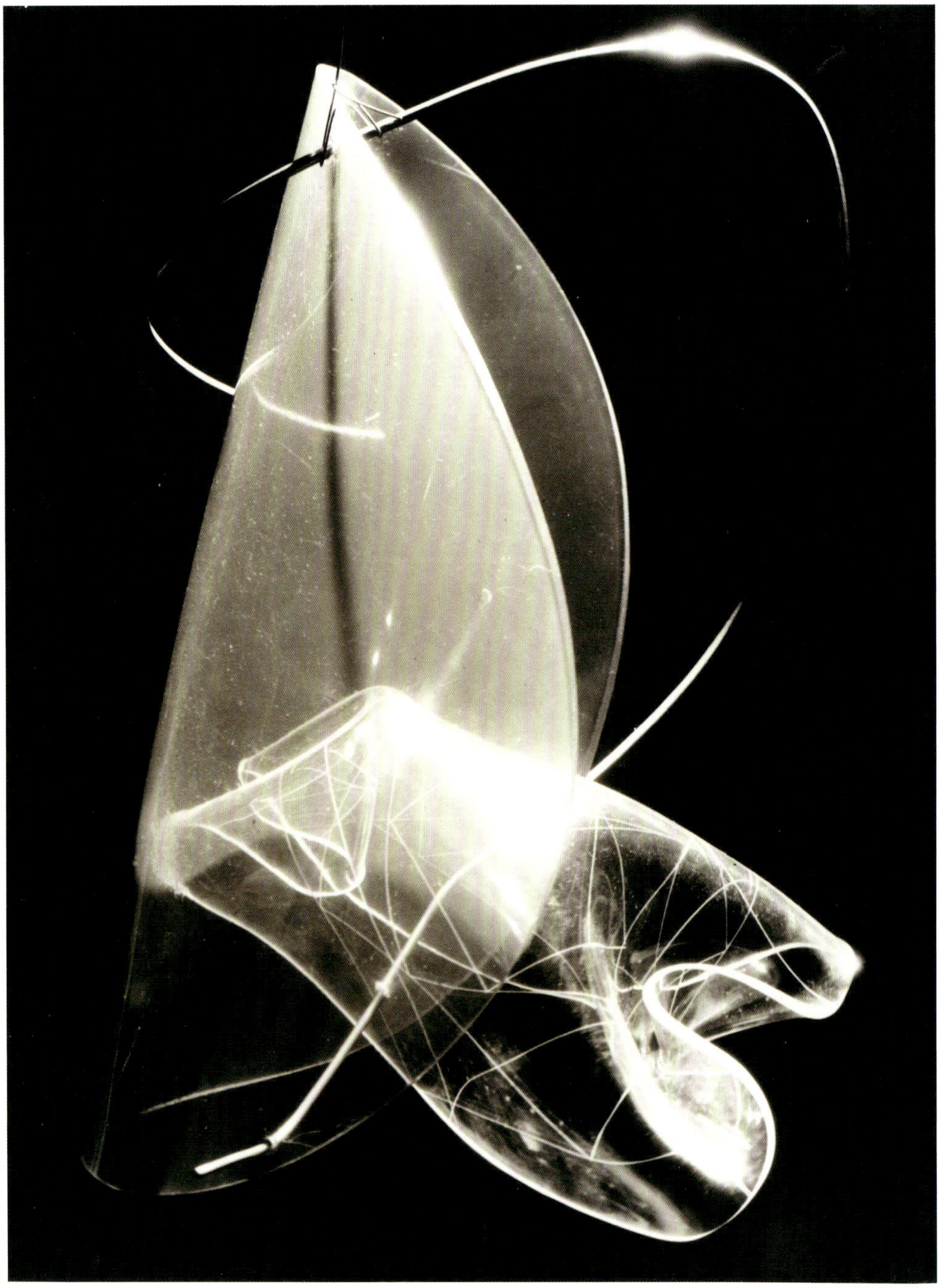

László Moholy-Nagy
Plexiglas sculpture, 1940
gelatin silver, 35.4 x 27.9 cm

György Kepes
Eggs and Strings, 1942, print of 1945
gelatin silver, 43 x 35 cm

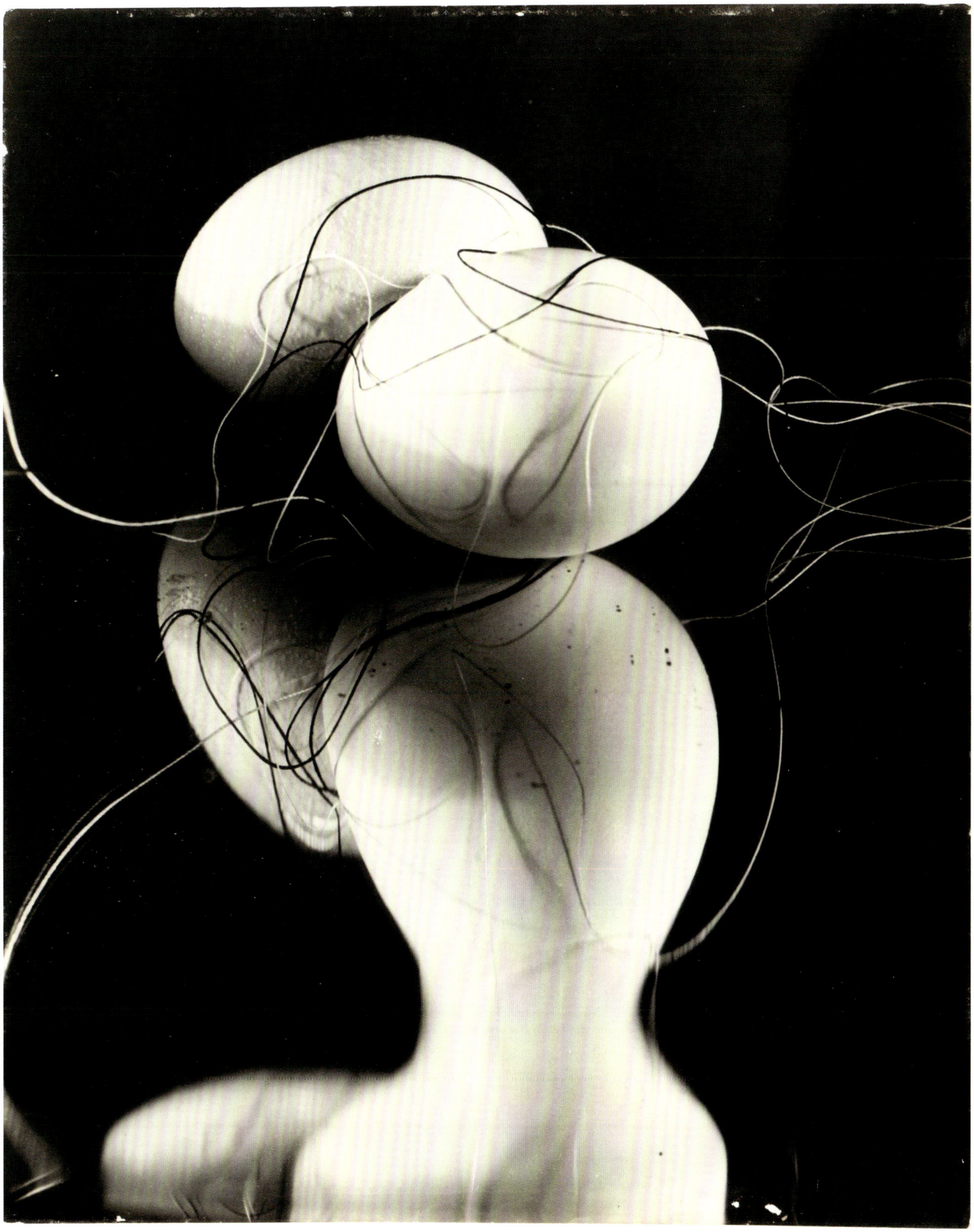

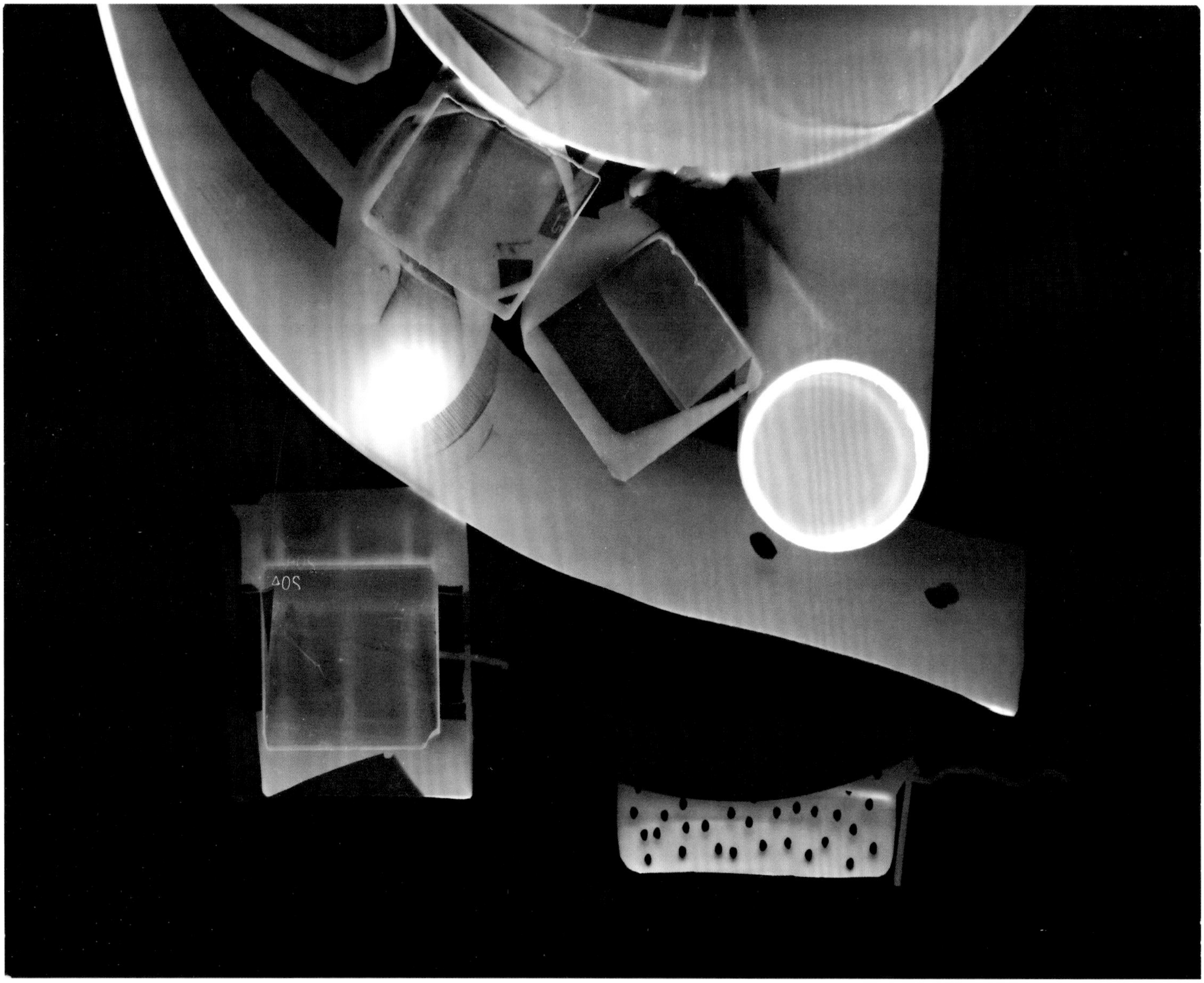

László Moholy-Nagy
Untitled, 1943
photogram, gelatin silver, 20.4 x 25.5 cm

László Moholy-Nagy
Untitled, 1943
photogram, gelatin silver, 25.5 x 20.4 cm

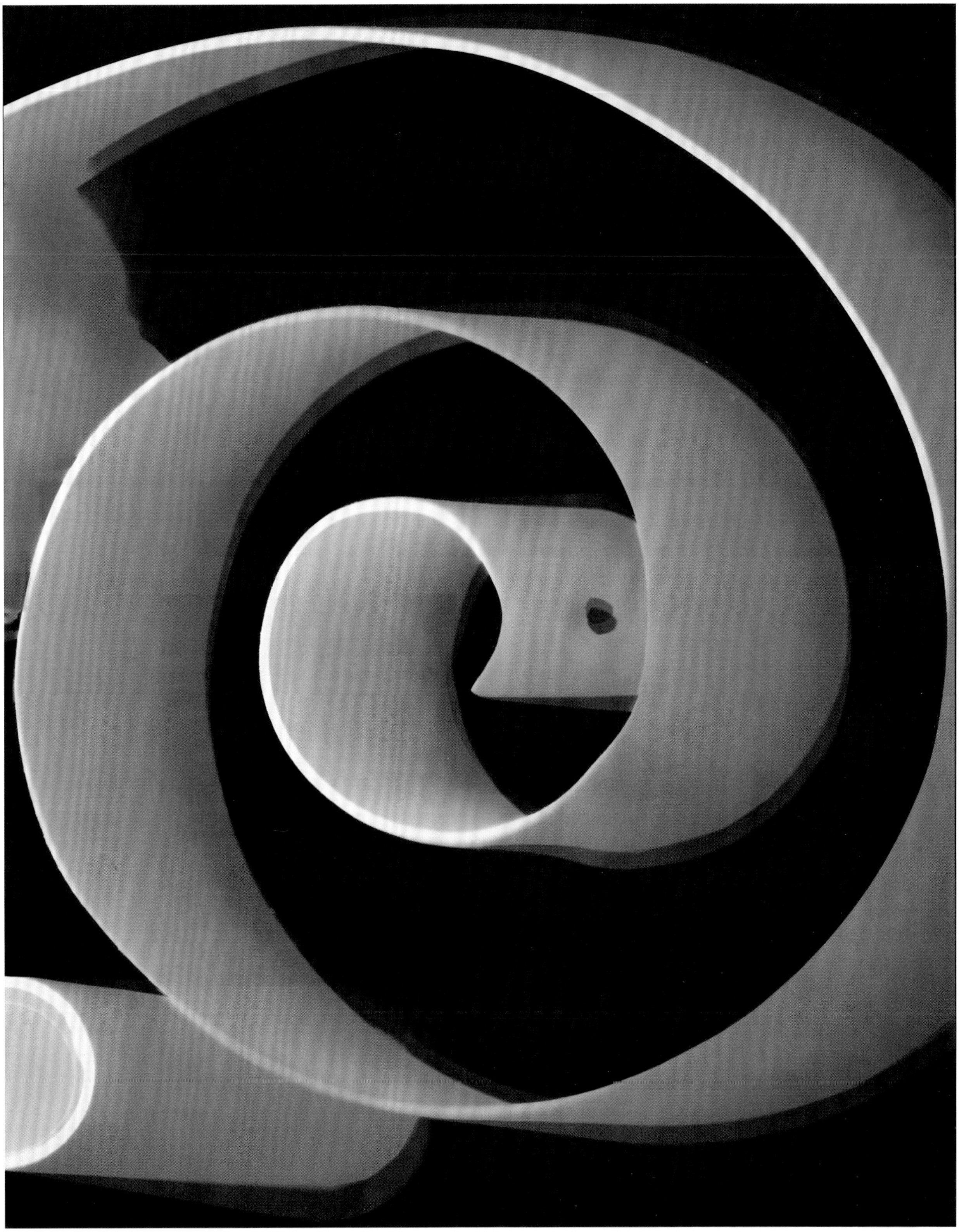

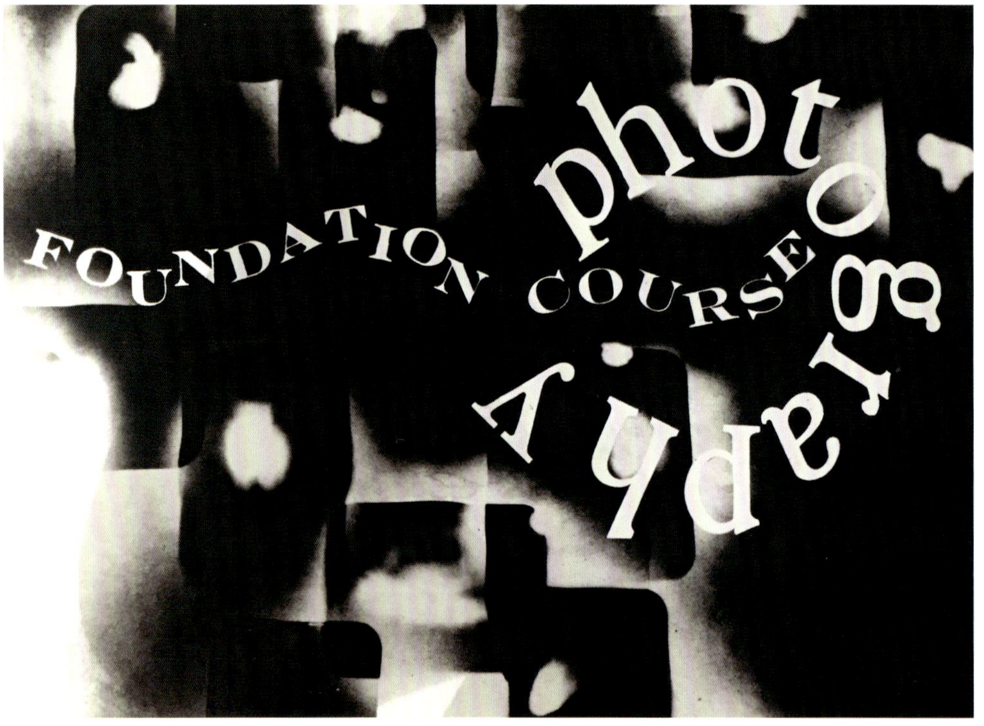

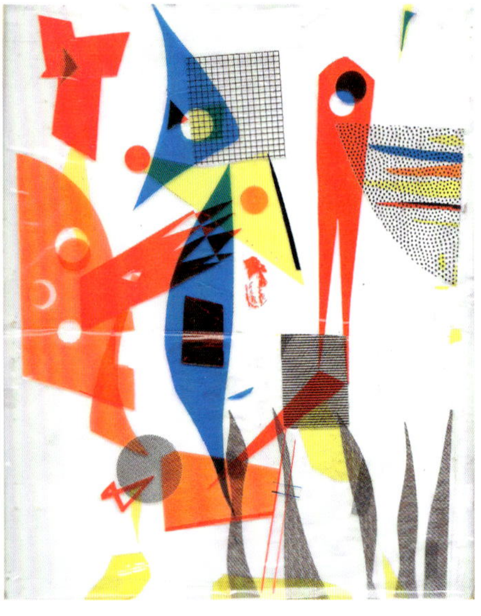

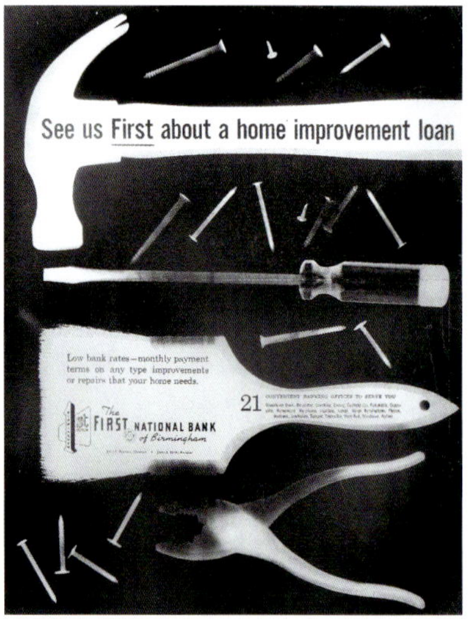

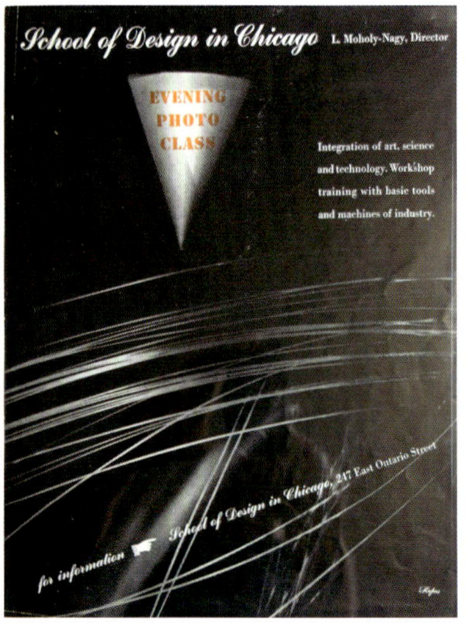

Joseph Jachna
The Foundation Course, early 1960s
spiral bound book maquette, 31 x 46 cm

Sumner Fineberg
Examples of materials used
for experimental photograms
1945–48
plastic stencils, 25.6 x 20.8 cm

Sumner Fineberg
First Bank photogram proof sheet, 1960/61
gelatin silver, 31.2 x 25 cm

School of Design in Chicago,
Evening Photo Classes, Chicago 1944
school brochure, cover

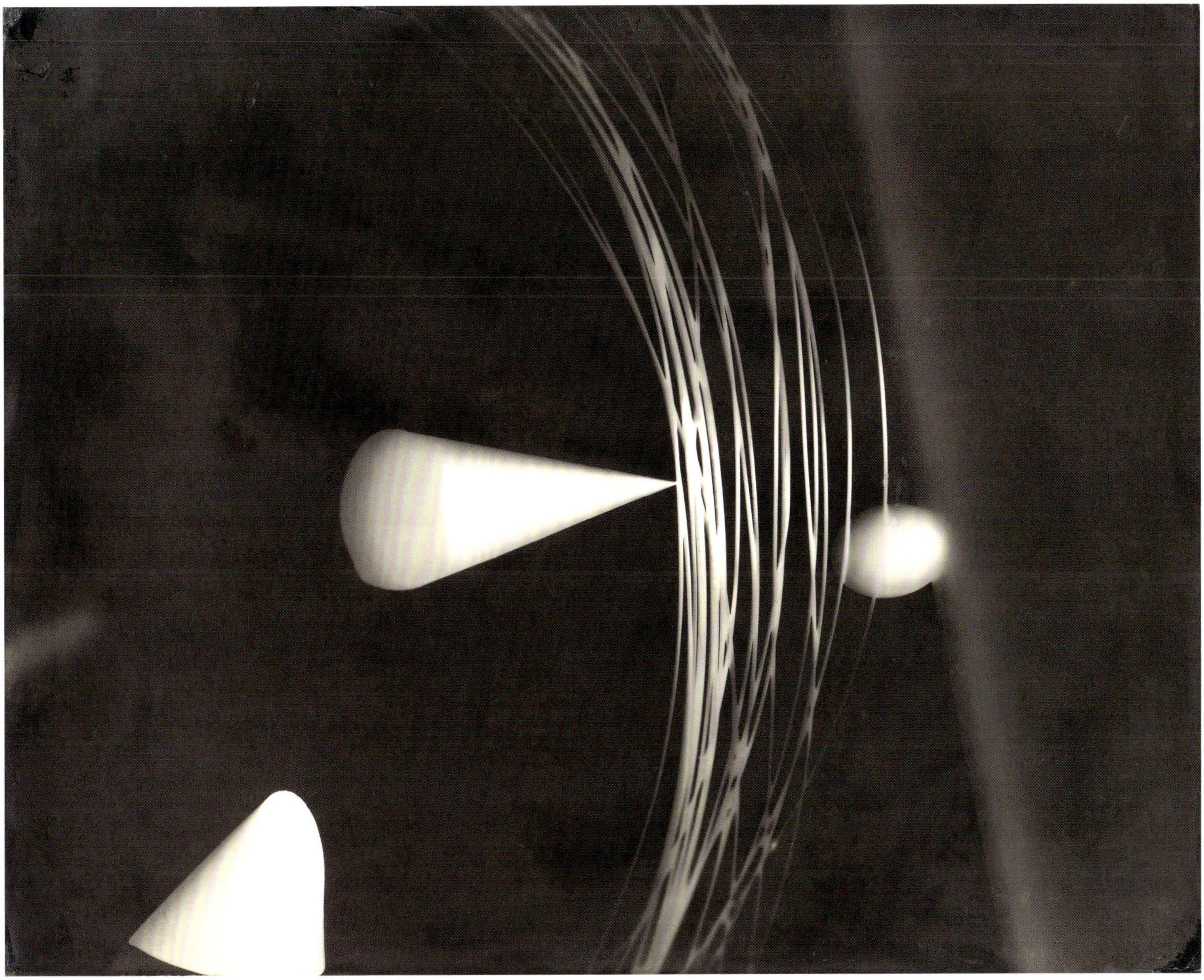

György Kepes
Untitled, ca. 1941
photogram, gelatin silver, 40.5 x 50.8 cm

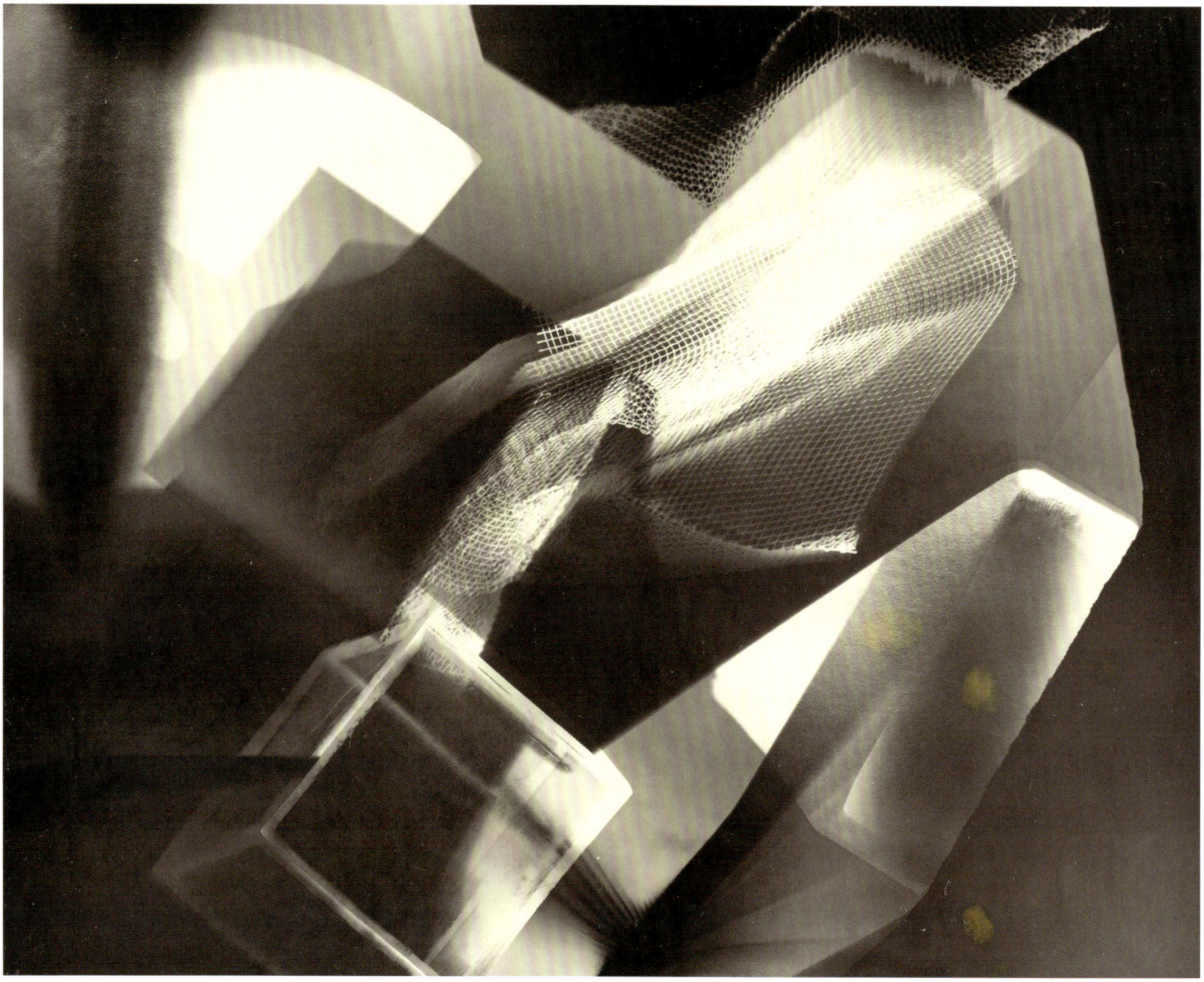

Anonymous
Untitled, between 1939 and 1944
photogram, gelatin silver, 20.4 x 25.3 cm

Arthur Siegel
Untitled, 1940s
photogram, gelatin silver, 27.8 x 22.8 cm

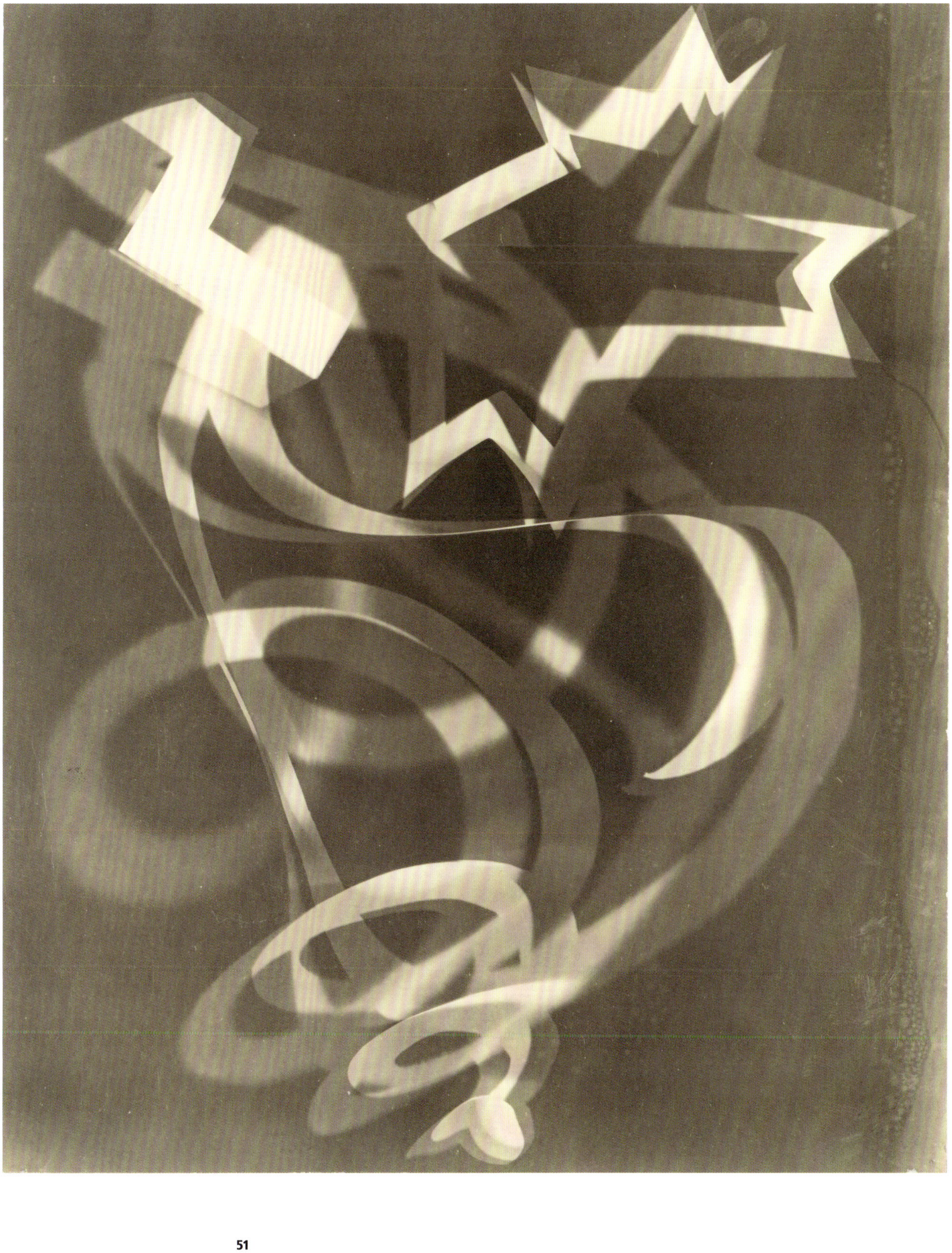

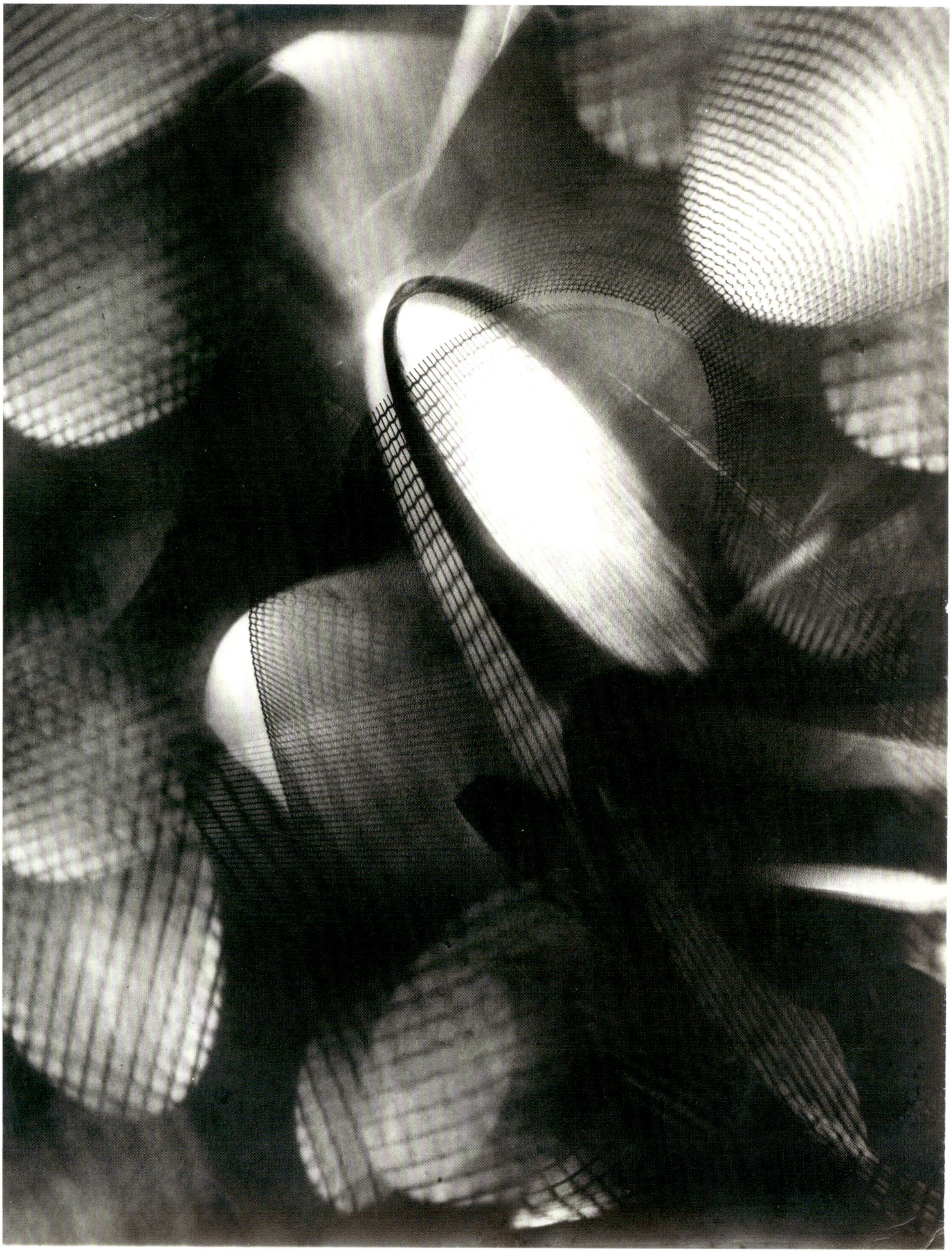

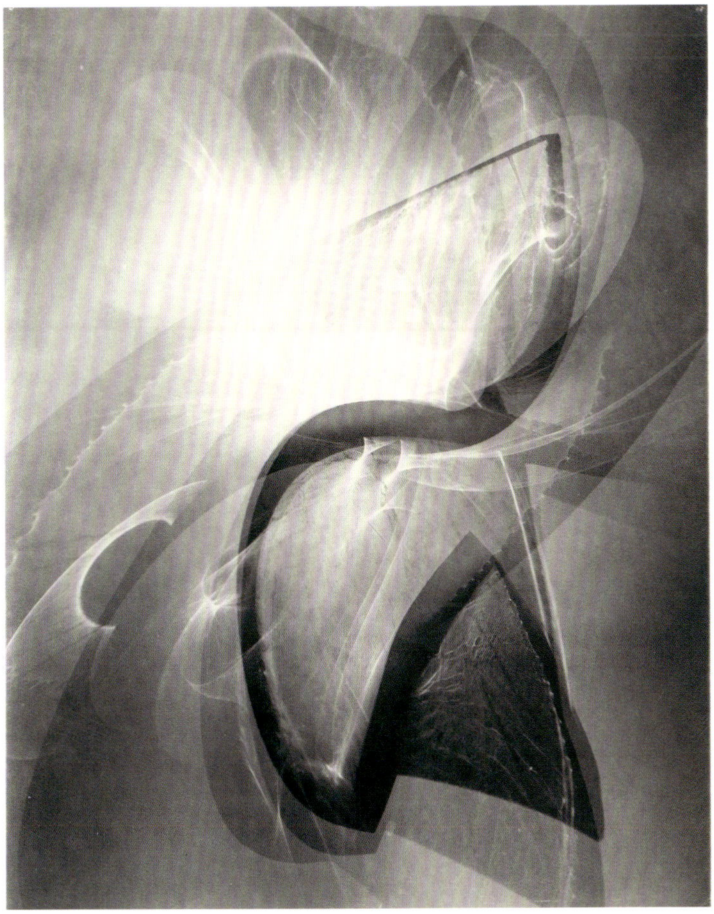

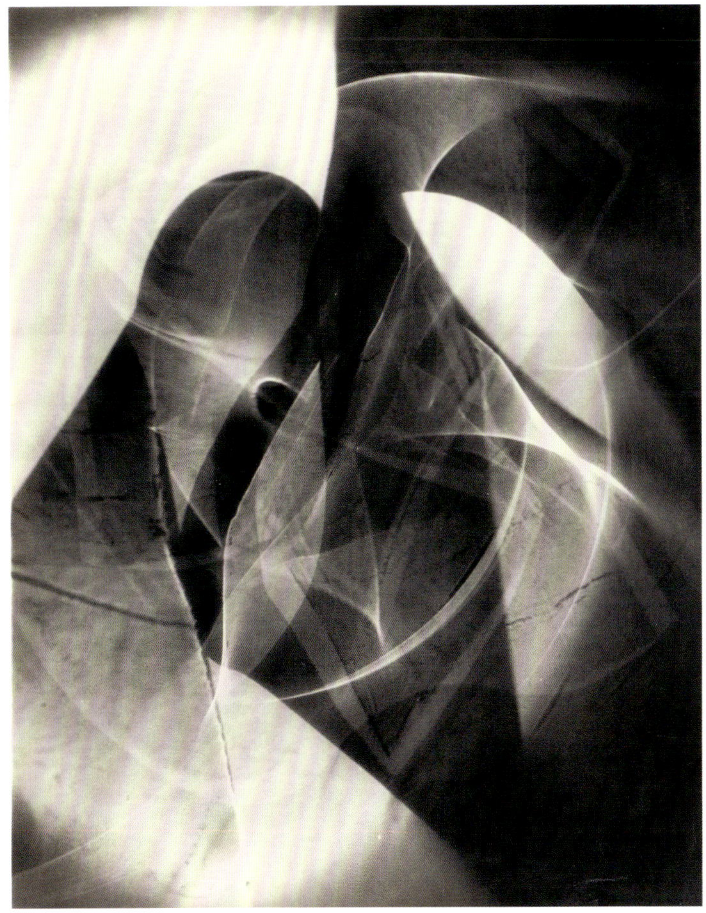

Arthur Siegel
Untitled, 1949
photogram, gelatin silver, 35.3 x 27.7 cm

Arthur Siegel
Untitled, 1949
photogram, gelatin silver, 35.3 x 27.9 cm

Arthur Siegel
Untitled, 1949
photogram, gelatin silver, 35.3 x 27.9 cm

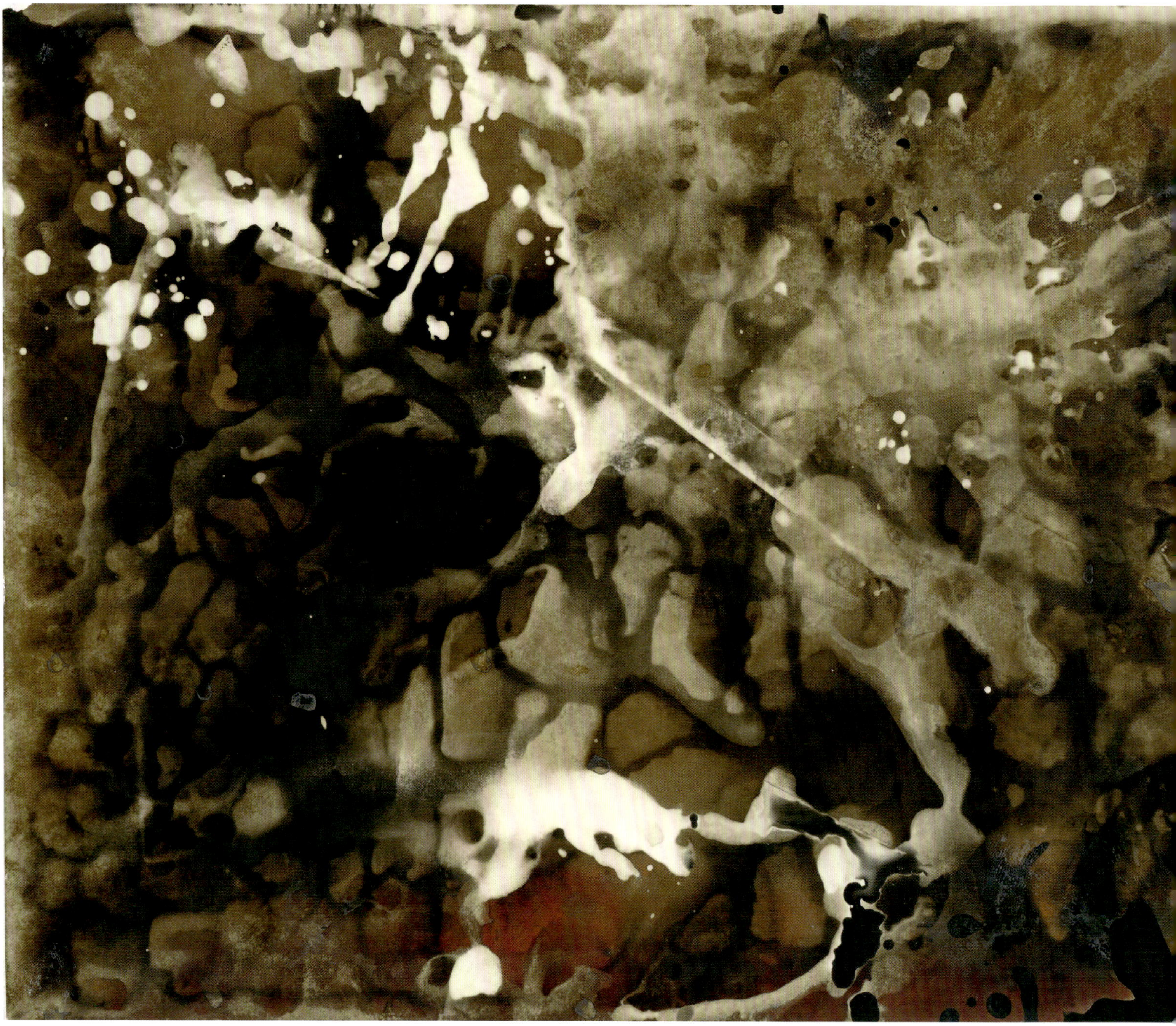

Myron Kozman
Untitled, 1938
chemical drawing, gelatin silver, 20.3 x 25.2 cm

Arthur Siegel
Untitled, 1940s
cliché verre, gelatin silver, 35.5 x 28 cm

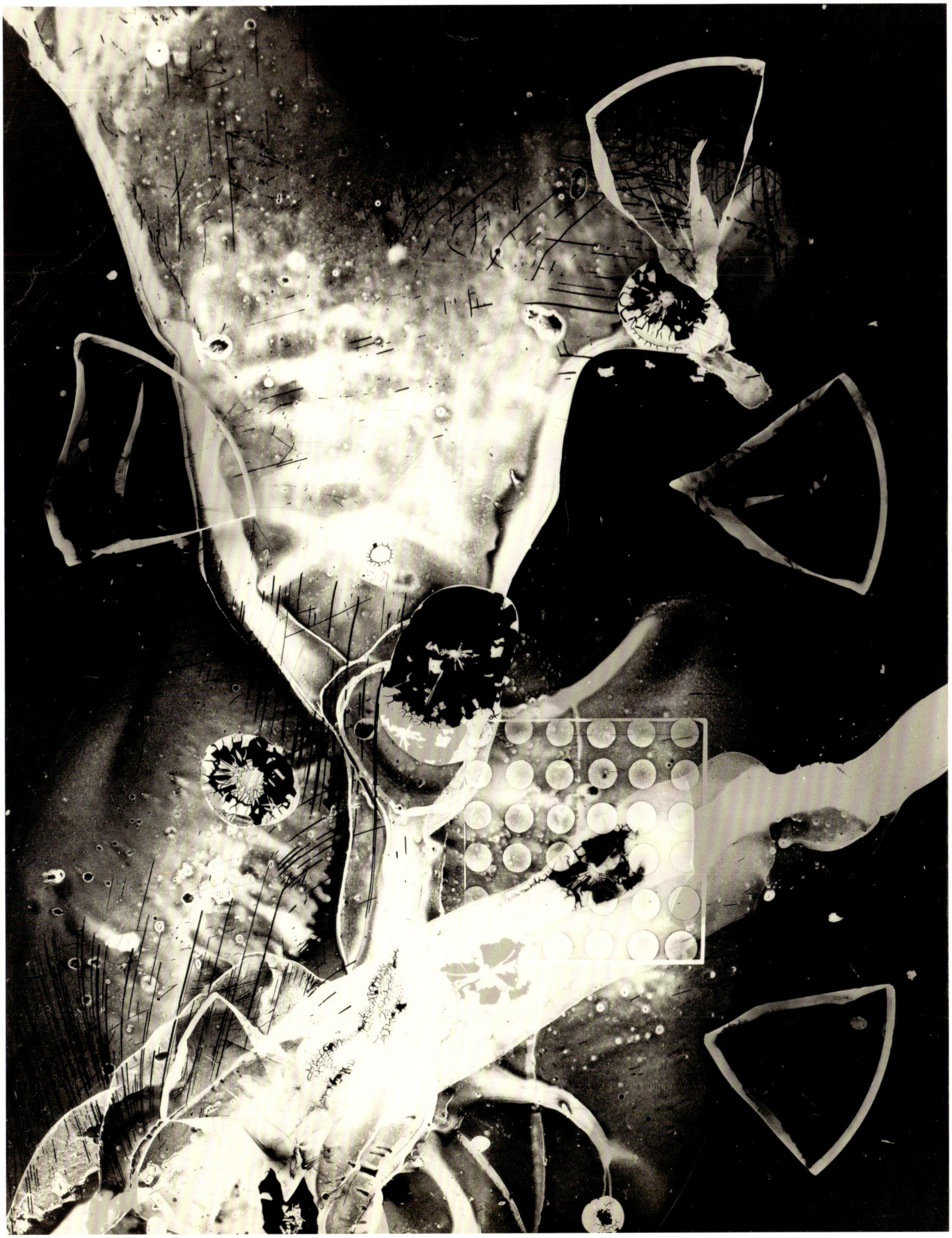

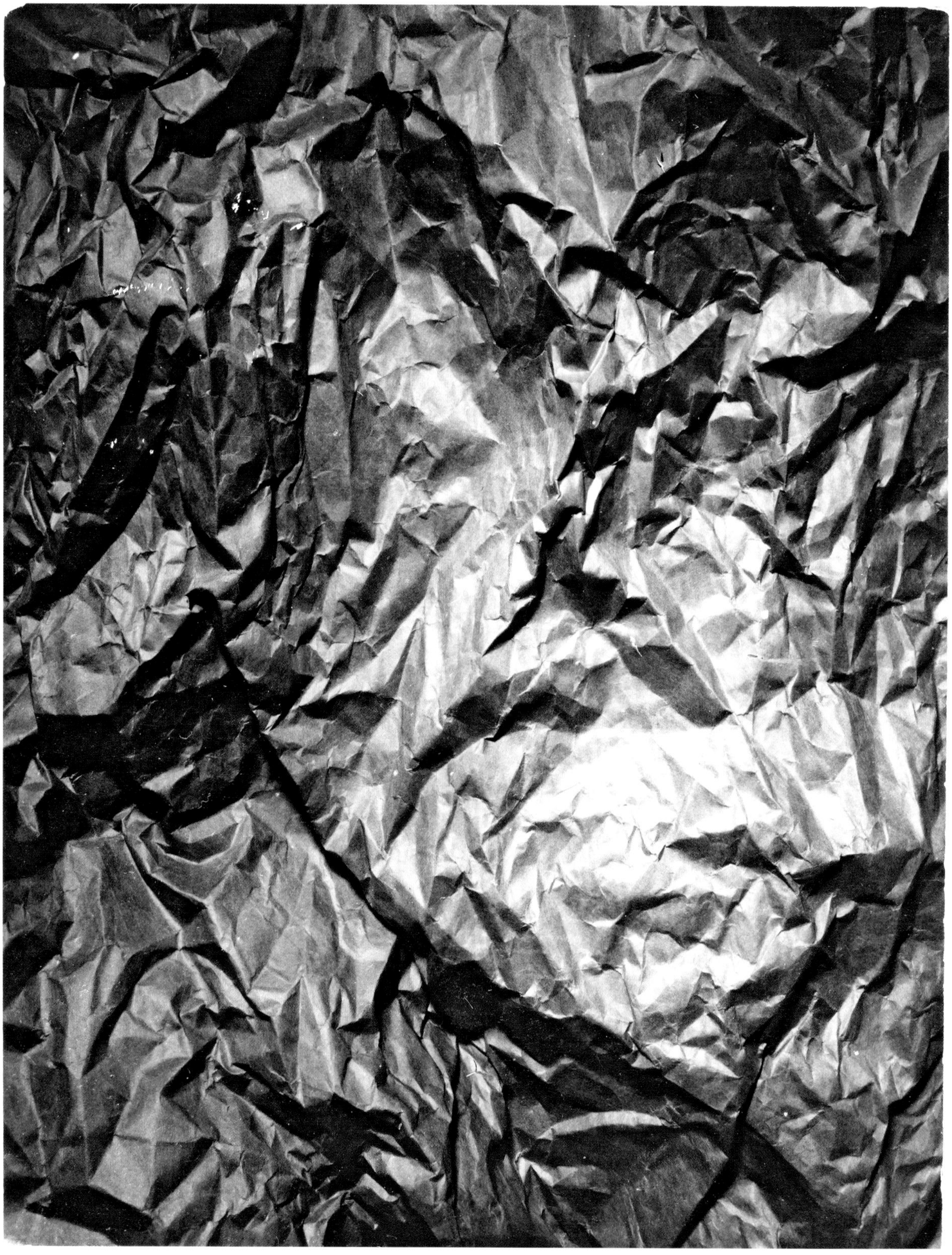

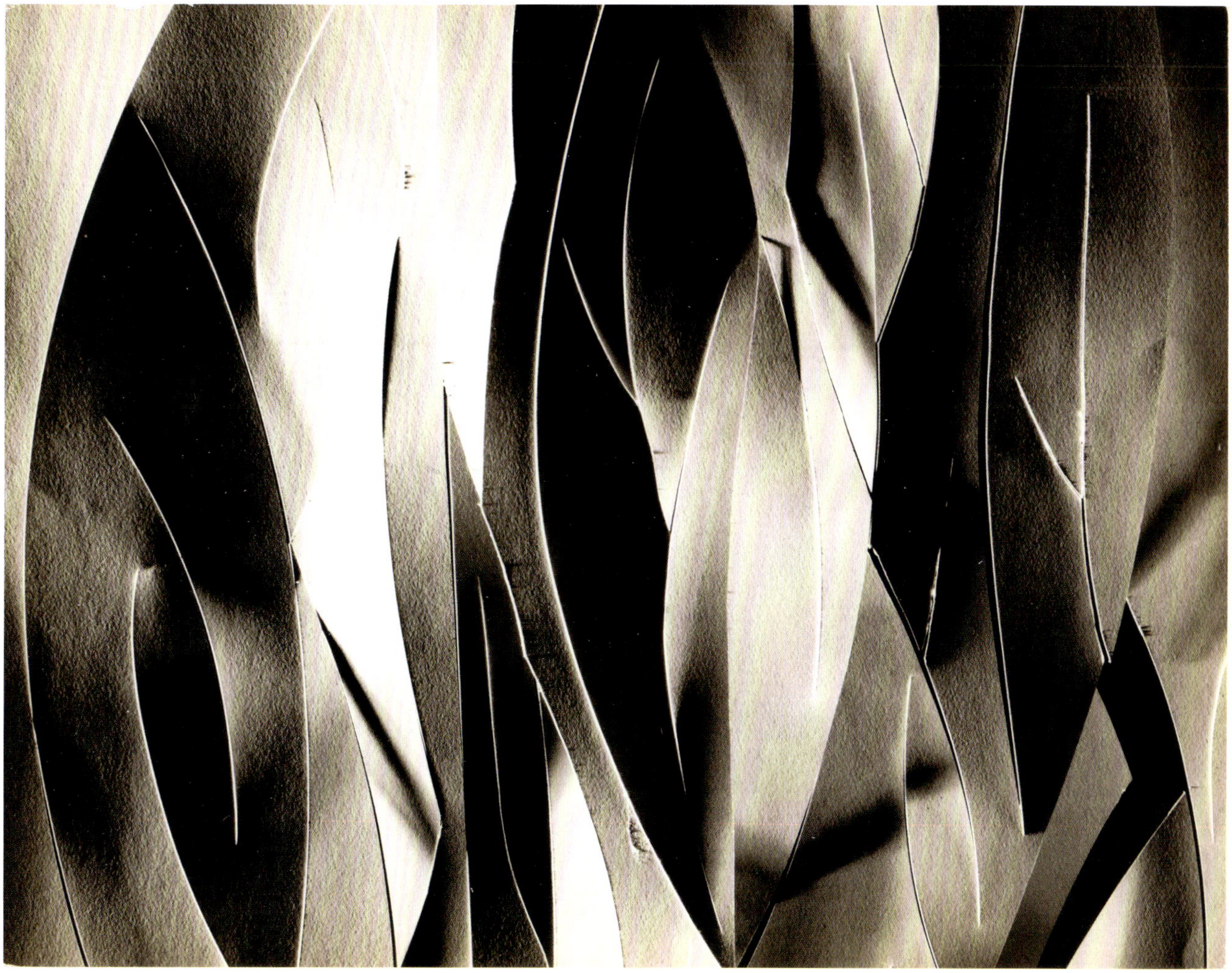

Jerome Sharff
Light modulator, ca. 1940
gelatin silver, 12 x 9 cm

Arthur Sinsabaugh
Untitled, ca. 1940
gelatin silver, 9 x 12 cm

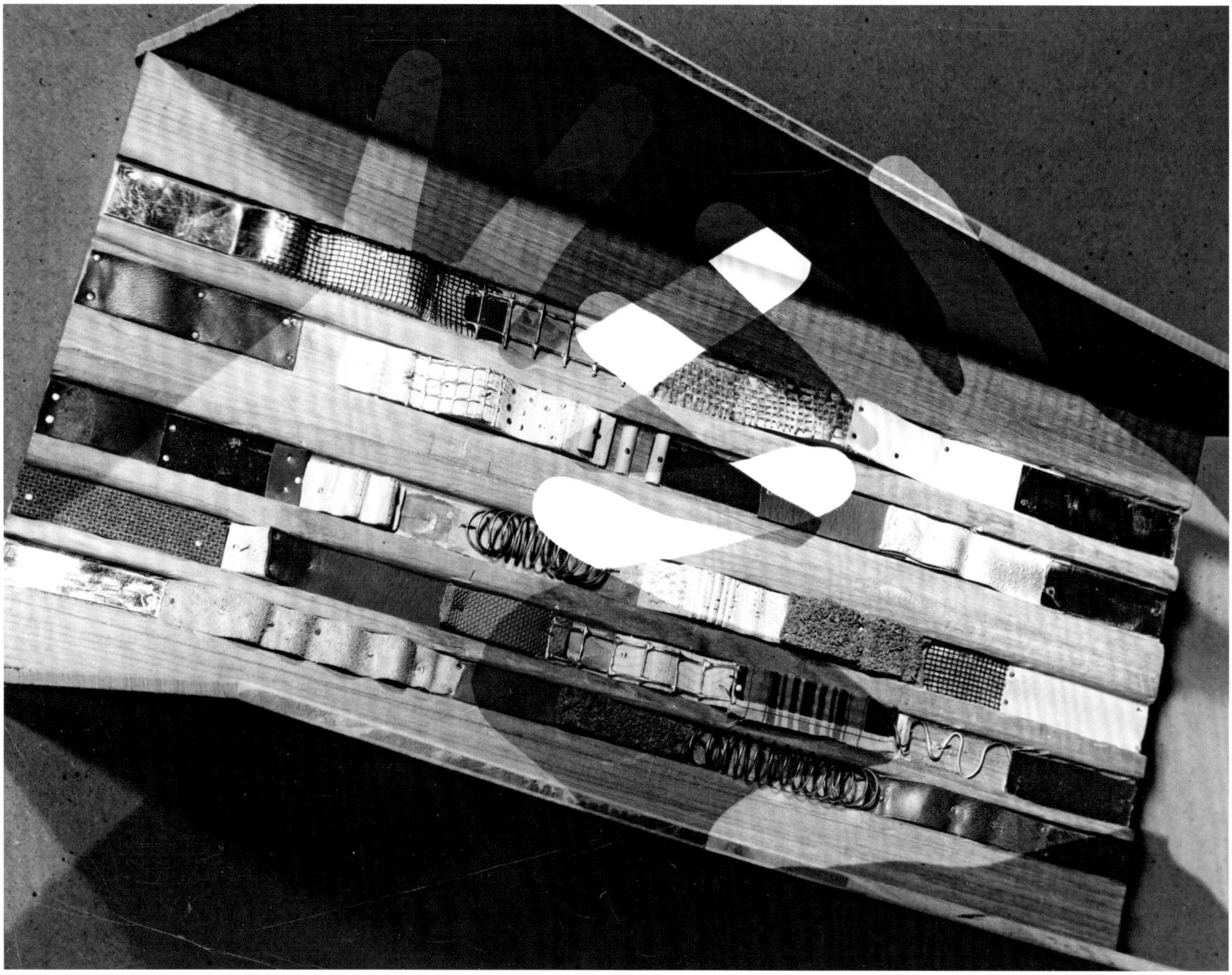

Eugene Whitehorn
Untitled, 1939/40
gelatin silver, 26.6 x 34.5 cm

Nathan Lerner
Light modulator, 1940, later print
gelatin silver, 31 x 20.2 cm

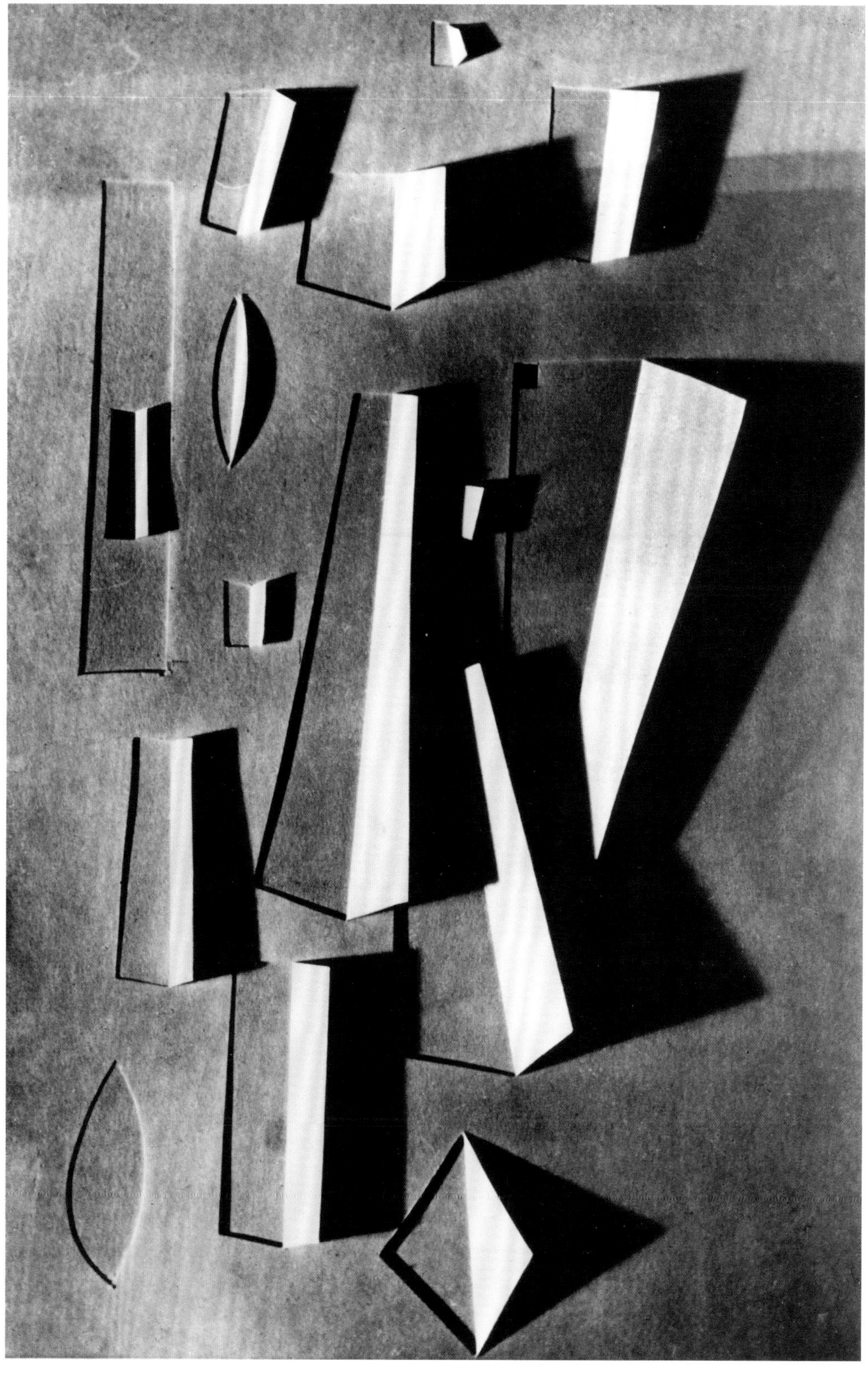

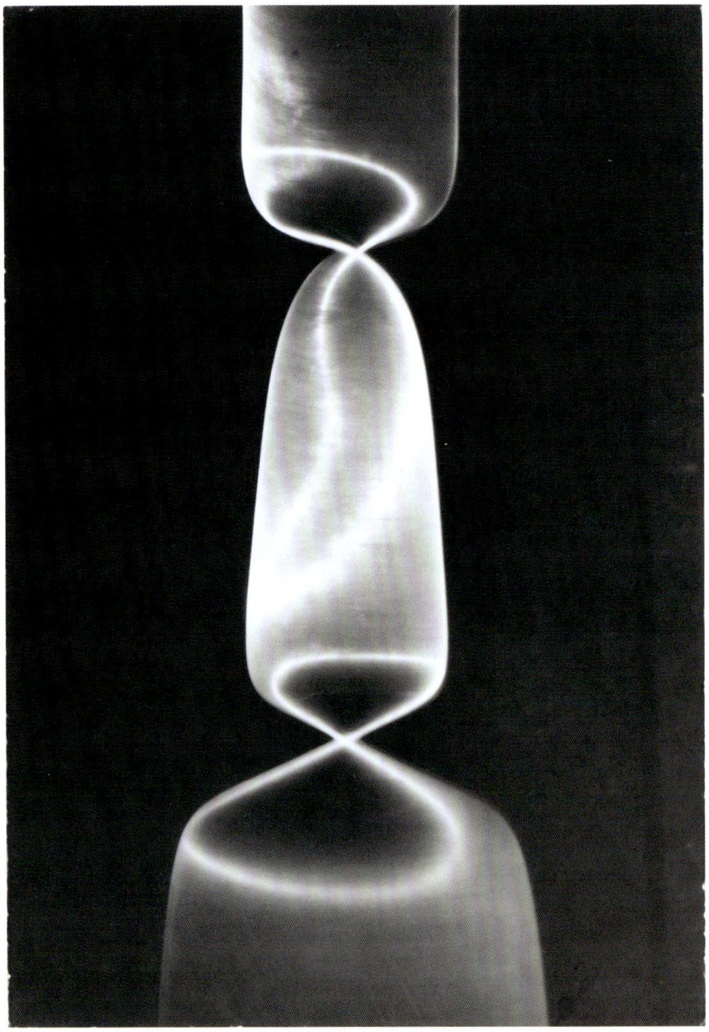

Anonymous
Untitled (Virtual volume), ca. 1940
gelatin silver, 12 x 9 cm

György Kepes
Simulated light effects with floating reflective buoys, 1967
gelatin silver, 50.5 x 40.2 cm

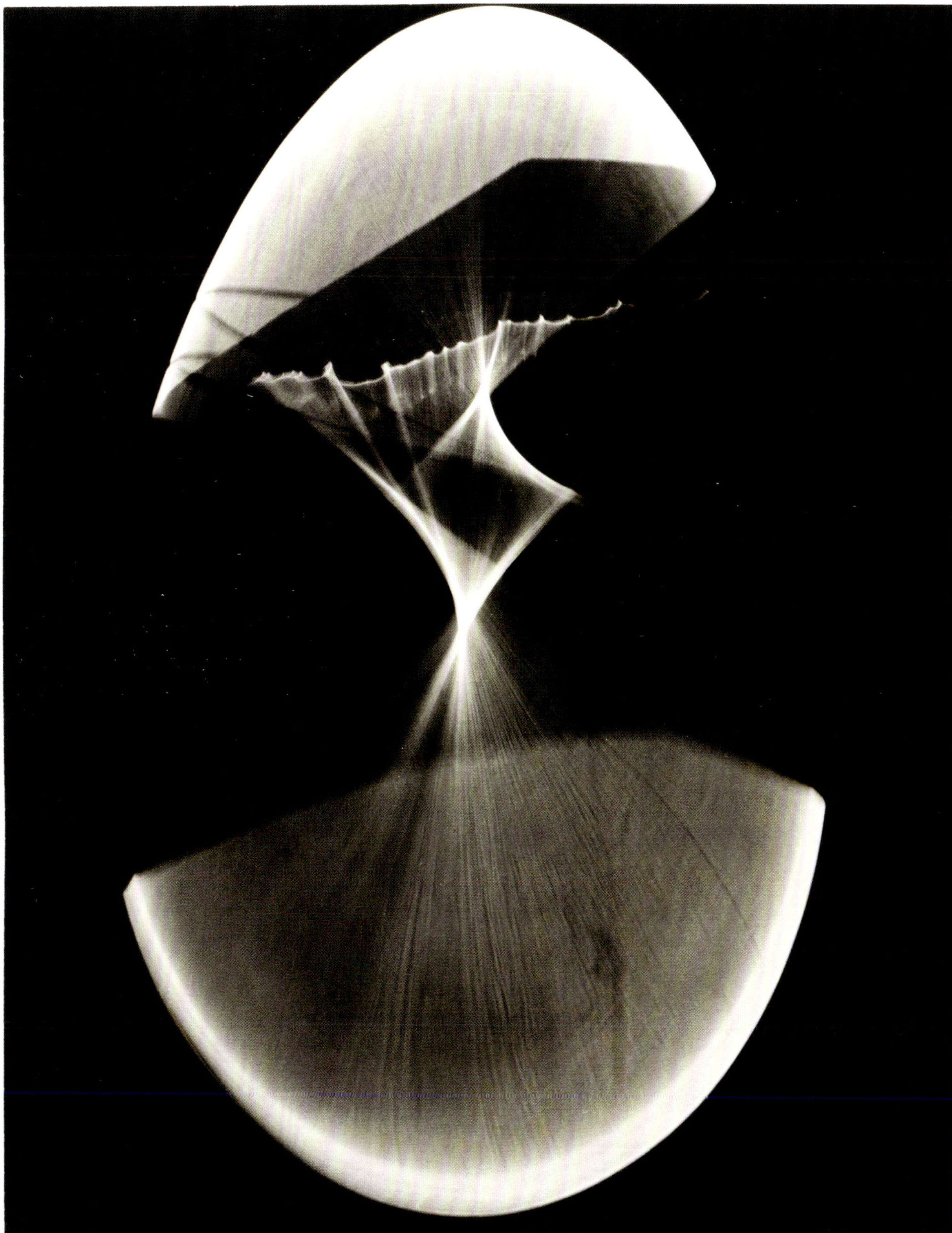

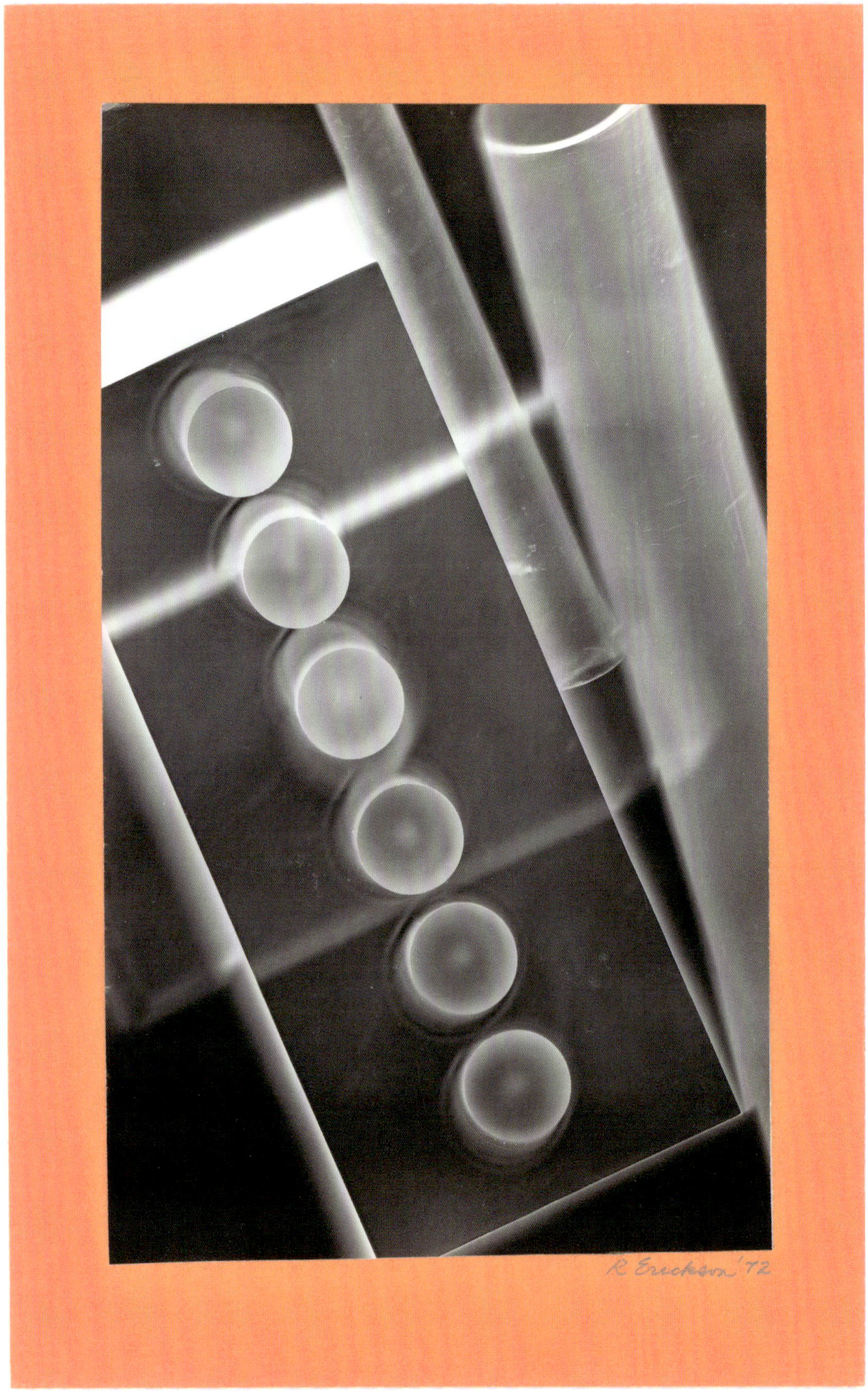

Robert Donald Erickson
Photogram # 10, Lucite Rods & Blocks, 1972
gelatin silver, 25.2 x 15 cm

Robert Donald Erickson
Untitled, 1970
photogram, gelatin silver, 25.1 x 19.8 cm

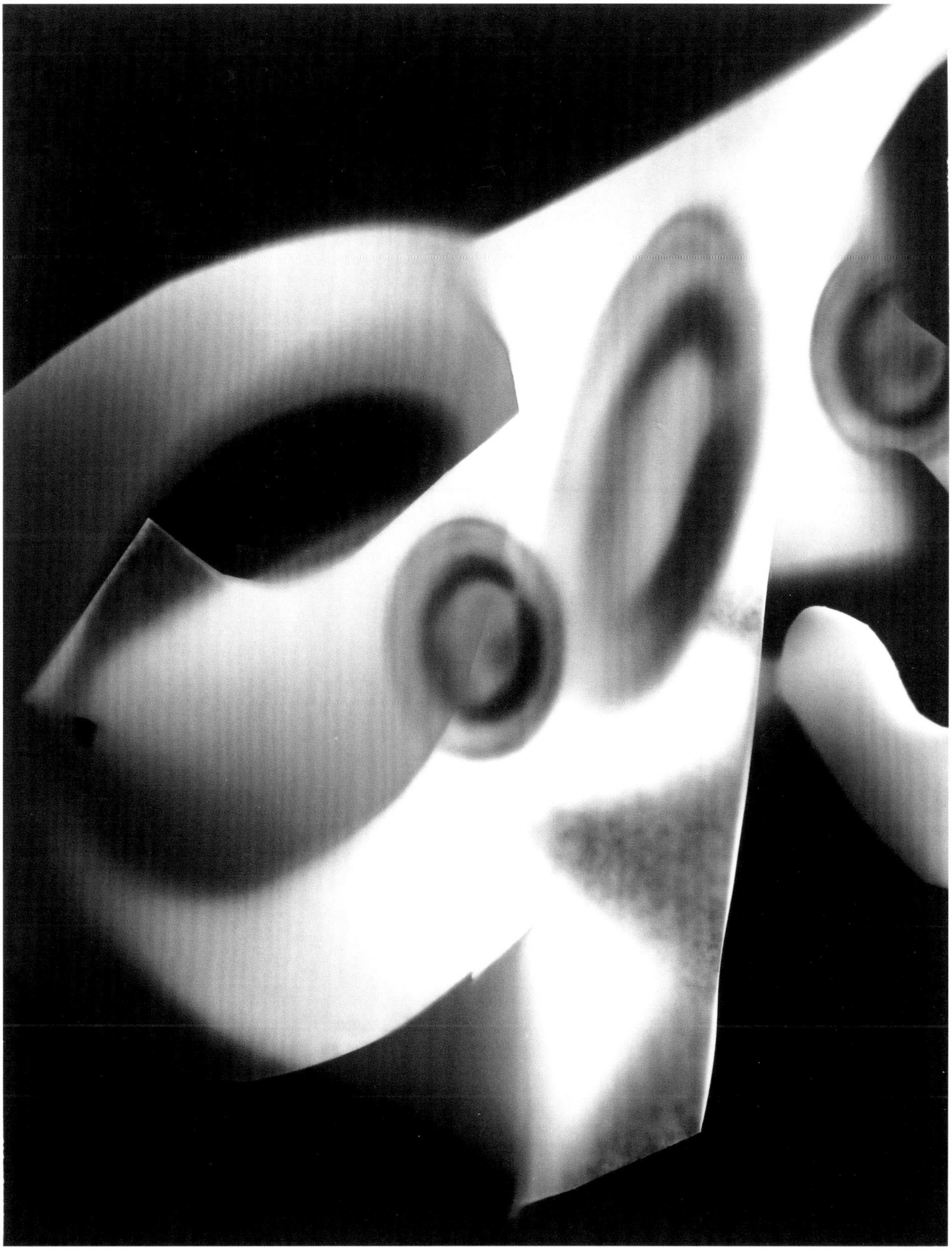

THE PHOTOGRAPHY PROGRAM AT THE INSTITUTE OF DESIGN

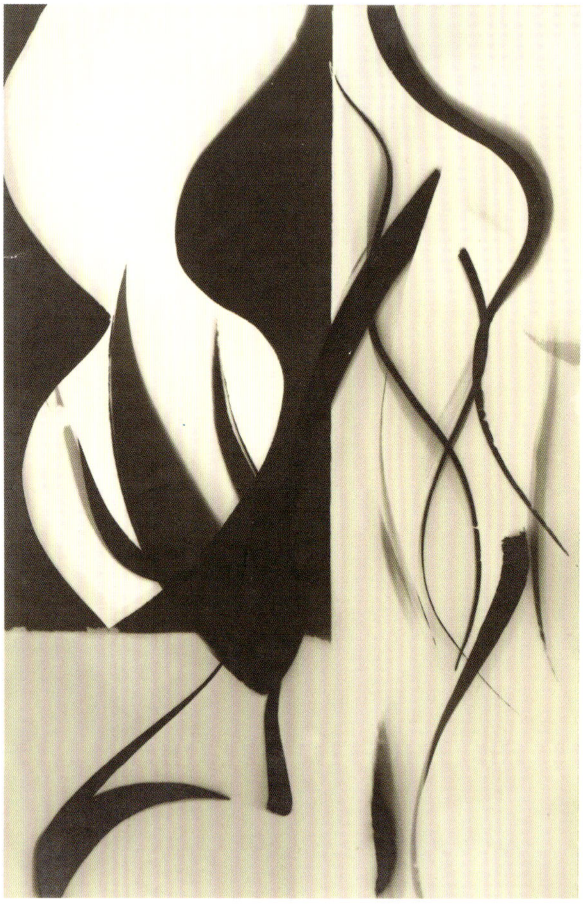

Arthur Siegel
Untitled, 1938
photogram, gelatin silver, 18.5 x 12 cm

John Grimes

Between 1938 and 2001 the Institute of Design (ID) produced over 200 photographers. At least 140 of these were or are working artists and teachers of photography in colleges and universities.

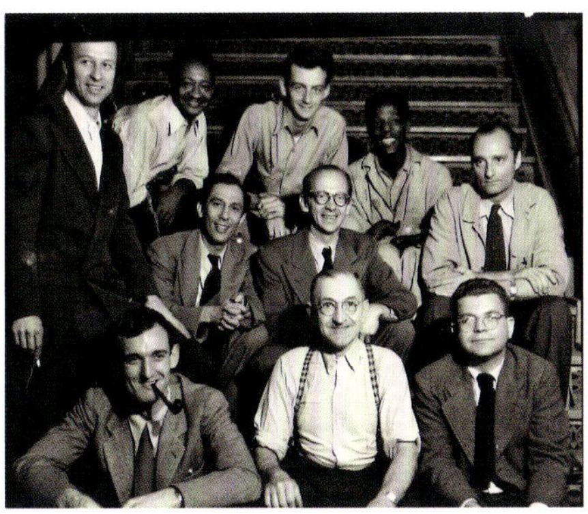

Mili Thompson
ID staff, top row: Harry Callahan, Huell Washington (janitor), John Reynolds, Jimmy Hargrove; middle row: Arthur Siegel, Frank Levstik, unknown; bottom row: Hugo Weber, Casey (surname unknown, carpenter), Nathan Lerner, ca. 1946–1949
gelatin silver, 10 x 12.5 cm

THE BEGINNING

Though photography was part of the Bauhaus's investigations, it was only formally taught there after László Moholy-Nagy had left the school. For Moholy-Nagy, photography was an essential component of "total education," and he made it coequal with the other parts of his foundation in the New Bauhaus as the Light Workshop, which would investigate the properties of light as a new medium of expression. The curriculum for the Light Workshop was based on a series of experiments built around Moholy's 'Eight Varieties of Abstract Photographic Seeing.'

In the *Annual of American Photography* (1944), Moholy-Nagy summarized his conception of the role of photography in the study of design and reported on the results thus far. Photography was the vehicle by which light, the fundamental "material" of the medium, would be investigated for its power to create new imagery. He concentrated on the photogram and the light modulator as the most basic explorations of photography and emphasized the interrelationship between drawing, typography, spatial form, and color study. While not stated in this article, it was the case that all the foundation workshops were linked together: less separate areas of study than a single experience finding an outlet in multiple forms. In the foundation course students took the products of the drafting course to the darkroom and made multiply exposed prints of them. Folded paper studies developing three-dimensional forms from two dimensions were taken to the photo studio and used as light modulators—as were three-dimensional hand sculptures (→ 56–59). In the Light Workshop they made photograms, light modulators, did close-ups, images that were almost all white, others almost all black (→ 66, 67), contrasts between near and far, large and small, positive and negative, they used fast shutter speeds to stop action and slow ones to expand time and create virtual volumes (→ 69), and they would print sandwiched negatives and make multiple exposures (→ 70).

Between 1938 and 1945 the number of students remained small. In 1946 everything changed: While in the spring, there were about thirty students enrolled, in the fall, there were over three hundred.[1] To handle the rush, at least in photography, Moholy-

1 Through the Servicemen's Readjustment Act of 1944, commonly known as the G. I. Bill, the government gave grants to veterans to pay tuition and living expenses at colleges and vocational/technical schools, including the Institute of Design.

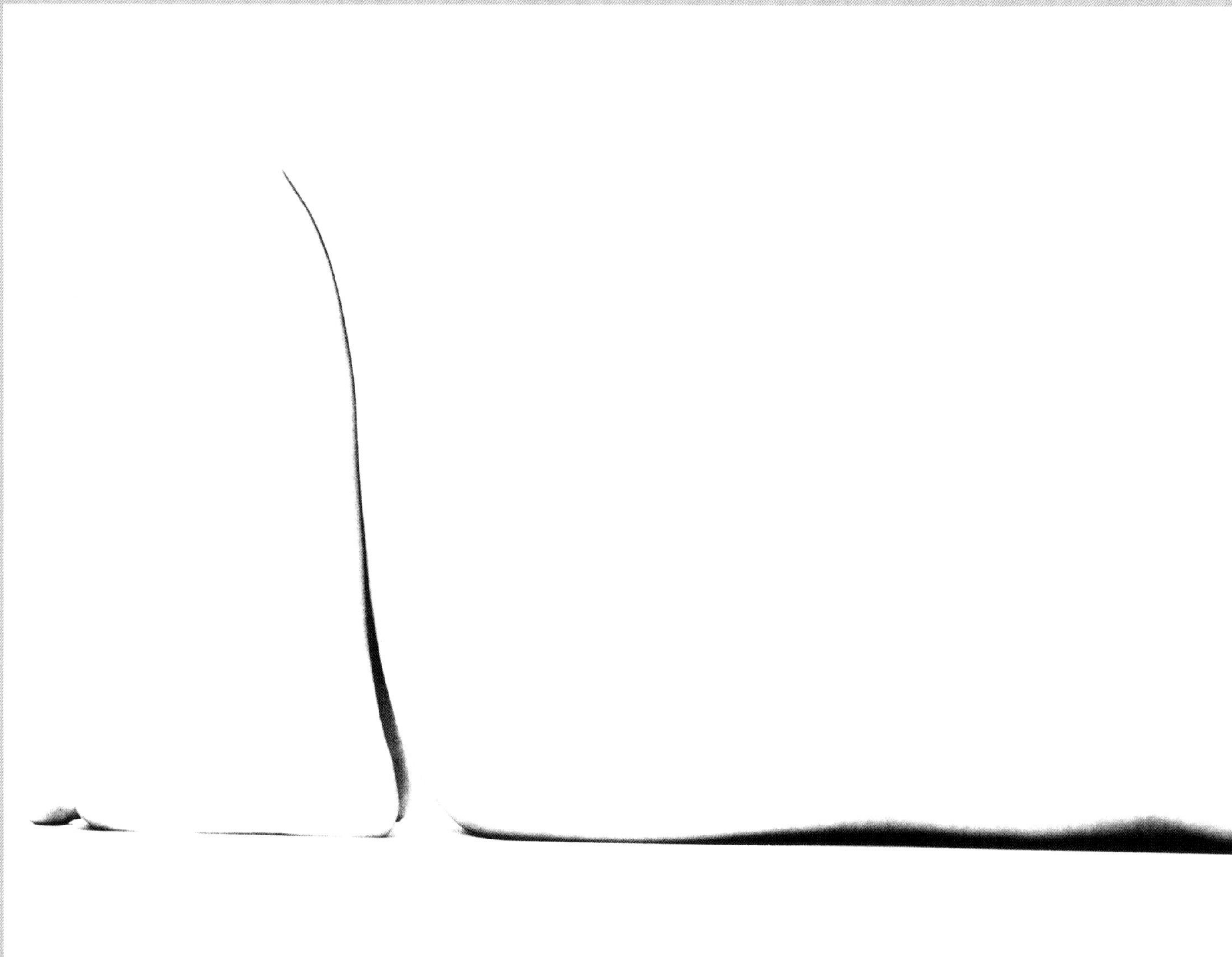

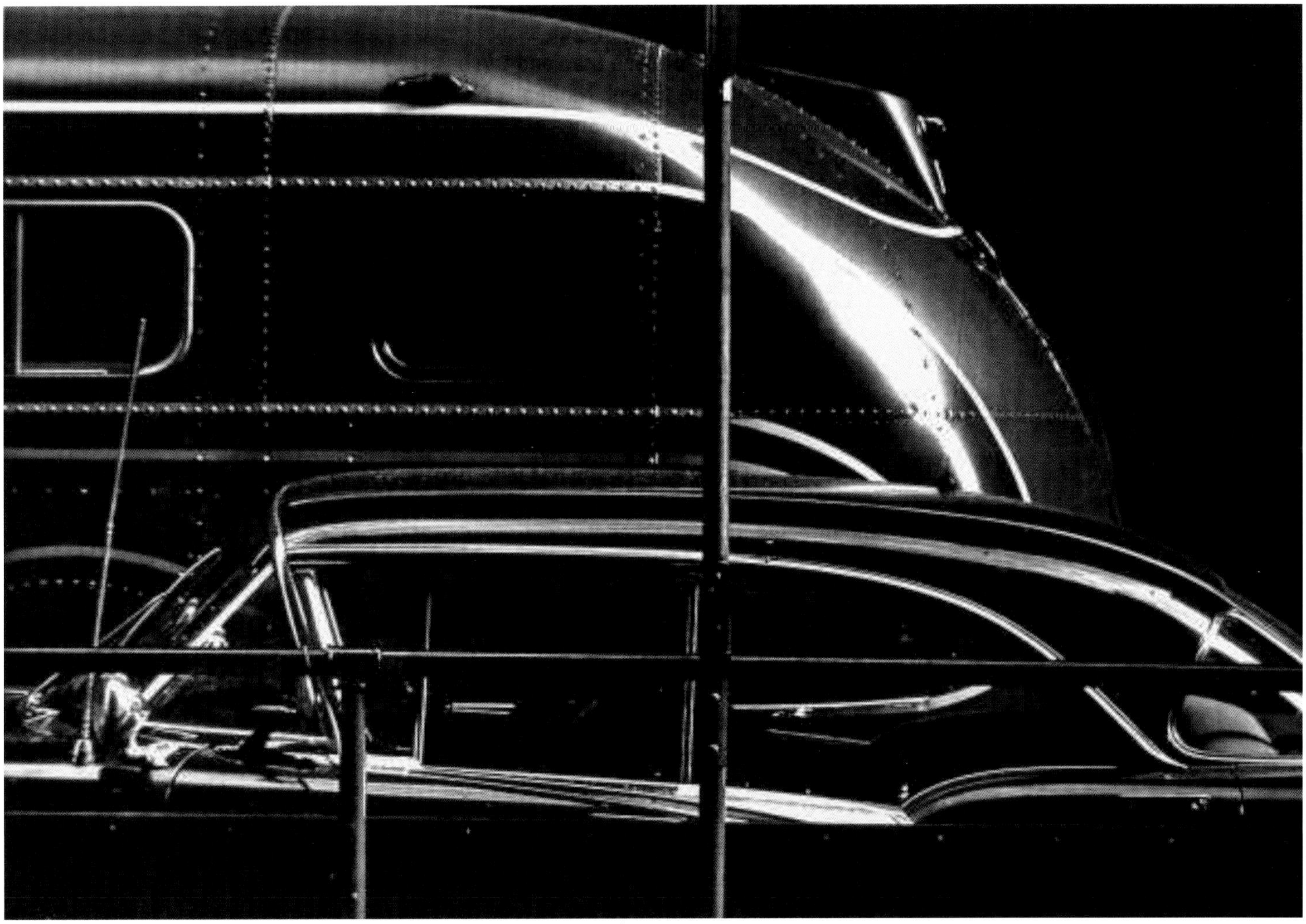

Barbara Crane
Untitled, from the series *Human Form*, from the portfolio *Institute of Design Student Independent 7*, 1965, print of 1969
gelatin silver, 17.8 x 23.6 cm

Ray K. Metzker
Chicago, Loop (58 AX-22), 1958
gelatin silver, 12.2. x 21.7 cm

Nagy had hired Arthur Siegel, a member of the first New Bauhaus class from 1937. With Harry Callahan, Siegel extended Moholy-Nagy's foundation to a four-year program, experimental throughout. After Siegel was forced out in 1949, Callahan ran the photography program as he saw fit, enriching and extending what Moholy-Nagy had taught.

In about 1982 Callahan told me that, when he got to the school, Siegel handed him a piece of paper describing the ten assignments for the coming year. He said that list was the "best way to teach then and the best way to teach now." It was a list of the various assignments Siegel, Nathan Lerner, and Moholy-Nagy himself had derived from the original 'Eight Varieties of Abstract Photographic Seeing.'[2]

Aaron Siskind replaced Siegel in 1951, bringing a strong connection to fine art in his association with the Abstract Expressionists in New York and credentials in social documentary from his work in Harlem.

THE GRADUATE PROGRAM IN PHOTOGRAPHY

Also in 1951, a graduating senior came to Callahan saying that he had enjoyed the program so much he wanted to continue for another year. In short order a graduate degree in photography was created, and in 1952 Jordan Bernstein became the first graduate.

The creation of a photography program for older students separated from the other parts of the school became the basis for the ID's prominence in the field—that and the lack of any fine arts department or college at the university that would have controlled and directed its development. Isolation was essential to fostering the uniqueness of the program though allowing it to become a sort of cult, sure of its own truth.

For the younger design students the foundation photo classes taught a formal vocabulary that explored the unique properties of the medium of expression. Subject and point of view were undefined or self-defined. The ID way of photographing could be applied to any project: commercial or personal, design or fine art.

The graduate program was different. Callahan and Siskind had little interest in design or commercial photography, so they trained their graduate students for careers similar to their own.

All of the graduate students were exposed to the ID foundation either by being forced to take it or by assisting in teaching it. Also, Callahan's own work was the ID curriculum flawlessly executed. Barbara Crane has said that since she wasn't required to take foundation, she did it as her thesis. Siskind valued the ID photo traditions because they gave students all sorts of different ways in which they could make images. The foundation assignments formed a lexicon to be used and extended by each student. There were only seven graduates from 1952 to 1959.

Although graduates were not very successful in finding employment in design, it must be noted that students of that time were delighted with their education and remained loyal to its experimental orientation, most for life. The graduate program started small as well, accepting a few, well-chosen people dedicated to the medium and attached to Callahan or Siskind as apprentices.

It is important to remember that photography was part of a design program and that design integrates physiology (ergonomics, anthropometrics), social science, tech-

2 See also contribution by Lowis.

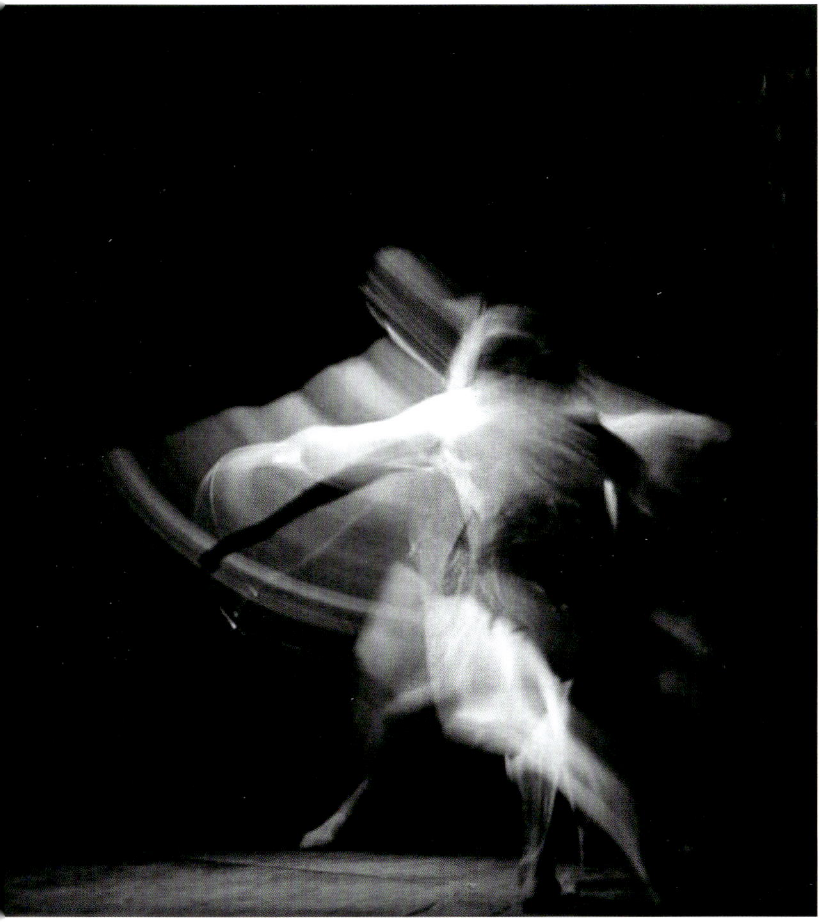

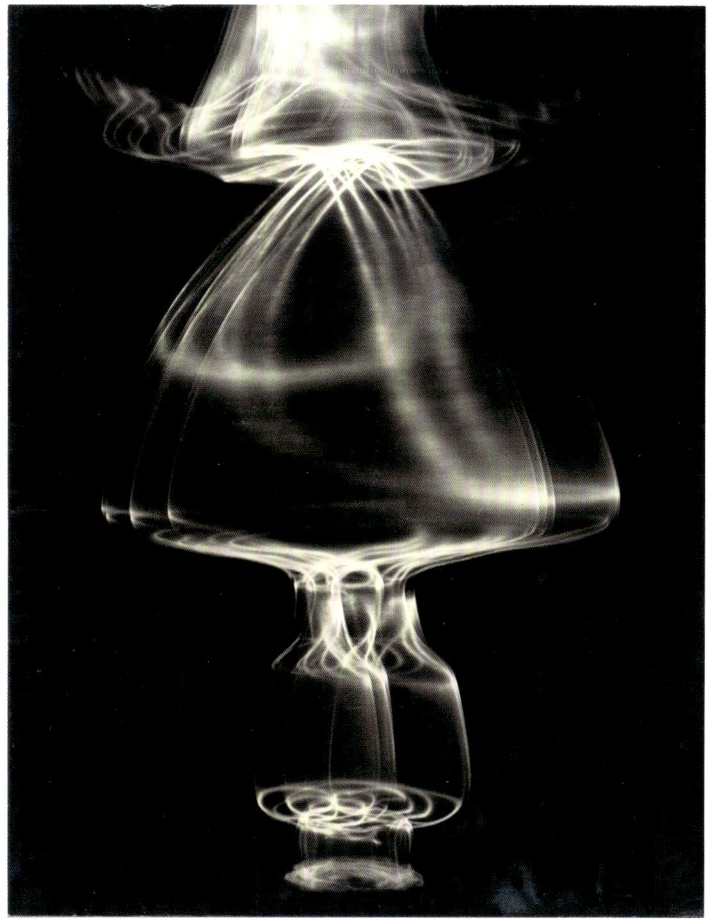

Anonymous
Slow Shutter, undated
gelatin silver, 16 x 16 cm

Eugene Harmon Godfrey
Virtual volume, ca. 1946
gelatin silver, 21.7 x 12.2 cm

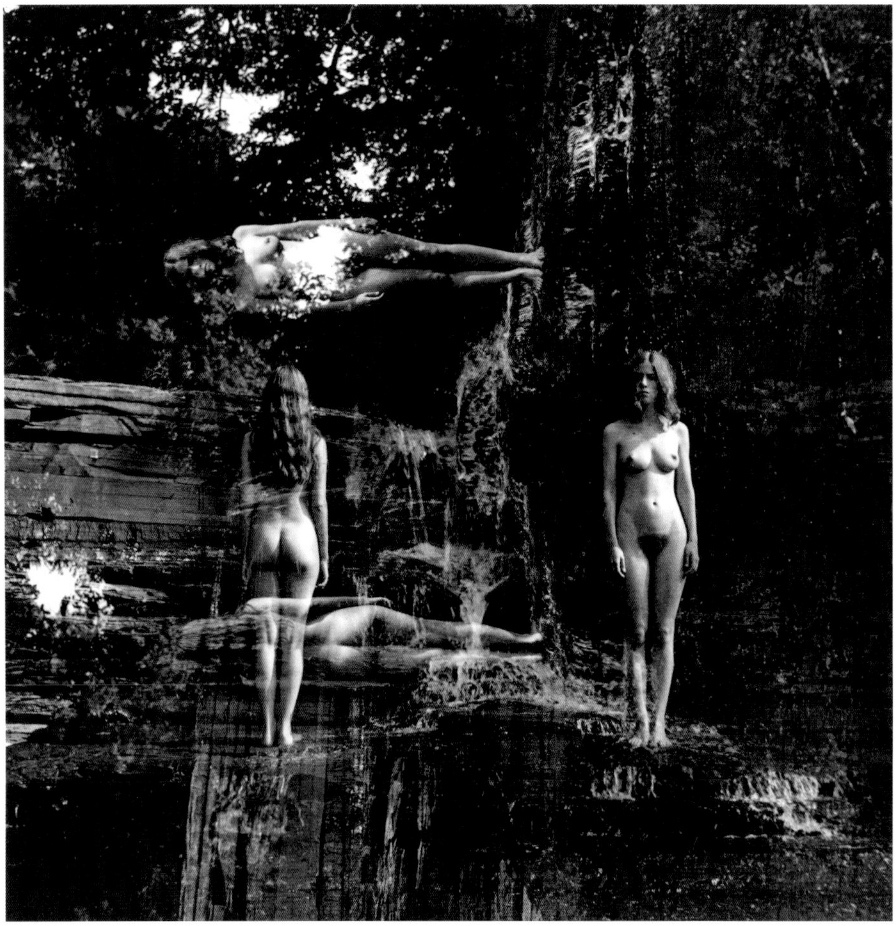

Charles Swedlund
Untitled, from the series *Multiple Exposure with the Figure*, ca. 1969
gelatin silver, 18.7 x 18.6 cm

nology, advocacy, art, and sometimes more. At least in the American context these are mixed in varying proportions depending on the designer or design school under consideration.

Between 1951 and 1955 the school drifted along as a slowly shrinking, experimental art school and was on the path to failure. The unilaterally appointed Jay Doblin came from the wholly commercial side of design, and he thought Moholy-Nagy was a "dilettante." Determined to professionalize the ID, basing instruction on rational rather than intuitive methods, he cut the foundation, which had expanded to fill the entire four years, back to two and built his product design program on top. He didn't care what other areas of the school did so long as they were successful. This decision allowed Callahan and Siskind full autonomy.

By 1959 the essential elements of the ID photo program were all in place. First, the photo program was the graduate program, which was separate from the rest of the school. Second, undergraduates would be mixed with graduate students in the upper-level classes and benefit from inclusion, but the graduate program was the center, focused on developing artists/photographers who would predominately take jobs teaching in other university-level photography programs and less frequently become commercial photographers. There was no stigma attached to commercial work, but the freedom to follow one's own assignments was more highly valued. Finally, a successful thesis was the essence of the graduate program. After the completion of class work each student would produce a body of work (usually 30–50 prints) consistent in subject, formal vocabulary, and point of view at a level of quality satisfactory to the student's advisor, Siskind in nearly all cases. Each thesis needed to be original, which meant not imitative or closely derivative of existing bodies of work: No work is strictly original. *My Camera and I in the Loop* (1959) was Ray Metzker's thesis. It was the model for all subsequent students and is the earliest in the ID archive.[3]

In 1961 Callahan left. Doblin was remaking the school again, this time with the idea of integrating all the undergraduate areas of the school under a concept called "universal design." Callahan got an offer from the Rhode Island School of Design, which he took.

SUCCESS

The results of the photo program started matching its goals in the 1960s, when the baby boomers reached college age possessing a set of attitudes that included a rejection of materialism and favored an alternative lifestyle enhanced by sex, drugs, rock music, and an embrace of new media, which included (a century late) photography. Rachel Carson's *Silent Spring* was published in 1962, causing a flood of Ansel Adams imitators into the woods and onto the mountains.

This enormous wave of youth led to a huge expansion of higher education sponsored by scholarships and grants from the federal government. The results were similar to those of the G.I. Bill in 1946. These students demanded painting, photography, and film. Moholy-Nagy's time had come. All the new and expanded departments of art needed to hire faculty to teach photography, and there were not that many candidates with the appropriate credentials.

3 See also contribution by Siegel.

ID may not have been the first graduate program in photography, but it was substantial and becoming famous through shows and the publication of student work in *Aperture* and elsewhere.[4] ID graduates were the perfect choice for new faculty hires since they knew how to teach all sorts of photographic techniques for the fine arts, commercial work, photojournalism, and more.

By contrast to the prevailing culture, the photographers of ID—graduate students and teachers—while open-minded, were not an active part of the counterculture. They were adults, many with families, dedicated to photography, and were more likely to have Beethoven playing in their darkrooms than rock and roll. Of the graduates between 1959 and 1985 about two thirds became university teachers. The graduate program at the ID was the leading force shaping photographic education during that time. Arthur Sinsabaugh, who had taught in the program from 1947 to 1961, came back to get a master's degree in 1967, despite his already notable achievements, because the University of Illinois demanded that he have an advanced degree to be eligible for promotion within the art department.

In 1967 Siegel returned to teach at ID after becoming bored with commercial work and having been successful enough to afford the pay cut. Though he had been teaching in the evening program sporadically since 1954, he was hired full time by Siskind to strengthen the documentary component of the program. In addition, he also taught a history of photography, which was not a conventional history but a series of brilliant essays about the known body of photographic precedent and provided a common vocabulary to which students could refer. At his best he was the most perceptive critic of bodies of work that photography has had, but this is only documented in his extensive tape recordings of his lectures and critiques.

When Siskind was mandatorily retired in 1971, Siegel took over the direction of the program until his death in 1978. In 1974 he hired me to teach foundation and large-format photography and Alan Cohen to investigate scientific and technical photography. To replace Siskind he hired a series of photographers, one per year. Of these the most influential was Garry Winogrand. His teaching was completely outside of the ID tradition, yet, he was a strong influence on the thesis work of the early 1970s and on his students long after they graduated. He also represented the incorporation of other photographic traditions into the ID program, in his case, street photography as practiced in New York. These inclusions, while strengthening the program, also made it less different from dozens of other graduate programs. Siegel, who also emphasized color, hired David Rathbun, who had been Elliot Porter's printer, to teach this process at ID. He also hired Patty Carroll to teach color using the more common methods. After 1974 there were many thesis projects in color.

CHANGES IN THE FIELD

When Siegel died in 1978, Carroll, Rathbun, and I remained. There weren't enough classes to afford four positions in photography in a shrinking undergraduate program. Since I was running photography, I could move on to explore other possibilities, multimedia at first and then digital imaging starting in 1985. These were areas needing attention, and by moving into them I also provided room in the program for the other faculty.

4 See also contribution by Bähr.

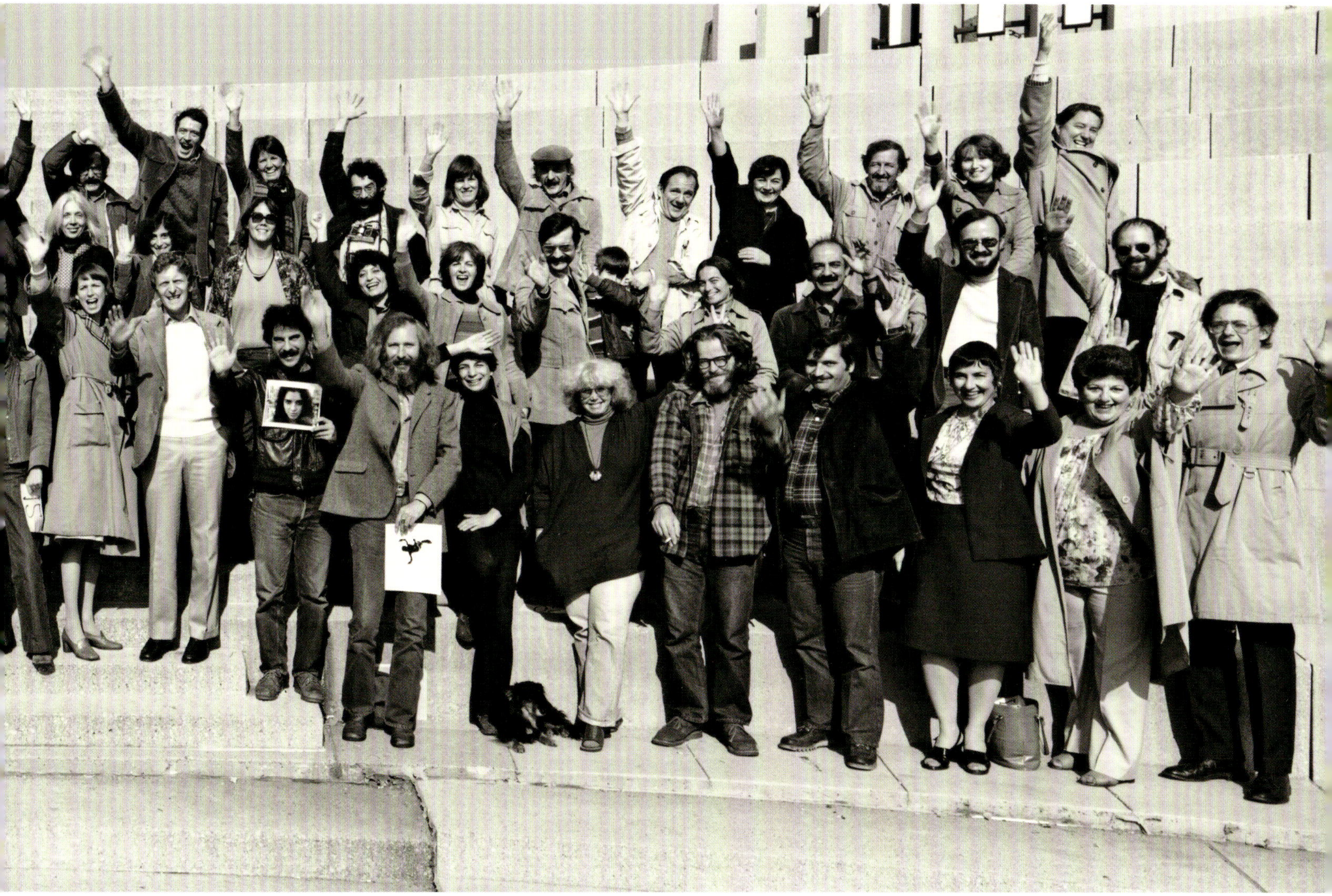

Anonymous
Faculty of the Institute of Design, 1970s
gelatin silver, 16.5 x 48 cm

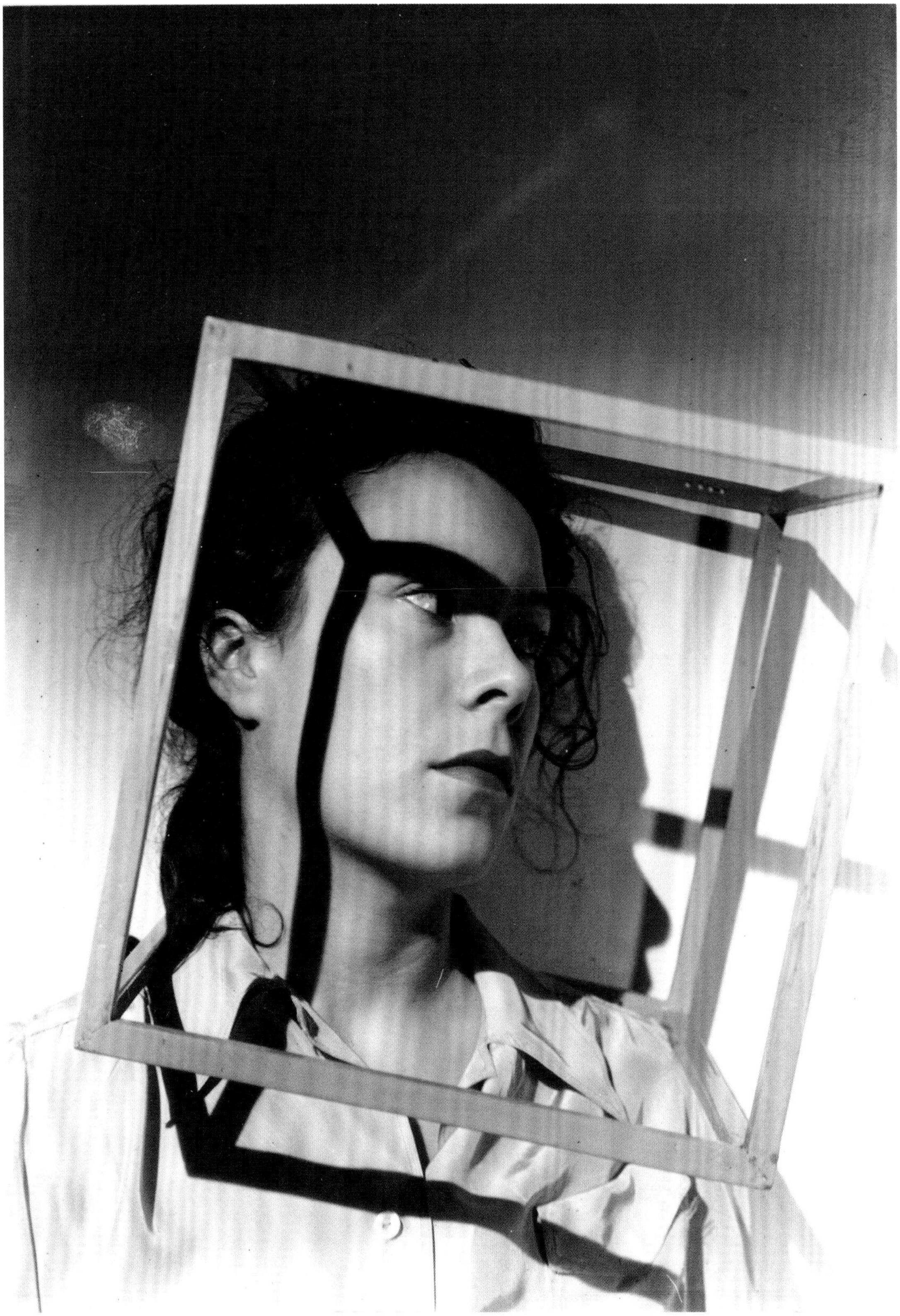

György Kepes
Portrait of Juliet Kepes, 1938, later print
gelatin silver, 18 x 13 cm

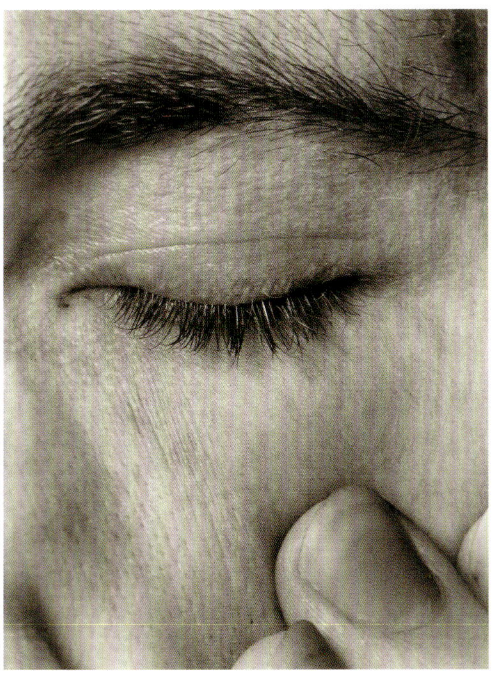

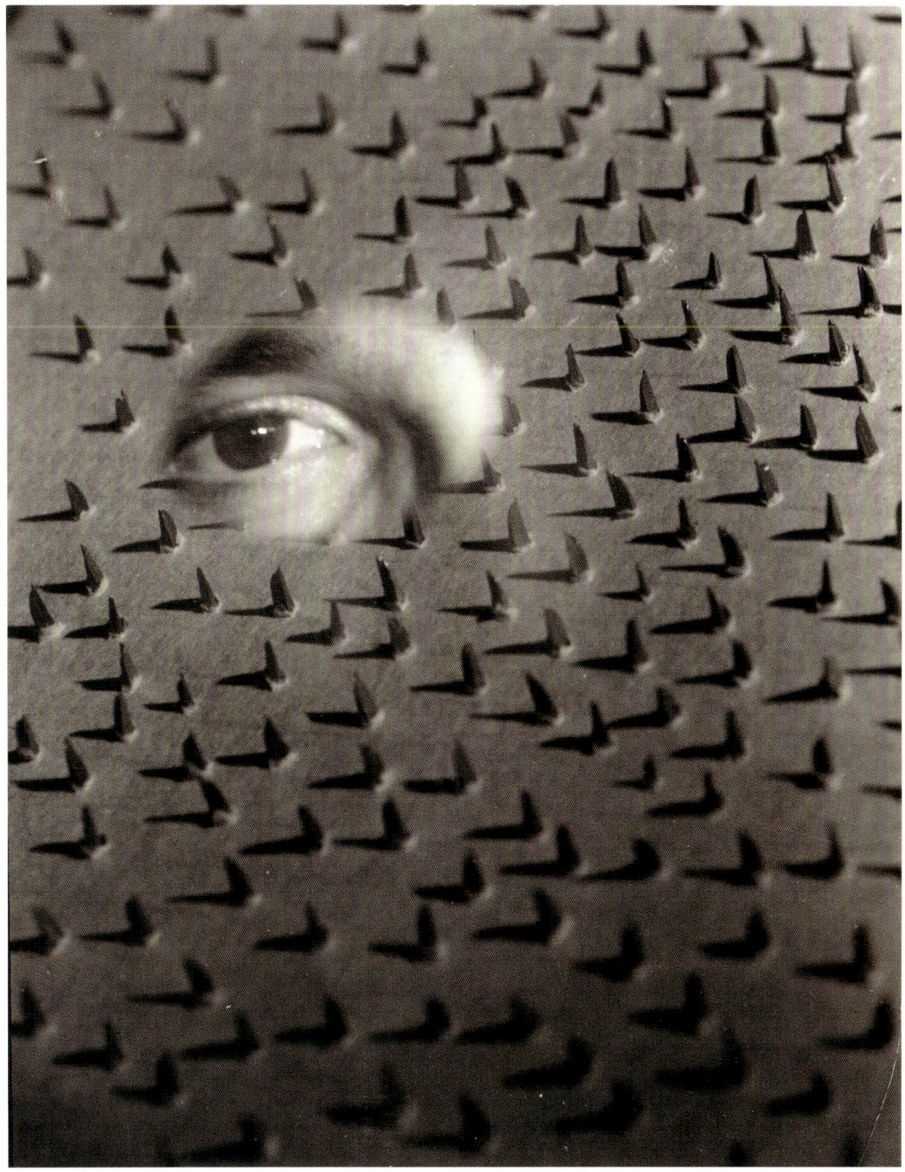

Nathan Lerner
Closed Eye, 1940, later print
gelatin silver, 35.5 x 27 cm

Nathan Lerner
Eye on Nails, 1940, later print
gelatin silver, 25.3 x 20.6 cm

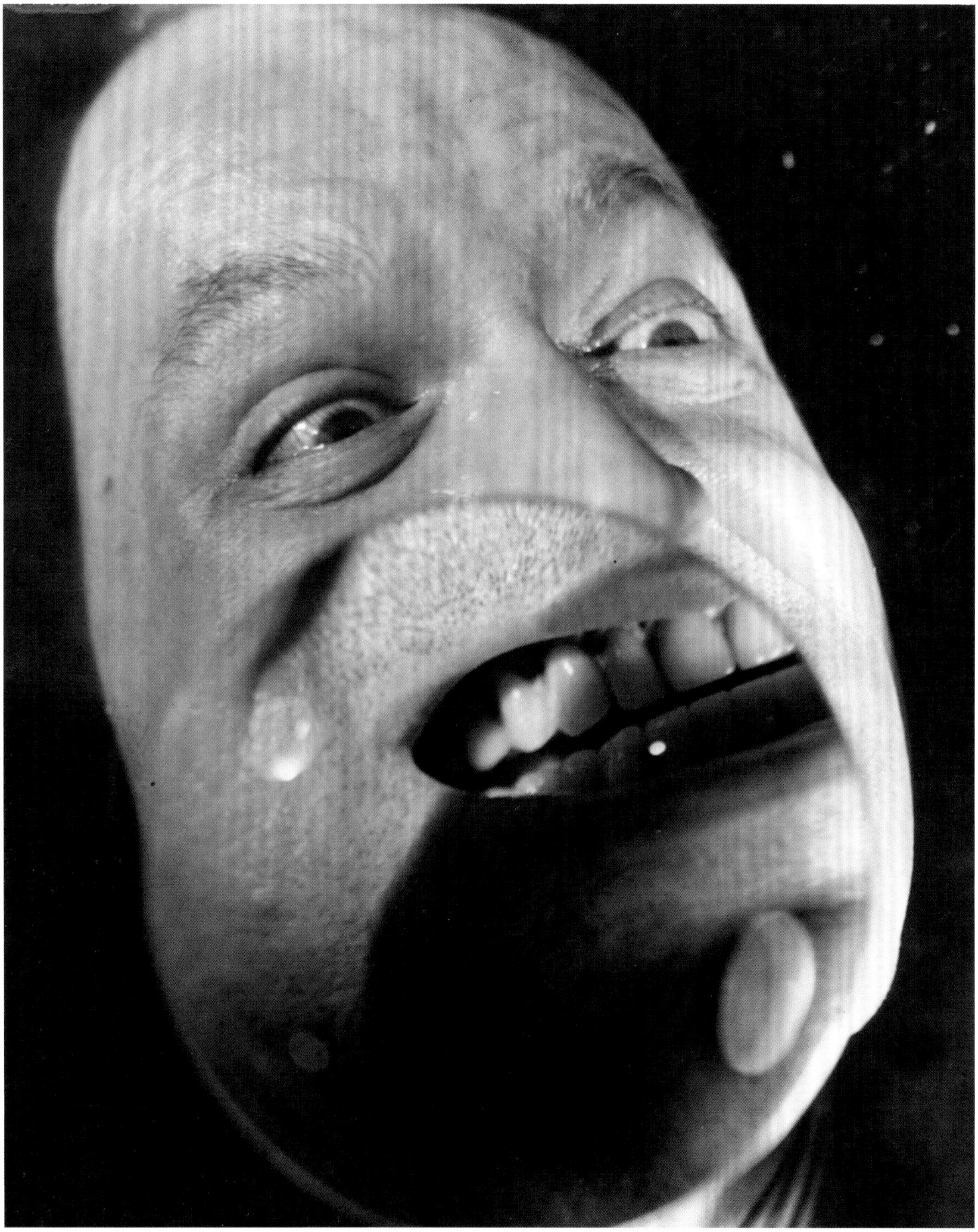

Nathan Lerner
Brown's Face, 1939, later print
gelatin silver, 23.5 x 19.2 cm

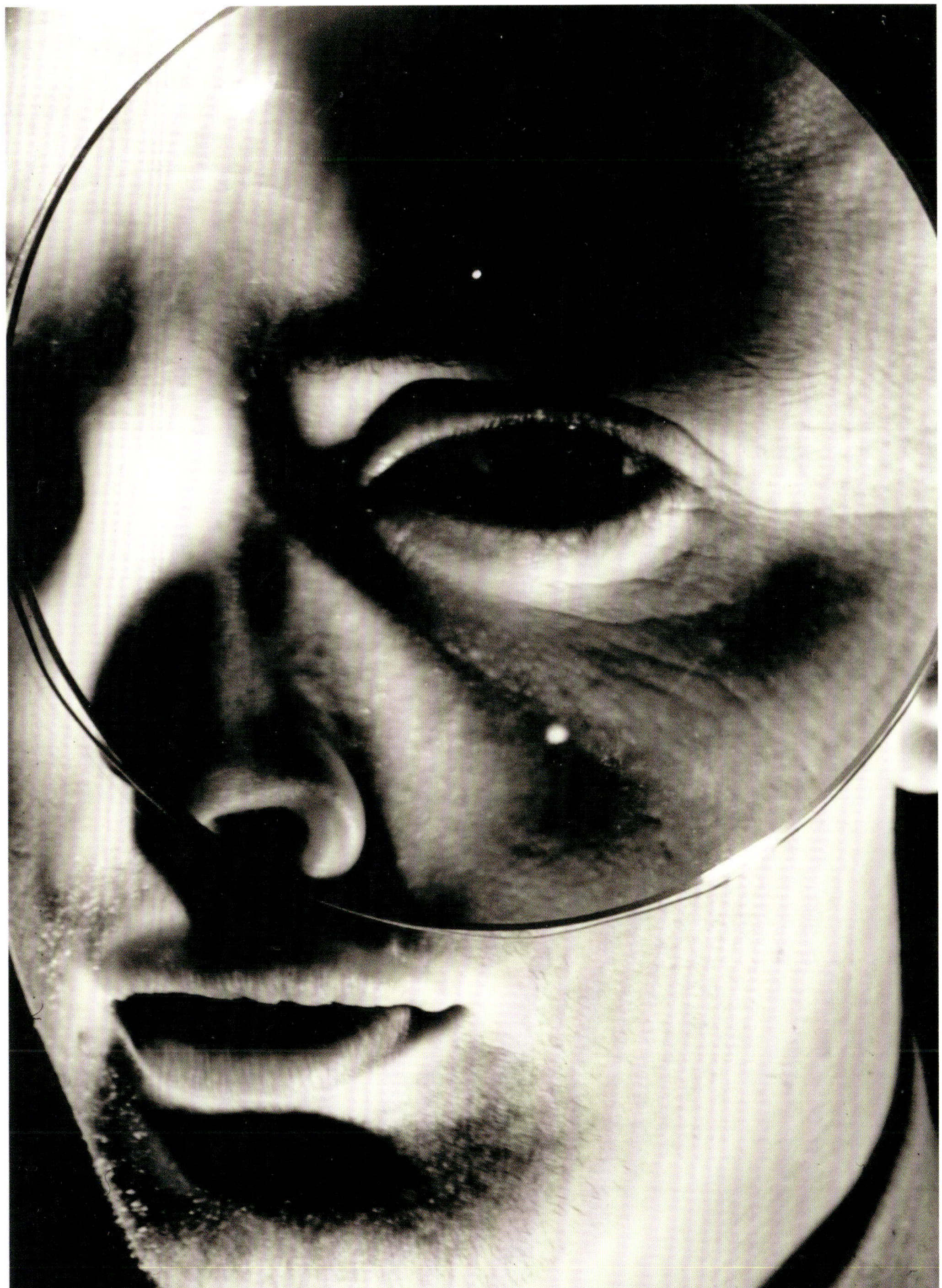

Nathan Lerner
Charlie's Eye, 1940, later print
gelatin silver, 35.5 x 27.7 cm

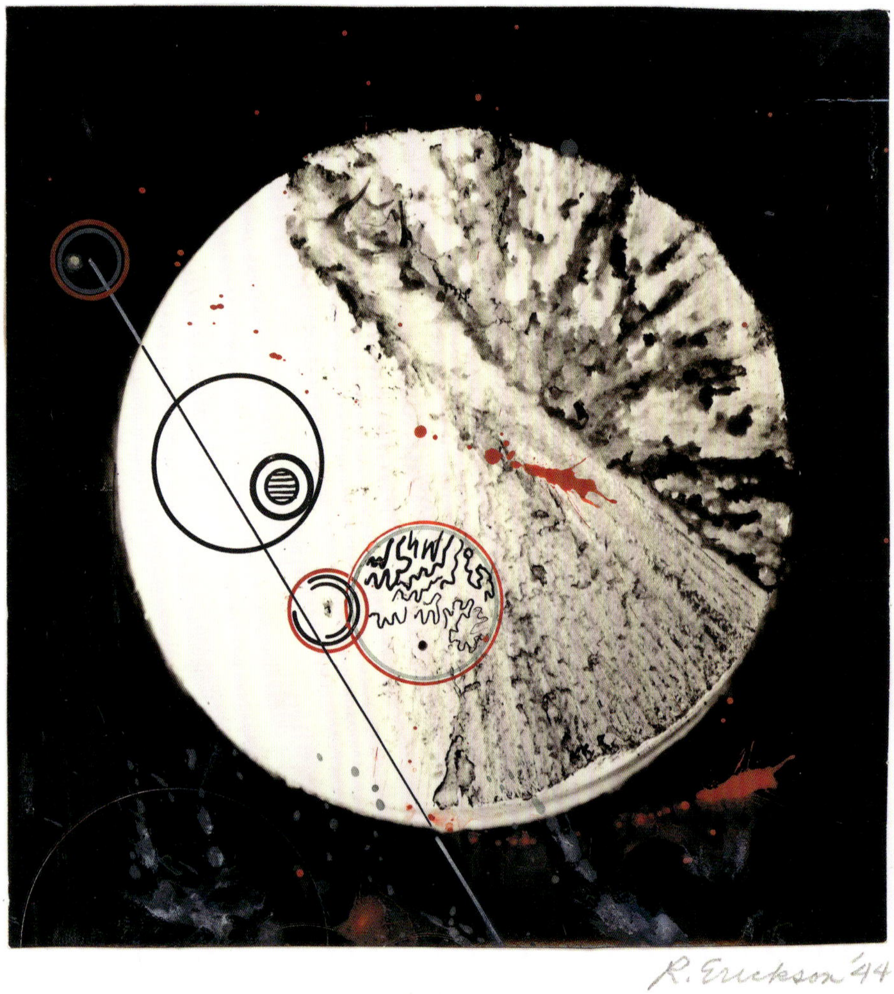

Robert Donald Erickson
Close-Up of Plastic Rod Plus Drawing, 1944
gelatin silver with tempera and ink, 12 x 11.5 cm

Nathan Lerner
Pen Light Drawing "Head", 1939, later print
gelatin silver, 25.5 x 20.5 cm

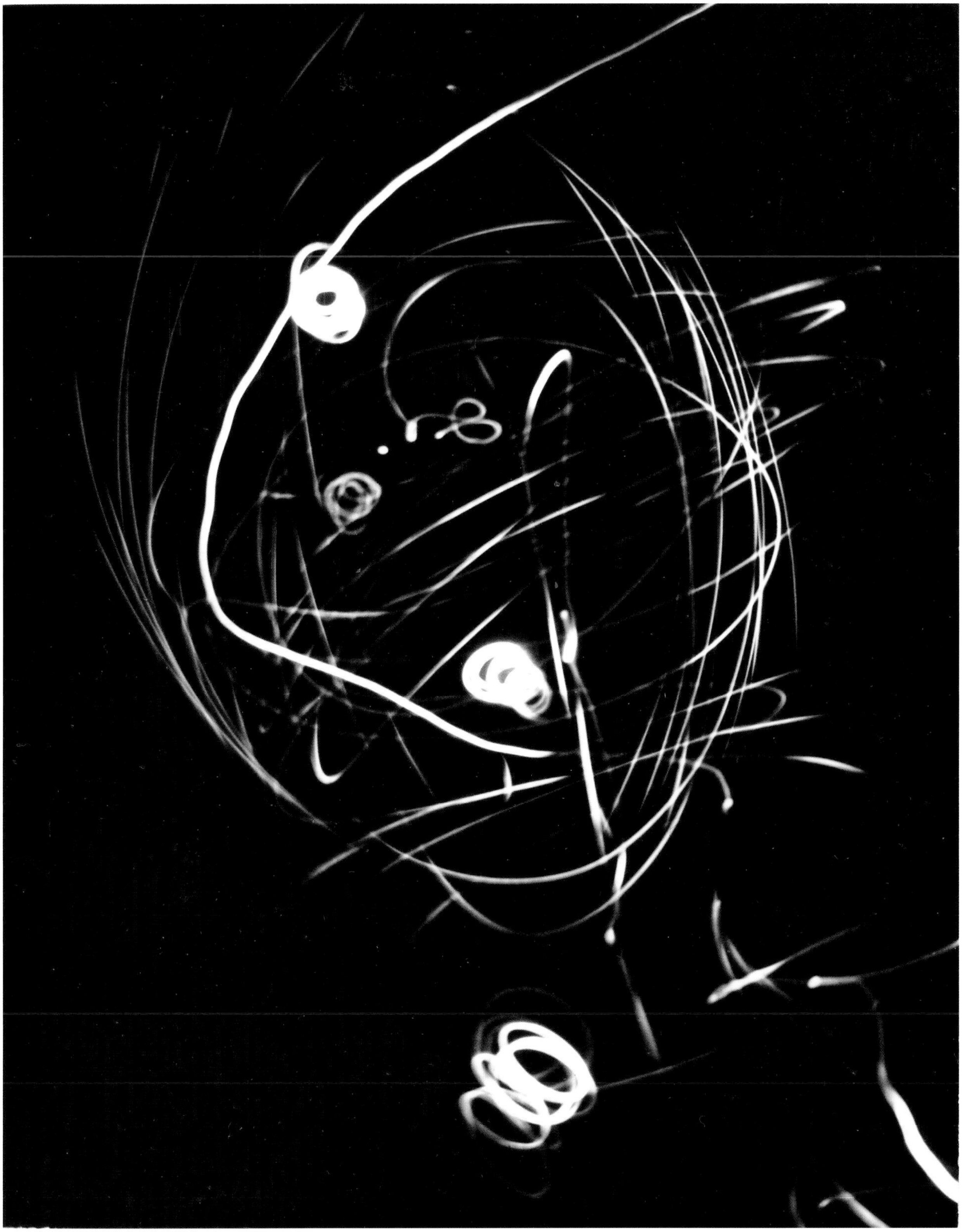

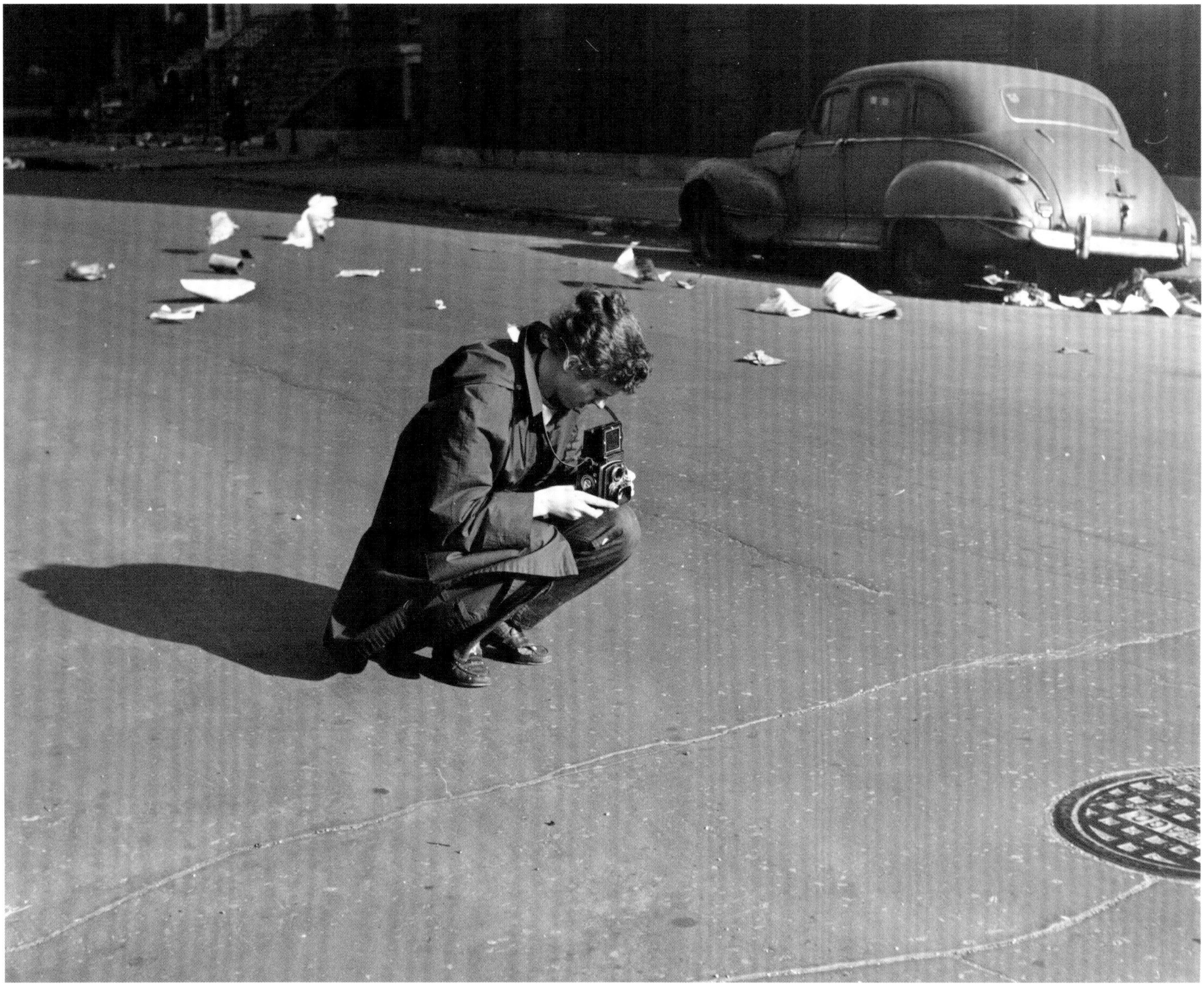

Anonymous
Else Tholstrup working on the assignment
"All that glitters is not gold," ca. 1952
gelatin silver, 20.3 x 25.2 cm

Else Tholstrup
"All that glitters is not gold," ca. 1952
gelatin silver, 19.7 x 24.5 cm each

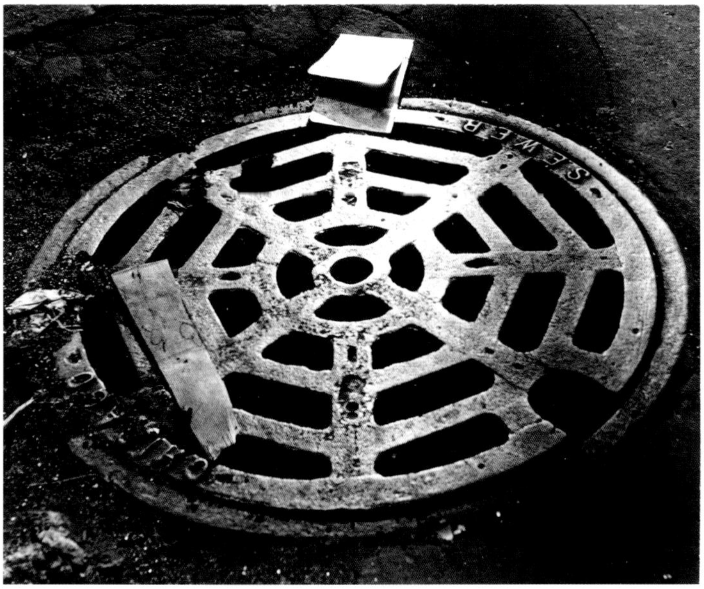
SEWER

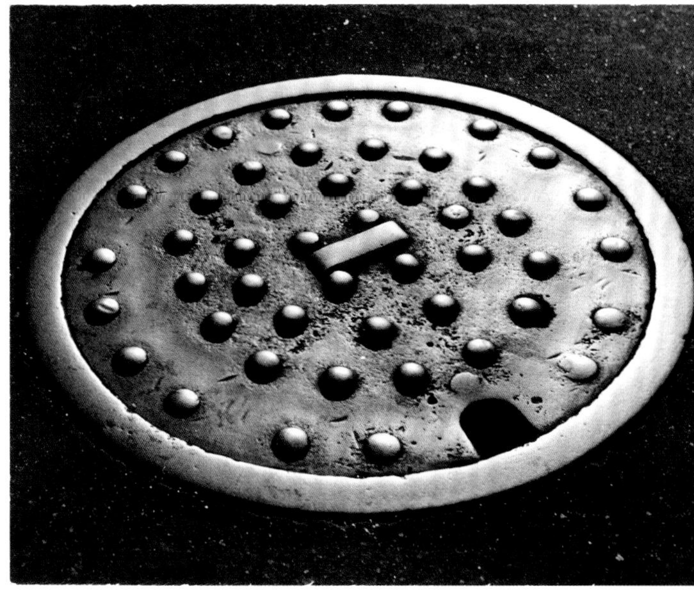

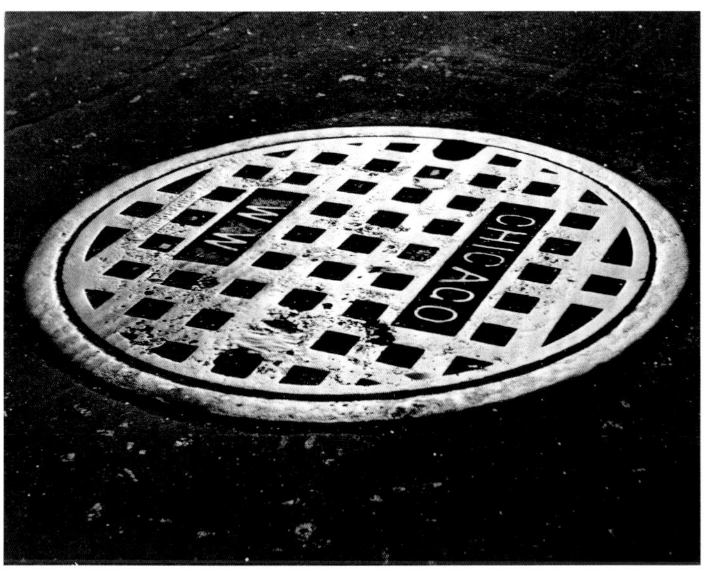
W W
CHICAGO

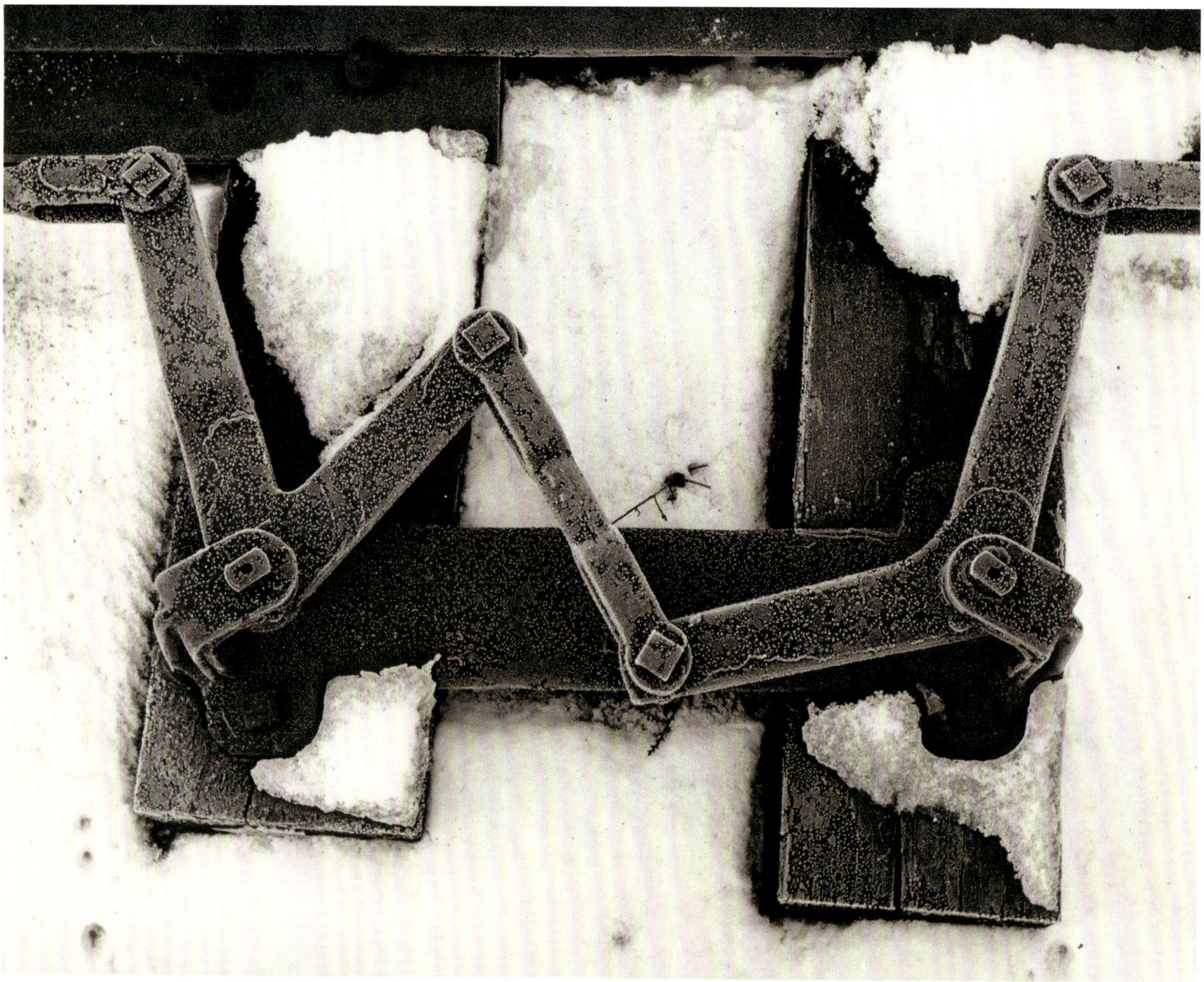

Joseph Jachna
W, 1957
gelatin silver, 18.7 x 23.5 cm

Joseph Jachna
R, 1957
gelatin silver, 17.8 x 17.4 cm

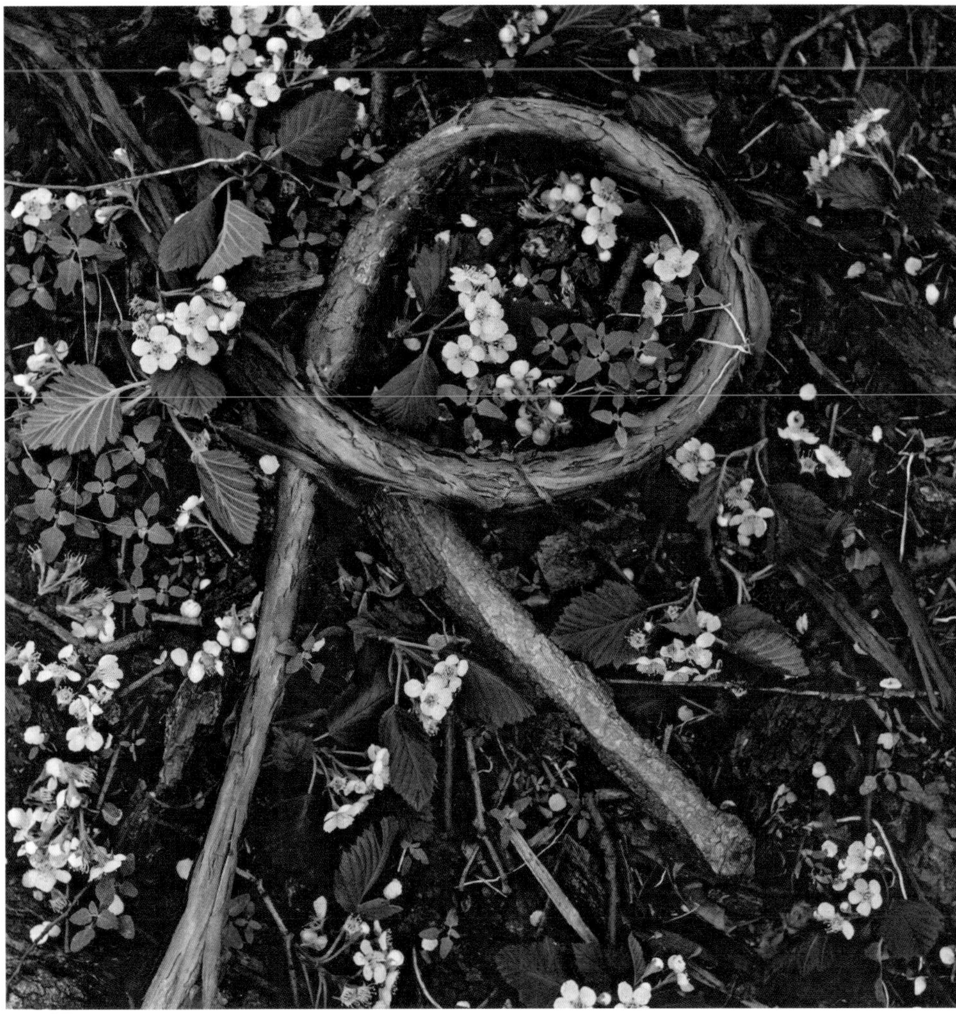

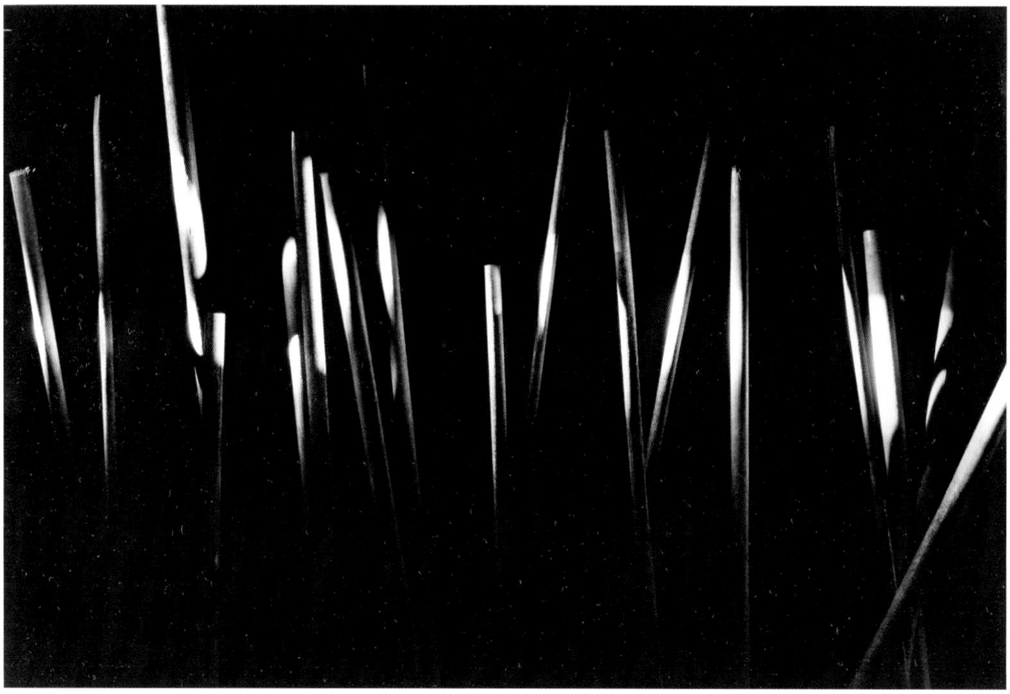

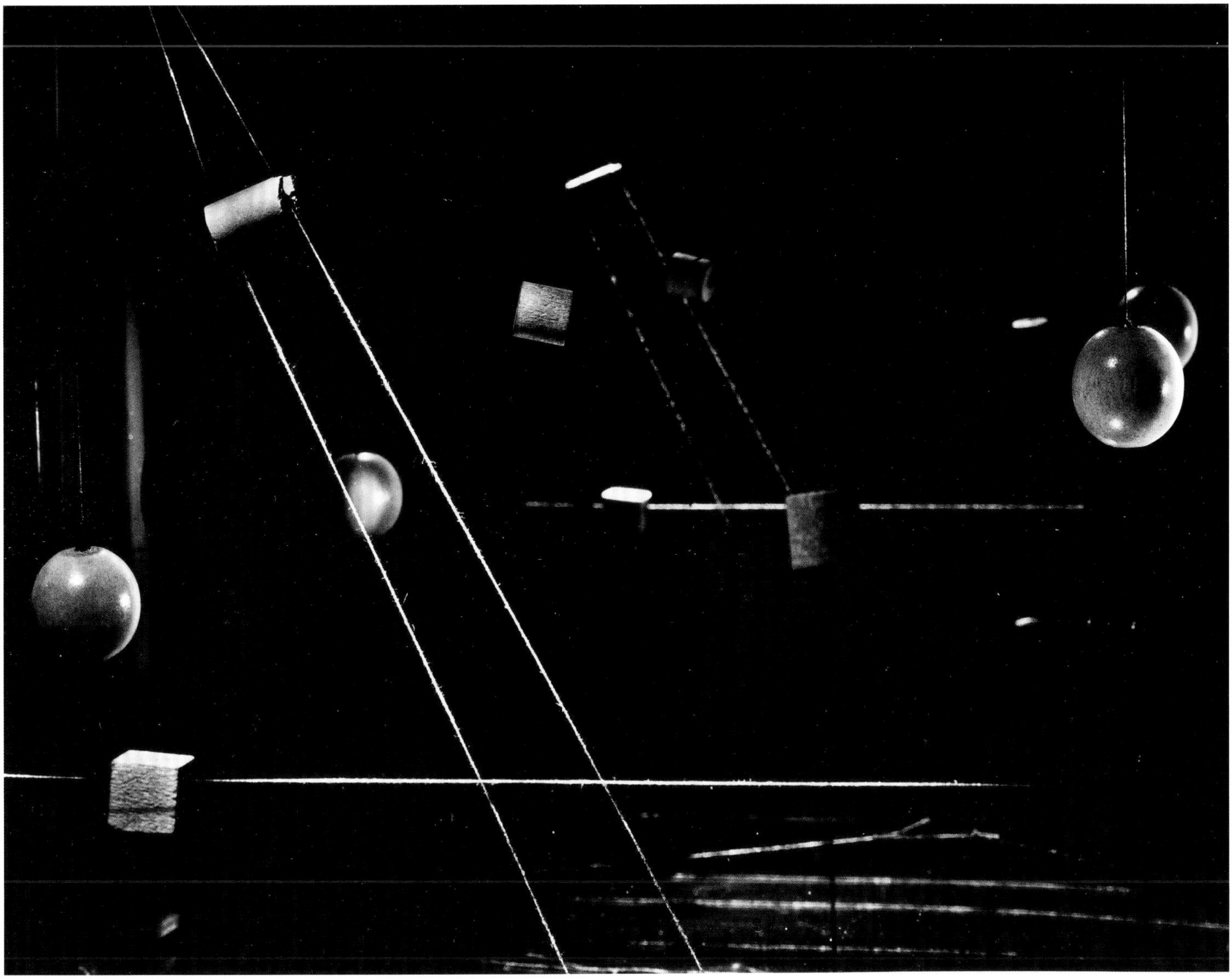

Nathan Lerner
Wooden Dowels, 1939, later print
gelatin silver, 17.9 x 27.5 cm

Henry Holmes Smith
Light Study, 1946, print of 1987
gelatin silver, 27.8 x 35.5 cm

Nathan Lerner
Light Box Study No. 4, undated
gelatin silver, 28.9 x 37.7 cm

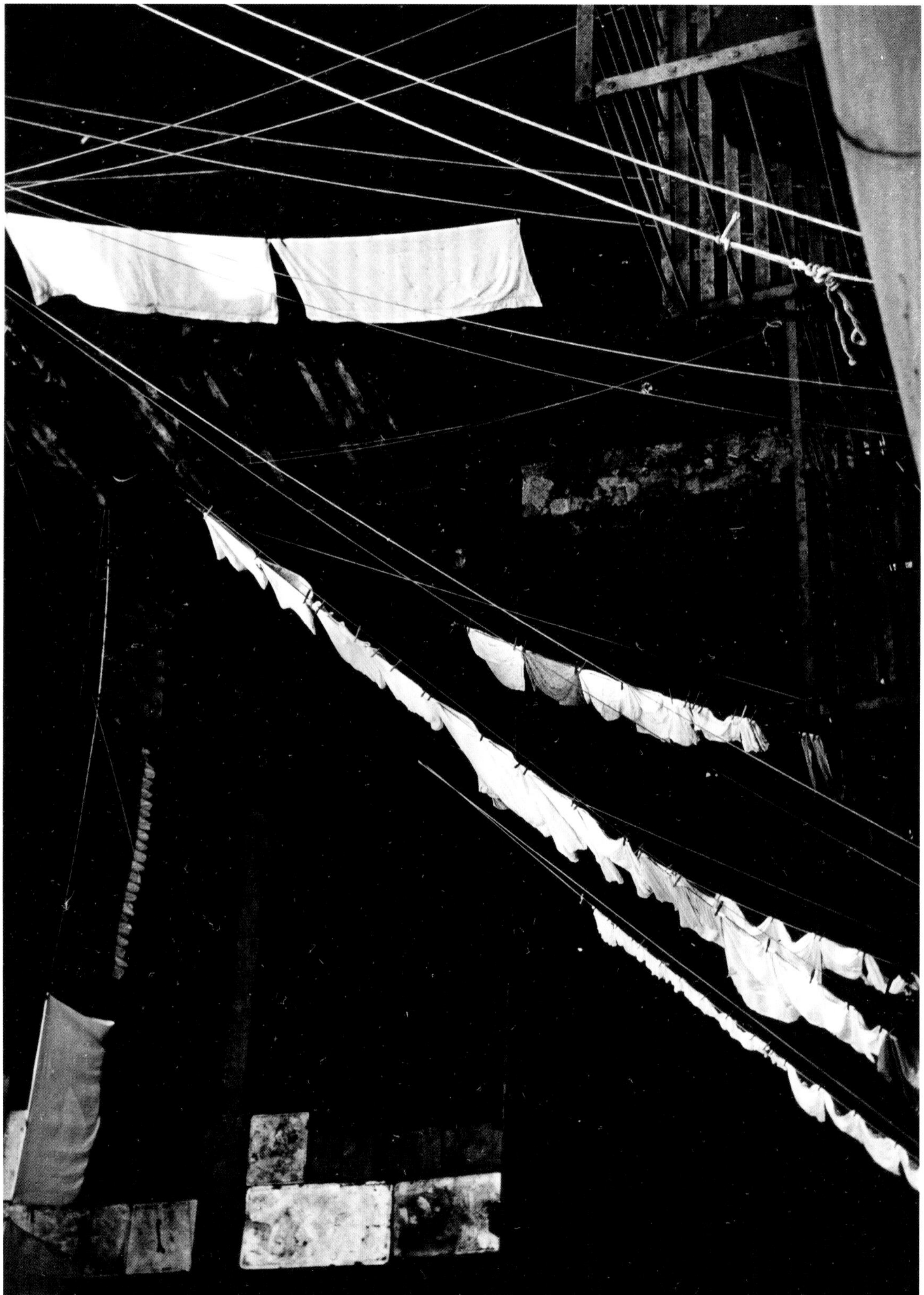

Nathan Lerner
City Light Box Study, 1944, later print
gelatin silver, 50.3 x 40.4 cm

William Keck
Dining Room Window, 1938/39, print of 1987
gelatin silver, 50.6 x 40.5 cm

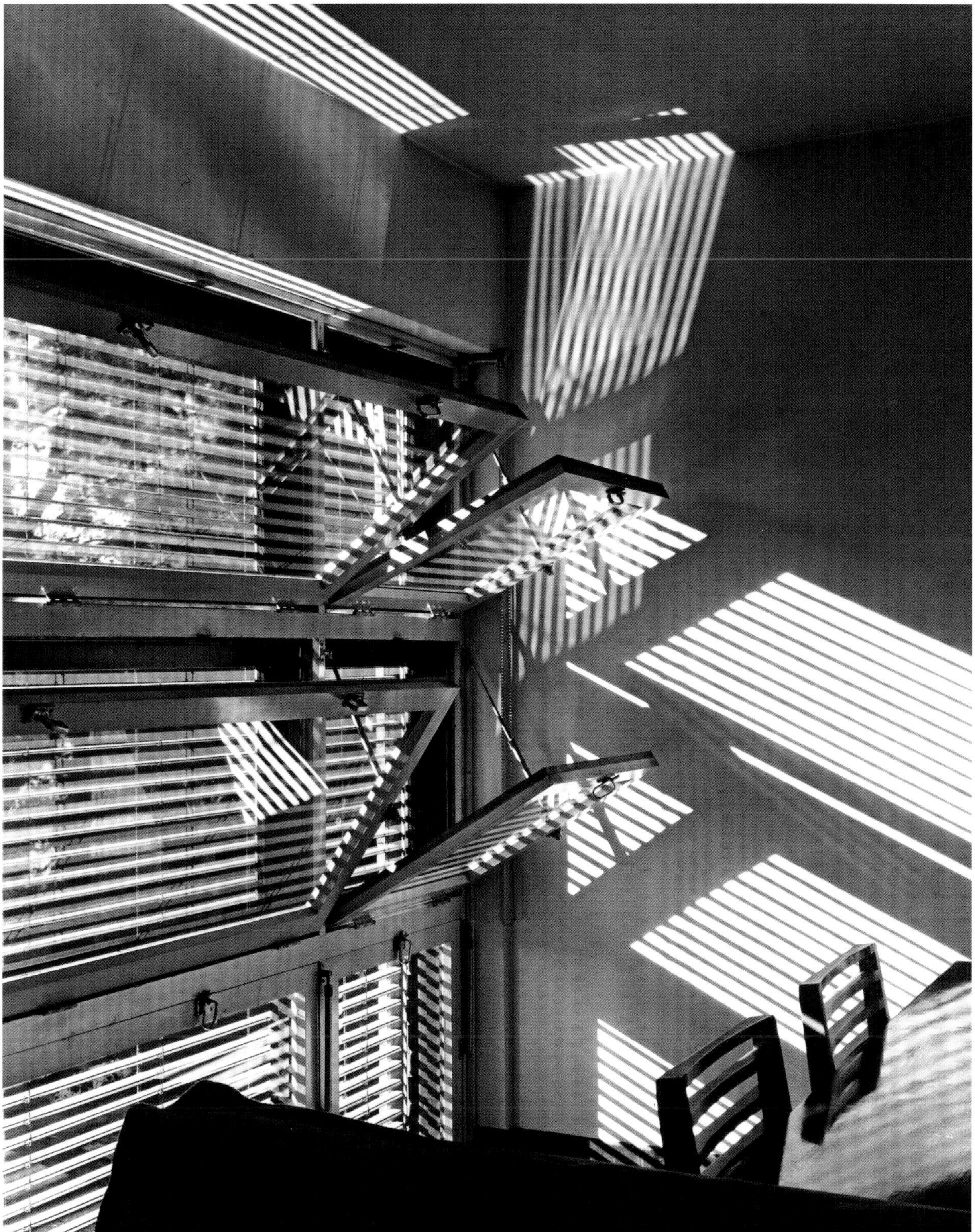

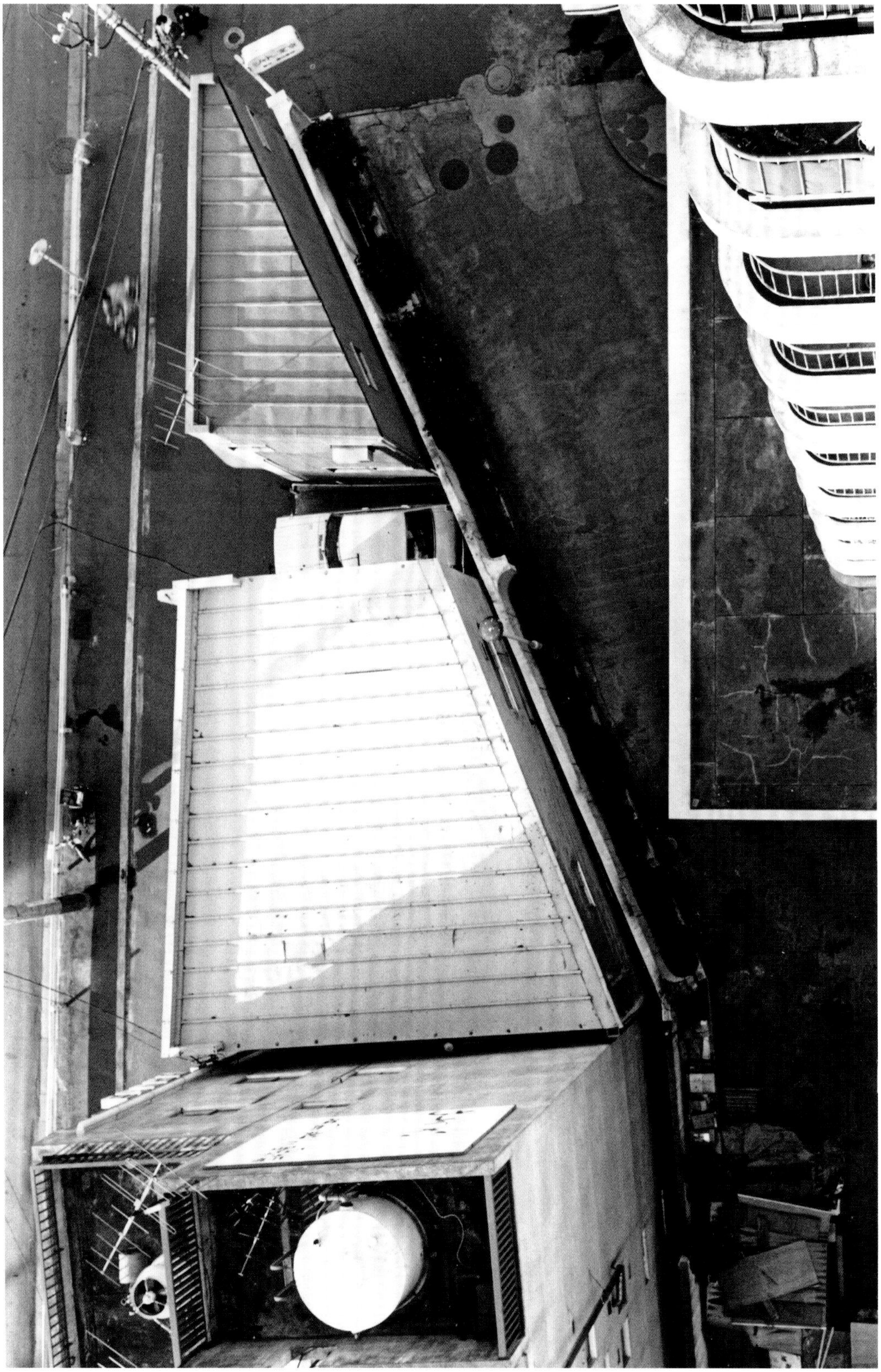

Nathan Lerner
Roof Patterns, 1986
gelatin silver, 22.7 x 14.9 cm

Allen Porter
From Lower Wacker, 1948, later print
gelatin silver, 24.2 x 19.4 cm

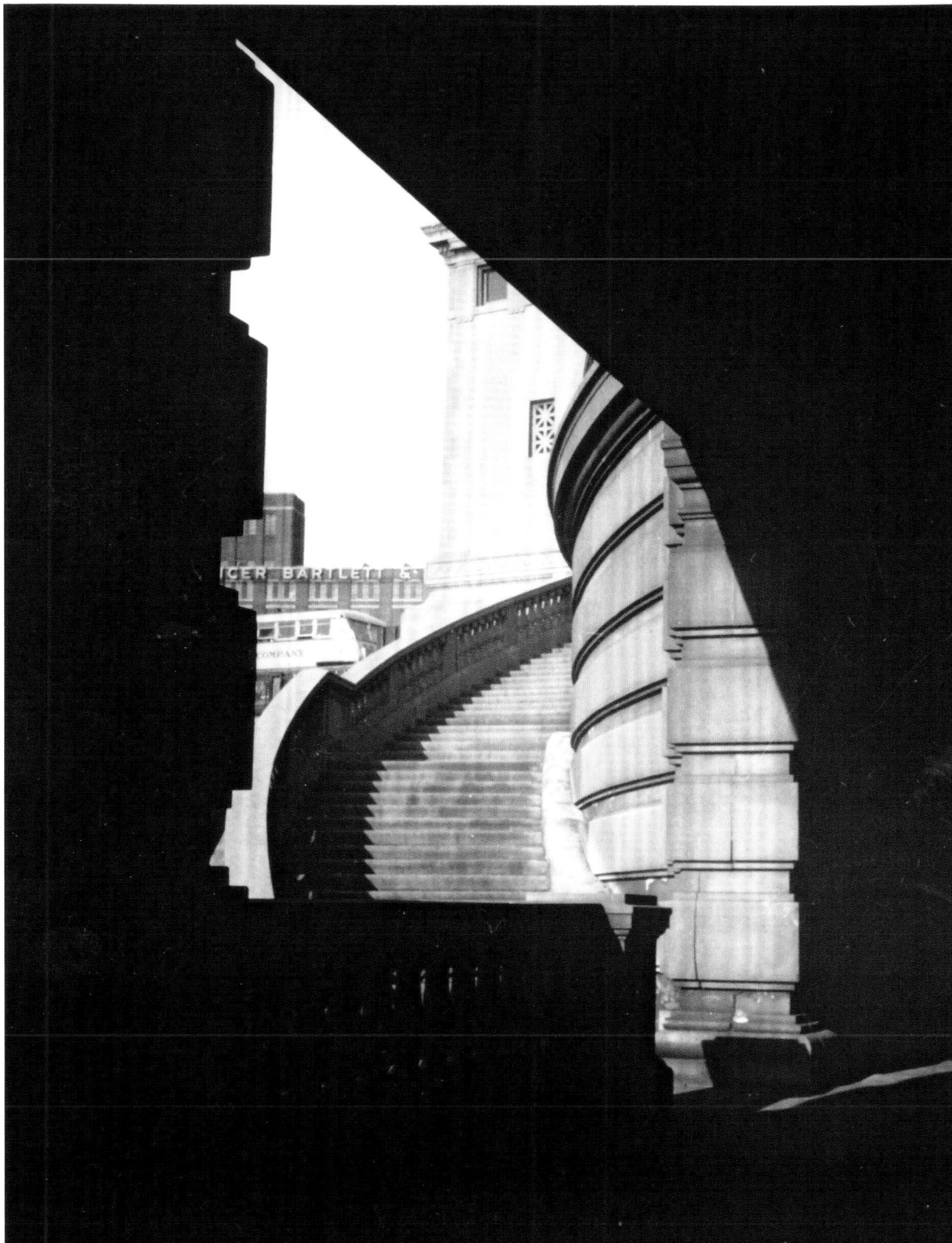
CER BARTLETT &
COMPANY

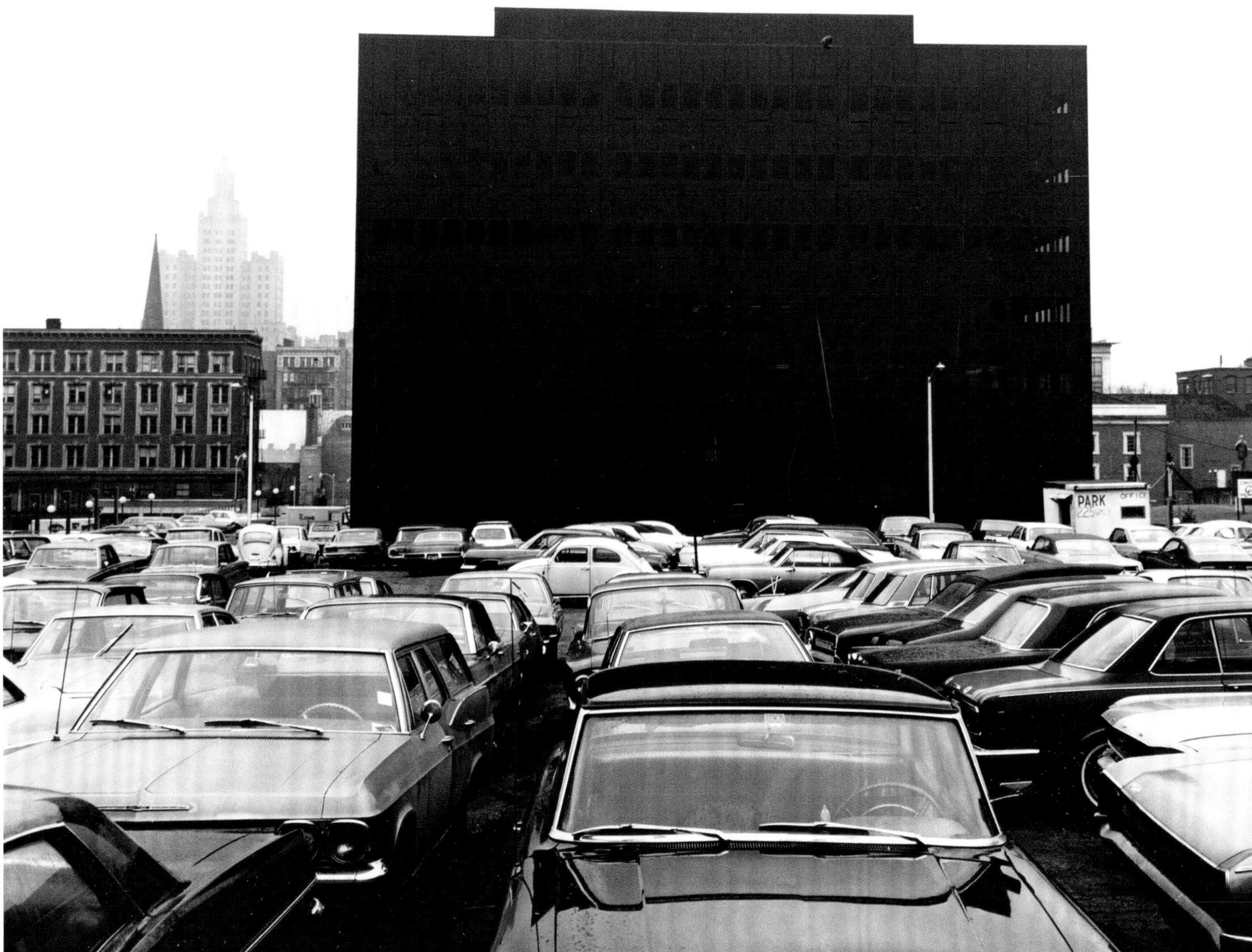
PARK
OFFICE

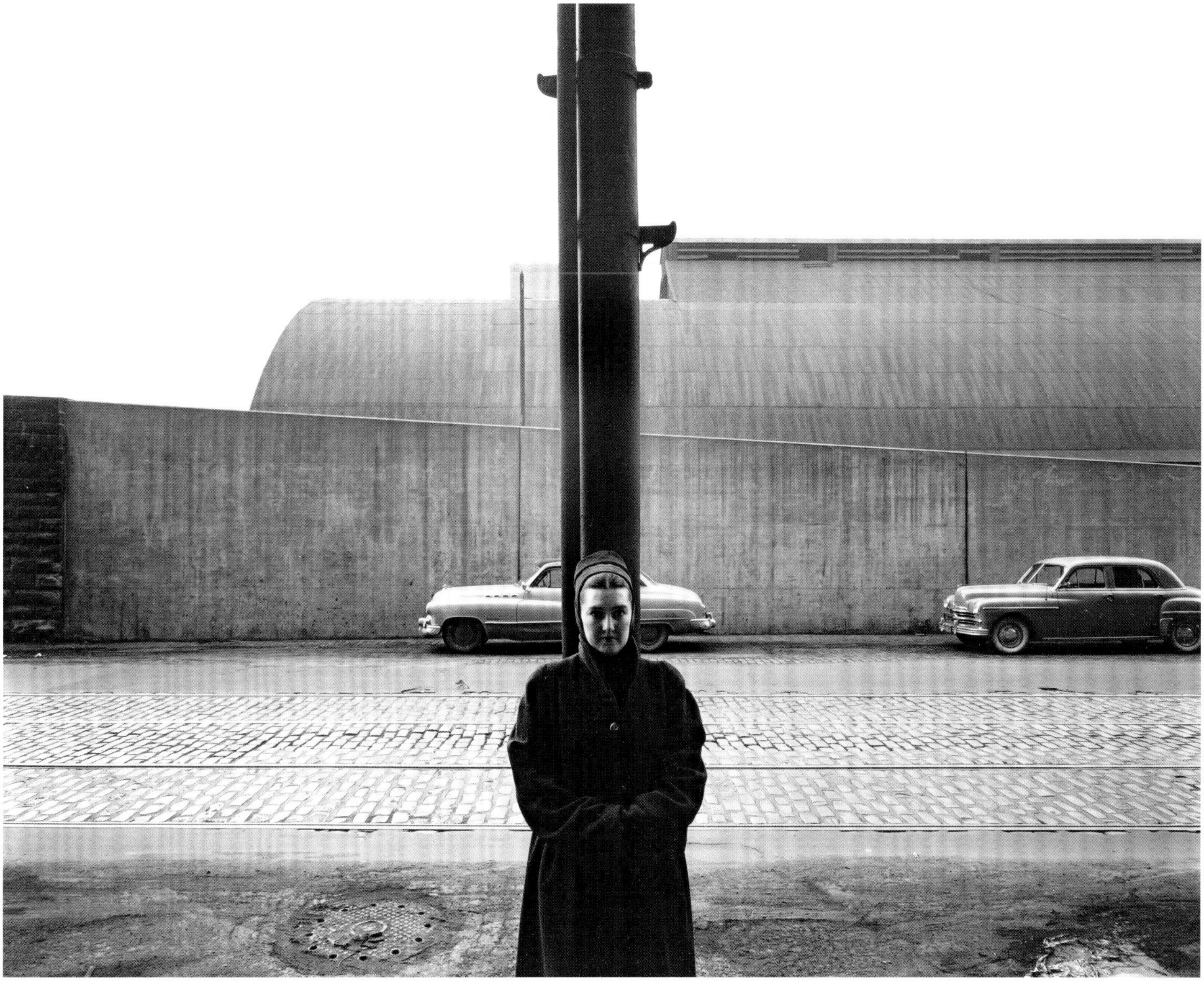

Harry Callahan
Untitled, undated
gelatin silver, 17.8 x 17.8 cm

Harry Callahan
Eleanor, Chicago, 1953
gelatin silver, 19.4 x 24.5 cm

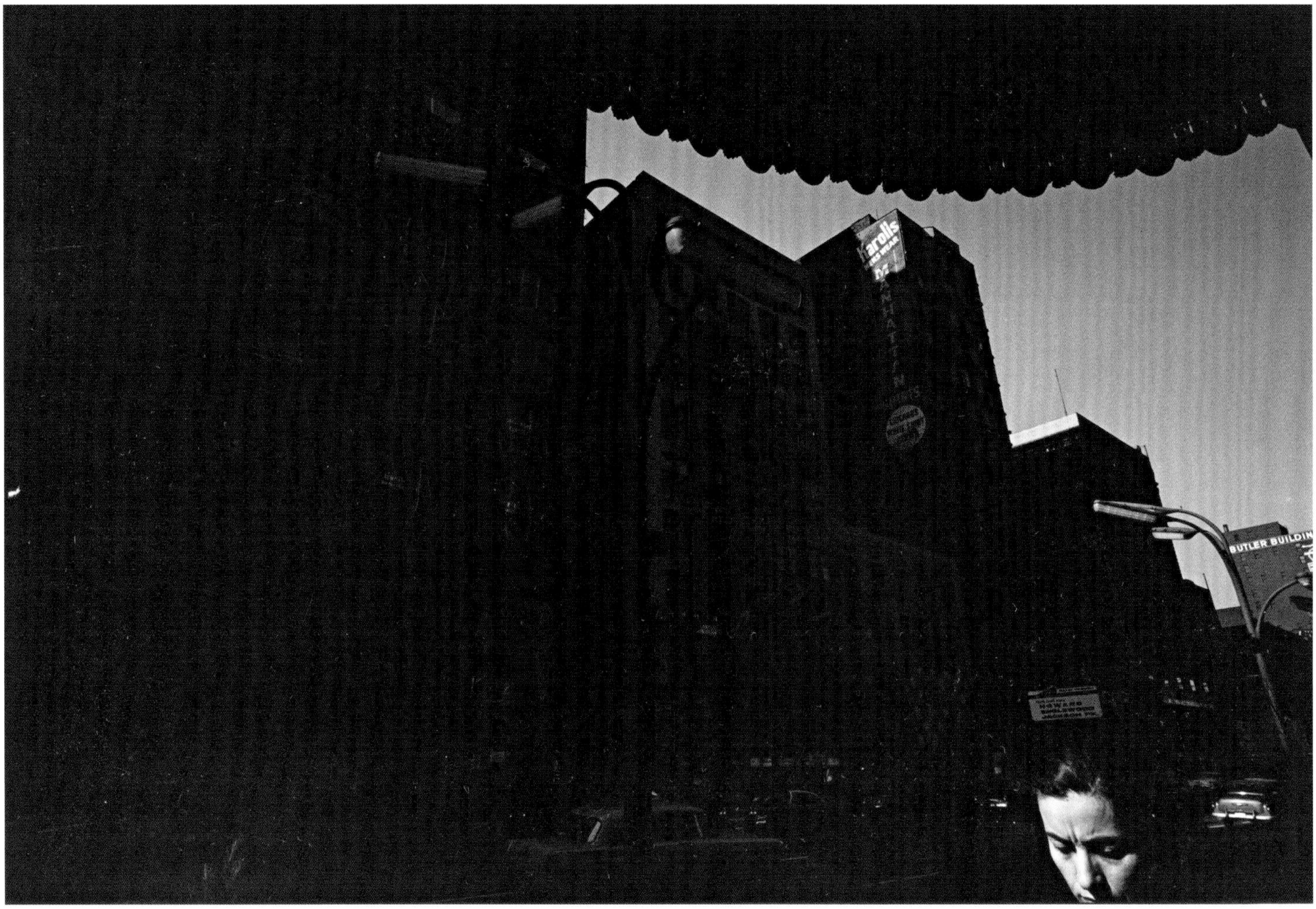

Harry Callahan
Chicago, undated
gelatin silver, 15.8 x 23.8 cm

Harry Callahan
New York, ca. 1968
gelatin silver, 18.1 x 18.4 cm

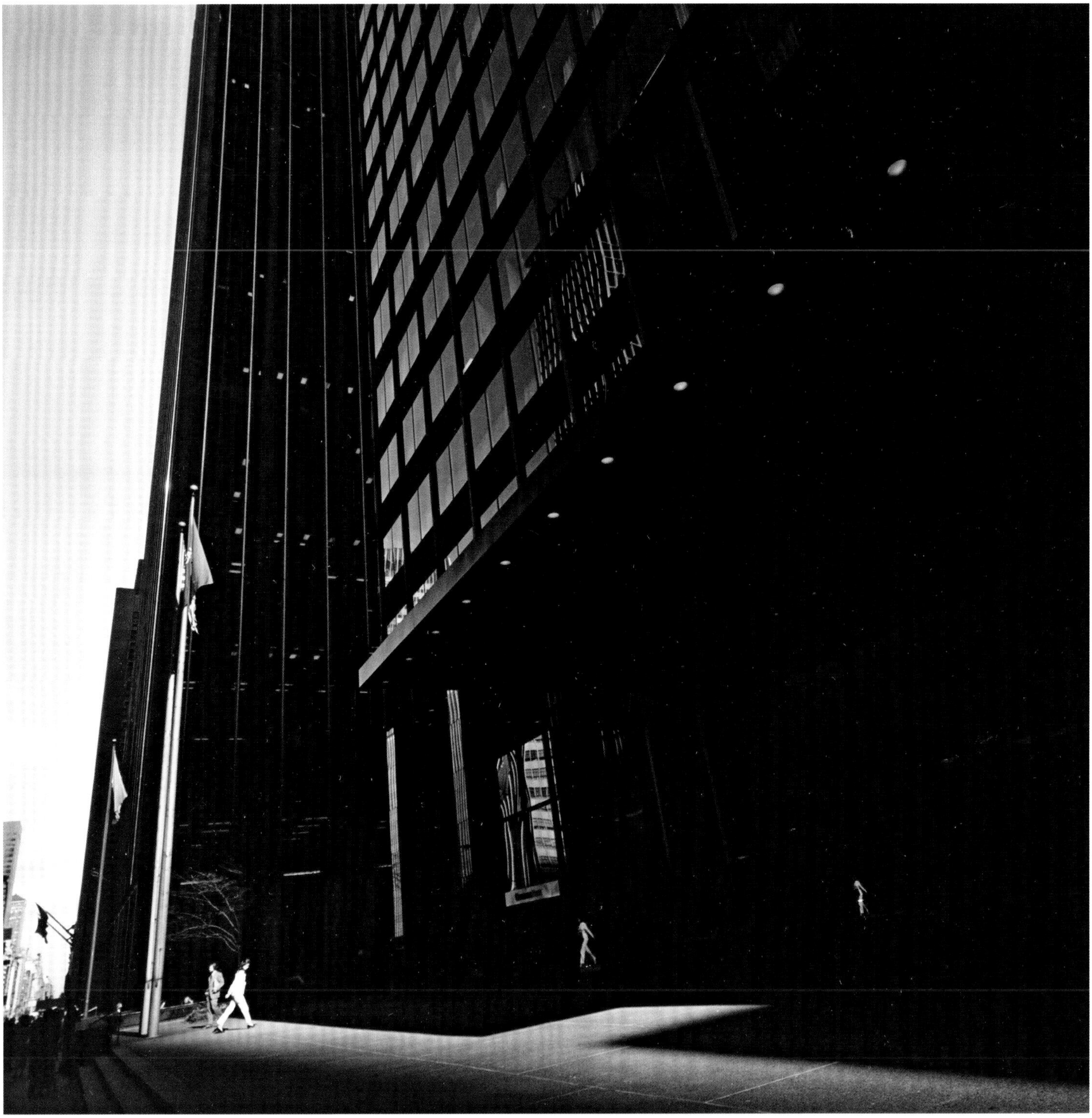

Photography

The School of Design introduces tasks from a new point of view in order to stimulate the student's own approach. Thus photography is taught at the start without camera, using instead only photo-sensitive emulsion, creating photograms.

This is the real key to photography. The next stage is to make a "light modulator" from a sheet of white paper as the principal material. Every student designs such an object to work with a single light source. As the planes of the light modulator are curved or straight, bent or perforated, light play results which may be translated by photography with camera into a series of black, white and gray gradations.

The next stage is the study of light volumes as a genuine means of expression. After this type of exercise, the student goes on field trips and learns to distinguish between structure, texture and surface aspects. He learns about superimposed images, multiple exposures, negative prints and principles of solarization, photomontage and color photography. After these studies, he works with motion picture cameras.

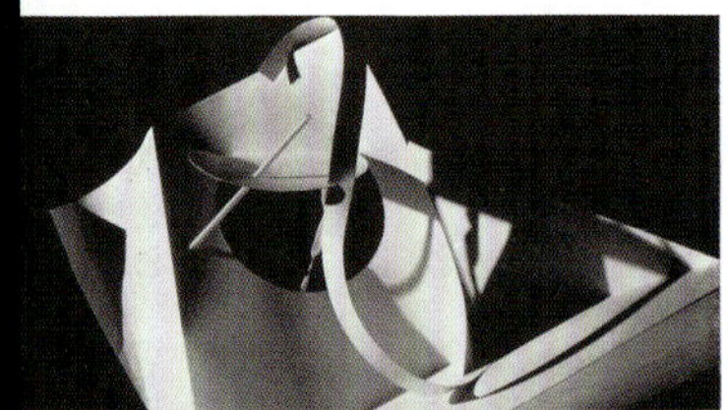

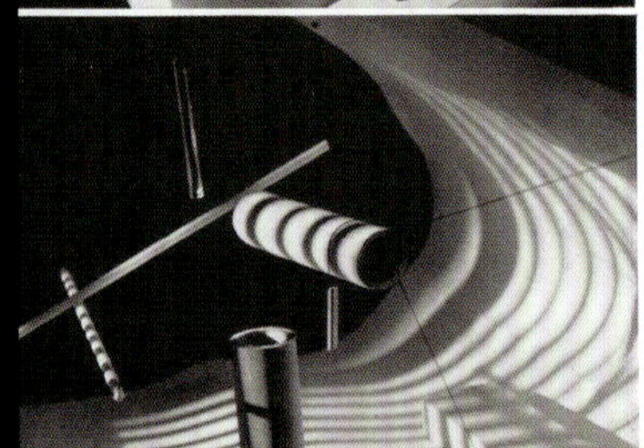

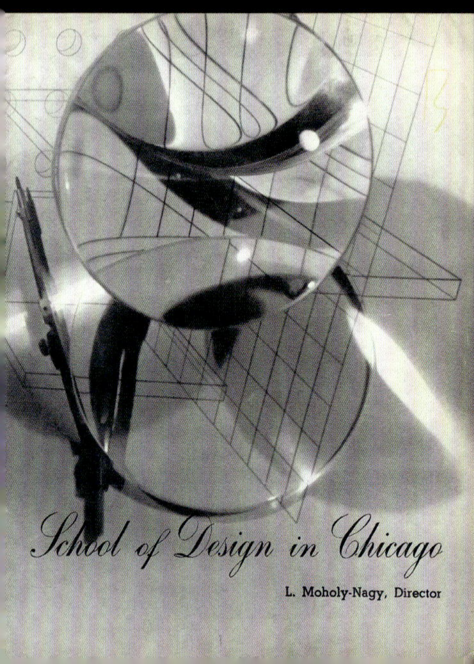

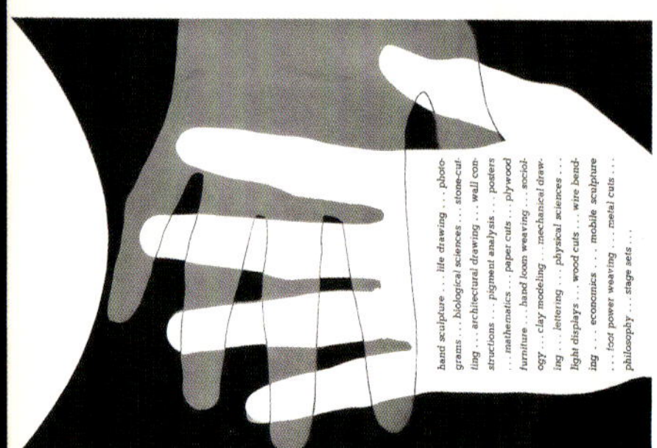

School of Design in Chicago

in focus

The picture reportage on the following pages portrays the spirit and activities of the school seen and expressed by the students themselves. And simply as students speaking to prospective students, it was not intended to give a detailed picture of the school but only its main current of activity. Text and plates were designed as a community project of the light and color workshop which, besides photography, the motion picture, and work in color, includes the advertising arts as well.

The Eye Opens . . .

We begin to see: with our own eyes. Our own signature, lines in our palms, veins of a butterfly wing, light on a surface, all are seen with a primal wonderment

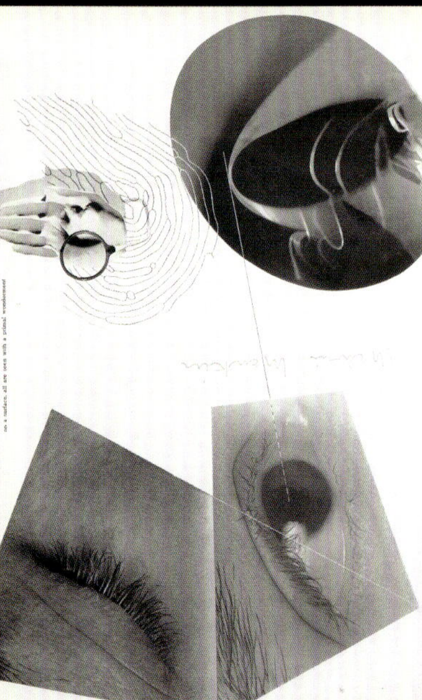

School of Design, Chicago, 1939
school brochure, cover and interior page

School of Design in Chicago: L. Moholy-Nagy, Director, Chicago, 1940
school brochure, cover and interior page

The Institute of Design, Chicago, 1948
school brochure, cover and interior page

id, Chicago ca. 1950
school catalogue, cover and fig. 43–44

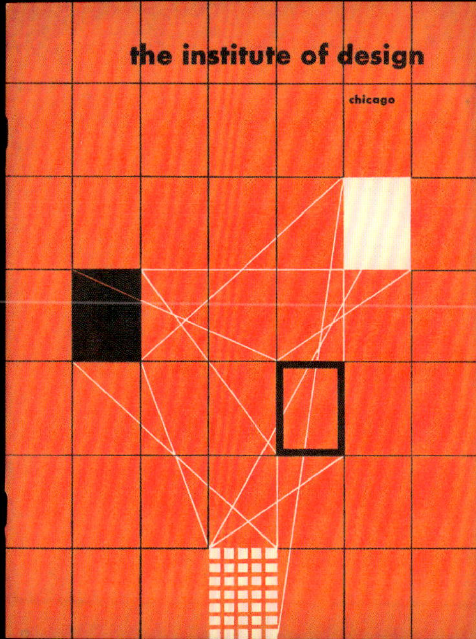

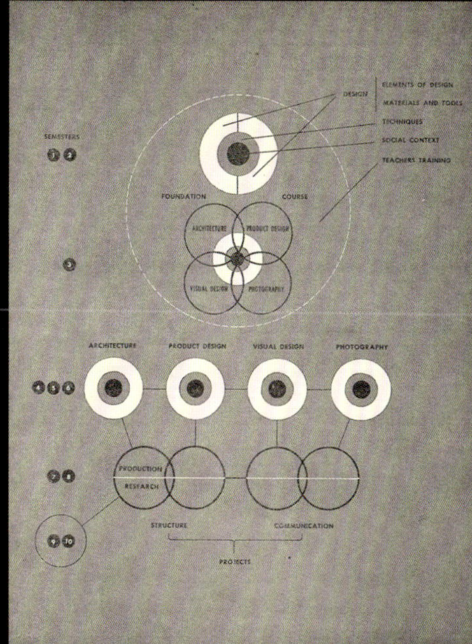

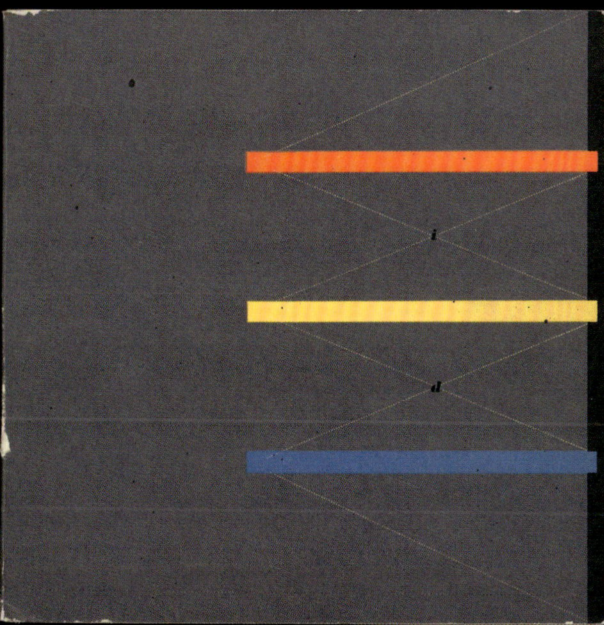

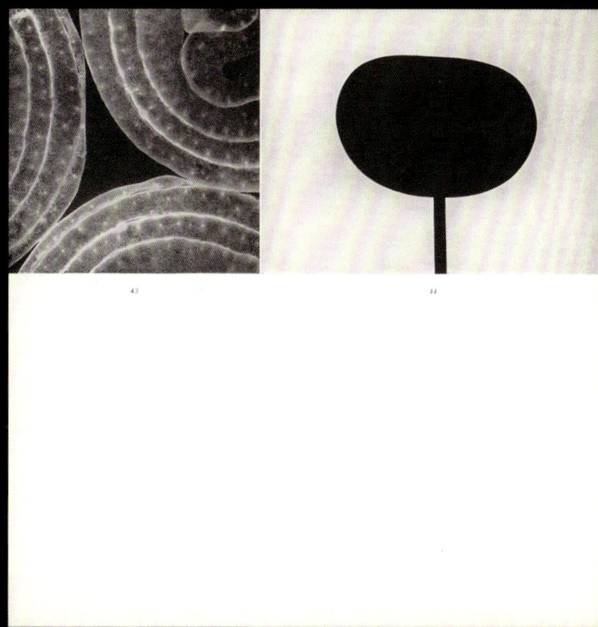

MOHOLY-NAGY'S LEGACY: THE SELF-PRESENTATION OF THE "AMERICAN SCHOOL OF DESIGN" IN ITS SCHOOL BROCHURES

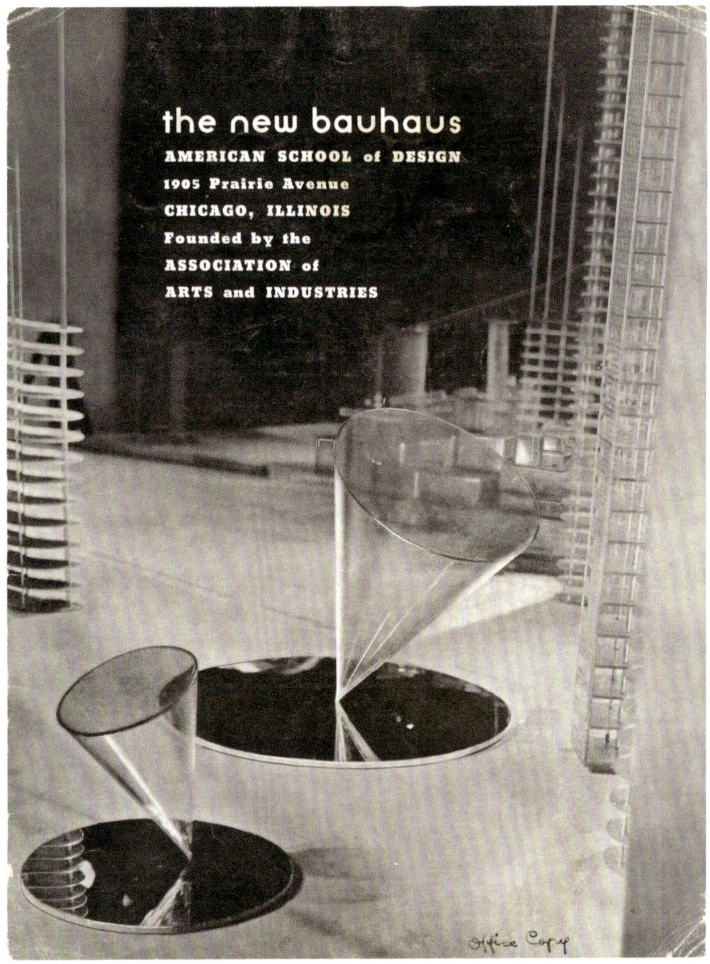

The New Bauhaus: American School of Design,
Chicago, 1937
school brochure, cover

Astrid Bähr

When László Moholy-Nagy opened the New Bauhaus/American School of Design in Chicago in October of 1937, he invoked not just the name and educational curriculum of the Bauhaus, which had been disbanded four years earlier in Germany, but also the PR techniques successfully employed by the school there.[1] He was also dedicated to using the school's brochures for its self-presentation; in doing so, he set standards for its communications and self-concept in the period that followed. Although the school brochures have never been subjected to a focused examination, they have always served as one of the central sources for assessing the institution and for its program. Here the brochures in the New Bauhaus collection of the Bauhaus-Archiv/Museum für Gestaltung will be used to trace these strategies, particularly with regard to perceptions about photographic education.[2]

The first brochure presented by Moholy-Nagy is already programmatic in character. In 1936 he had designed models of a city, based largely on abstract light-and-space sculptures, for Alexander Korda's science-fiction movie *Things to Come*, but these were only used for a short sequence in the film. However, a still shot of this utopian environment wraps around the front and back covers of the school's first publication (→ 100). The central disciplines of the school are interwoven at first glance: film, photography, sculpture, and theatrical as well as exhibition design provide a sense of the possibilities for future artistic work. Moholy-Nagy has additionally used the concise presentation of his educational program to lay the cornerstone for the school's orientation: a broadly conceived, experimental introduction to every art form intended to develop the creative potential inherent within everyone by means of a precise knowledge of materials and techniques. Concrete, applied training in the workshops was to follow. This curriculum was to enable a linking of previously unconnected paths to knowledge, in order to attain new creative achievements and develop the socially responsible designers of the future. Moholy-Nagy emphasizes the close connection with the German Bauhaus, which simultaneously provides legitimation and demonstrates quality, on a number of levels. It is not just the printed text of the commentary by the

1 Regarding the Bauhaus's PR work, see esp. Rössler 2009, and for its reception in the US, Grawe 1994.

2 The school brochures continued to be relatively comprehensively collected until into the 1950s; however, for later years, the collection primarily contains illustrated brochures and no pure course descriptions.

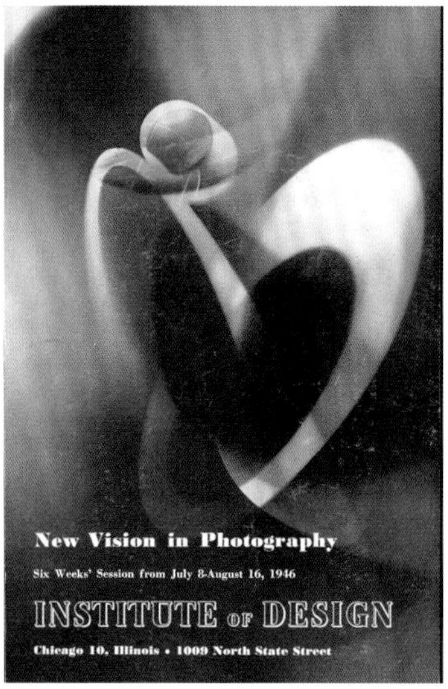

New Vision in Photography: Six Weeks' Session from July 8–August 16, 1946, Institute of Design, leaflet

absolute authority on the Bauhaus—Walter Gropius—on Moholy-Nagy's 1936/37 exhibition at London Gallery that provides a professional guarantee for the new director: Oskar Schlemmer's 1922 Bauhaus seal (inverted into its negative image) serves as a logo, and the curriculum, which displays only a few modifications compared to the German school, was also reprinted (→ 18).[3] Like Moholy-Nagy, the philosopher Charles W. Morris saw an intellectual understanding of the modern world, nurtured by familiarity with contemporary science, as the prerequisite for any kind of work as an artist, and a short text by Morris supports Moholy-Nagy's educational concept.
Moholy-Nagy's pursuit of these strategies of establishing a connection with the German Bauhaus and substantiating his educational theses by means of selected photographs can be seen particularly clearly in the two school brochures developed for the following school years, which were also carried out in a large format (→ 98). Renamed the "School of Design" in 1939/40, "Bauhaus" may have disappeared from the brochure's title, but the reprinting of Alfred Barr's text "Why is the Bauhaus so important" (originally published in the catalogue of the MoMA's 1938 Bauhaus exhibition) emphasizes the school's roots and its role as the "American Bauhaus."
The texts of the following year, largely borrowed from previous years, are supplemented by the newly introduced section "Objectives." In addition to Moholy-Nagy and György Kepes, authorities like Gropius and Morris once again provide support for the educational profile. At a visual level, Moholy-Nagy is able to illustrate the theoretical program through student works. With Nathan Lerner's Light Box[4] and another complex, three-dimensional light modulator, these present some of the most important exercises in the Light Workshop (→ 98): Complemented through a work by Kepes on the cover,[5] these present the photo program in a concentrated visual form.
With a generous two-page design, the 1940/41 school brochure boldly links image and text, thus once again taking up a technique that had already been utilized in the magazine *More Business*:[6] With photographs (many of them by Kepes), photomontages, line drawings, and collages focusing predominantly on the eye and hand as well as material and form, students from the Light Workshop show what they have learned—together with advertising specialists, in keeping with the curricular goal of workshop collaboration during the practical application of learning (→ 98). Kepes's cover illustration features magnifying lenses, a compass, and graph paper defamiliarized into reflecting, arcing, and mysterious forms through their enlargement and distortion, suggesting an education that will enable students to create new visionary worlds out of elementary materials and tools. With their experimentation, playful use of the elements of design, and images repeatedly used in different contexts to convey new content,[7] the school brochures became a visual and textual artistic vehicle for Moholy-Nagy's thought.
The following years' brochures for the summer-school sessions, evening and children's courses, and for the war and camouflage classes held during the final years of World War II only feature variations on previously published texts and usually display photographs solely on their covers.[8] However, the 1944 brochure issued under the school's new name, the Institute of Design (ID), once again presents student works (→ 103). The reproductions here primarily show the furniture and handmade sculptures that had become central to the occupational therapy program and work with veterans. For the Light Workshop, Lerner's *The Photo Studio*—a glimpse inside a studio animated by

3 These modifications consisted primarily of the expansion to include concrete and practical applications (e.g., from "textile" to "weaving and fashion"), a stronger emphasis on the sciences, the more prominent use of mechanical tools, and the introduction of the relatively new media of photography and film. Regarding the film program's significance and development, see Siegel 2002.
4 Of all the student works, Moholy-Nagy seems to have been particularly impressed by this one: He not only included the photo in *The New Vision* of 1938 as fig. 164, he also selected it for the catalogue accompanying the MoMA exhibition as a central work of the Light Workshop as well as for his programmatic essay "New Education—Organic Approach," see Moholy-Nagy 1946, p. 71.
5 Kepes was responsible for the entire brochure's design.
6 See *More Business* 1938, where the emphasis is placed on the commercial orientation of education.
7 For example, the photogram of the crossed hands in *The New Vision* 1938, fig. 176, which was used to illustrate the phenomenon of spatial vision; it was also used in the school brochure as a background for the photographic educational program as well as on the cover of the 1940 summer school brochure.
8 Here the brochures are mostly printed in an A5 booklet format, some of them without any illustrations at all. Those for the summer school sessions usually show students working outside; the covers of the evening-class brochures for 1941/42, and 1943/44 feature photographs by Kepes.

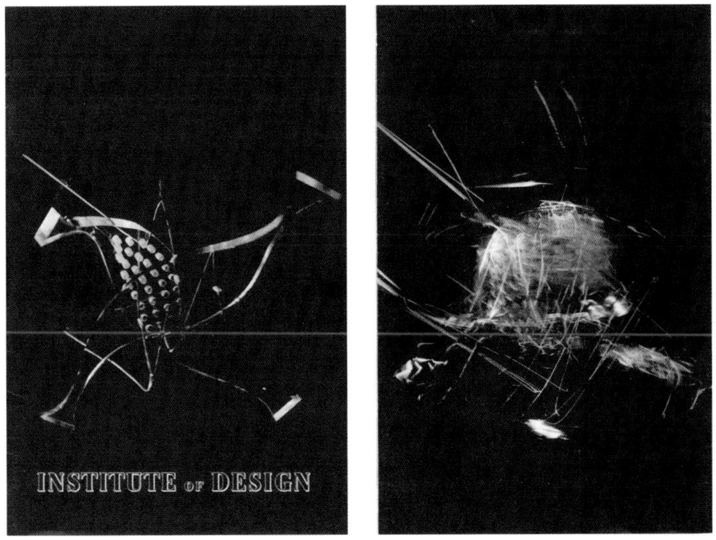

Institute of Design formerly School of Design, Chicago, 1944
school brochure, front and back page

numerous students and richly supplied with photo and film cameras (→ 30)—emphasizes the educational program's potential. In William Keck's *Light Display* (→ 91), light enters the room through windows tilted at different angles and blinds closed to varying degrees, generating a play of different gray values and realizing the central aspirations of Moholy-Nagy's photographic teaching. Moholy-Nagy's photographs of a mobile at rest and in motion on the front and back covers also concisely present his concept of the multidimensional, visionary gaze.

Moholy-Nagy used *New Vision*—the 1946 summer program led by the newly hired head of the Light Workshop, Arthur Siegel—to strengthen photo education at the ID.[9] The department was able to broaden its perspective not just by introducing a nationally recognized, four-year bachelor program, but particularly by opening itself up to different directions in photography, as would also be demonstrated by Harry Callahan's hiring that year. Visually, however, the brochure's cover featuring Siegel's abstract light study of interlocking, spherically revolving rings is once again clearly focused on an experimentally oriented understanding of photography (→ 102).

From the very beginning, Moholy-Nagy used complementary strategies to help insure the success of his mission to create a pioneering school of design with the New Bauhaus. His busy activity as a lecturer,[10] the summer school in California, the successful press relations with various national newspapers and magazines,[11] and the exhibitions[12] all insured that the school's fame spread far beyond Chicago. Moholy-Nagy also reached a large audience with his book publications; based on his experiences at the Bauhaus, he conceived these in the form of series. The final volume of the original "Bauhausbücher" series, *Von Material zu Architektur* (From material to architecture), had been translated and published in the US in 1930 under the strikingly succinct title *The New Vision*; in 1938 Moholy-Nagy announced the release of its second edition as the first volume of the "New Bauhaus Books."[13] In the expanded American edition, he extensively discusses the significance of the German Bauhaus

9 See also Pohlad 2000.
10 See Engelbrecht 2002, p. 30.
11 See the extensive bibliography in *50 Jahre New Bauhaus* 1987 as well as Moholy-Nagy's laboriously composed scrapbook at the Bauhaus-Archiv Berlin, in which he pasted newspaper articles and letters to the ID.
12 See the contributions here by Hoiman and Siegel as well as Siegel 2016.
13 For the announcement of the "New Bauhaus Books," see School brochure 1937, p. 12.

and its continuation as the New Bauhaus. To illustrate this, he scattered works created at the New Bauhaus throughout all the chapters, thus reconfirming the continuation of his theoretical conviction. Moholy-Nagy began a second book series in 1945 under the title "id Book, Institute of Design," whose first volume was Gropius's *Rebuilding Our Communities*. In 1947 Moholy-Nagy's *Vision in Motion* was released as this series' second volume: It offers a summary and analysis of the most important milestones in modern art and of his own artistic and pedagogical ideas. These are once again extensively illustrated using student works and, as a result, the book can be read as his ID legacy. In addition, these publications also continued to be listed for decades as recommended reading in the ID's school brochures.

After the Moholy-Nagy era, this form of design closely interlinking image and text disappears from the school brochures preserved at the Bauhaus-Archiv and is replaced by a reductive, purely typographical concept that primarily presents the overarching teaching concept without using images to shed light on the individual departments. Serge Chermayeff's directorship began in 1948, more than a decade after the school was founded; during this period, Moholy-Nagy had himself grown into a historical figure. As one of the minds responsible for the German Bauhaus's educational program, he embodied its legacy and Gropius's succession.[14] Under the motto "think comprehensively and act effectively," practically applicable design was now emphasized over experimental design, and the unity of "artistry, technology and science" was highlighted. The modified teaching model now consisted of a three-semester foundation course, which formed the basis for four majors that stood alongside one another on equal terms: architecture, product design, graphic design, and photography (→ 99). The 1950 issue of the *Bulletin of Illinois Institute of Technology* devoted to the ID (which had been incorporated into IIT in 1949) also largely reiterates this educational principle—although here its status is further enhanced through the portrait of founding father Moholy-Nagy in the pose of the thinker (→ 104). He sits in front of the educational model drawn in chalk on the blackboard: In reality, though, the model had become increasingly distant from his pedagogical conviction regarding creative self-development and was moving toward a program of studies based on a valid system of academic credits.

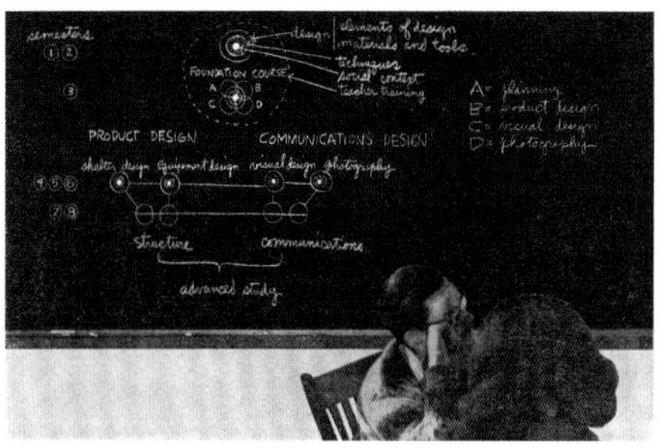

Bulletin of Illinois Institute of Technology, Institute of Design, Chicago, 1950
school brochure, interior page

An exception among the brochures up to 1956 is presented by a catalogue that serves not to provide an overview of the curriculum and course offerings but solely to convey the image of the ID as a "complete laboratory of design education," while relying entirely on the visual idiom of photography to do so (→ 99).[15] Without distinguishing between the individual departments, it features a total of forty-five photographs dealing with every area of specialization and concise statements about the goals of design education. Here the ID presents itself in the tradition of Moholy-Nagy in its experimental exploration of construction, structure, movement, and volume. In photography this is demonstrated in particular by images of the light, contrast, and motion studies. Amazingly, the ID brochures contain no echo of the introduction of the US's first graduate program in photography in 1952 and the resulting increase in this department's significance.

In mid-1956 the ID's relocation to Crown Hall, which Ludwig Mies van der Rohe had built on the IIT campus, began to make its mark visually. Whether as a graphic silhouette in the header of the accordion book on the different courses and majors or as a

14 The design of the 1948 school brochure is based closely on the Harvard Exhibit that Chermayeff assembled in 1947/48; see *50 Jahre New Bauhaus 1987*, fig. 7.33. The depiction of Moholy-Nagy as the inventor of the preliminary course (Vorkurs) can be traced back to Gropius's 1937 letter of recommendation to Norma K. Stahle: "He was my nearest collaborator in the Bauhaus, built up the preliminary courses and was head of some of the workshops," see Walter Gropius to Norma K. Stahle am May 18, 1937, Scrapbook, BHA, NB-Archiv (→ 134).

15 Like most of the brochures from the 1950s to 1980s, this catalogue does not indicate its date of publication; on the basis of the listed address, it can be dated between 1946 and 1956.

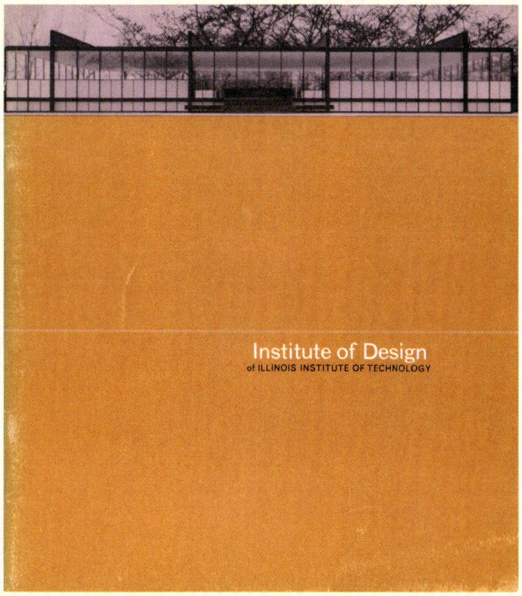

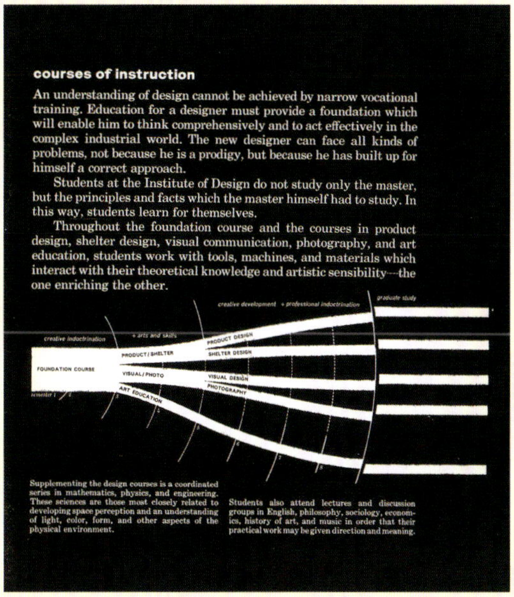

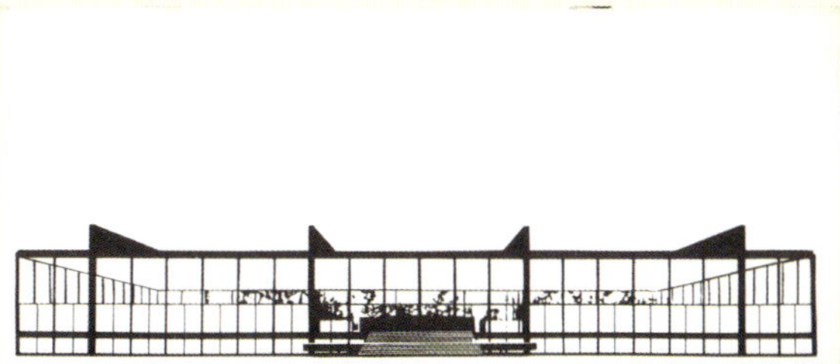

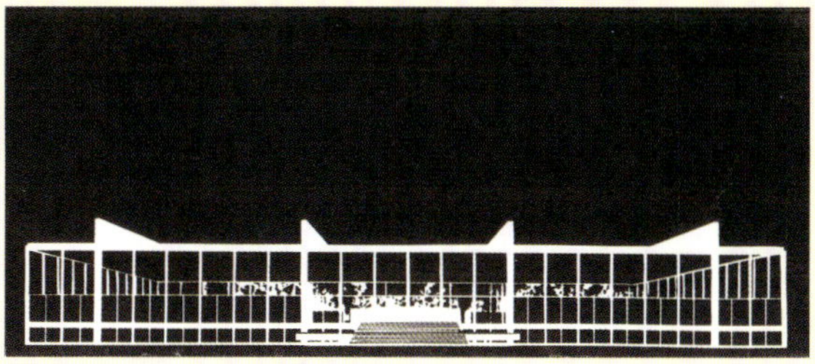

Institute of Design of Illinois Institute of Technology, Chicago, ca. 1956, cover and interior page

Your career in design, Chicago, ca. 1956 school brochure, front and back page

cover photograph (→ 105), institution and location are visually merged into a unity in which the ID presents itself as a site of modern creation. Even under director Jay Doblin, who was controversial because of his close ties to industry,[16] the references back to the school's founder and his historical legacy remain explicit.[17] The aspiration to foster creativity through experimentation remained in place, and the camera—simultaneously "technique and tool"—was specifically seen as a central means for developing individuals' personal potential. However, the principal emphasis was on the focused professional training of designers, as the celebrated industrial designer Henry Dreyfuss underscores in his 1956 opening address devoted to "public taste."[18] The foundation course was once again two semesters long and was followed by the initially combined areas of product/shelter and visual/photography; these split off into independent courses (and were joined by art education) after the fourth semester and enabled students to study in a graduate program after their eighth semester. The photography program had been headed by Callahan since 1949—with the assistance of Siskind since 1951—and its expansion to encompass the investigation of contemporary life as well as its practical use is clearly expressed:[19] "The camera in the hands of

16 Particularly the press eyed Doblin with suspicion, see Chancellor 1955.
17 "Today [...], the ID still carries the imprint of this great man—who [...] was unrelenting in his attempts to penetrate conventional design barriers." School brochure 1956, unpag.
18 Henry Dreyfuss, "What's happening to public taste: Address delivered at the dedication of the new Institute of Design—Illinois Institute of Technology, Chicago, April 30, 1956."
19 This brochure also emphasizes the teachers' accomplishments: Callahan, with "many one-man-shows [...] constantly on exhibit in leading museums," and Siskind, with works in the "permanent collection of the Museum of Modern Art" as well as being mentioned in numerous journal articles devoted to his work.

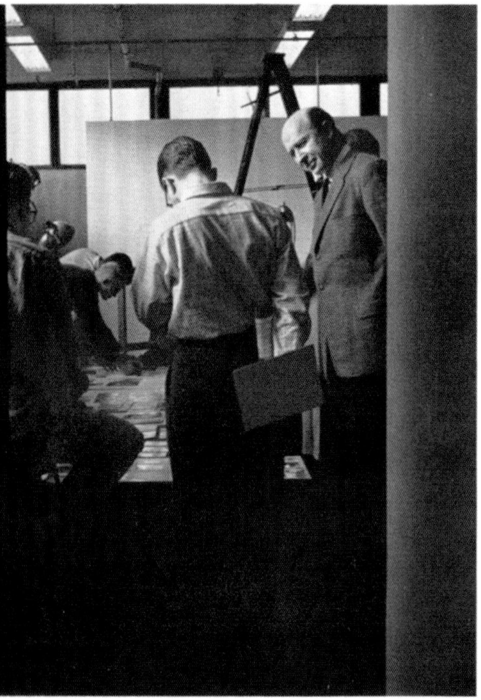

The camera in the hands of a person with a developed creative sense is much more than an unbiased mechanical instrument. It is the medium for interpretative recording of contemporary life for journalistic, documentary, illustrative, or pictorial purposes.

The aim of the Institute of Design's photographic department is to develop this interpretative sense in the student while teaching the use of equipment and technique. Through a carefully-graded series of problems, the student masters the machine, but always in relation to the expression of the problems.

The department is more than adequately equipped with cameras, enlargers, lighting and other equipment.

All photographs in this catalog were taken by students of the photography department.

1 experimental studies: **a/b/c** photograms, **d/e** virtual volumes, object movement. **2** lip expression, one of a series. **3** from a definitive study the architecture of Adler and Sullivan (Horizon Press, fall, 1957). **4** evidence of people. **5** product analysis, negative print. **6** plant forms, one of a series. **7** documentary series, from a study made for the Chicago Housing Authority.

1 a/b/c/d/e

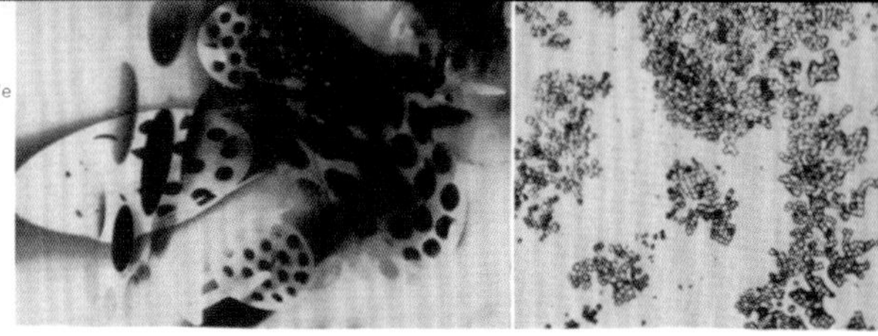

2

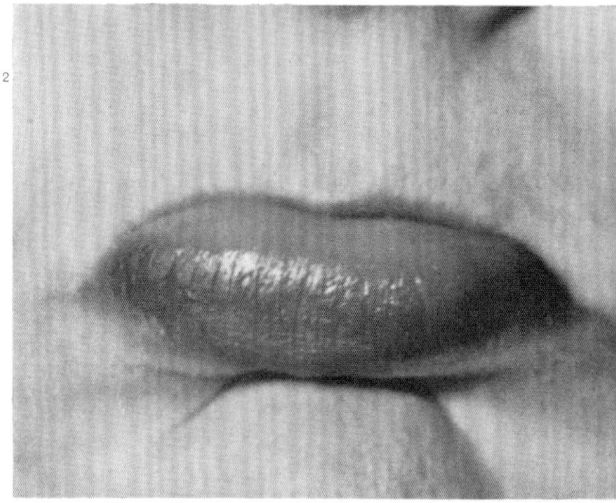

4

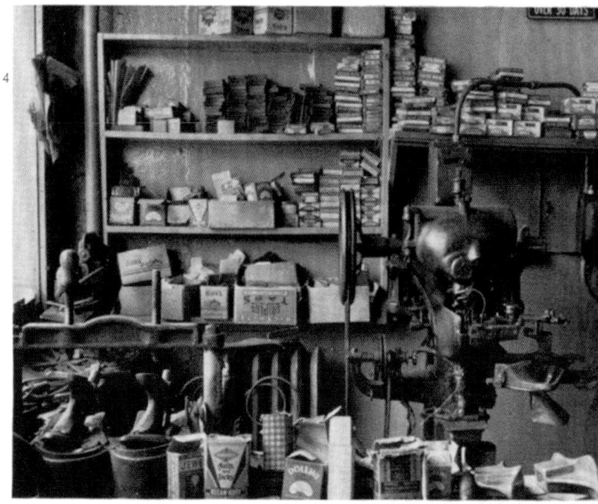

7

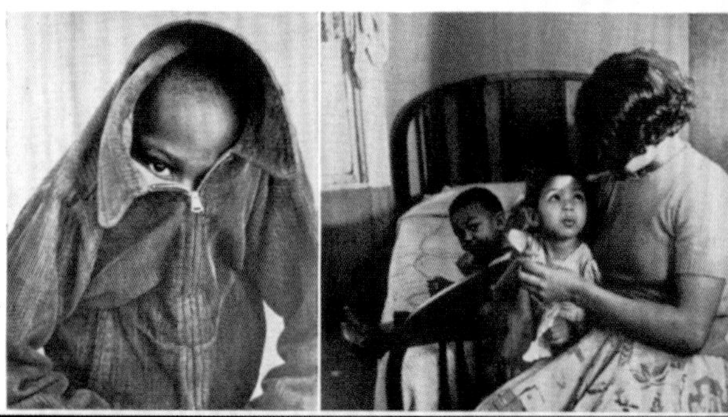

Institute of Design of Illinois Institute of Technology
Chicago, ca. 1956
school brochure, interior page

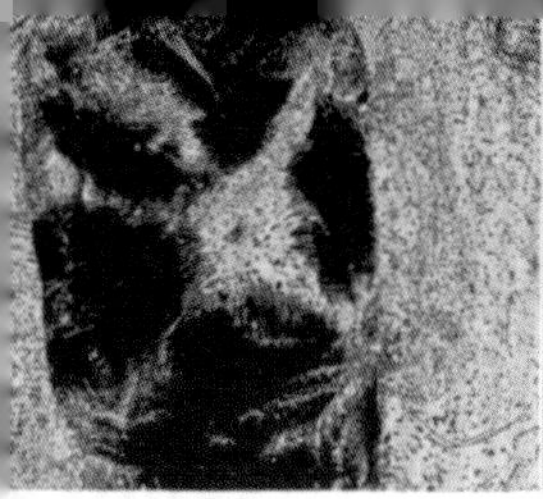
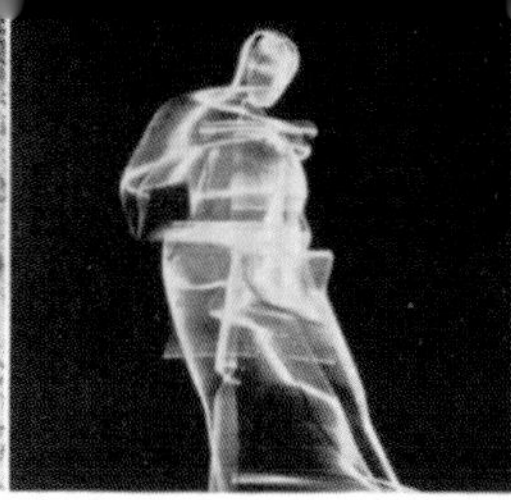
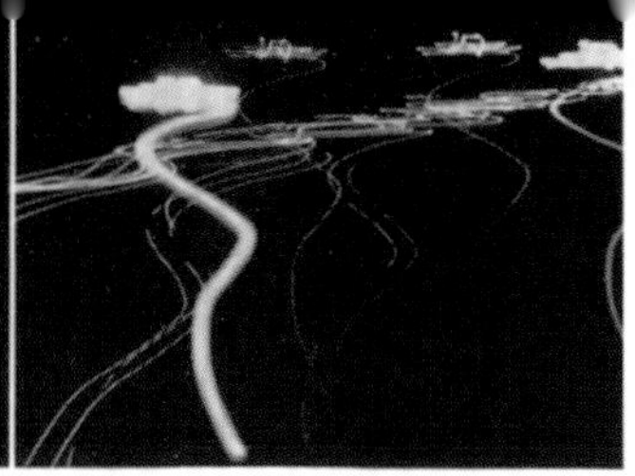
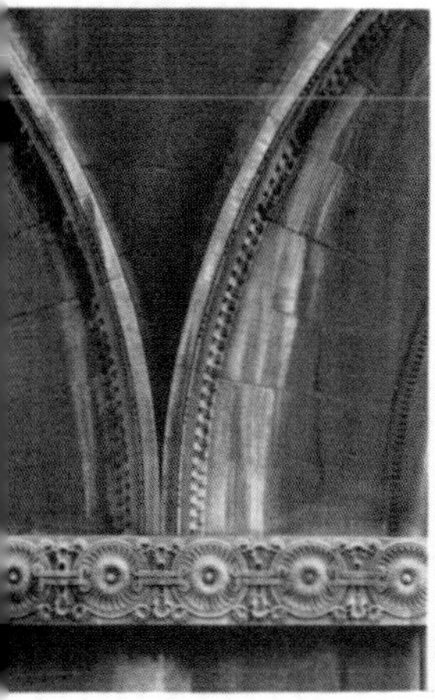
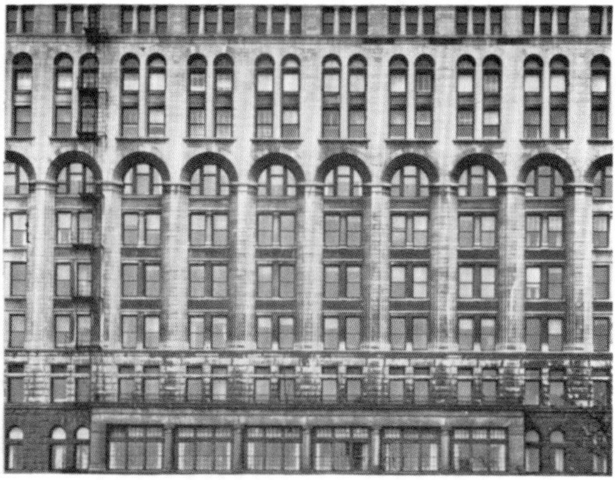

3

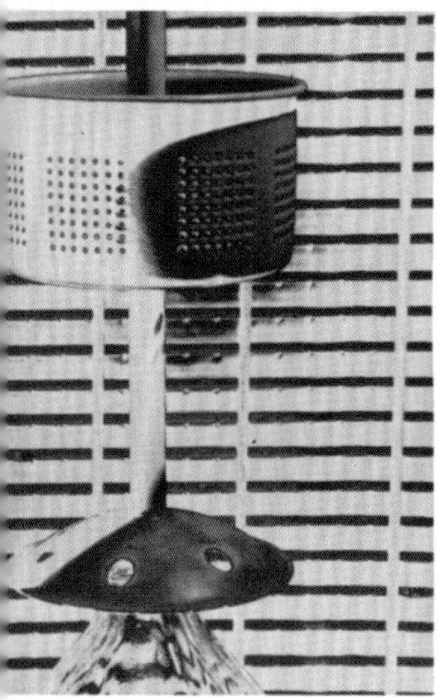
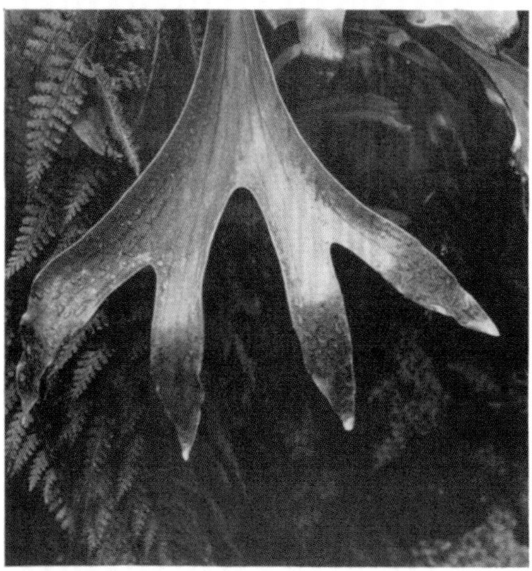

5/6

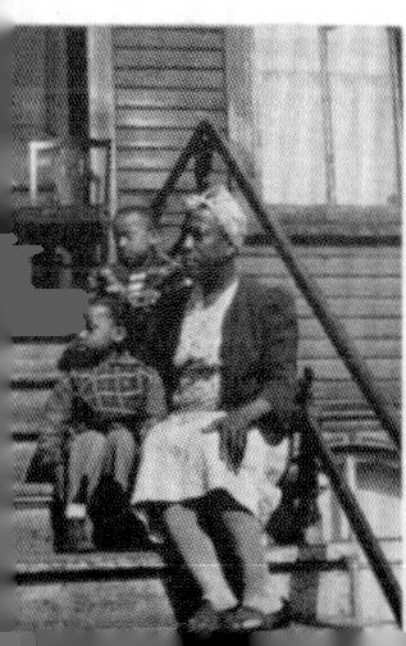
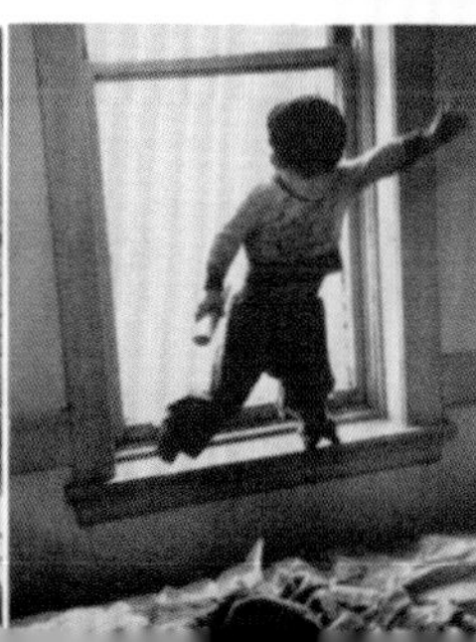
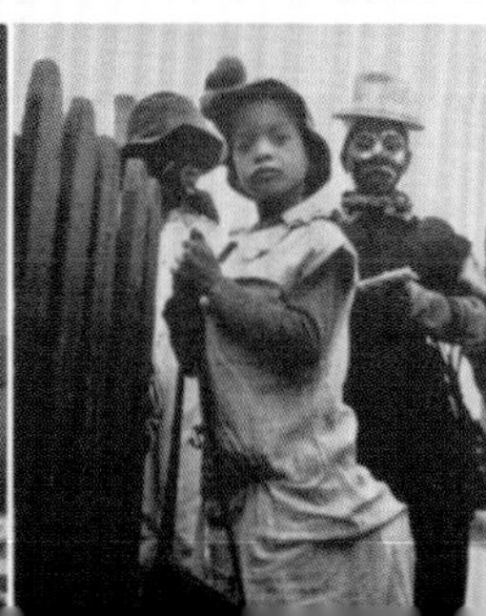
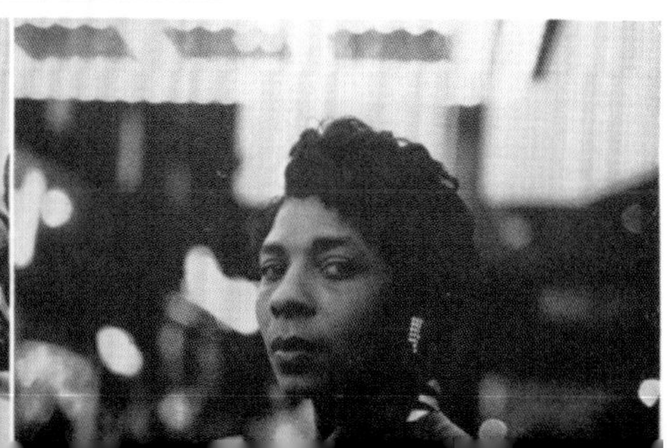

PHOTOGRAPHY

	lecture (hours per week)	laboratory (hours per week)	credits
second year			
Introduction to Literature	3	—	**3**
General Physics	3	—	**3**
History of Art	6	—	**6**
Basic Visual Design	5	21	**11**
Methods of Photography	5	21	**11**
liberal elective	3	—	**3**
totals	25	42	**37**
third year			
Principles of Economics	6	—	**6**
Public Speaking	2	—	**1**
The American Const'l. System	3	—	**3**
Music Appreciation	2	—	**2**
Photography	4	42	**18**
Drawing & Color	1	5	**3**
totals	18	47	**33**
(optional) Film History	4	—	**4**
totals	22	47	**37**
fourth year			
Humanities Elective	3	—	**3**
Photography	8	28	**18**
Photo Workshop	—	24	**8**
liberal elective	3	—	**3**
totals	14	52	**32**

Semester hours per week and semester credits may be determined by dividing the above figures by two.

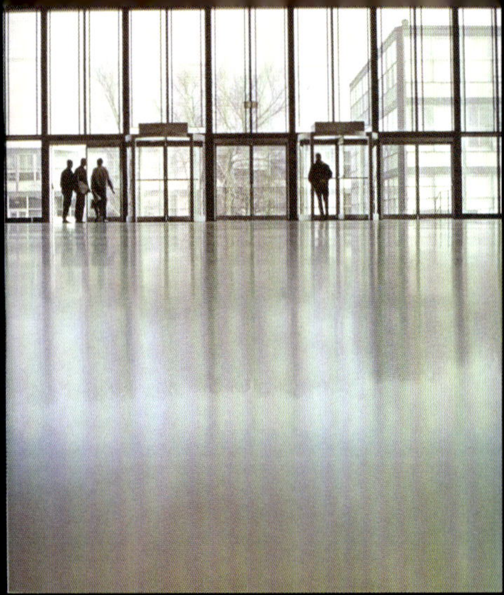

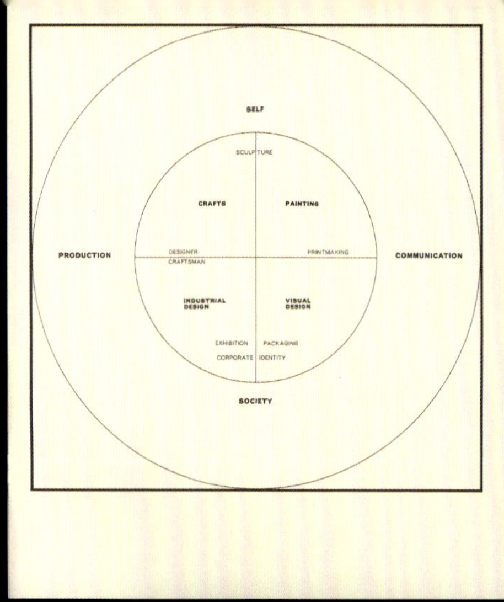

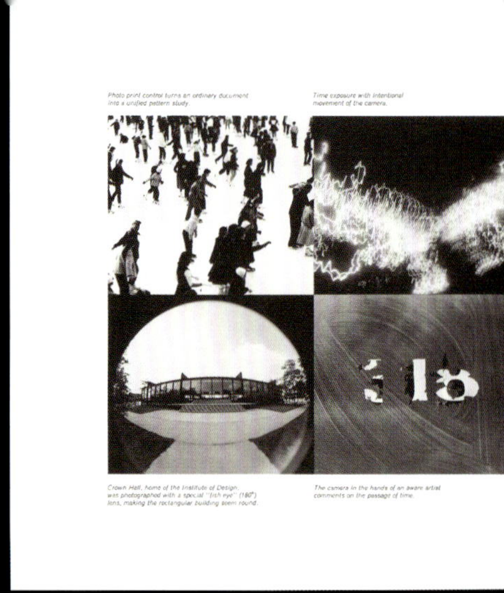

Institute of Design, Illinois Institute of Technology, Chicago, ca. 1966
school brochure, cover and interior page

a person with a developed creative sense is much more than an unbiased mechanical instrument. It is the medium for interpretative recording of contemporary life for journalistic, documentary, illustrative, or pictorial purposes."[20] The anonymous student works (→ 106–107) demonstrate this spectrum, which was far broader than that of the 1940s. In addition to photograms and experimental studies of space and motion, we also find photographic details of human physiognomies and plants, photographs from Siskind's documentary project on the architecture of Adler and Sullivan, and images "from a study made for the Chicago Housing Authority." These also reflect the two photography teachers' areas of interest: fundamental experiments and the learning of documentary forms as well as working in series, photographs of plants and architecture, and group projects.[21]

To the degree that photography disappeared from the ID's brochures, its teachers now published their work in specialized periodicals.[22] In their 1956 *Aperture* essay, Callahan and Siskind see photo education as an independent program of study: At the ID it offers the advantage of profiting from other areas of design education, but it nonetheless aims at a specific and broad-based professionalization.[23] This may also

20 See School brochure 1956, unpag.
21 The same text—accompanied by a similar mixture of experimental and documentary photographs—also appears in the thin leaflet *ID + IIT*.
22 Regarding these exhibitions and publications, see also Davis 2002, p. 84.
23 See Siskind/Callahan 1956. Regarding the program presented there, see Davis 2002, p. 87.

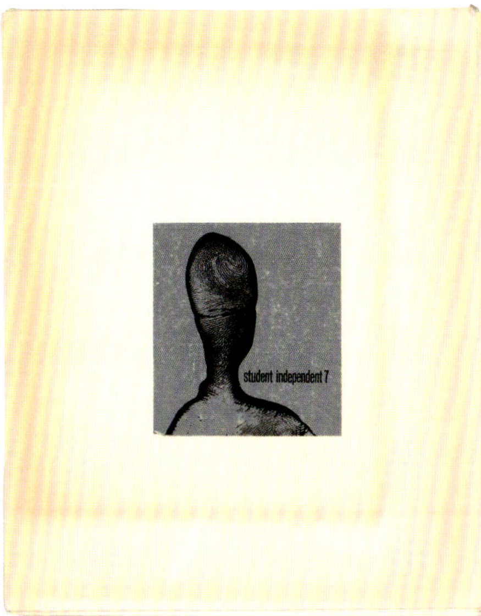

Institute of Design Student Independent 7, 1965
portfolio, 36 x 29.5 cm

be the reason why the unique nature of the education in the foundation course—a form of introducing students to their studies that had by then spread to many other US universities and colleges—is no longer emphasized, but evaluated as "largely traditional." Siegel also wrote in *Aperture* and presented five of his graduates (→ 177).[24] In an ironic introduction to the development of photography, he names the fundamental goal of this "school of subversion": to unite the photography developed in Europe, which was oriented around experimentation and painting, with the achievements of the American technique of "object transformation," that is, to take up a path that went much further than Moholy-Nagy's program and was specifically focused on photography. The seven documented portfolios of the series *Student Independent* (→ 109), which were issued between 1953 and 1969, are not ID publications either, as their initiator Siskind decidedly emphasized. The photographs—and the graphic works in some issues—were created independently of the curriculum and are meant to present and foster students' talents. Featuring unconventional supports (various papers, synthetic materials, and textiles) and elaborately printed, they are among the most important works created at the ID. While Callahan's catalogue *The Multiple Image* was published by the ID in 1961 and privately financed by Doblin,[25] it nonetheless advanced his own artistic career more than anything else.

After the individual, specialized majors within the bachelor program were eliminated and replaced by the single, comprehensive design degree awarded from 1966 onward,[26] illustrated brochures appeared only very sporadically. Among these, a booklet whose cover features an anonymous, painterly-looking color photograph of Crown Hall stands out: Looking out from the building's interior and across the finely graduated tones of the flooring, it focuses on the building's entrance façade (→ 108). At this point, the central legacy of the Bauhaus had become the teachability of design. While familiarity with "media and art" had replaced that with "technique and tool," the designer's sense of social responsibility still remained the educational goal. A graphic diagram of the curriculum positions the "self" of the designer in relationship with society, production, and communication. However, the field of photography has disappeared entirely from the divisions of design as well as the forms of its application. Photography's concrete application is nonetheless presented by a five-page photo sequence in which the serial working process has come to serve as the basis of photography. The experimental occupation with light, space, contrast, and perspective has also been maintained and expanded to include an exploration of overarching concepts like "passage of time" or "tool of our memory."

While the school brochures still continued to paraphrase Moholy-Nagy's program into the 1970s,[27] using keywords like "experiment," "creative potential," and "social responsibility," their design had become far removed from his avant-garde image brochures presenting the Light Workshop. An accordion booklet from the late 1980s demonstrates the great degree to which the school's self-image was nonetheless still fed by this heritage, in spite of its transformed understanding of its pedagogical orientation and educational programs: The "New Bauhaus" logo, the cover of the first school brochure from 1937, and photographs by Keck, Lerner, and Siegel stand for the identity of the ID as the American Bauhaus and form the background for everything that has happened since.

24 See *ID5* 1961.
25 See Grimes 2002, p. 156.
26 See ibid., p. 165.
27 School brochure 1974.

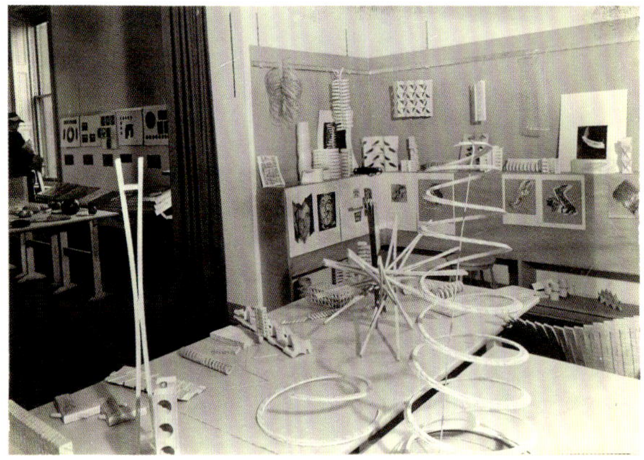

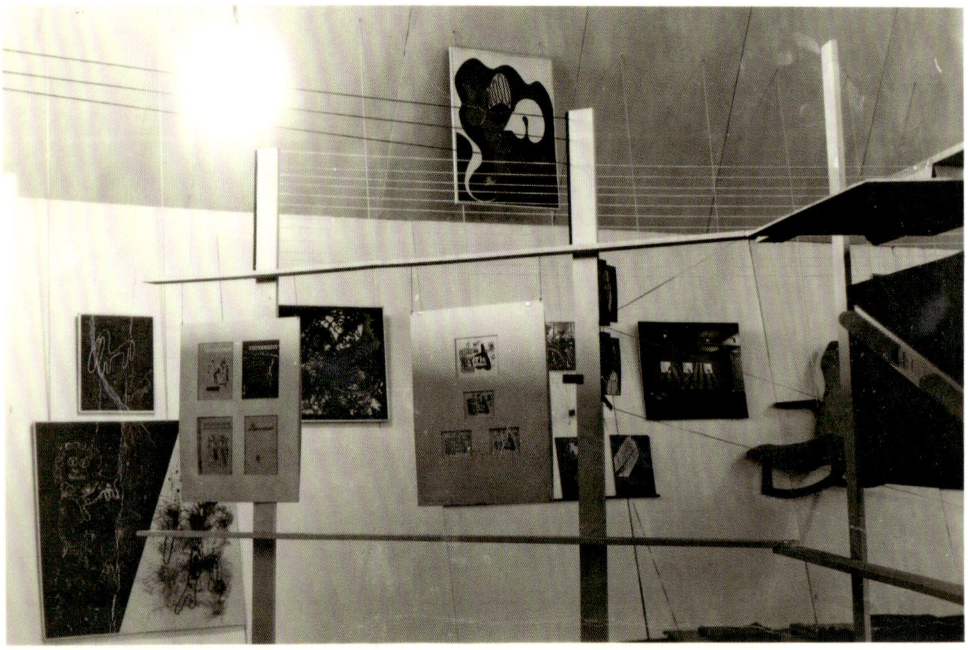

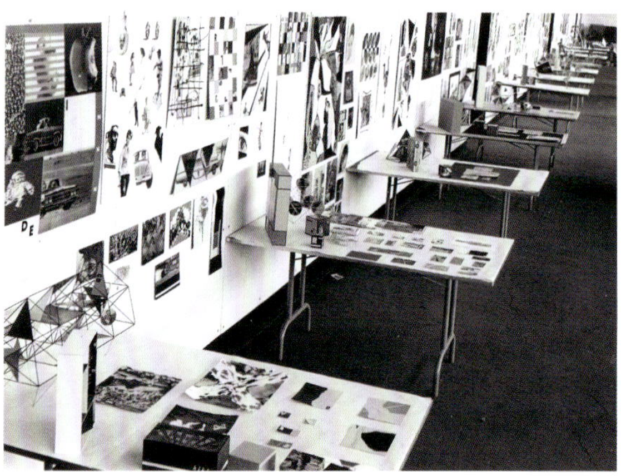

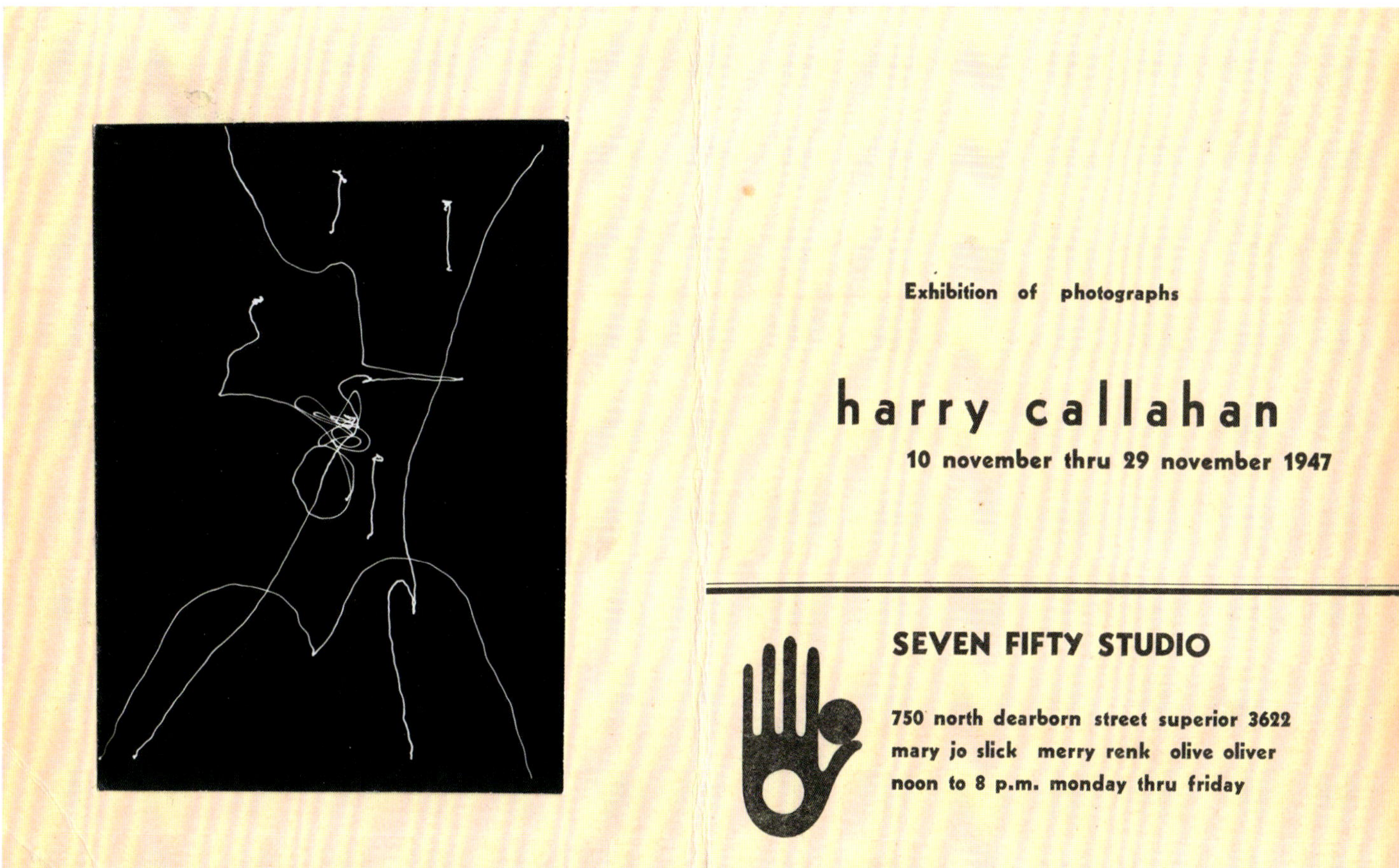

Hin Bredendieck
Exhibition of works from the foundation course at the New Bauhaus, 1937/38
gelatin silver, 9.5 x 11.4 cm

Anonymous
View of the faculty show at the ID
1943 or 1944, print of ca. 1975
gelatin silver, 12.5 x 18 cm

Richard Koppe
Works from Koppe's class at the IIT between 1955 and 1963, later print
gelatin silver, 28.2 x 35.5 cm

Invitation to the exhibition *Harry Callahan* at the student run 750 Studio, with original print, 1947
15.4 x 25.4 cm

THE INSTITUTE OF DESIGN: BALANCING EDUCATION, COMMERCE, AND ARTISTIC EXPRESSION

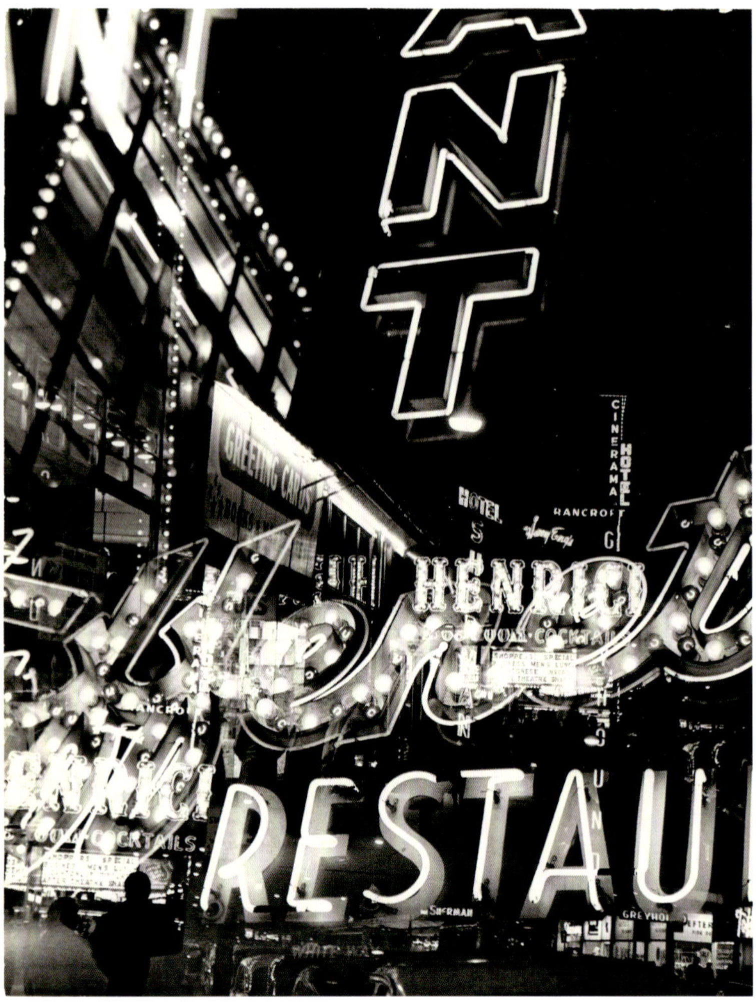

Charles Swedlund
Chicago, Multiple Exposure, ca. 1955
gelatin silver, 24.1 x 19 cm

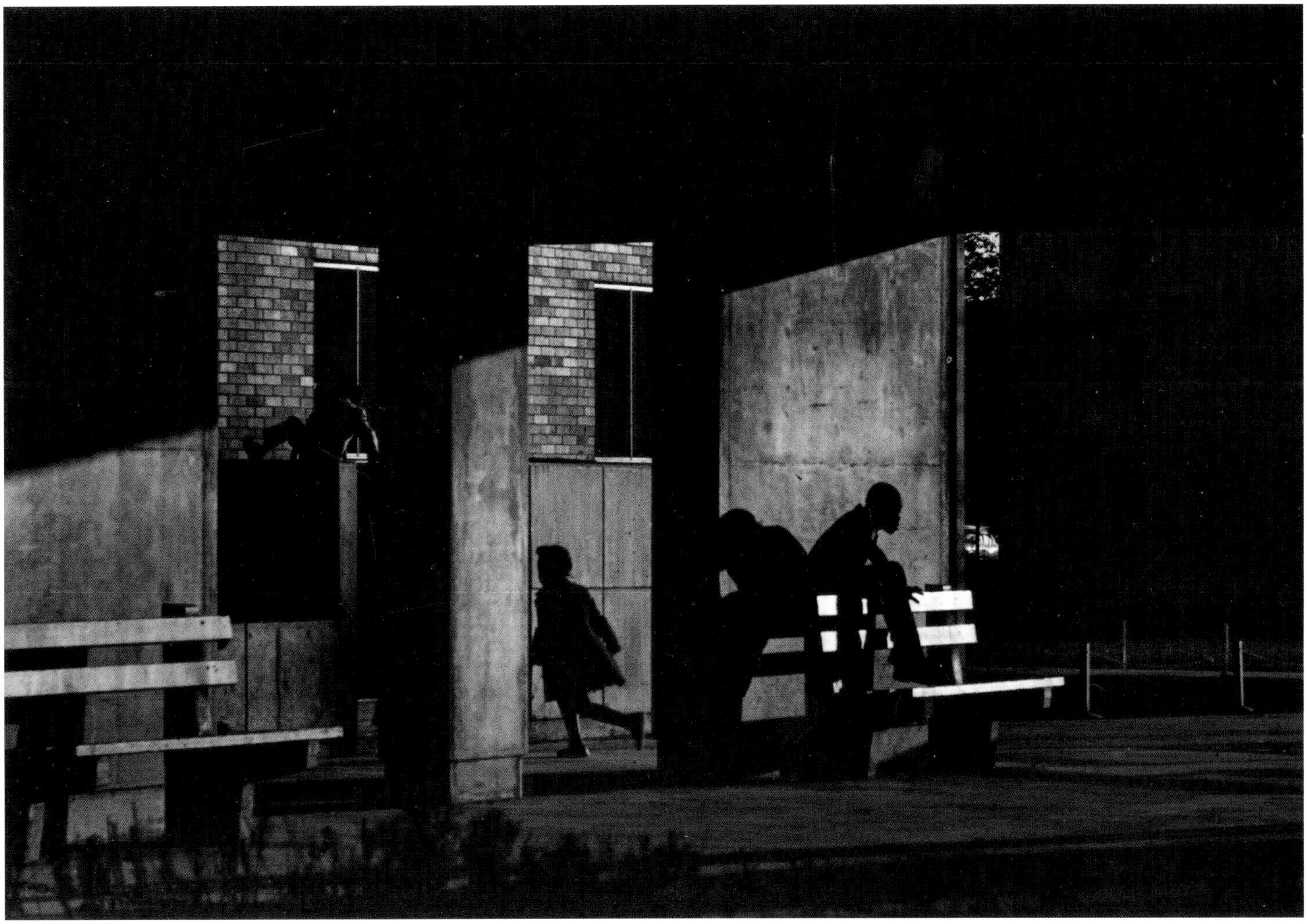

Ray K. Metzker
Chicago (58 AC-28), 1958
gelatin silver, 14.6 x 21.3 cm

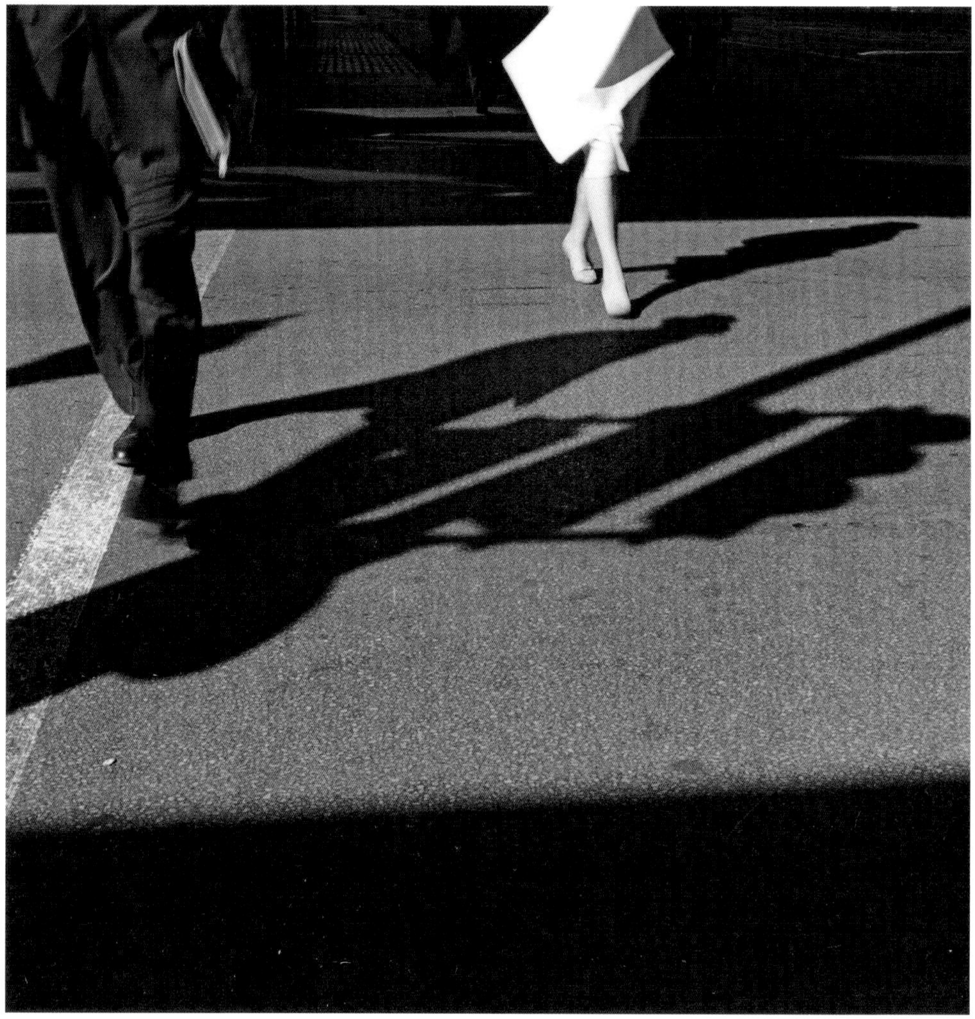

Ray K. Metzker
Chicago, Loop (57 HK-3), 1957
gelatin silver, 19.2 x 19.2 cm

To highlight the importance of where you work and who you network with, I will compare the careers of three ID photographers—Ray Metzker, Kenneth Josephson, and Charles Swedlund, who were contemporaries, comparable artistic talents, and among the best and most creative photographers that the post-WWII ID has produced. Their paths to artistic recognition and commercial success are very different. In the 1960s and 1970s all three exhibited and published widely, securing serious teaching positions. Since the 1970s their paths to commercial and broad artistic recognition have diverged in part due to their career priorities and in part to where they lived and worked.

Ray Metzker has had the most long-term commercial, collecting, and institutional success of the three (→ 117–118). After graduation from the ID (MA, 1959) he moved to Philadelphia (1962) to teach. In the 1970s Metzker began and then maintained a gallery relationship in New York—first with Light Gallery and then Laurence Miller Gallery. He has been vigorously promoted for over thirty years by Miller (averaging a one-person exhibition every eighteen months to two years) and they have been adept at connecting with museums, for exhibition and acquisition, and in getting Metzker's work published. Metzker's accomplishments include: one-person museum exhibitions (Art Institute of Chicago in 1959 and 1991,[29] MoMA in 1967, International Center of Photography in 1978, Museum of Fine Arts Houston in 1984,[30] Nelson-Atkins Museum[31]), eight books, and successful placement into many notable institutions and private collections at very strong market prices. Metzker's proximity to New York enabled him to regularly engage with the art and photography world.

Kenneth Josephson stayed in Chicago after finishing his training at the ID (MA, 1960) (→ 122–125). He started the photography department at the School of the Art Institute Chicago and spent over thirty-five years teaching there. Chicago is not New York in terms of opportunity and exposure and Josephson is not big on self-promotion, perhaps because of his classic Midwestern humility. Rhona Hoffman Gallery, a high-profile Chicago contemporary art gallery, represented Josephson for two decades, along with a number of other crossover photographer/artists (e.g. Carrie Mae Weems, Cindy Sherman, Jenny Holzer, Barbara Kruger, Vito Acconci, Robert Heinecken), but she never felt she was successful in marketing Josephson's work until the Art Institute (1999) and Whitney exhibitions (2001). The Whitney show and book generated considerable interest in Josephson's work, and sales increased—in part through my gallery and a New York gallery. In 2006 my gallery took over primary representation of Josephson from Hoffman,[32] and we have helped publish four books,[33] exhibited his work regularly in galleries and at major international art fairs,[34] and helped arrange museum exhibitions.[35] The increased public awareness has yielded a consistent growth in sales and prices for his work. Recently Josephson's prices reached rough parity with Metzker's.

Charles Swedlund attended the ID, receiving a BA (1958) and an MA (1961) (→ 112, 121). He had a passion for teaching and was quite good at it. He began teaching part time at the ID, followed by full time at State University College at Buffalo (1963–1969), the ID (1969–1971), and finally at Southern Illinois University, where

29 *My Camera and I in the Loop.* 1959; *A New Leaf,* 1991.
30 *Unknown Territory: Photographs by Ray K. Metzker 1957–1983*, November 17, 1984–January 29, 1985. Travelled to MOMA, Art Institute of Chicago, High Museum, San Francisco and Philadelphia Museums of Art; George Eastman House; Smithsonian.
31 *The Photography of Ray K. Metzker and the Institute of Design,* January 15–June 5, 2011. Travelled to J. Paul Getty Museum, Los Angeles, and Henry Art Museum, Seattle.
32 With Gitterman Gallery in New York.
33 *Kenneth Josephson* 2008; *Kenneth Josephson* 2012; *Kenneth Josephson* 2014; *Kenneth Josephson* 2016.
34 AIPAD, Art Basel, Art Chicago and Paris Photo.
35 Denver Art Museum October 11, 2015–May 8, 2016; *Kenneth Josephson: Photography Is*, New Orleans Museum. of Art September 9, 2016–February 19, 2017, Museum of Contemporary Art, Chicago, 2018.

he remained for twenty-nine years, until his retirement in 2000. Swedlund was isolated from the art world in Carbondale and as a result his opportunities to sell and publish nationally dwindled after the 1970s. As a photographer Swedlund was endlessly creative and experimented obsessively, with film, lenses, paper stock, exposures, and chemical processes as well as subject matter. He wrote a seminal textbook on photography,[36] created wide-ranging art that included limited-edition publications or portfolios, color and black-and-white photographs made by various alternative processes, curious perceptual phenomena, a series of photo buttons, and unique photo-puzzles. Despite his massive creative output he never focused on marketing himself until we encouraged him to about six or seven years ago. Since then we have had success selling individual photographs, book maquettes, his games and toys, and his works in series to museums and collectors. Despite this success, we have not secured one-person museum exhibitions and major book contracts, in large part because he had been off the art world grid for over 30 years.

Over the years my gallery has consistently tried to educate the public about ID artists and help them develop a strategy to present and market their work to a broader public. We have been a meaningful voice in the US promoting the work of early ID faculty, including György Kepes, László Moholy-Nagy, Aaron Siskind, and Harry Callahan, as well as many of their esteemed students: Barbara Crane, Joseph Jachna, Kenneth Josephson, Arthur Siegel, Joseph Sterling, and Charles Swedlund, among others. Thankfully, in 2017, it finally seems like public awareness, recognition of the influence of the ID, and acceptance of ID photographers is broadening and beginning to reach a mainstream audience.

36 *Photography Handbook* 1974

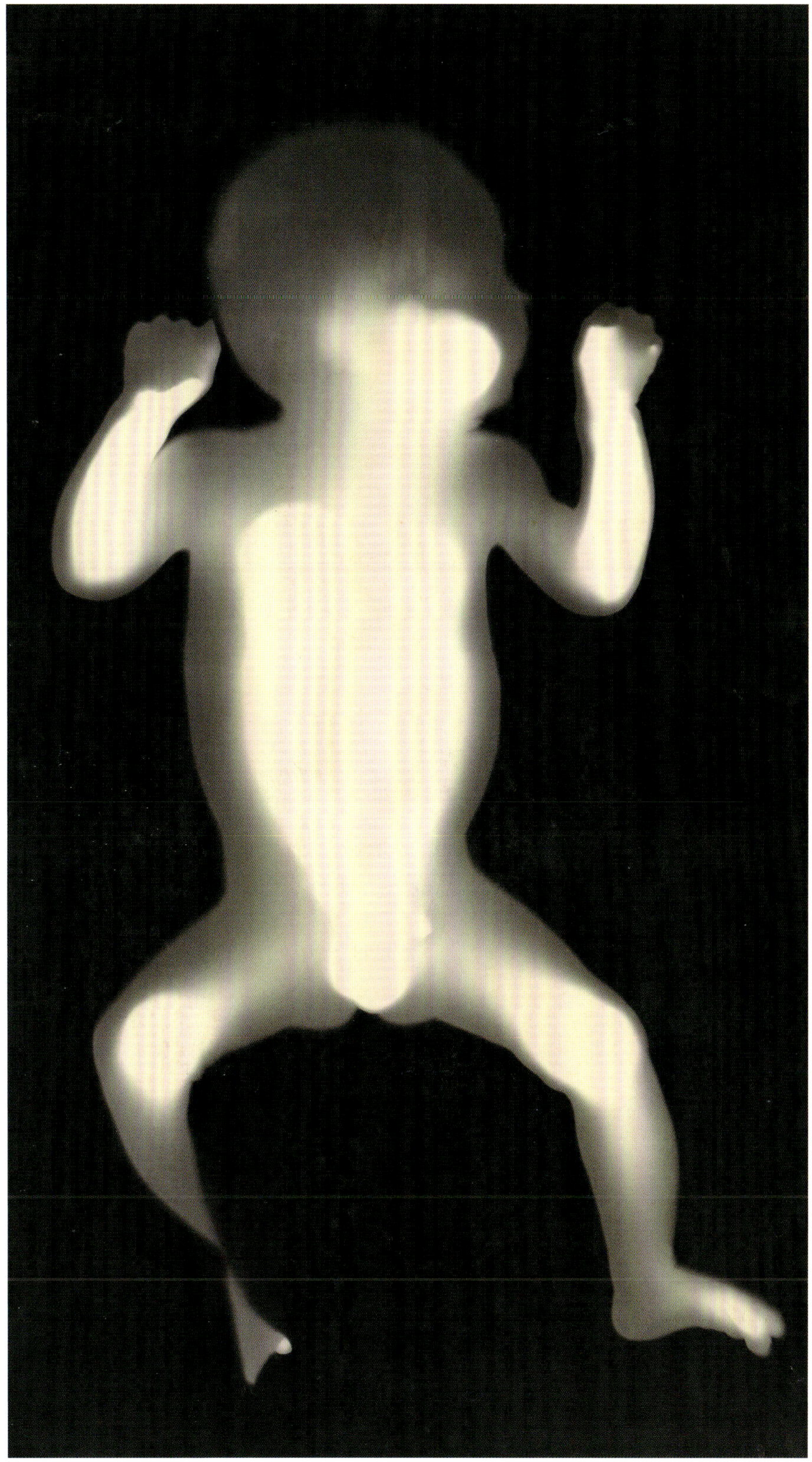

Charles Swedlund
Untitled, 1957
photogram, gelatin silver, 68.3 x 38.7 cm

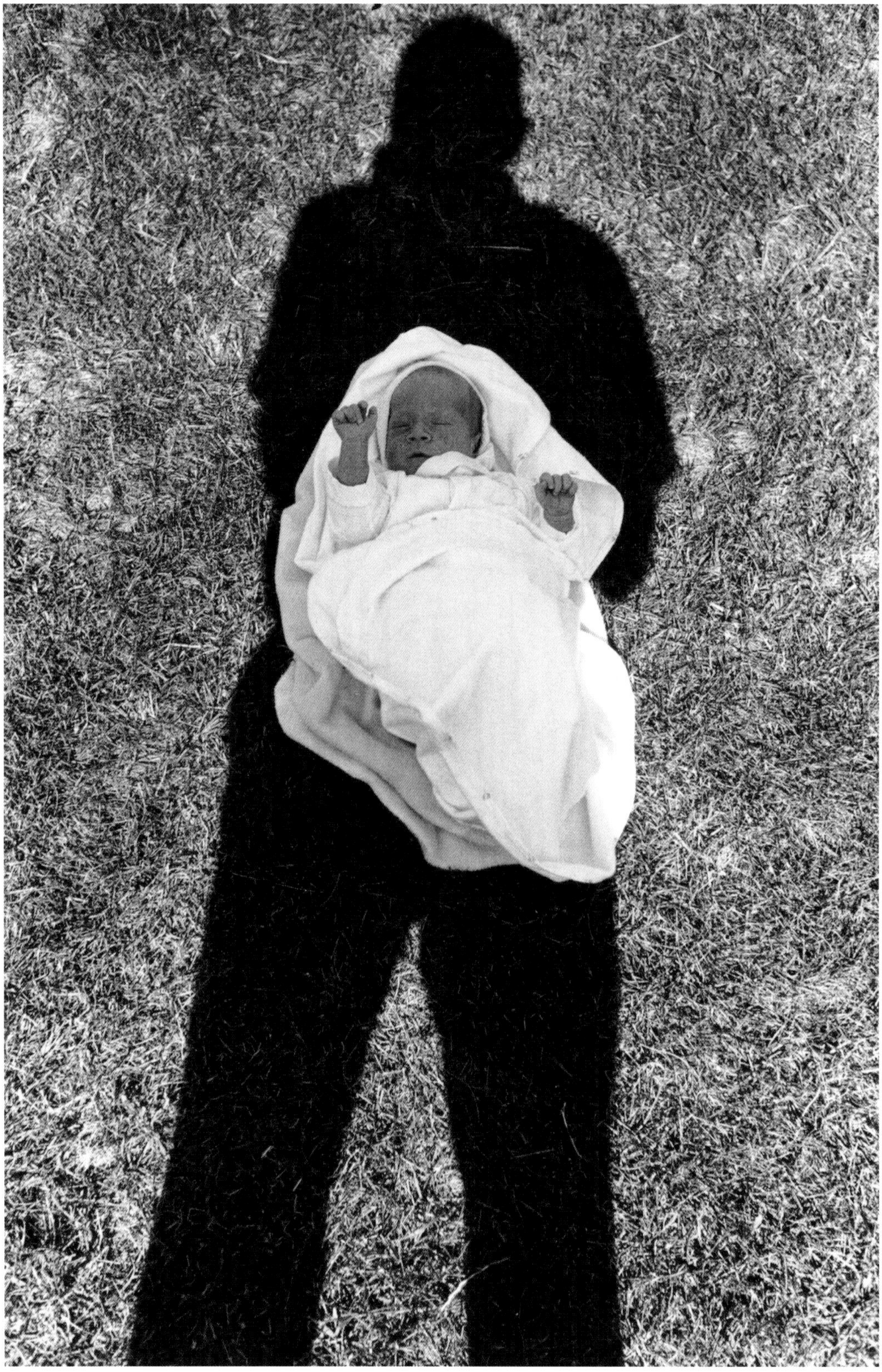

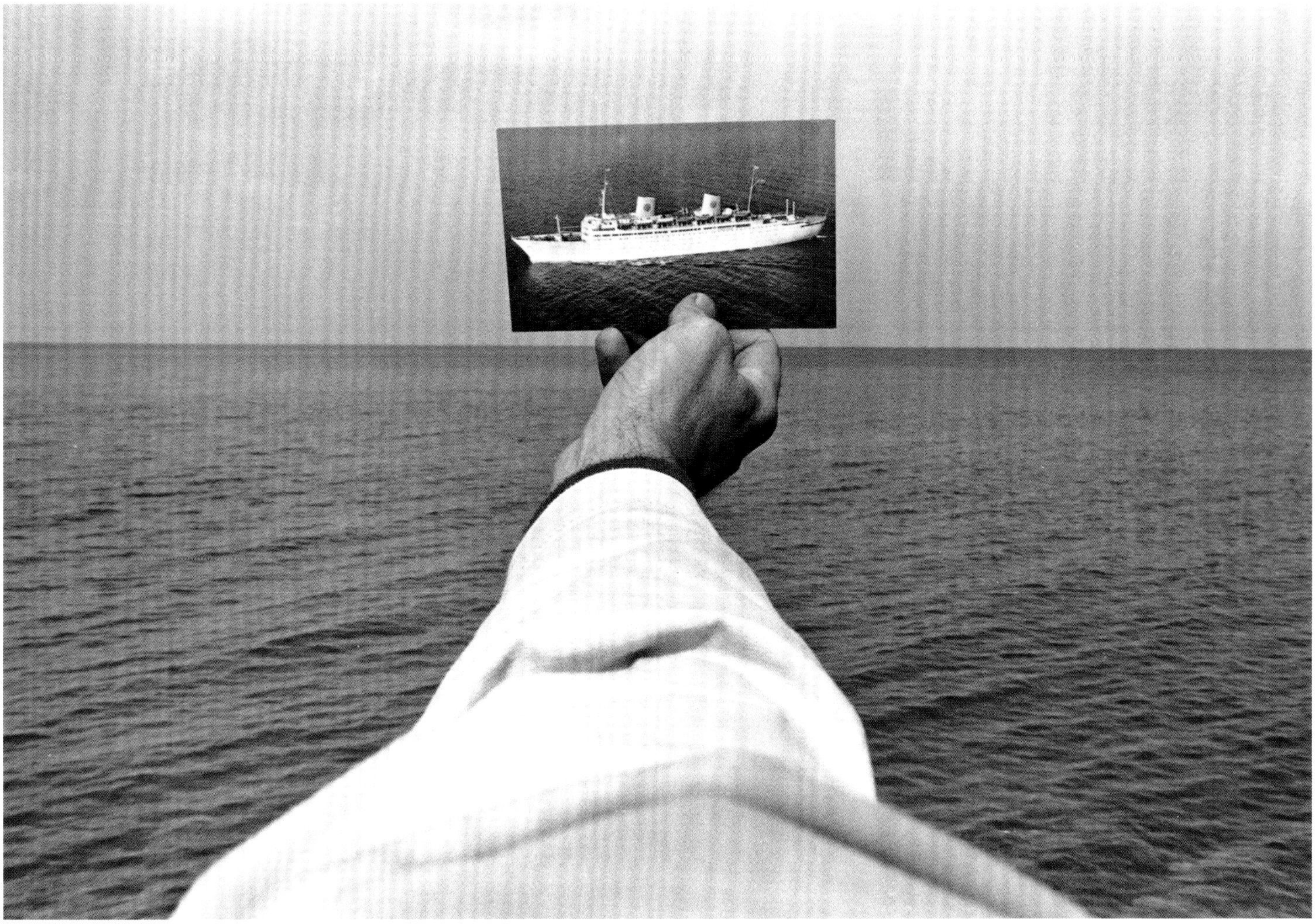

Kenneth Josephson
Matthew, 1963
gelatin silver, 30.5 x 20.2 cm

Kenneth Josephson
New York State, 1970, print of 1975
gelatin silver, 28 x 35.6 cm

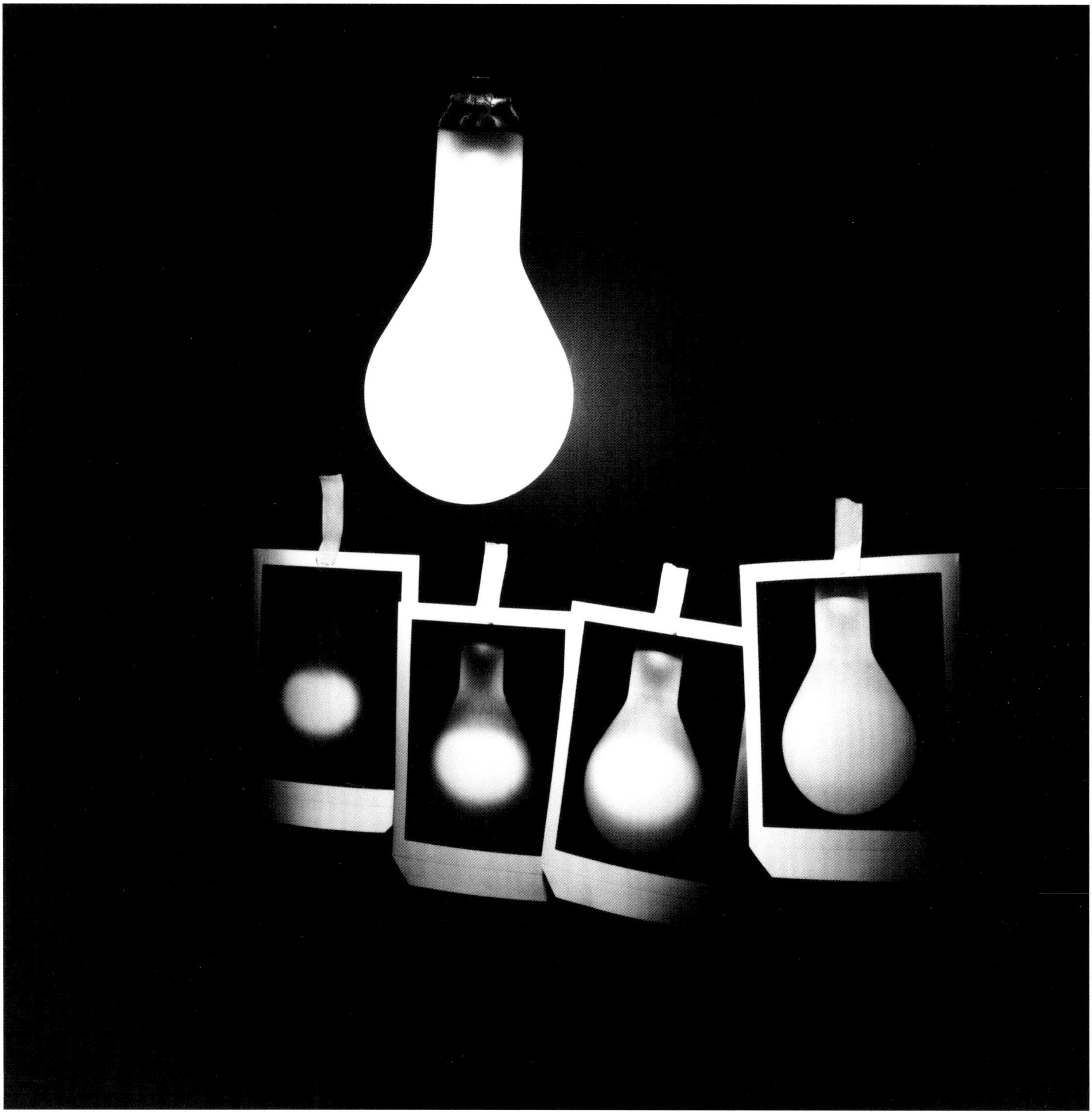

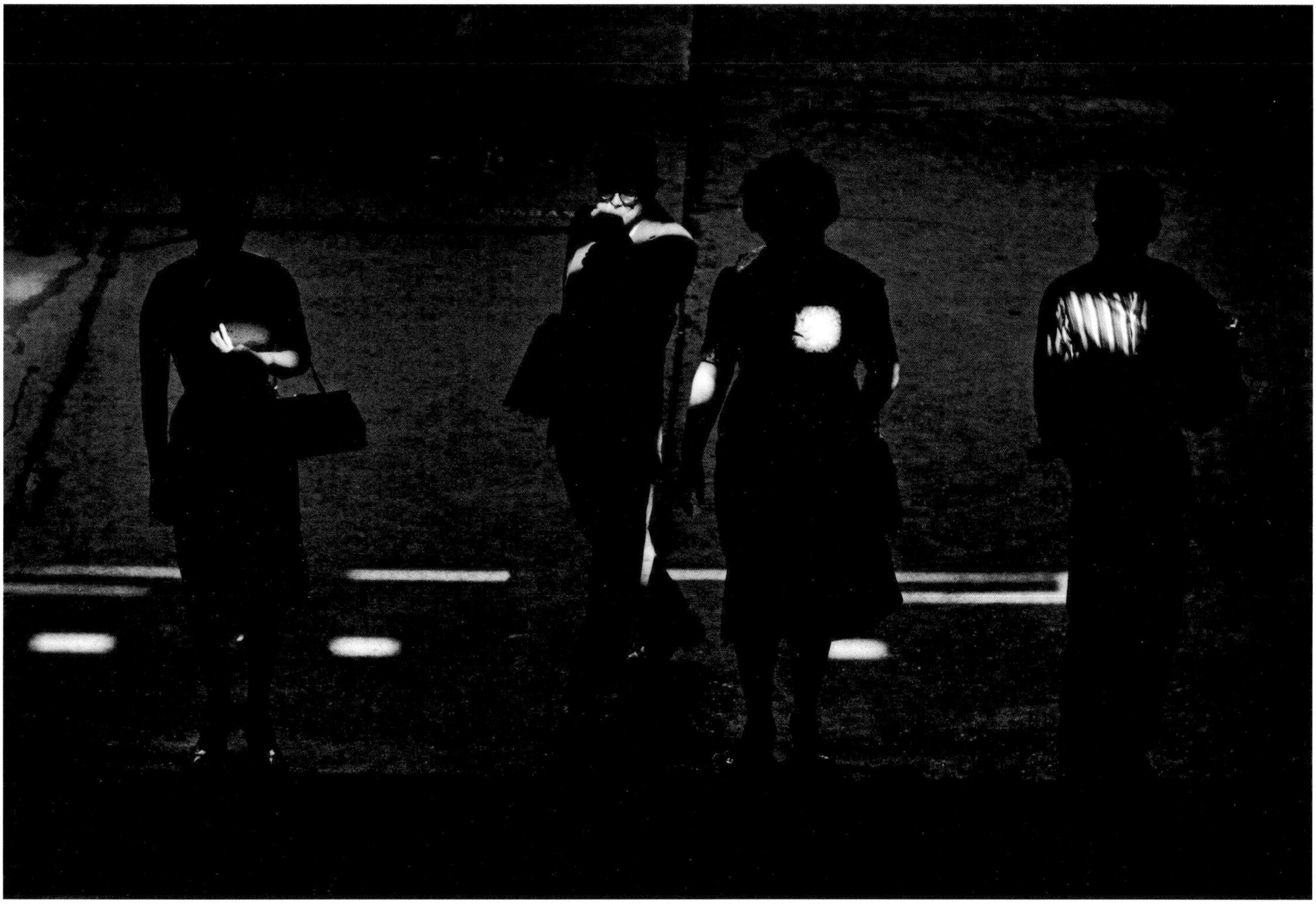

Kenneth Josephson
Polapans, 1973
gelatin silver, 22.9 x 22.9 cm

Kenneth Josephson
Chicago, 1961
gelatin silver, 20.3 x 30.5 cm

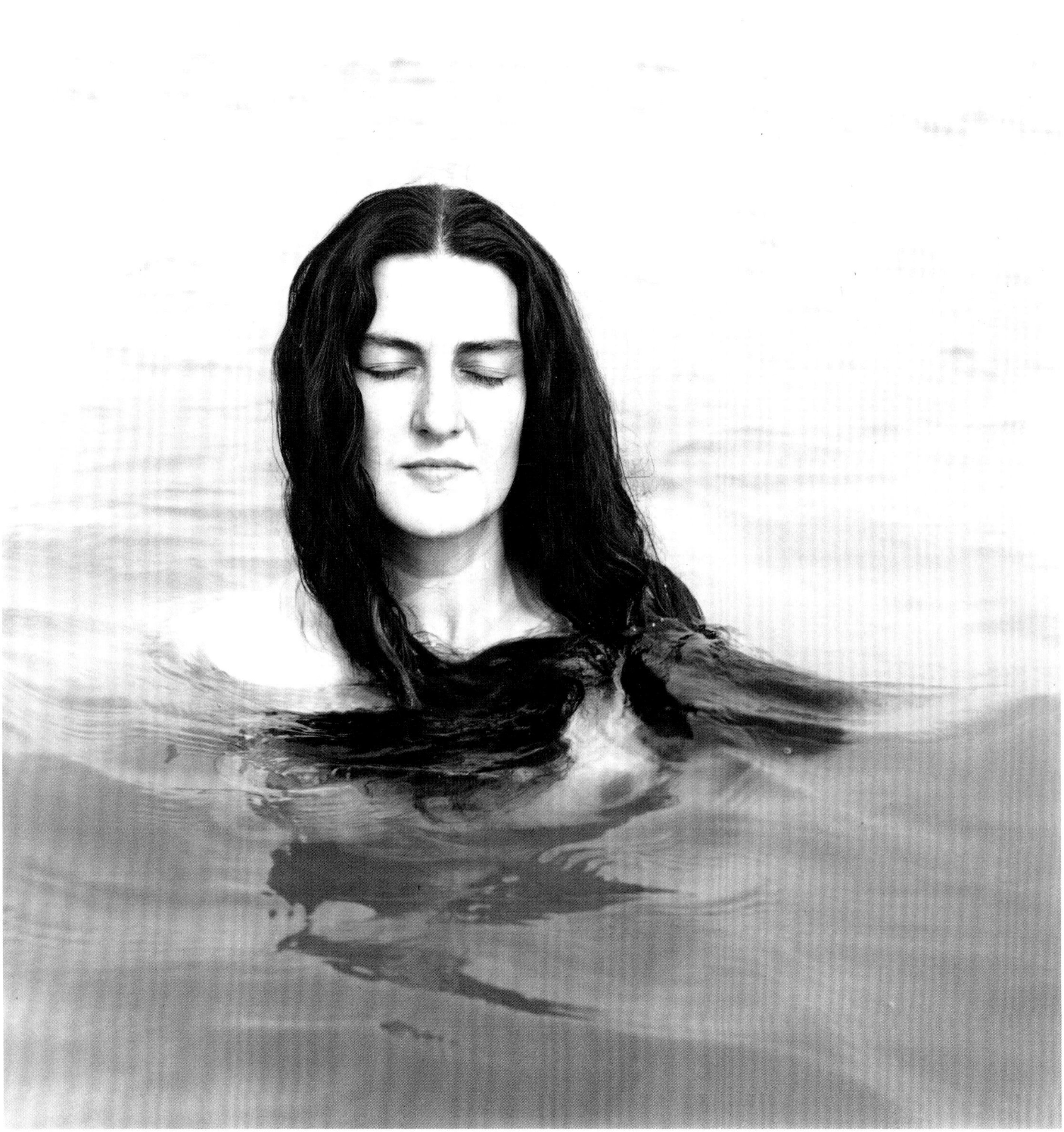

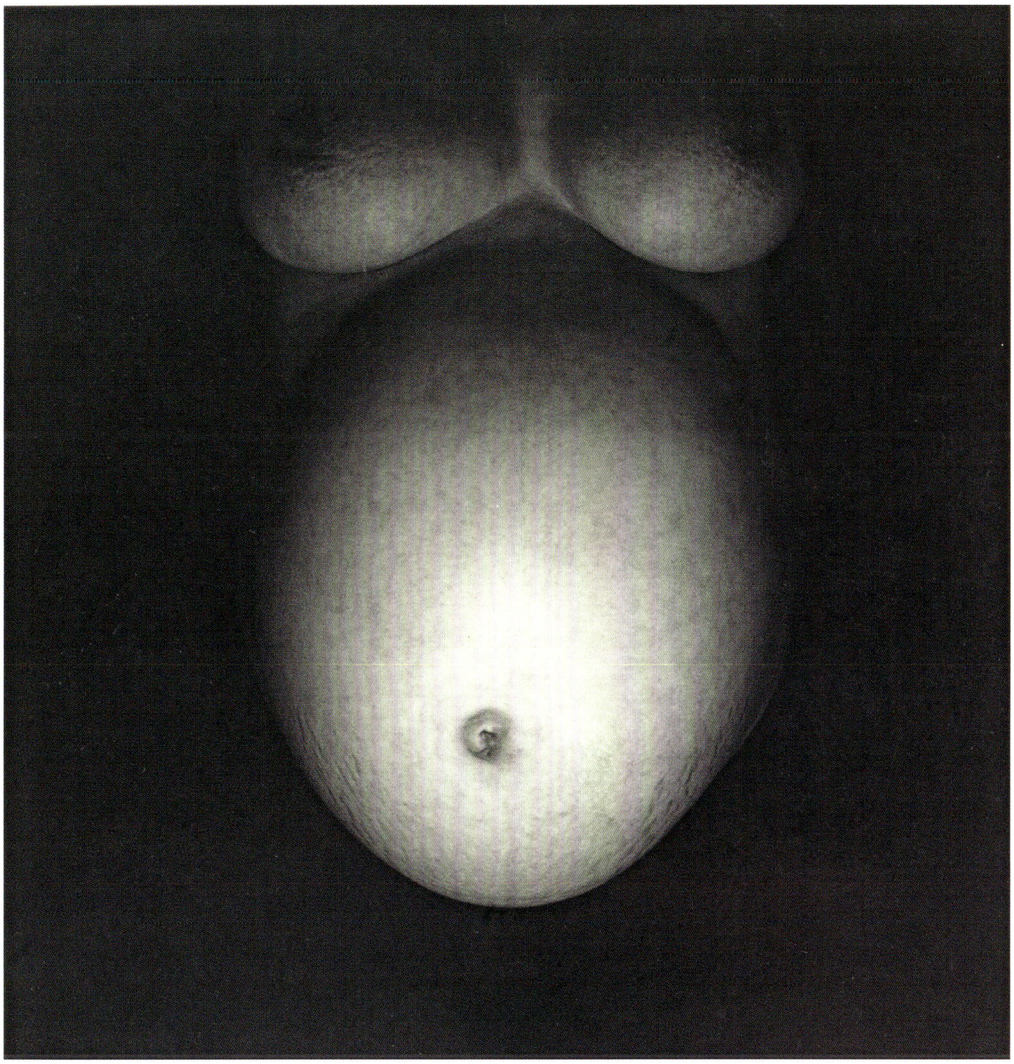

Harry Callahan
Eleanor, Chicago, 1949, later print
gelatin silver, 25.4 x 27.9 cm

Harry Callahan
Eleanor, 1949, later print
gelatin silver, 25 x 20 cm

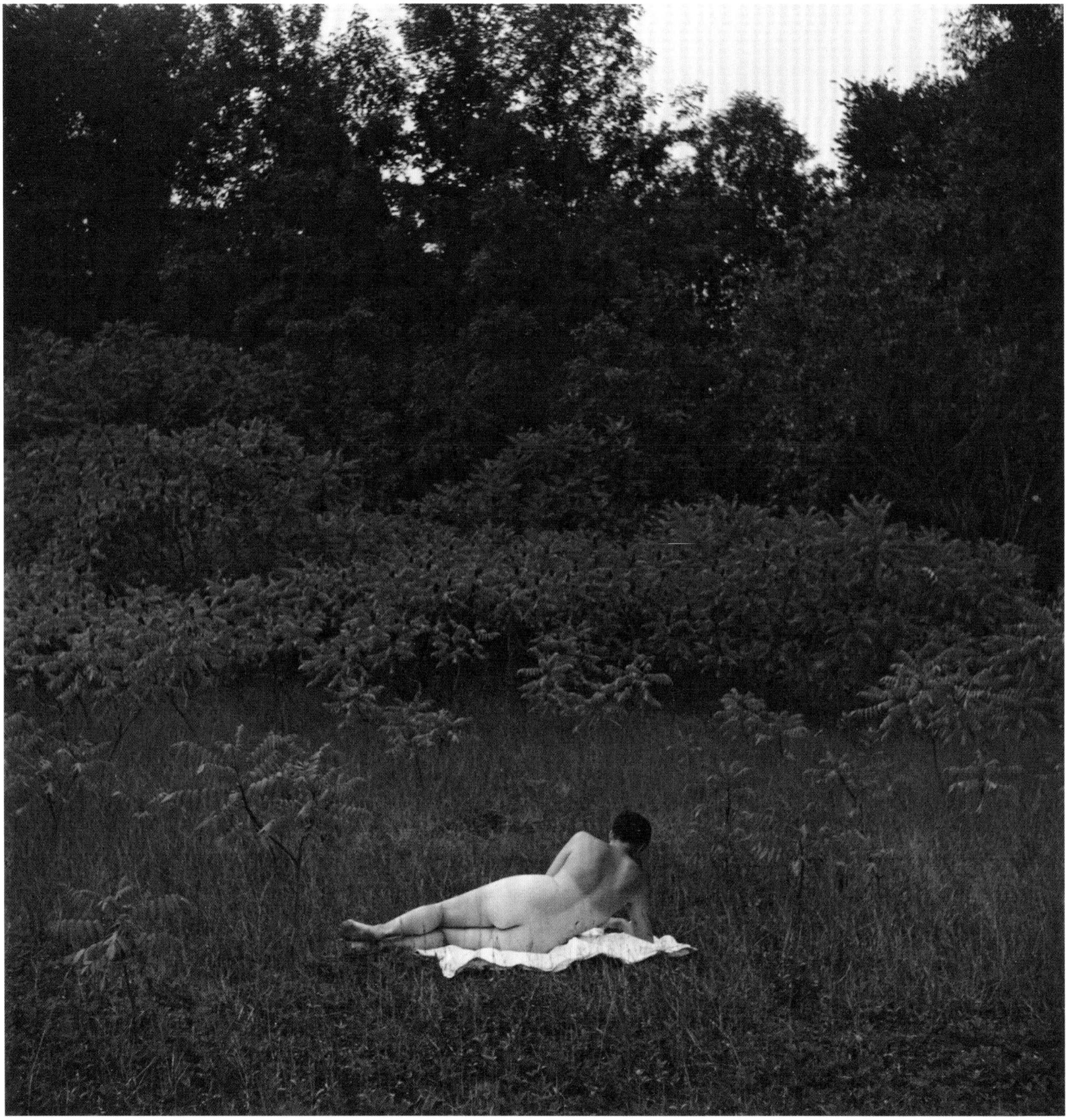

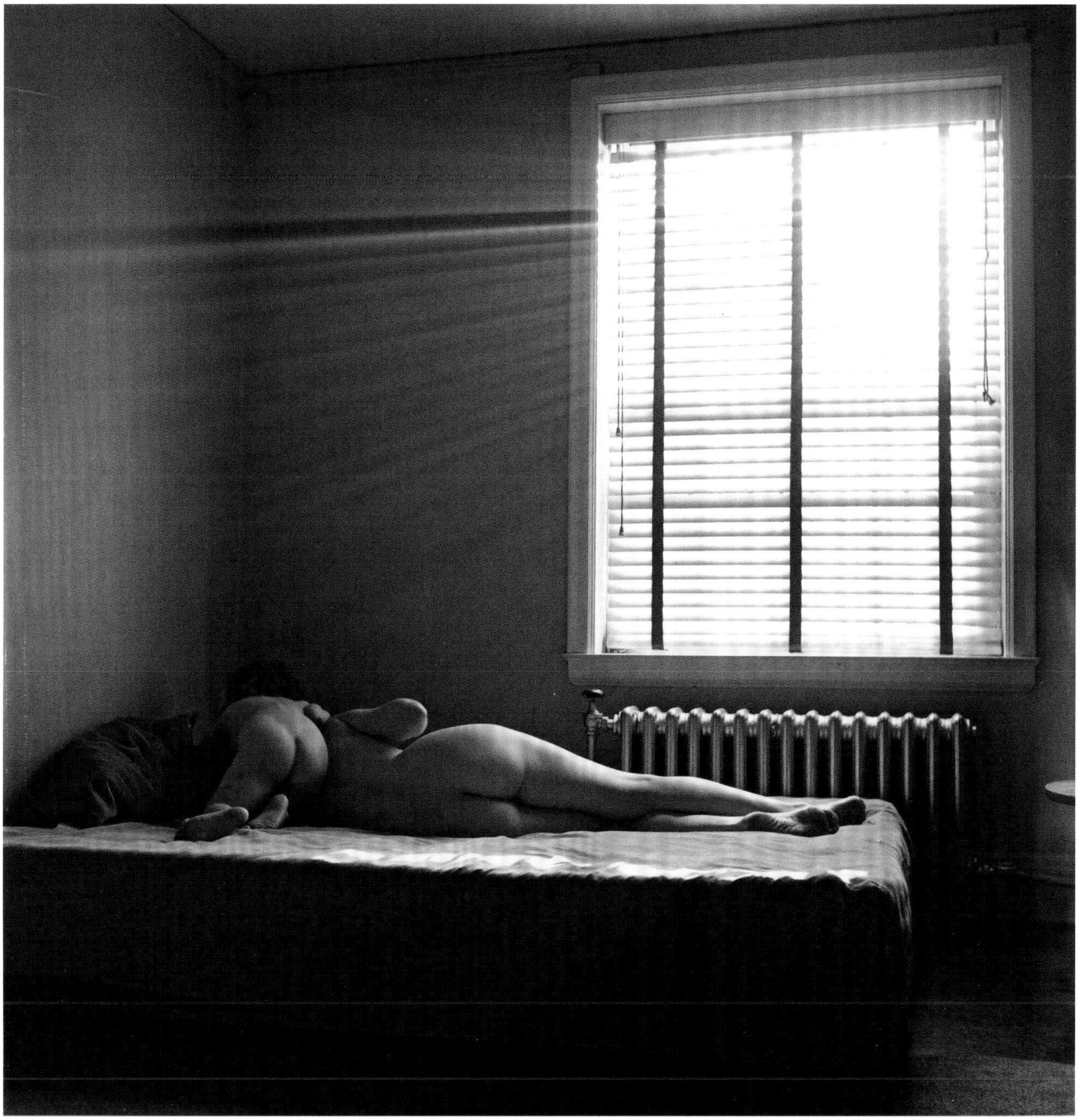

Harry Callahan
Eleanor, Port Huron, 1954, later print
gelatin silver, 25.3 x 20.3 cm

Harry Callahan
Eleanor and Barbara, Chicago, 1954, later print
gelatin silver, 30.1 x 27.9 cm

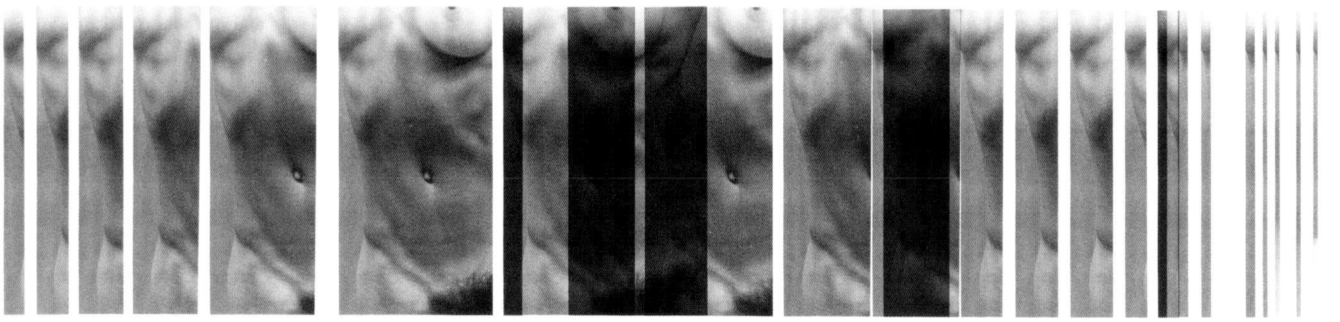

Tadao Takano
Nude.2.Lines, 1980/81
Staromat print on gelatin silver, 20.3 x 50.9 cm

Charles Swedlund
Untitled, from the series *Multiple Exposure with the Figure*, ca. 1967
gelatin silver, 18.7 x 18.4 cm

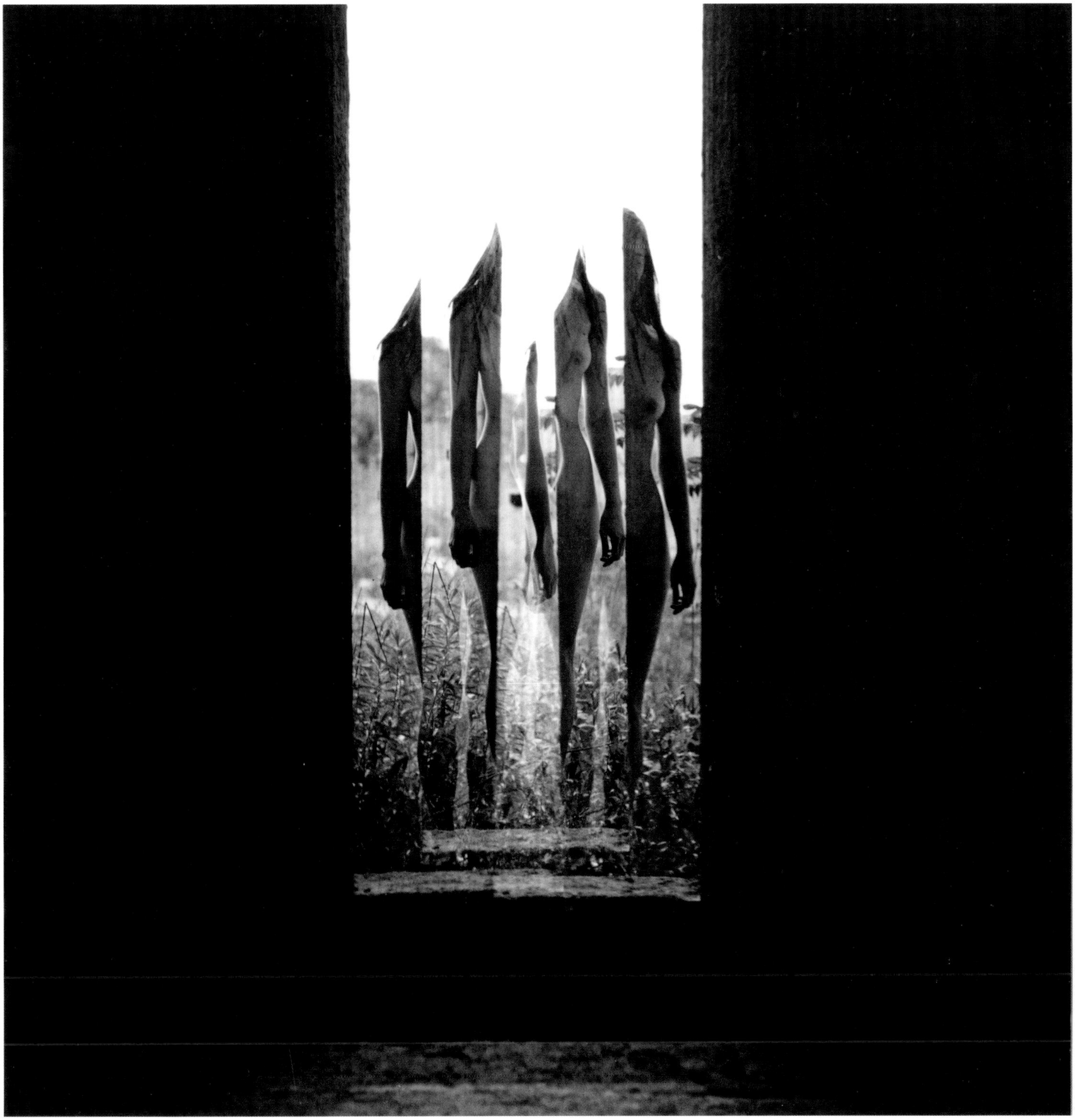

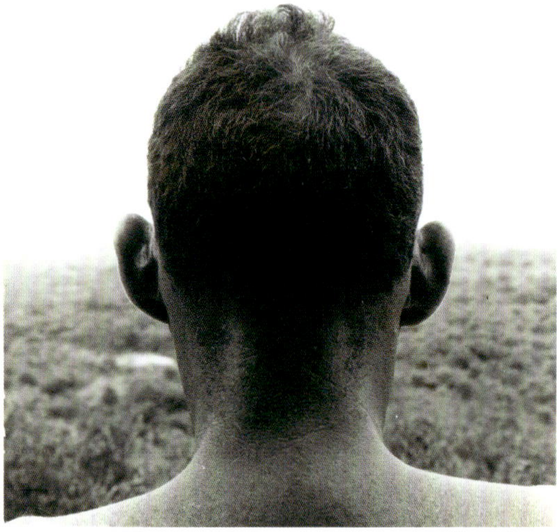

Greetings! - Christmas, 1960 - Aaron

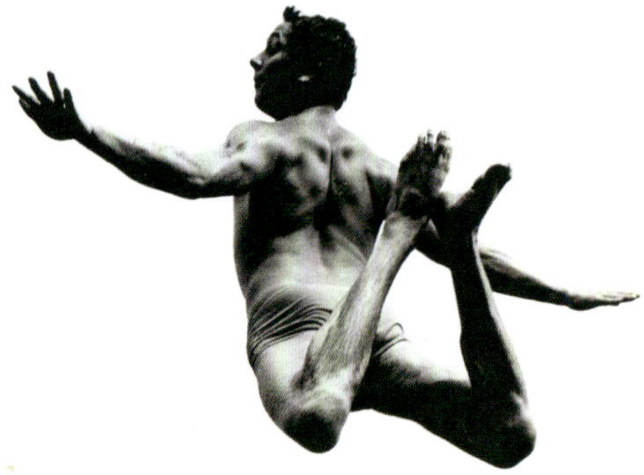

Xmas, 1961 - Greetings! - Aaron

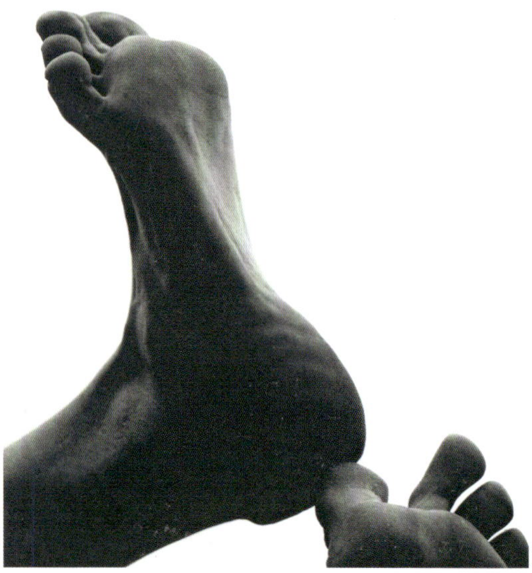

Xmas, 1957 Greetings! Aaron

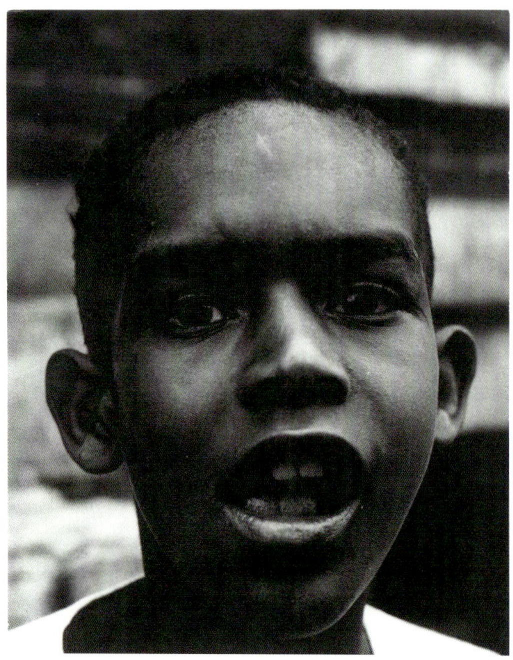

Xmas 1959 Greetings! Aaron

Aaron Siskind
Greeting card, 1960
gelatin silver, 17.2 x 11.7 cm

Aaron Siskind
Greeting card, from the series
Pleasures and Terrors of Levitation, 1961
gelatin silver, 17.3 x 11.9 cm

Aaron Siskind
Greeting card, 1957
gelatin silver, 17.4 x 11.8 cm

Aaron Siskind
Greeting card, 1959
gelatin silver, 17.9 x 11.9 cm

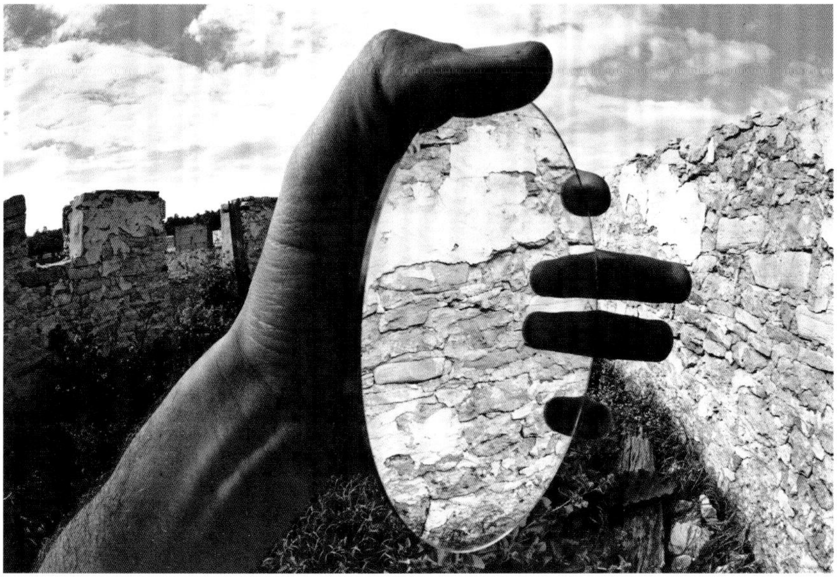

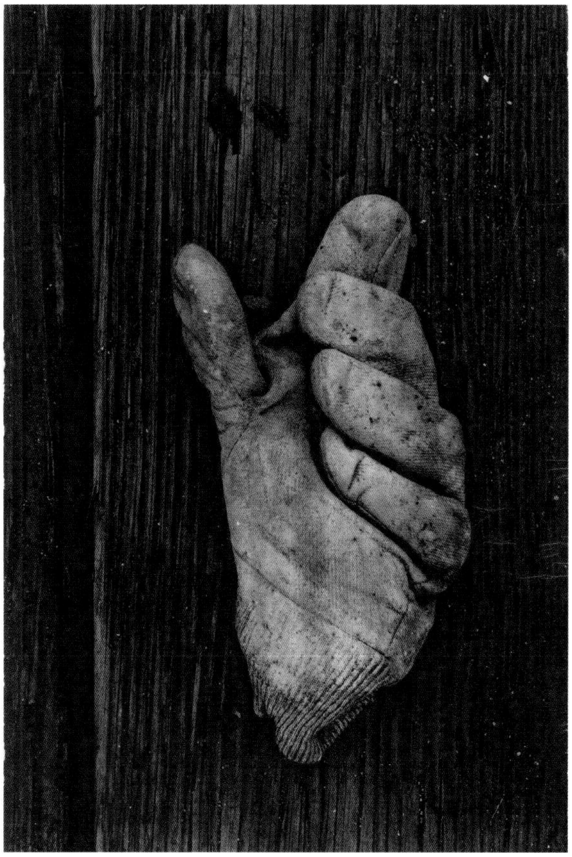

Joseph D. Jachna
Barn Foundation Wall, Door County, 1970
gelatin silver, 17.3 x 25.7 cm

Aaron Siskind
Greeting card, 1956
gelatin silver, 17.5 x 11.4 cm

HARVARD UNIVERSITY
CAMBRIDGE
MASSACHUSETTS

GRADUATE SCHOOL
OF DESIGN

DEPARTMENT OF
ARCHITECTURE

May 18, 1937

Miss Norma K. Stahle
700 North Michigan Avenue
Chicago, Illinois

Dear Miss Stahle:

Thank you very much for your letter of May 14th telling me about the new School of Industrial Design to be put up in Chicago. I think it is a splendid idea, and there is a real need for this sort of school in every country. I shall watch your endeavourings with greatest interest, but I am afraid I shall not be able to take part in them personally as I have accepted an appointment for an indefinite period at the Harvard Graduate School of Design.

However, as you are looking for a head of this school, I should like to suggest Professor Moholy Nagy. He was my nearest collaborator in the Bauhaus, built up the preliminary courses and was head of some of the workshops. He is the best man you can get, has had very wide experiences and is endowed with that rare creative power which stimulates the students. He is not only a painter of international fame, his recent exhibitions at London and Bâle were very successful, but he has worked for years with industrial firms--in glass, metal, textiles, and wood and is equally skilled in photography, films, typography and commercial advertising. In all these branches he did pioneer work in Germany, and recently in England. This versatility, combined with a delightful and most energetic character, qualifies him very highly as a teacher and organizer. He is about forty-five years old, Hungarian by birth, and speaks English. At present he lives in London, Golders Green, 7 Farm Walk. He might be willing to accept an appointment in the States. If you should succeed in getting him over, I am certain he would develop a most remarkable institution.

May I refer to his book "The New Vision", published in the States, which gives an impression of his thoroughly creative mind. Finally, may I draw your attention to my

Dr. Walter Gropius
recommended L. Moholy-Nagy
as the best person
we could get for the
director.

Sibylle Hoiman

THE NEW BAUHAUS COLLECTION AT BERLIN'S BAUHAUS-ARCHIV IN THE CONTEXT OF COLLECTION STRATEGY AND HISTORIOGRAPHY

In May of 1935, two years after the disbanding of the Bauhaus he had founded in 1919, Walter Gropius sent a circular letter from London to his former students and colleagues requesting that they fill out a questionnaire and send him reproductions of works from the Bauhaus period (→ 136). He was determined to pursue the project of "once again clarifying the image" of the Bauhaus and "providing a response in the form of a cohesive and authentic collection—initially of slides, later in book form—that will show how far-reaching an influence the work of the bauhaus has had on the production of the present period." Simultaneously, he asked for information about their period at the Bauhaus (point in time and duration), what work they were doing at the moment, and the realization of the "bauhaus idea."[1] The response was good; however, the context in which Gropius evaluated the results is unknown.[2] Over the following decades, this methodological approach to collecting knowledge and objects would repeatedly be utilized by those occupied with this growing collection. The present essay outlines the consequences this involved for the inheritance, those who passed it on and the inheritors themselves.

It was in Darmstadt in 1960 that the Bauhaus-Archiv was constituted as an organization dedicated to gathering the legacy of the Bauhaus, which was scattered around the world, in a single place authorized by the school's founder. This initiative can essentially be traced back to the art historian Hans M. Wingler.[3] From the very beginning, Wingler received substantial support from Gropius in realizing this project. The latter laid the cornerstone for the collection with his own archive, which additionally contained the results of his 1935 call to former members: "As founder and former head of the Bauhaus, I therefore call everyone interested in the continued dissemination of the idea of the Bauhaus to place Bauhaus products, models, designs, letters, manuscripts, and printed materials at the disposal of the new Bauhaus archive in Darmstadt. I will personally get things started by transferring to the archive the collection of press articles, printed materials from the Bauhaus, photos, etc., which I have been systematically compiling since 1919."[4]

Prior to the organization's founding and its collecting activities, Wingler had spent

1 Walter Gropius, Rundfrage an die Bauhäusler, May 1935, BHA, GS 16 / Folder 120, unpag.
2 It nonetheless seems logical to assume that the material was used for the Bauhaus exhibition developed a few years later by MoMA in close collaboration with Gropius.
3 The meeting that was decisive for the archive's founding took place in Darmstadt in the fall of 1959.
4 Walter Gropius, An die Freunde und ehemaligen Mitglieder des Bauhauses, June 1960 (folded circular), BHA, Nachlass (estate of) Hans M. Wingler, Part 2, Folder 103, unpag.

years occupied with the topic, finally culminating in his pioneering publication *Das Bauhaus 1919–1933: Weimar, Dessau, Berlin*, whose first edition was published in 1962. An expanded new edition was released three years later and was supplemented by an additional section: *Nachfolge in Chicago seit 1937* (Successor in Chicago since 1937). When the book was published in English for the first time in 1969, its title displayed what Wingler saw as the logical merging of all its locations and no span of years was indicated at all: *The Bauhaus: Weimar, Dessau, Berlin, Chicago*. Wingler had conducted research and collected material during numerous trips and also met with and interviewed former Bauhaus members who were still alive.

Gropius and Wingler presumably met in person for the first time at the opening of the 1957 International Building Exhibition in Berlin's Hansaviertel (Interbau). Gropius subsequently helped Wingler to secure a two-month travel grant from the Rockefeller Foundation in 1957/58: This research fellowship at Harvard provided him with an opportunity to gain an important look inside American archives. For Wingler, Gropius became a mentor with whom he maintained an active dialogue from then on. For Gropius, Wingler was in turn the right person to keep the memory of the Bauhaus alive for the future in the form of publications and, in addition, a collecting institution that would later serve a museological function.

Thus, the idea of founding an archive in Germany gradually became more definite in the course of the late 1950s. It was to be devoted to the school in all its facets, including its successors, which had particularly made a mark in America. Accordingly, it was noted in the bylaws of the newly founded Bauhaus-Archiv: "The area of activity furthermore encompasses those cultural manifestations that [...] are to be seen as preliminary stages leading toward the Bauhaus or (right down to the current situation at the given time) as its consequences."[5] From the very beginning, Wingler's concept encompassed the activities of former Bauhaus members in America—whether in the sense of a history of ideas, institutions, reception, or emigration—and he collected accordingly (→ 139).[6]

The Bauhaus-Archiv's founding under the directorship of Wingler and the publication he created parallel to this were the decisive contributions of postwar West German historiography on the Bauhaus. This historical narrative adeptly influenced by Gropius also obviously included the image of the school's seamless continuation in the US, the place he had chosen to carry out his work since 1937 and—beyond that—the country to which West Germany felt itself deeply indebted after the war. "As you can imagine, the opening of the Bauhaus-Archiv provides me with a great sense of fulfillment and pleasure. [...] In this way, a legend is being transformed into tangible reality [...]. My own interest in further developing the Bauhaus idea is more alive today than ever."[7]

During the preceding years and decades, Gropius had already been largely successful in exercising his influence over the dissemination and interpretation of "his" Bauhaus in America. In 1937, when the Association of Arts and Industries in Chicago wanted to appoint him director of the soon to be refounded "the new bauhaus – American School of Design,"[8] he had just accepted a position at Harvard and he suggested they ask László Moholy-Nagy, who was working in London at that time. They immediately followed his advice. Gropius remained active as a consultant in Chicago until 1955, and he had a high regard for Moholy-Nagy, who had taught at the Bauhaus in Dessau from 1923 to 1928 and fundamentally shaped the Bauhaus's influence as an avant-

5 Satzung des Bauhaus-Archivs e.V. von 1960, section 2, paragraph 2.
6 See also Grawe 1994 and Grawe 2002.
7 From Gropius's address on the occasion of the official opening of the Bauhaus-Archiv in Darmstadt on April 8, 1961, Nachlass Wingler, Part 2, Folder 9, unpag. Before Wingler and Gropius met, the latter had planned to transfer numerous documents from emigrated members of the Bauhaus to the Busch-Reisinger Museum in Cambridge, Mass., and to additionally donate his own archive to them. The Houghton Library and the Busch-Reisinger Museum at Harvard do, in fact, contain material from the estate of Walter and Ise Gropius.
8 This was the first official name of the school of design founded in 1937; from here on, it will be abbreviated as the New Bauhaus, which also includes the successor institutions that appeared under different names.

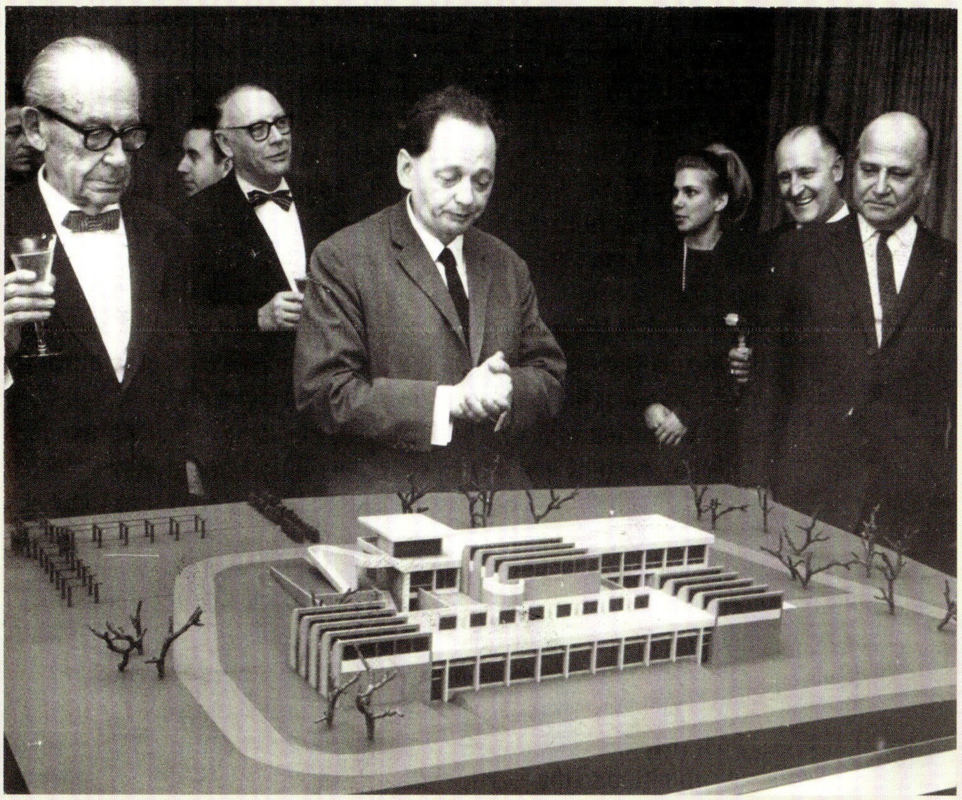

Anonymous
Hans M. Wingler and Walter Gropius at the presentation of the mock-up for an archive of the Bauhaus at Darmstadt, 1964
photograph for the *Darmstädter Tagblatt*
gelatin silver, 10.2 x 12.6 cm

garde school. The institution resumed its work in America in apparent continuity with the German Bauhaus—despite the fact that the revival of the American Bauhaus was separated from Moholy-Nagy's departure from the Bauhaus by nine years and from the end of the German Bauhaus by no less than four. Initially, Moholy-Nagy not only based the fundamental content of his work on the curriculum of the Dessau Bauhaus: In promoting the school, he also deliberately took up the name "Bauhaus" as well as visual formal devices in order to profit from the German institution's positive reception and to gain legitimacy (→ 18).

The history of the Bauhaus's influence on both sides of the Atlantic as told and vehemently shaped by Walter Gropius had a powerful impact on publications and exhibitions. Wingler and Gropius primarily used the media of publications and exhibitions for the process of historicizing the Bauhaus. The images of the school produced in this way provided decisive support for the history of the Bauhaus's influence as dictated by Gropius, who was active in every area.[9] Throughout his life, he sought to popularize the Bauhaus and to combat the diminishing importance of his school as well as criticism expressed toward it. One of the milestones in the context of this promotional self-representation was the 1938 exhibition *Bauhaus 1919–28*, held in New York at the MoMA's temporary headquarters in the Time & Life Building in Rockefeller Center.[10] While it certainly received critical reviews in the American press, it was evaluated as a success in retrospect. The accompanying catalogue was edited by Walter and Ise

9 See Grawe 2002, p. 22.
10 See Bergdoll 2016.

Gropius as well as Herbert Bayer, who was also responsible for designing the book and exhibition. In the catalogue's foreword, museum director Alfred H. Barr programmatically asserts: "The Bauhaus is not dead!" This position is underlined by the fact that Chicago's New Bauhaus is represented through student works, although the title's restriction to the period until 1928 does not suggest this in any way. In addition, in April of 1938, the New Bauhaus had already opened a photography exhibition with works on loan from the MoMA. On the one hand, the links between New York and Chicago document Gropius's successful networking; on the other hand, they served to promote the continuation of the increasingly adapted Bauhaus educational program in America after the political situation in Germany had taken away its future there.

It was this guiding concept of the Bauhaus as a victim of political circumstances that would manifest itself a few decades later in Germany, in Wingler's research as well as his collecting activity: "In particular, the achievements of the more recent centers of design teaching and design experimentation created since the period of emigration—some of which have already ceased to exist—are now to be examined as well: The achievements of Black Mountain College, the New Bauhaus, and the Institute of Design […]."[11] In numerous promotional texts as well as his publications and the decisive catalogue accompanying the 1987 exhibition *50 Jahre New Bauhaus: Bauhausnachfolge in Chicago* (50 years of New Bauhaus: The Bauhaus's successor in Chicago), shown at Berlin's Bauhaus-Archiv, he states: "With this exhibition, the Bauhaus-Archiv commemorates the founding of the New Bauhaus in Chicago in 1937 and, with it, the school that directly succeeded the Bauhaus after it was driven out of a Germany that had submitted to the Nazis."[12] While Gropius was primarily concerned with the continuity of "his" school and its undiminished influence, Wingler's interest in the New Bauhaus was intimately linked with his research on art-school reform in general: "The more the gaps in our Bauhaus collection become filled, the more emphatically we will be able to occupy ourselves with institutions like the New Bauhaus, the Institute of Design, Black Mountain College, the Vereinigte Staatsschulen [for fine and applied art] in Berlin, Ulm's Hochschule für Gestaltung and Gropius's circle of students in America. For us, the educational aspects will always be the defining and central ones. We see it as one of our fundamental tasks to sort through and (where this seems worthwhile) preserve art school materials that were created *ad hoc* and usually possess little physical durability. After all, the materials' authenticity is essential to the unique nature of our collection of works from the Bauhaus's preliminary course. We want to provide access to the original materials that render didactic and critical insights comprehensible and verifiable."[13]

Another important event in connection with the history of the Bauhaus's reception was the exhibition *50 Jahre Bauhaus* (50 Years of Bauhaus), which opened in Stuttgart in 1968 and subsequently traveled around the world. In late August of 1969, it also stopped in Chicago, where it was shown at the IIT's Crown Hall, which had been designed by Ludwig Mies van der Rohe. Ludwig Grote was responsible for developing the concept for the travelling exhibition. He had already planned the 1950 Munich exhibition *Die Maler am Bauhaus* (The painters at the Bauhaus) and, as Anhalt's state superintendent of cultural heritage, he had maintained close contact with the Bauhaus. A supplement "on the occasion of the exhibition at illinois institute of technology in chicago, illinois, 1969" was added to the catalogue and deals extensively

11 Hans M. Wingler, Ansprache zur Grundsteinlegung zu dem von Walter Gropius entworfenen Museumsgebäude des Bauhaus-Archivs am Tiergarten in Berlin, May 8, 1976, Nachlass Wingler, Part 2, Folder 9, unpag.
12 *50 Jahre New Bauhaus* 1987, p. 7.
13 Hans M. Wingler, Ansprache zur Eröffnung des Museumsgebäudes des Bauhaus-Archivs held in the Staatsbibliothek, Berlin, December 1, 1979, Nachlass Wingler, Part 2, Folder 9, unpag. See also *Kunstschulreform 1900–1933* 1977; this volume was published as a "handbook" accompanying the exhibition of the same name at the Bauhaus-Archiv that year.

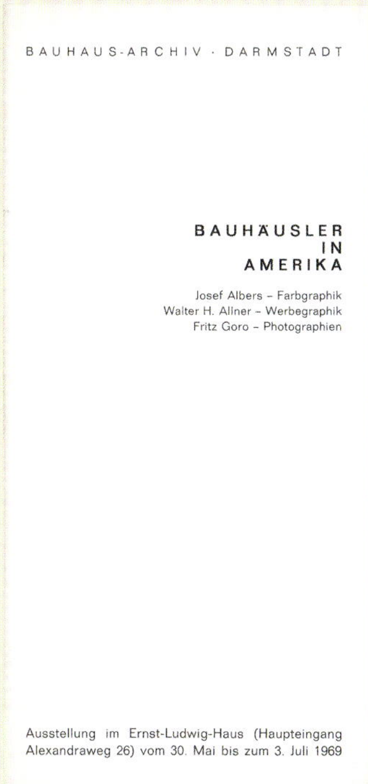

Hans M. Wingler
Bauhäusler in Amerika, 1969
leaflet

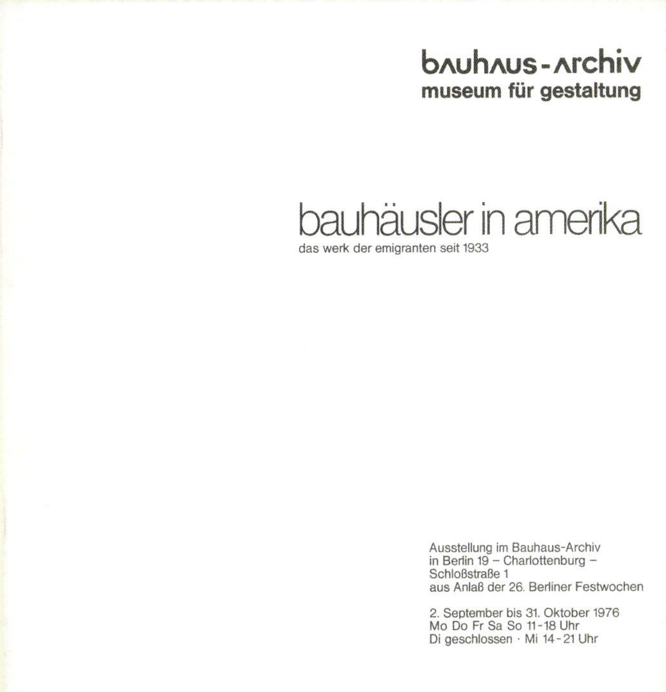

Hans M. Wingler
Bauhäusler in Amerika, 1976
brochure, cover

(among other things) with the influence of Mies van der Rohe, who—like Gropius—died that year.[14] The English translation of Wingler's Bauhaus book was published at the same time: There was an enormous advance in the Bauhaus's reception both in North America and West Germany.[15] In 1969 the Bauhaus-Archiv in Darmstadt also organized an initial exhibition on this topic, under the title *Bauhäusler in Amerika: Josef Albers – Farbgraphik / Walter H. Allner – Werbegraphik / Fritz Goro – Photographien*. *Bauhäusler in Amerika* followed in 1976 as a preliminary overview of the research that had already been going on for several years at the Bauhaus-Archiv (→ 141). Besides *50 Jahre New Bauhaus* (1987), noteworthy later exhibitions presented in the new museum building of the Bauhaus-Archiv in Berlin included *Vision in Motion* (2002), *New Bauhaus Chicago* (2004), and *Color in Transparency* (2006).

Beyond these general surveys, at irregular intervals, the Bauhaus-Archiv also presented exhibitions of individual artists who had worked at the New Bauhaus. These included *Nathan Lerner: Fotografie am New Bauhaus* (1974) and *György Kepes* (1977), for example (→ 142). Regarding Kepes's significance, Wingler notes: "It is important to us to show this exhibition at the Bauhaus-Archiv, because Kepes not only adapted Bauhaus ideas, he also fundamentally and creatively developed them. Kepes creatively contributed to the dissemination and familiarization of essential elements of the Bauhaus's intellectual heritage through his theory and his artistic work." Wingler goes on to say that "the Bauhaus, if it still existed, would have to occupy itself with similar

14 One of the essays was by Howard Dearstyne, a student of Mies van der Rohe who was at the Bauhaus from 1928 to 1932 and wrote a history of the Bauhaus at around the same time as Wingler; it was finally published posthumously in 1986, under the title *Inside the Bauhaus*.
15 See Grawe 2002, p. 212. For the reception of architecture connected with the Bauhaus and built in America, see Kentgens-Craig 1993 and Kentgens-Craig 2003.

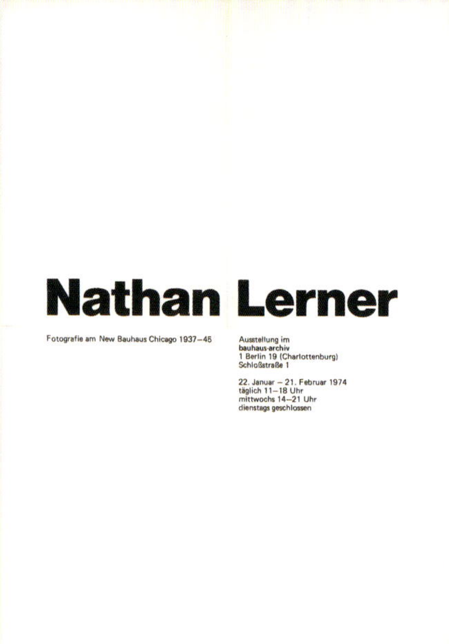

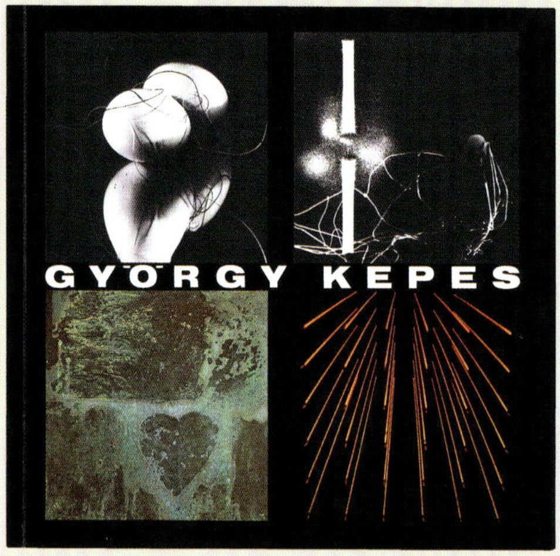

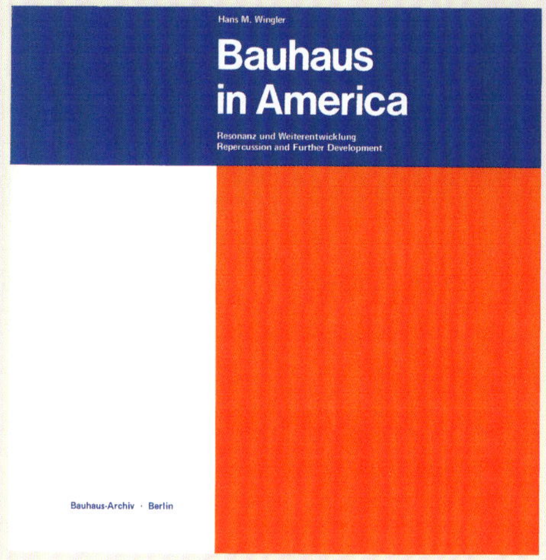

Hans M. Wingler
Nathan Lerner, 1974
leaflet

Hans M. Wingler et. al.
György Kepes, 1977
brochure, cover

Hans M. Wingler
Bauhaus in Amerika, 1972
brochure, cover

artistic and technical problems" like those explored by what he referred to as the "successor institutes" in the US: "If, continuously remaining in existence, the Bauhaus had wished to maintain its original intellectual aspirations, it could have—would even have to have—gone through a development similar to that of its American successor institutions."[16]

As Peter Hahn later explained: "the New Bauhaus was not the only institution where Bauhaus ideas remained influential after 1933 in America: Black Mountain College [...], the Harvard Graduate School of Design [...], and the Illinois Institute of Technology [...] pursued similar aims in specific areas, and many exiled members of the Bauhaus also gained recognition working in their given professions. Nonetheless, it was only at the New Bauhaus [...] that the full educational program developed in Weimar and Dessau was continued and further developed as a matter of principle."[17] German scholars' perspective on the Chicago school corresponded to its own self-perception: In Chicago they directly referred back to the period in Germany, which was perceived as successful and, in a sense, served to guarantee the quality of a "bauhaus education."[18] One of the school's promotional brochures states: "It [the New Bauhaus] embodies the principles of the famous bauhaus founded by Dr. Walter Gropius in Weimar in 1919 according to which the principles of design and scientific subjects are taught coordinated with workshop practice." Here, the talk of "bauhaus training" or also of "bauhaus students" is seen as obviously appropriate.[19]

16 Wingler, in: *György Kepes* 1977, unpag. The attribution of significance to Kepes is also interesting insofar as he was never at the Bauhaus and had, instead, only worked together with Moholy-Nagy for a short time during the period he spent in London. Kepes is also represented by the volume *Sprache des Sehens* (the 1971 German translation of the 1944 English original *Language of Vision*) in the series *Neue Bauhausbücher*, which was edited by Wingler and published by the Florian Kupferberg Verlag.
17 Hahn, in: *50 Jahre New Bauhaus*, p. 7.
18 See typescript "EXHIBITION: Work from the Preliminary Course, 1937–1938, The New Bauhaus," anonymous [Moholy-Nagy], undat., unpag., BHA, NB-Archiv.
19 Cover of the evening-course brochure of 1938.

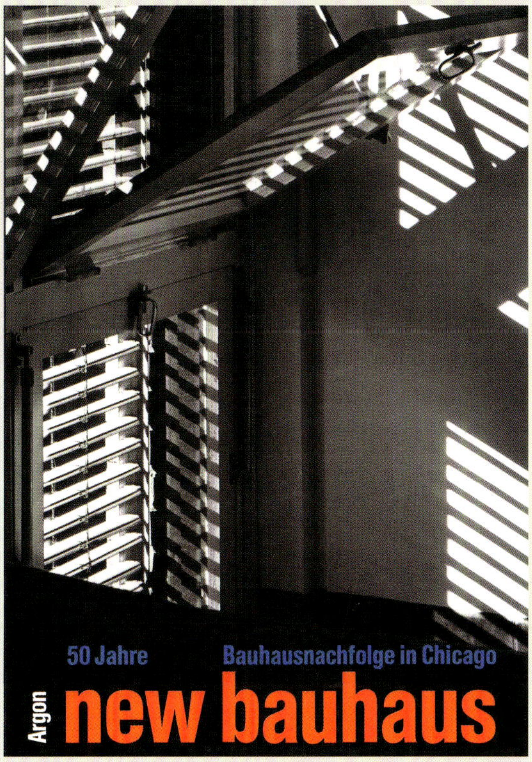

50 Jahre new bauhaus, Berlin, 1987
cover

Wingler had already republished his essay "Bauhaus in America: Repercussion and Further Development," written for the 1968 Stuttgart catalogue, as a separate publication in 1972. Beginning in 1974, he made efforts to develop a comprehensive and scholarly presentation of the New Bauhaus (→ 142). This intention finally culminated in the research project "Chicago Bauhaus," which he realized together with Peter Hahn and Lloyd C. Engelbrecht with funding from the German Research Foundation (DFG) in the framework of their support for research on exiles. Not only was the school to be examined in a "historical-critical" sense, they wanted to engage in "museological-collecting" activity.[20] In 1975, within this context, Wingler sent out a call in English "to the former members and all friends of the New Bauhaus Chicago, the School of Design, and the Institute of Design". Under the ambitious title "A Museum for the Chicago Bauhaus Movement," he sought to obtain information and materials (→ 136). He refers to the Chicago institutions as "the legitimate heirs of the Bauhaus," because they had taken up the concept of the "old" Bauhaus and continued to dynamically develop it: "As a natural consequence, the American Bauhaus Movement will have its own department in the research institute and museum which is concerned with the Bauhaus: the Bauhaus-Archiv in West Berlin." He announced the development of an extensive collection consisting of documents, letters, printed materials, instructional materials, exhibition catalogues, publications, and three-dimensional objects along with their industrially manufactured realization.[21]

20 Wingler, in: *György Kepes* 1977, unpag. In doing so, however, they limited themselves to the period up to 1951.
21 "As a natural consequence, the American Bauhaus Movement will have its own department in the research institute and museum which is concerned with the Bauhaus: the Bauhaus-Archiv in West Berlin." Aufruf Hans M. Wingler an alle ehemaligen Mitglieder des New Bauhaus, 1975, BHA, NB-Archiv. The systematic examination by means of sending questionnaires to people formerly involved had already led to a certain amount of success in relation to the Bauhaus. Wingler had begun the questionnaire initiative "An alle ehemaligen Mitglieder des Bauhauses" (To all former members of the Bauhaus) in February of 1962.

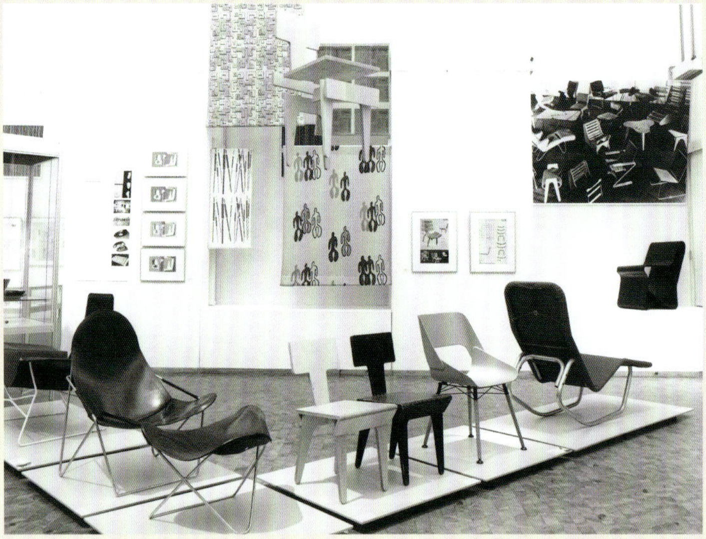

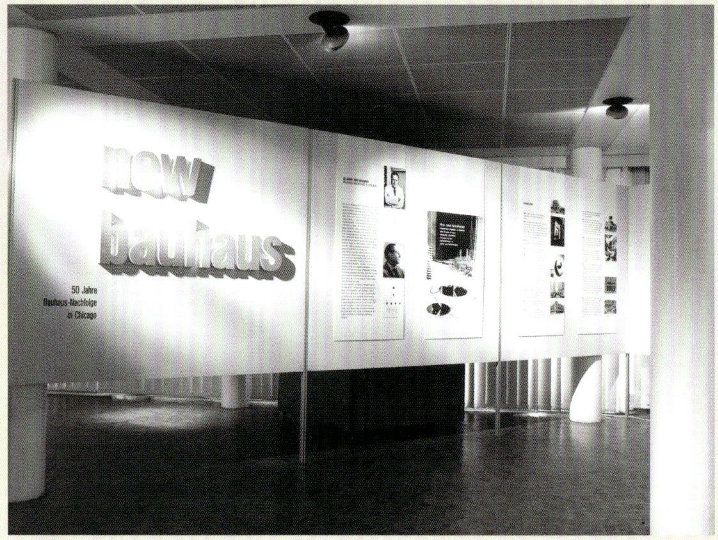

Anonymous
Views of the exhibition *50 Jahre new bauhaus*, 1987
gelatin silver, 18 x 24 cm each

A second request followed in 1976. It systematically asked about contact information, status, and the length of time spent at the given institutes, participation in courses, teachers and fellow students, projects, exhibitions, existing materials, thesis works, photographs taken for classes, previous education, professional work after the program, museums owning or exhibiting their works, and the significance of their studies/training. This research and these inquiries resulted, on the one hand, in a 1987 exhibition and accompanying catalogue marking the 50th anniversary of the New Bauhaus: Presented by the Bauhaus-Archiv in Berlin, they provided Germany's first comprehensive exploration of the school and thus also the indispensable foundation for all subsequent research (→ 143–144). Beyond this, the Bauhaus-Archiv was able to establish a great number of important contacts; it was particularly beneficial that many of those involved were still alive and eagerly provided not just information but, above all, extensive donations. A not insubstantial portion of the material to be found in the Bauhaus-Archiv's New Bauhaus collection derives from this context. These include numerous documents, exchanges of letters, extensive groups of photographs, and occasionally objects by students and teachers at the New Bauhaus. The exhibitions already mentioned, which were often presented by the Bauhaus-Archiv in close interaction with the corresponding artists or their families, also frequently led to donations or purchases (→ 145). As is to be expected, the quality of this collection that has grown

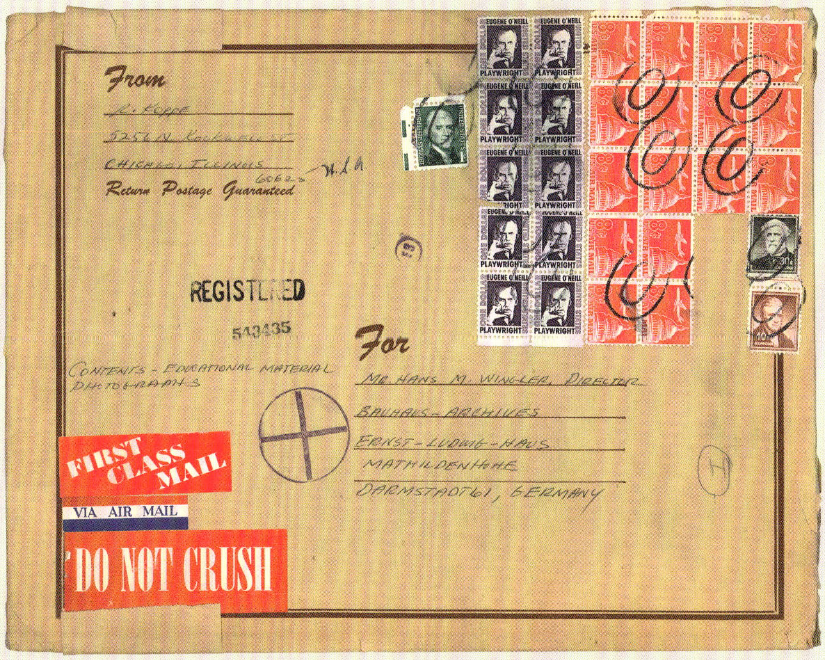

Richard Koppe to the Bauhaus-Archiv
envelope, 1968
24.8 x 32 cm

over the decades is certainly heterogeneous, but it is of incalculable value as a general overview of the school.

In the early 1970s, the collection entitled NB/SD/ID-Archiv (New Bauhaus/School of Design/Institute of Design) initially comprised works by the "most important key figures [...], particularly: Moholy, the founder; Gropius, the most important consultant; Paepcke, the most important benefactor; Chermayeff, Moholy's successor as director; and additionally the institute's most important teaching staff."[22] They were subsequently joined by more and more people and works clearly related to the school. Among these, the important photographs by Nathan Lerner and György Kepes are to be emphasized: The majority of these have entered the collection in a number of steps, thanks to generous donations. Today the holdings related to the New Bauhaus have achieved a scope that indubitably makes them a focal point among the various areas of the Bauhaus-Archiv's collections, which they complement in an outstanding manner. And it seems reasonable to hope they will also continue to grow in the future. The Bauhaus-Archiv has embraced the material legacy of both the Bauhaus and the New Bauhaus and constantly finds itself faced afresh with the challenge of dealing critically with heritage, with the "relationship between those who pass on an inheritance, the inheritance, and the heirs."[23]

22 Ibid.
23 Richter 2016, p. 11.

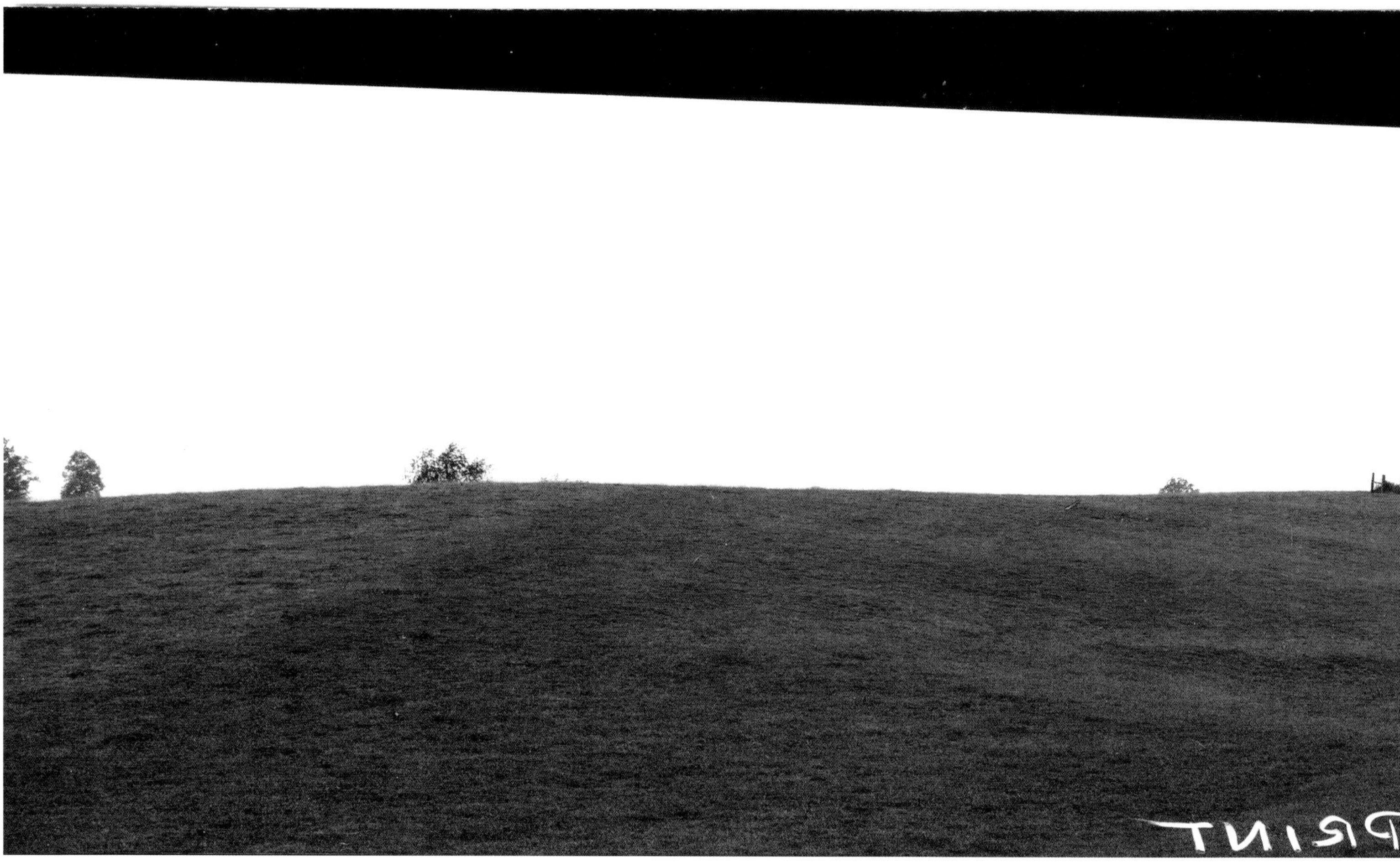

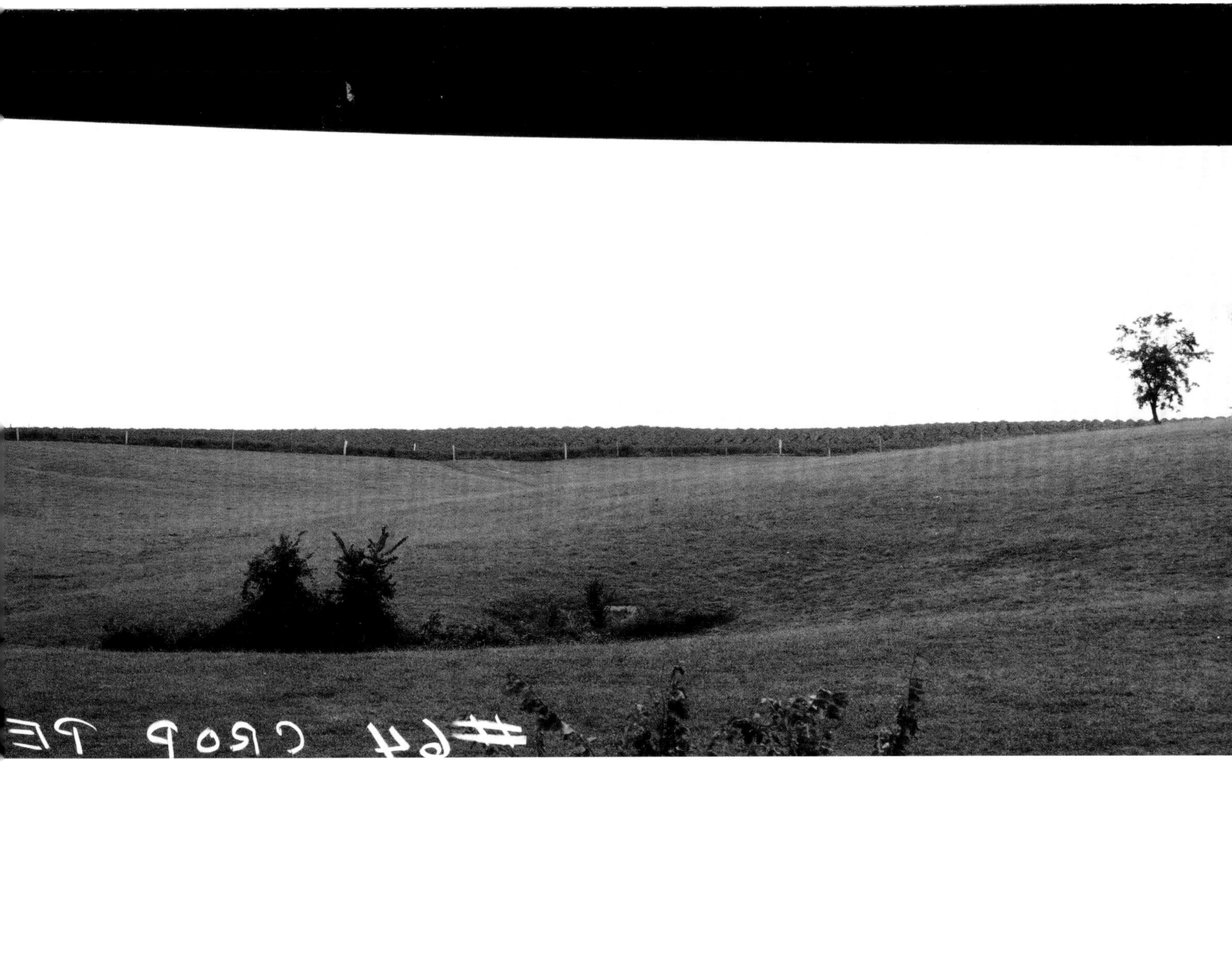

Arthur Sinsabaugh
Untitled, 1960s
gelatin silver, 14.6 x 50.6 cm

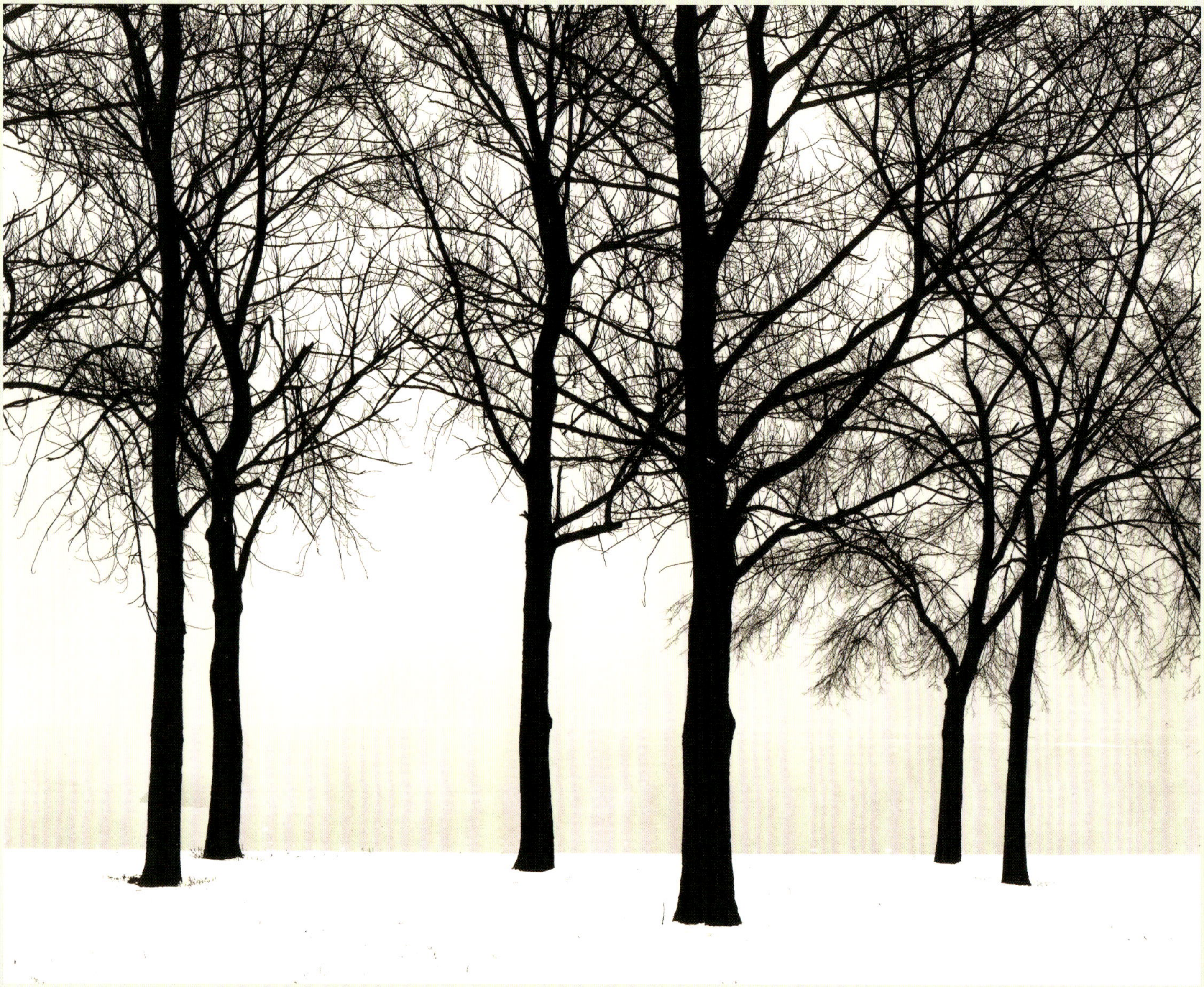

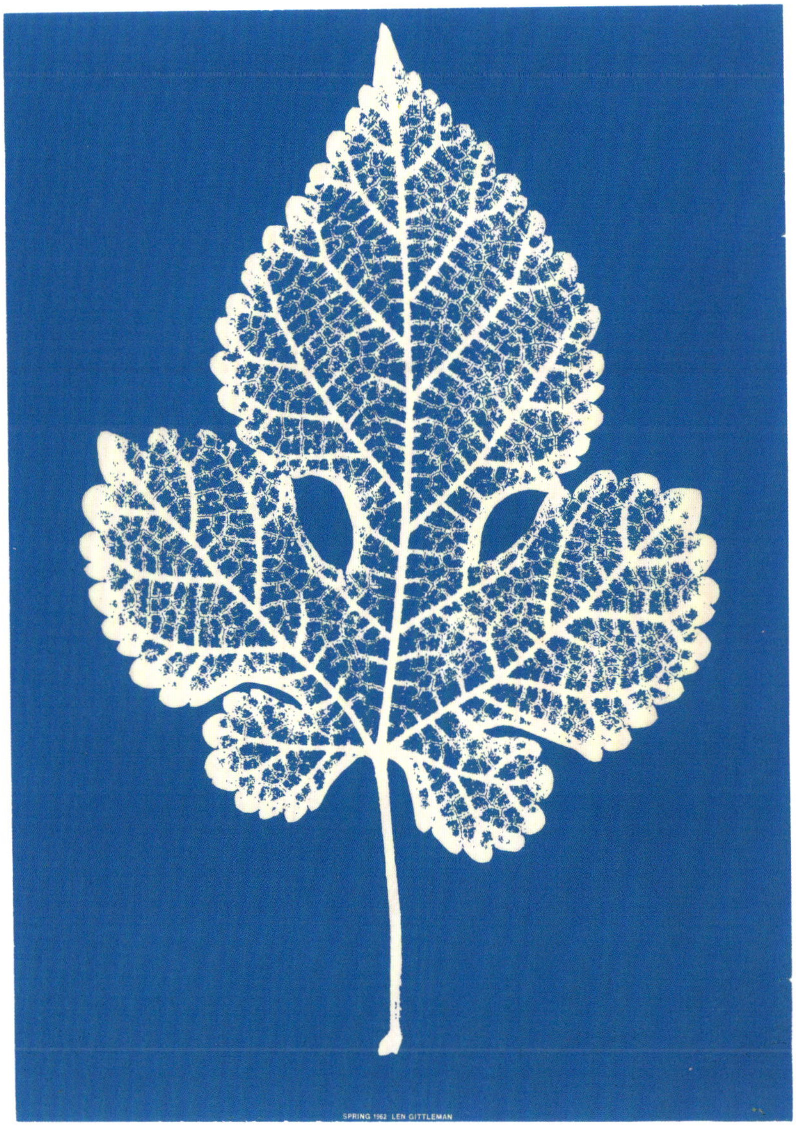

Harry Callahan
Chicago, ca. 1950
gelatin silver, 20 x 25.3 cm

Len Gittleman
Untitled, 1962
photogram, relief print in color, 35.4 x 25.4 cm

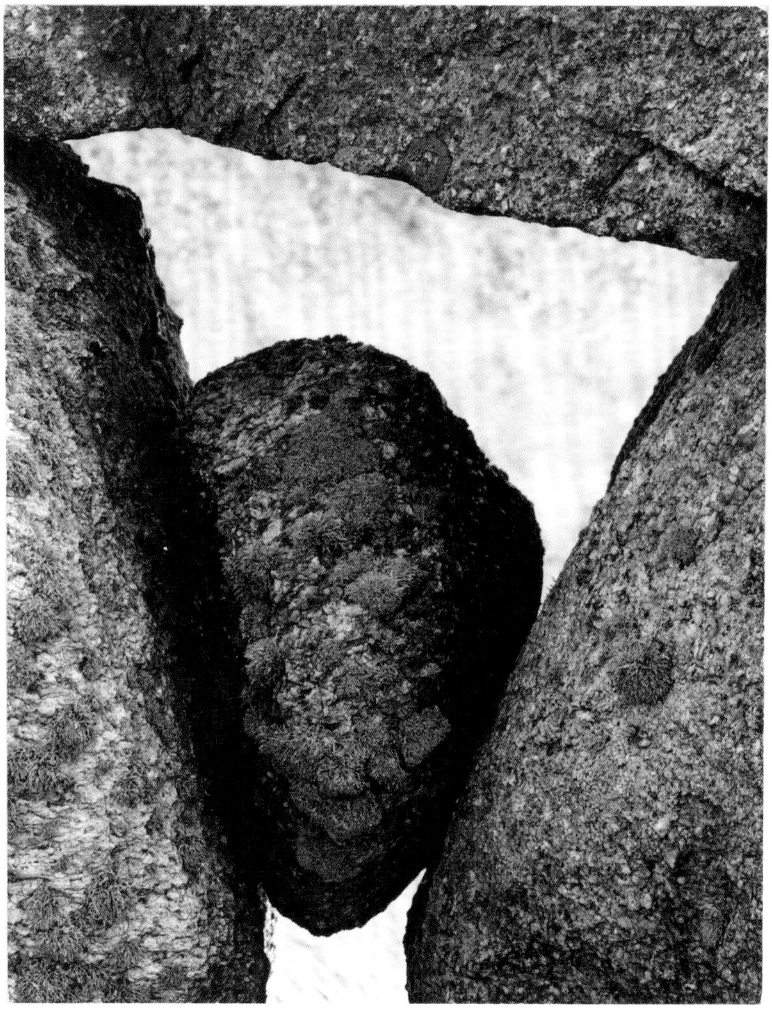

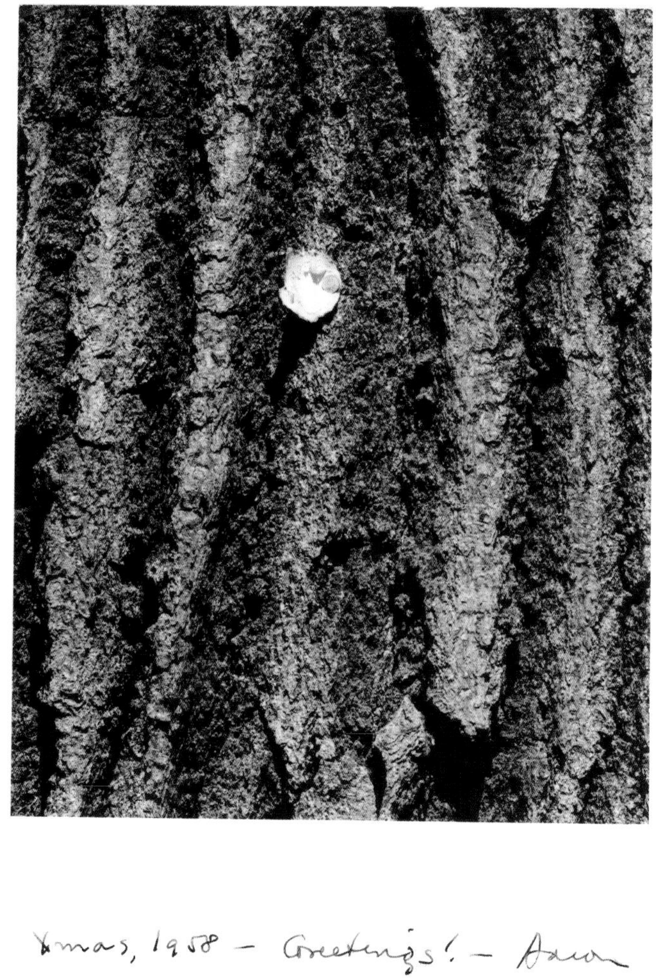

Aaron Siskind
Greeting card, 1956
gelatin silver, 16.5 x 12.9 cm

Aaron Siskind
Greeting card, 1958
gelatin silver, 17.8 x 11.6 cm

Aaron Siskind
Untitled, 1949
gelatin silver, 34.8 x 46.5 cm

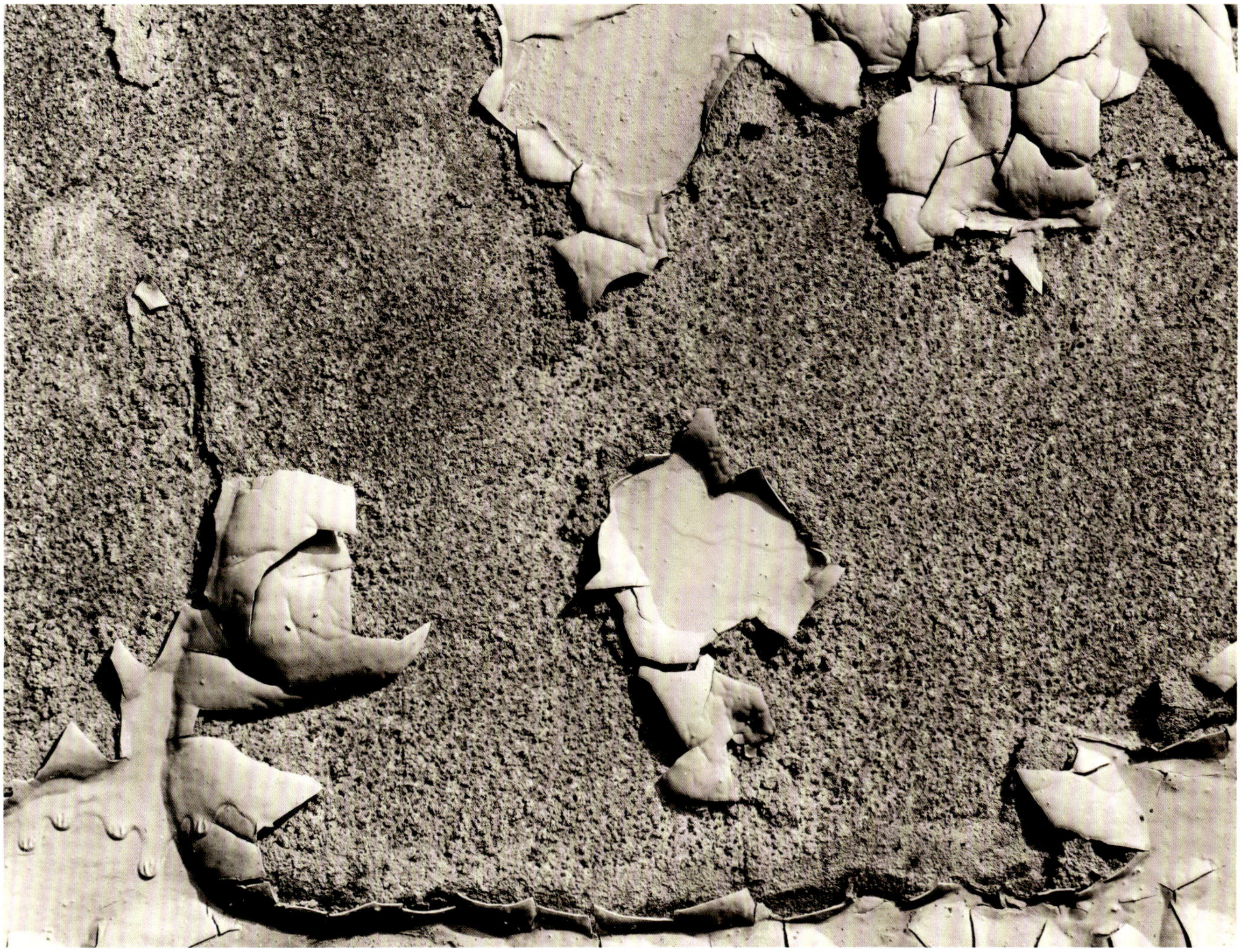

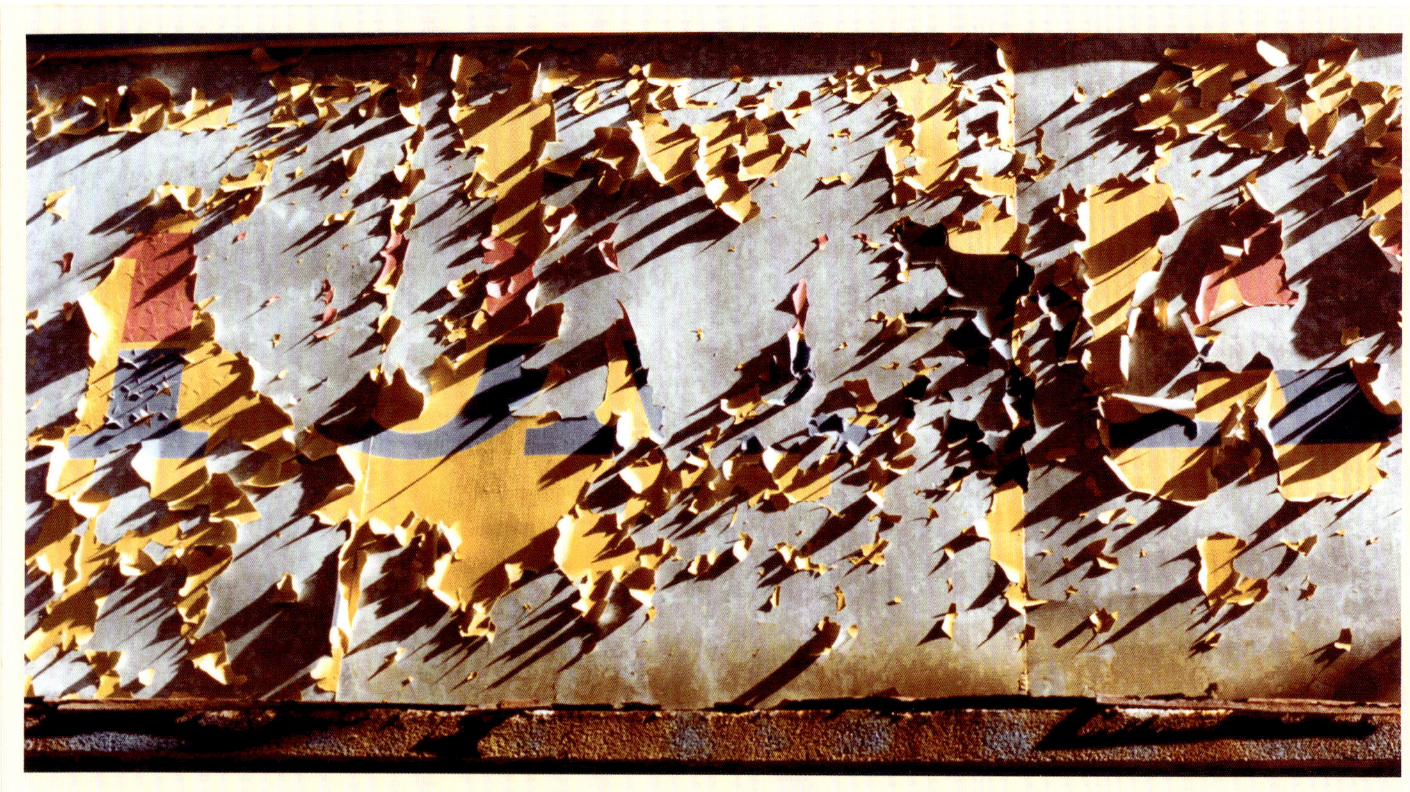

Nathan Lerner
Untitled, 1970s
chromogenic print, 19.2 x 35.1 cm

Nathan Lerner
Green Image, 1976
Cibachrome (silver-dye bleach process), 19.8 x 25.2 cm

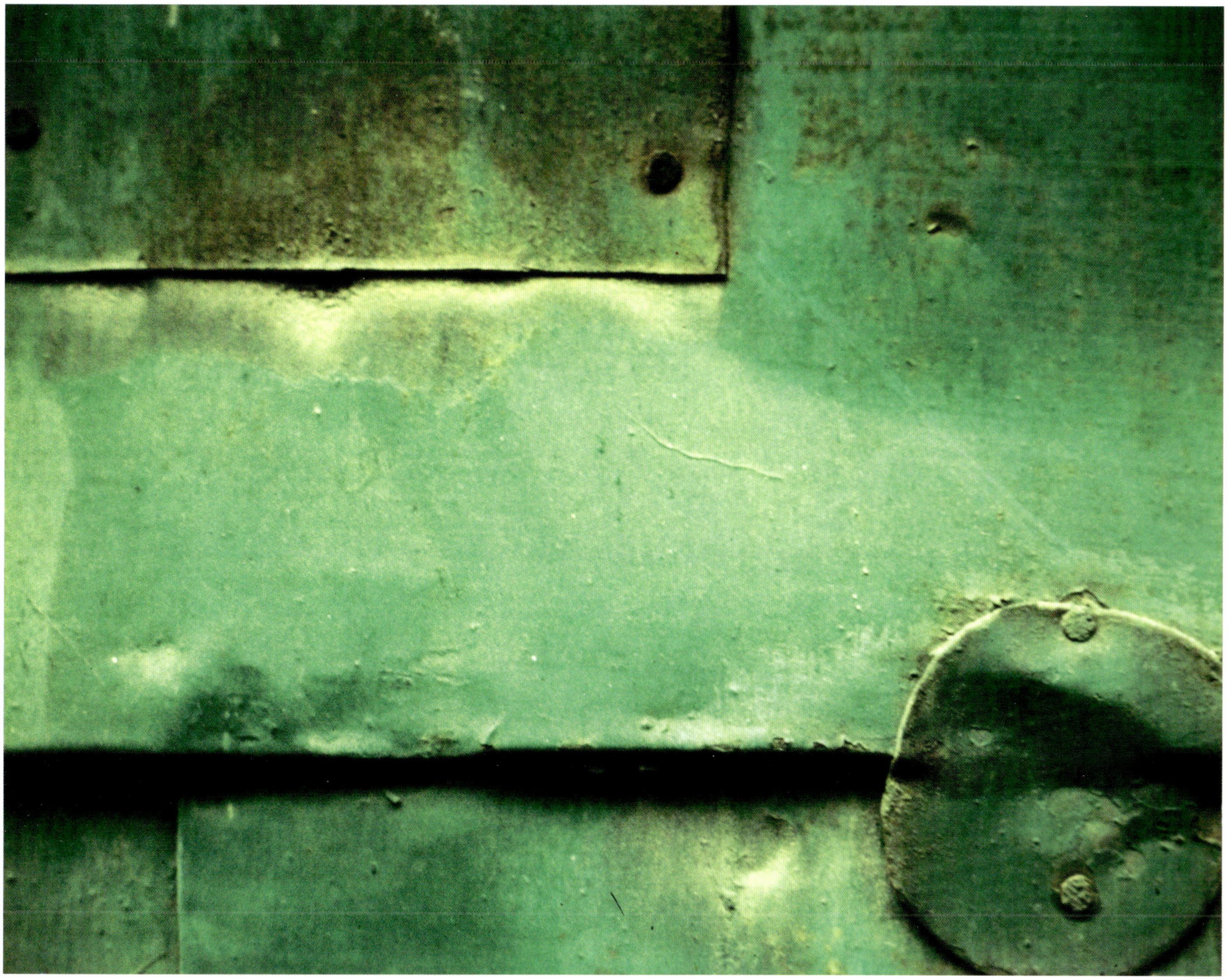

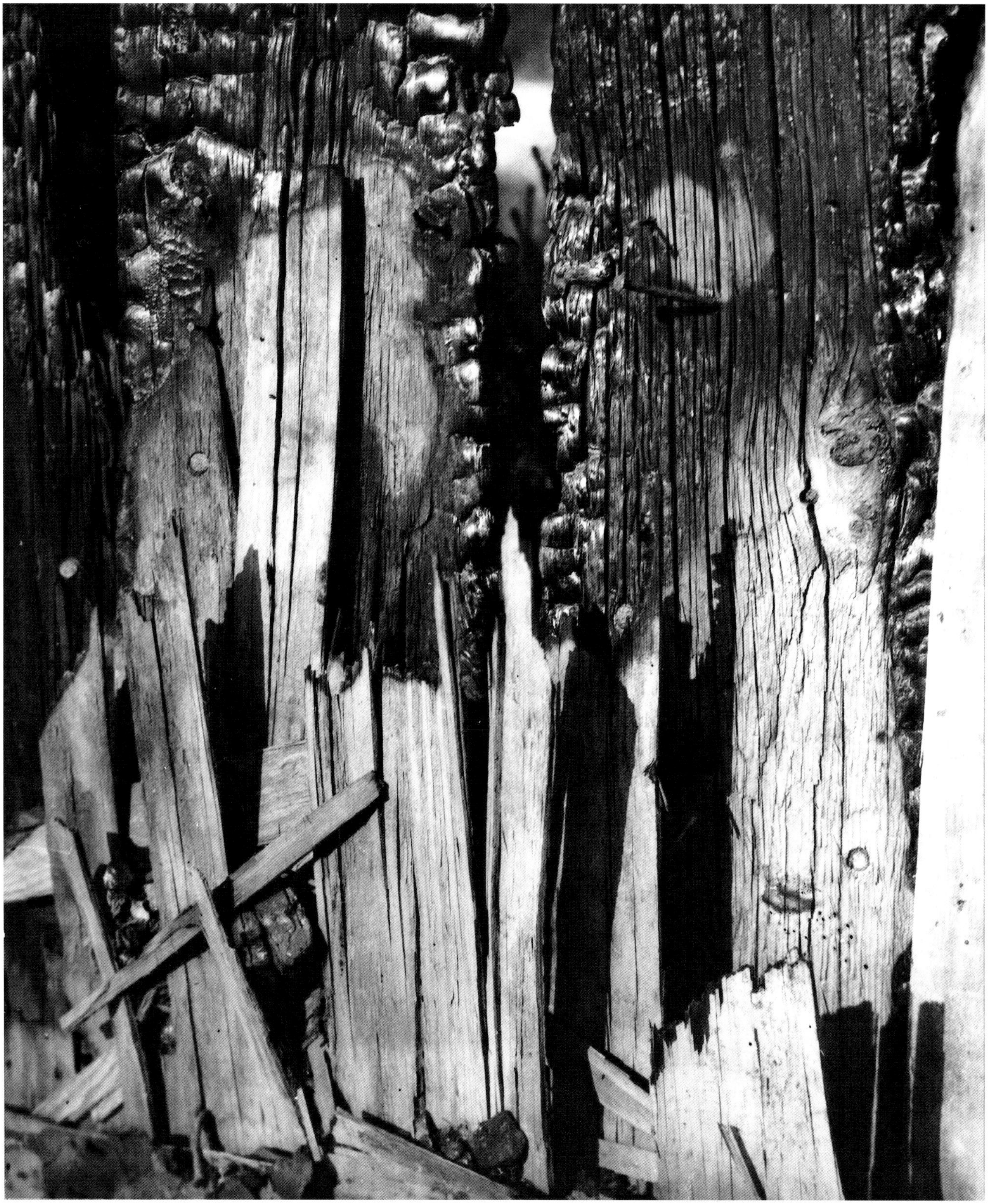

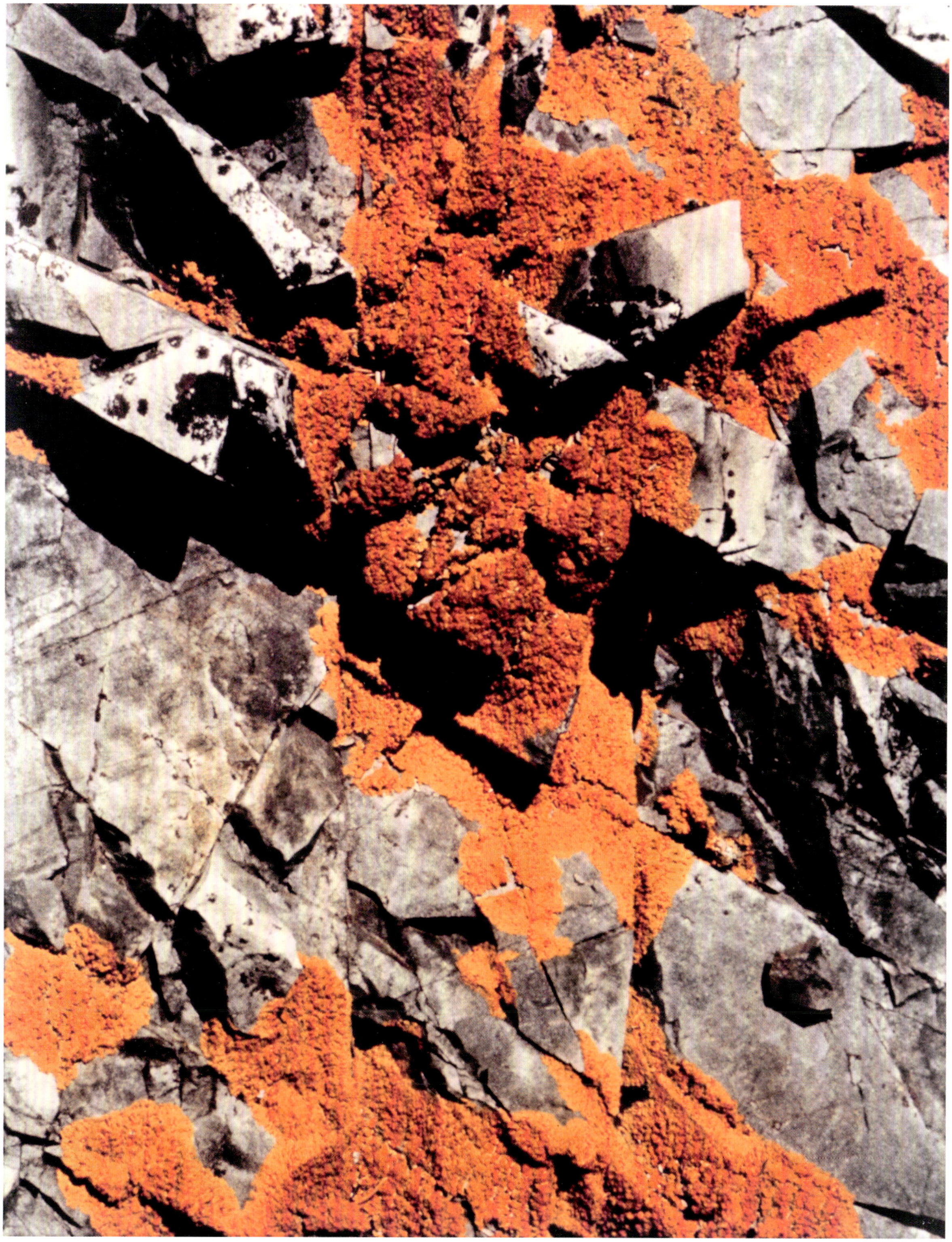

Robert Donald Erickson
Charred Fence, 1946
gelatin silver, 20.8 x 17.5 cm

Albert Szabo
Untitled, 1960
color photograph, 25.5 x 20.3 cm

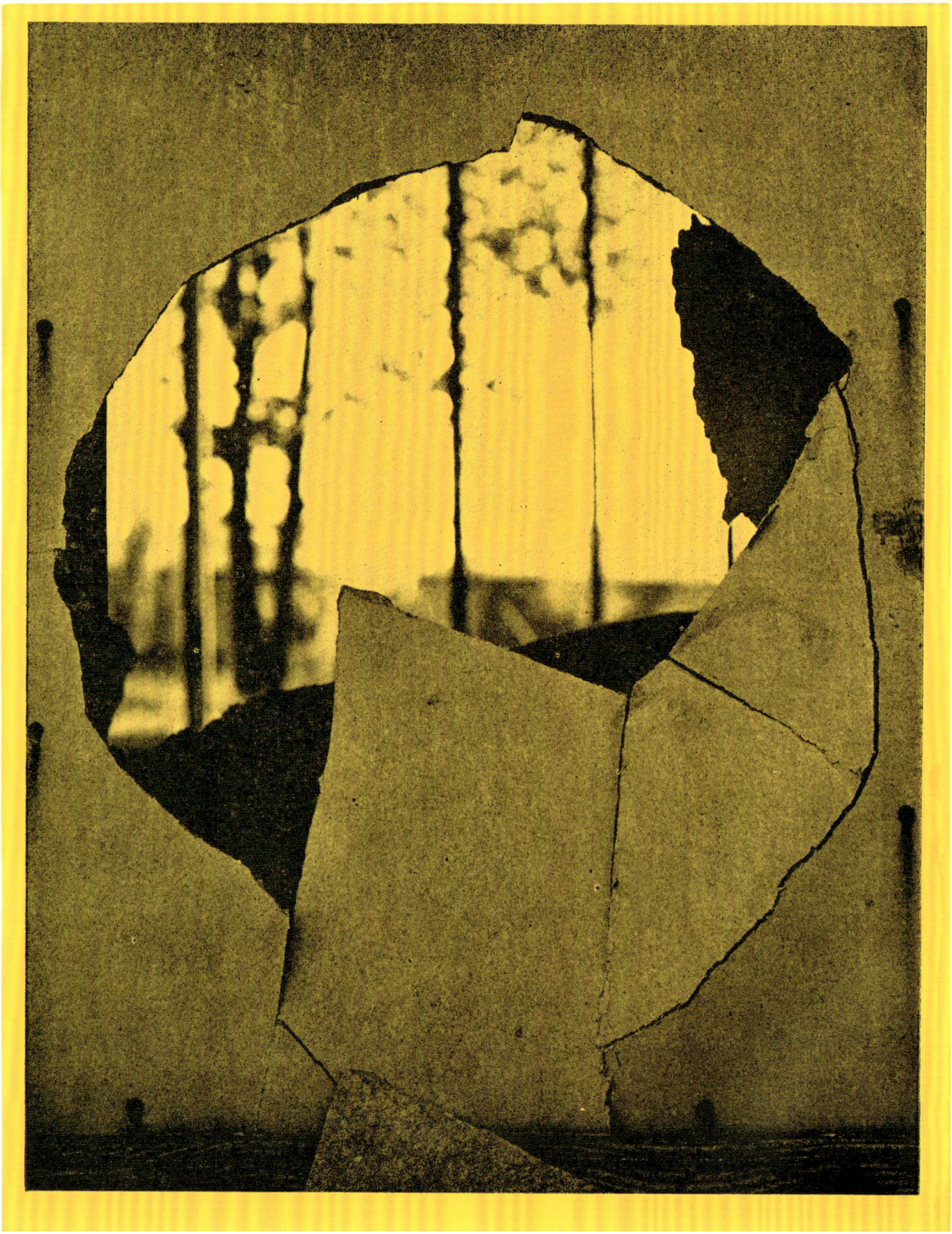

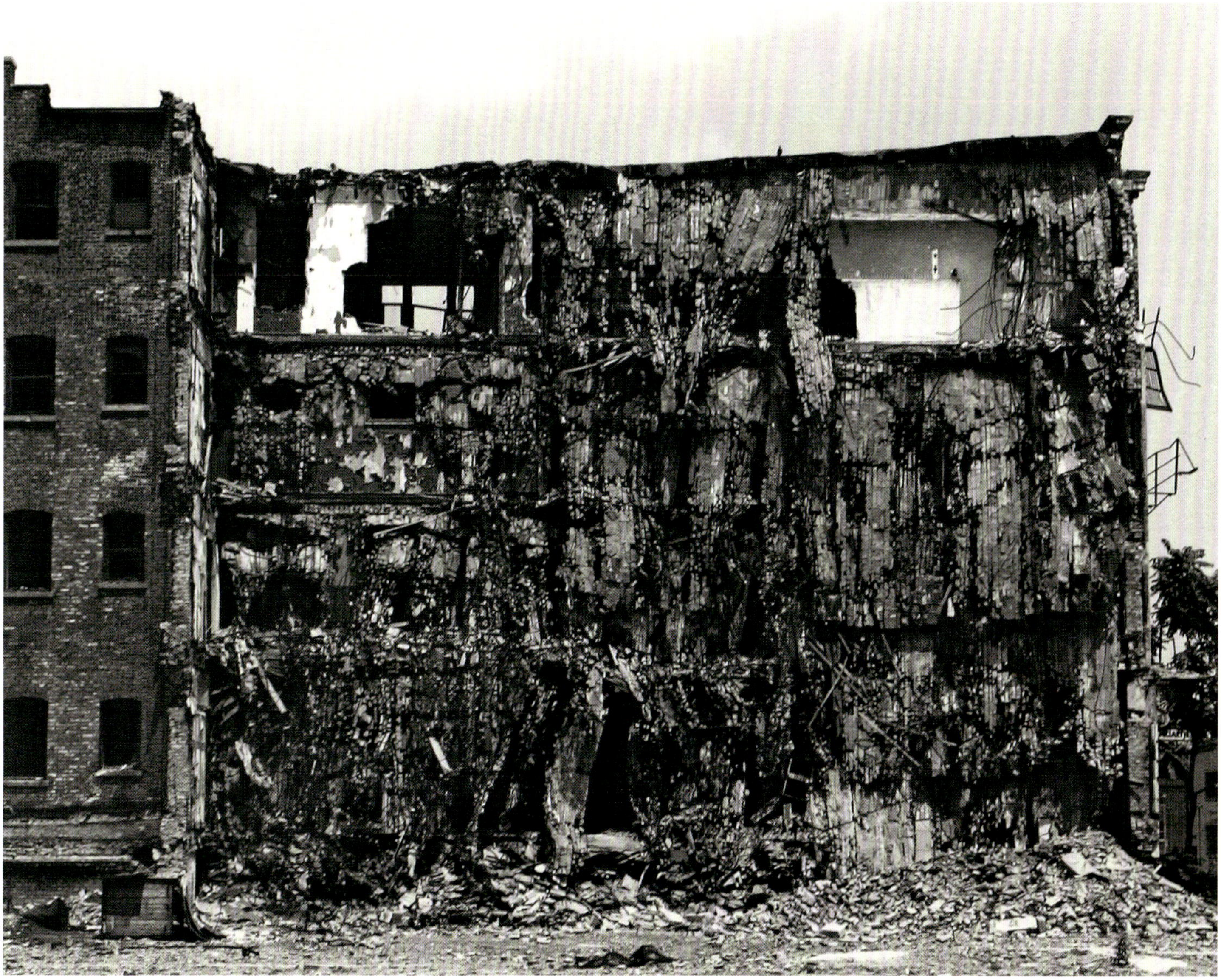

Charles Swedlund
Untitled, from the portfolio *Institute of Design Student Independent 2*, 1957
print on colored paper, 33.5 x 27.5 cm

Aaron Siskind
Chicago Façade, ca. 1965
gelatin silver, 40.5 x 50.5 cm

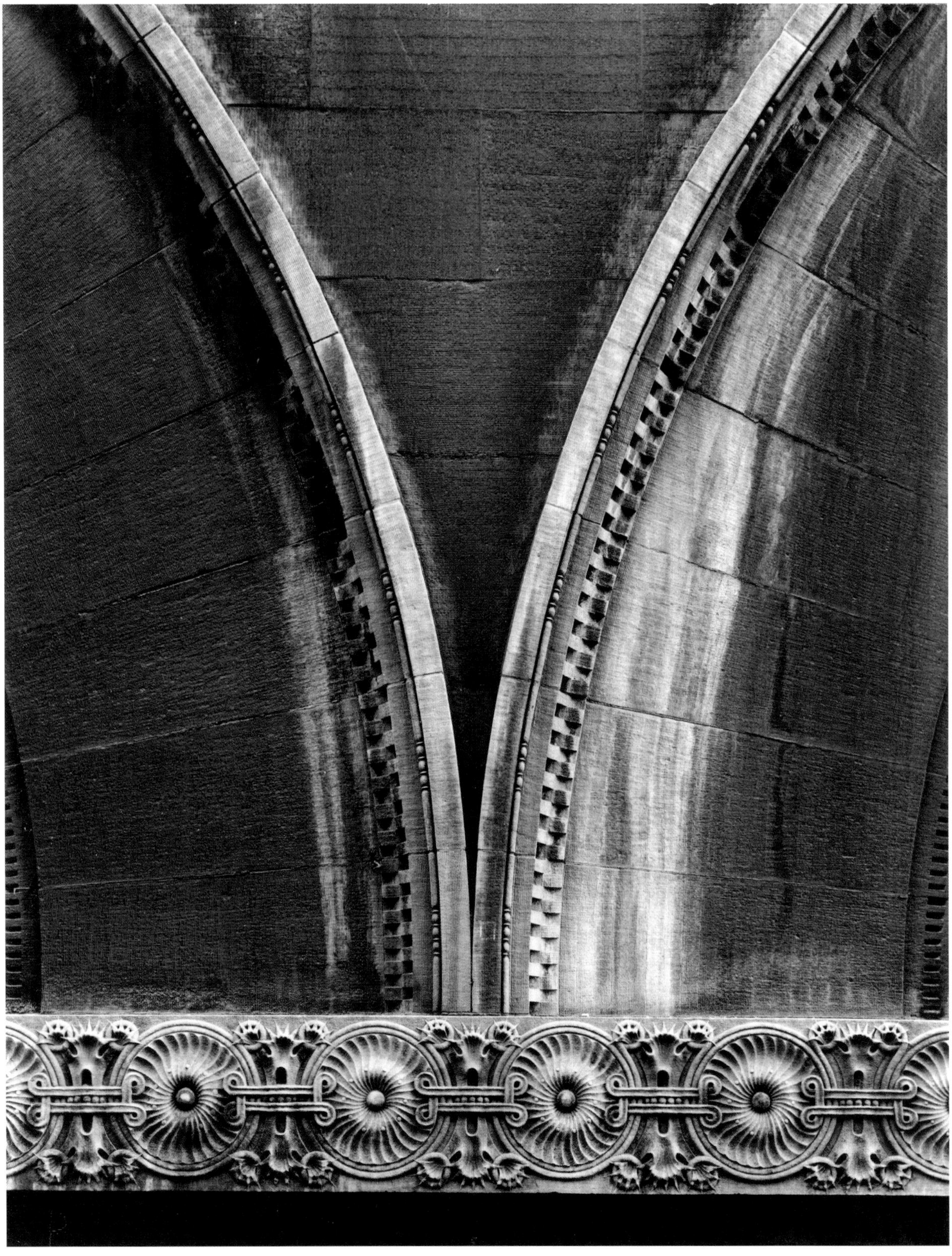

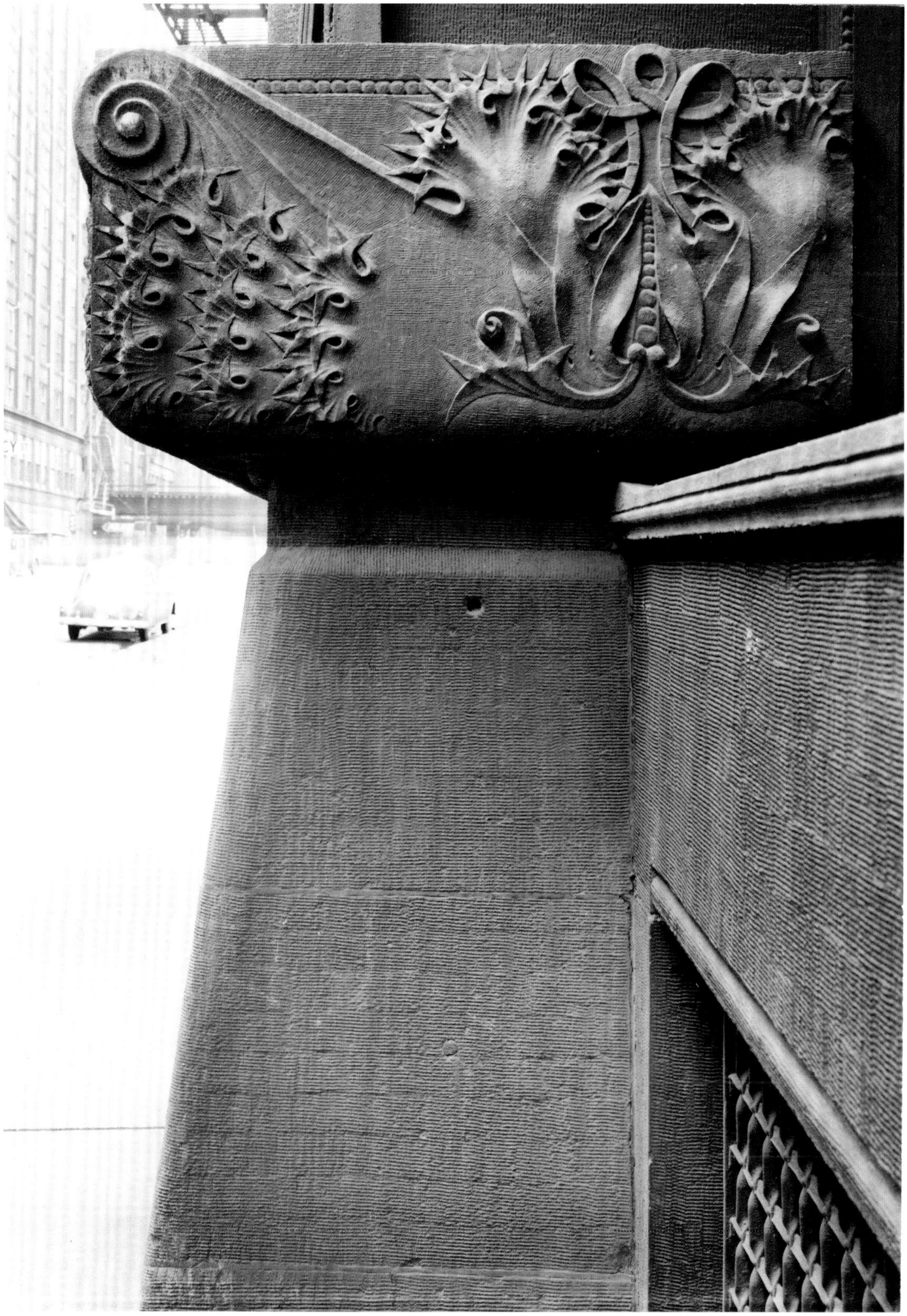

Aaron Siskind
Walker Warehouse, 1952/53
gelatin silver, 35 x 27.5 cm each

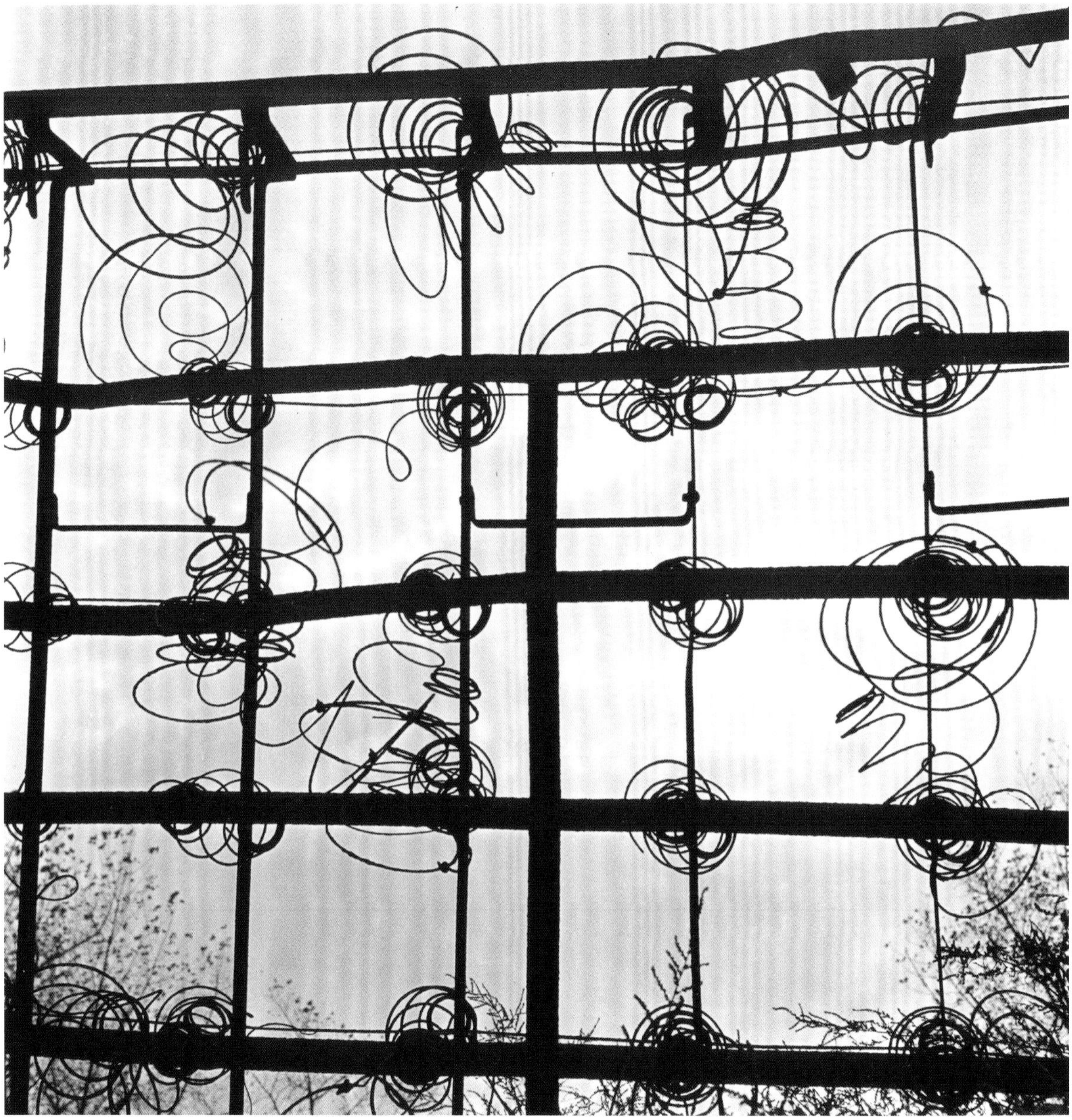

Frank Levstik
Untitled, between 1940 and 1950, print of 1987
gelatin silver, 22.8 x 22.8 cm

Robert Donald Erickson
Railroad Grating, 1947, later print
gelatin silver, 22.2 x 14.6 cm

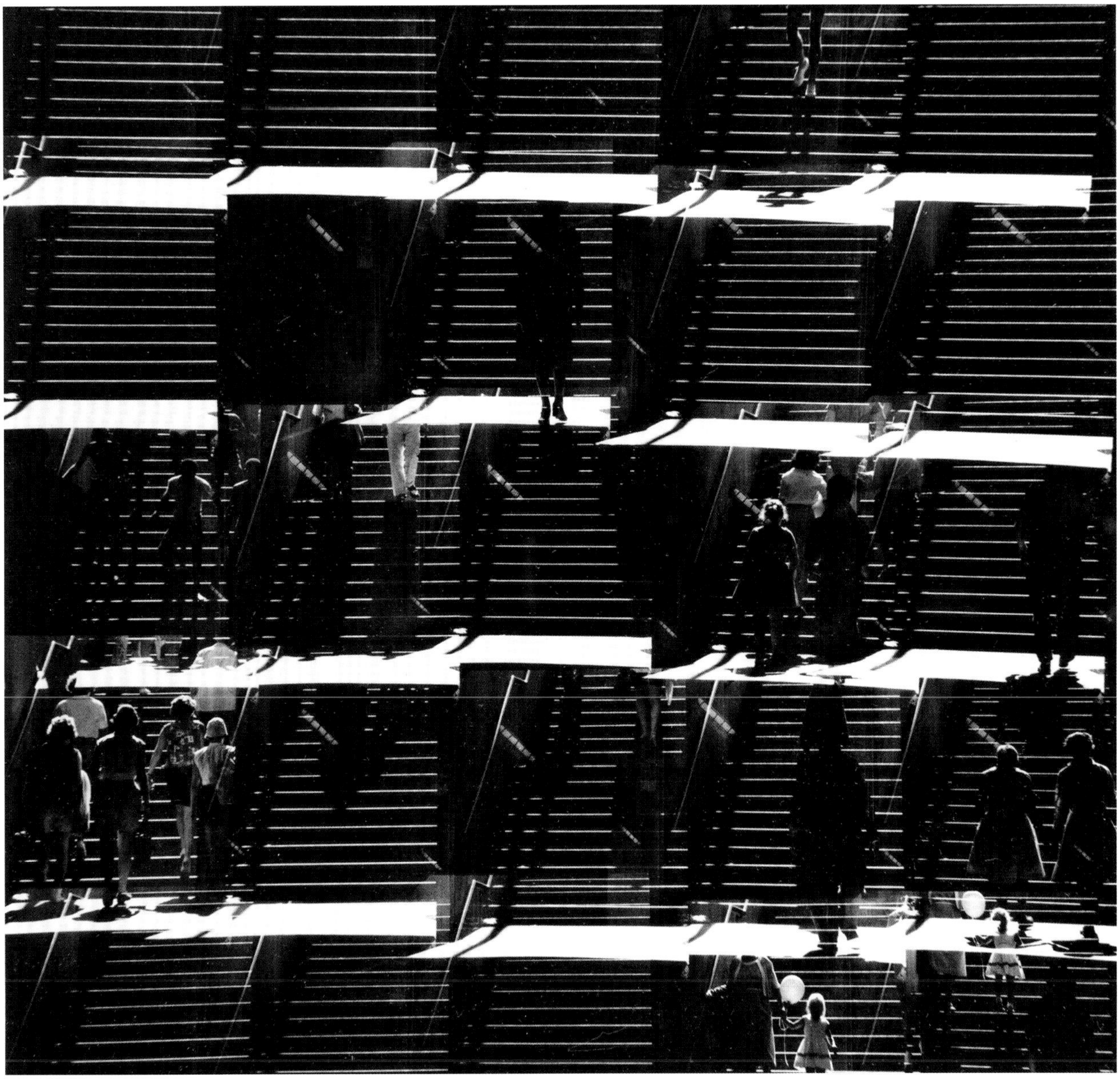

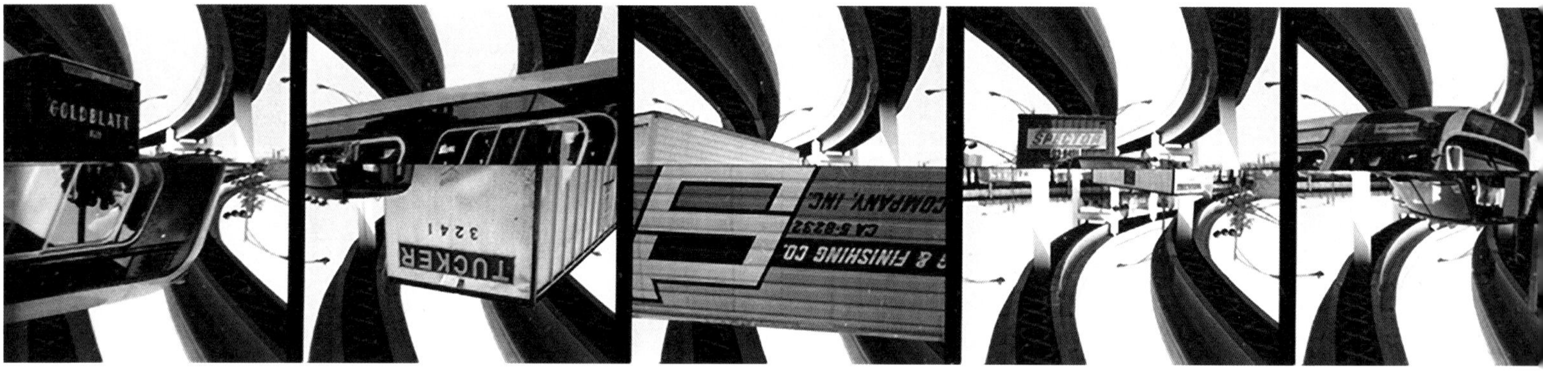

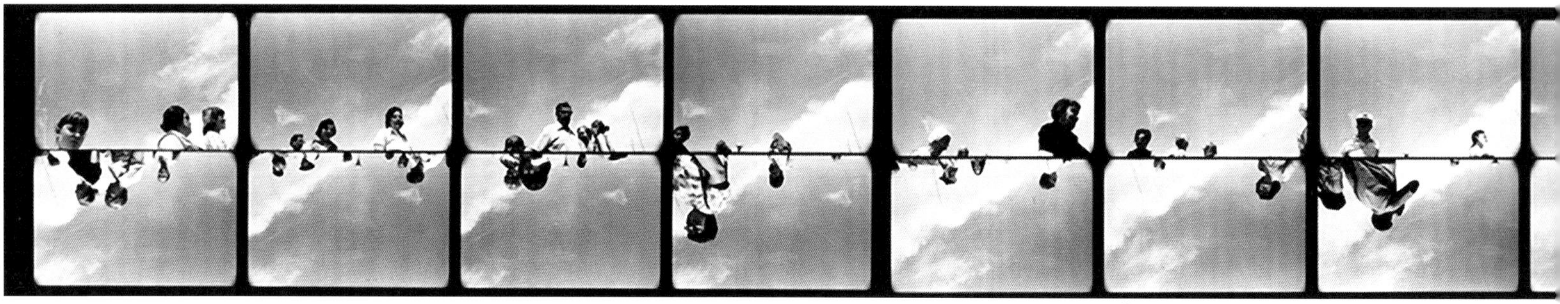

Barbara Crane
Dan Ryan Expressway, from the series *Repeats*, 1975
gelatin silver, 4.4 x 37.5 cm

Barbara Crane
Peoplescape, from the series *Repeats*, 1975, print of 1986
gelatin silver, 5 x 56.8 cm

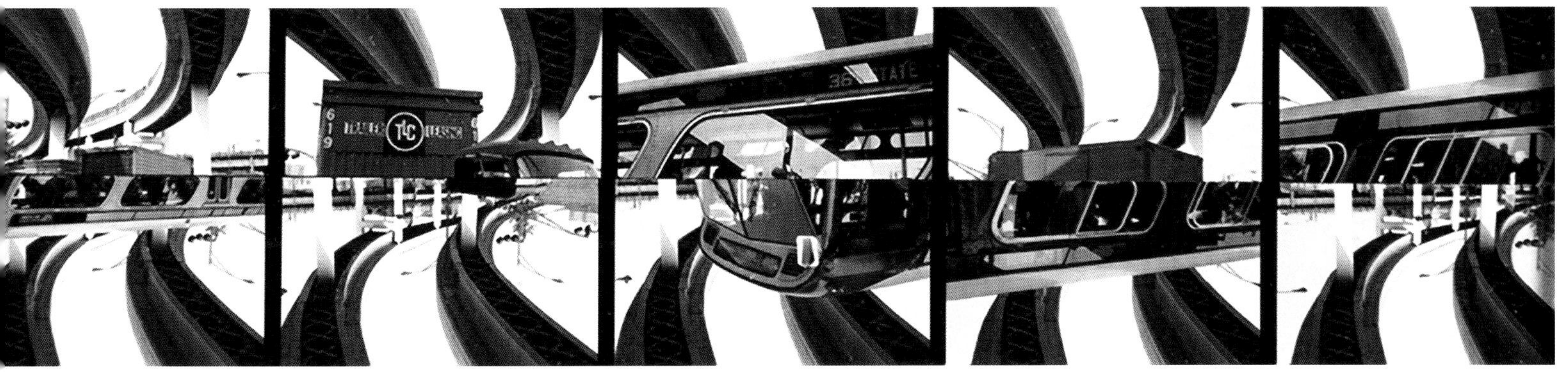
619
TLC

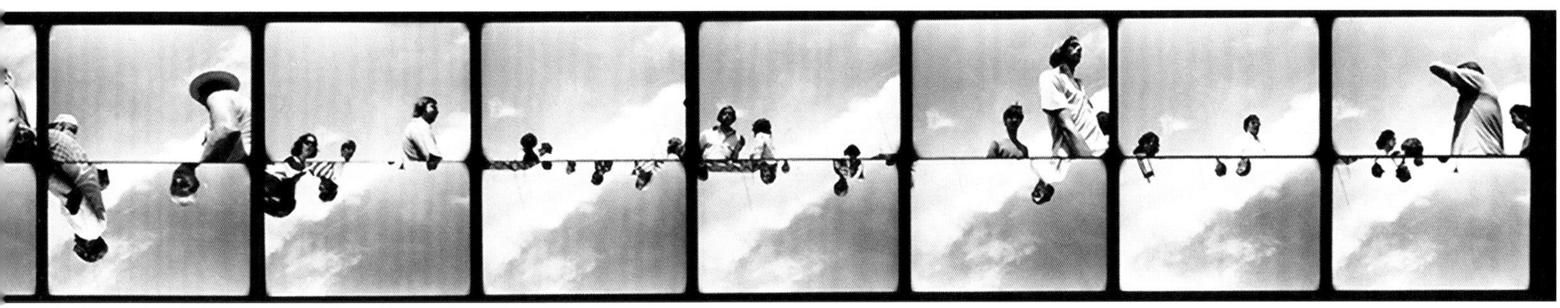

Barbara Crane
Tar Findings, from the series *Whole Roll*, 1975
gelatin silver, 26.2 x 24.1 cm

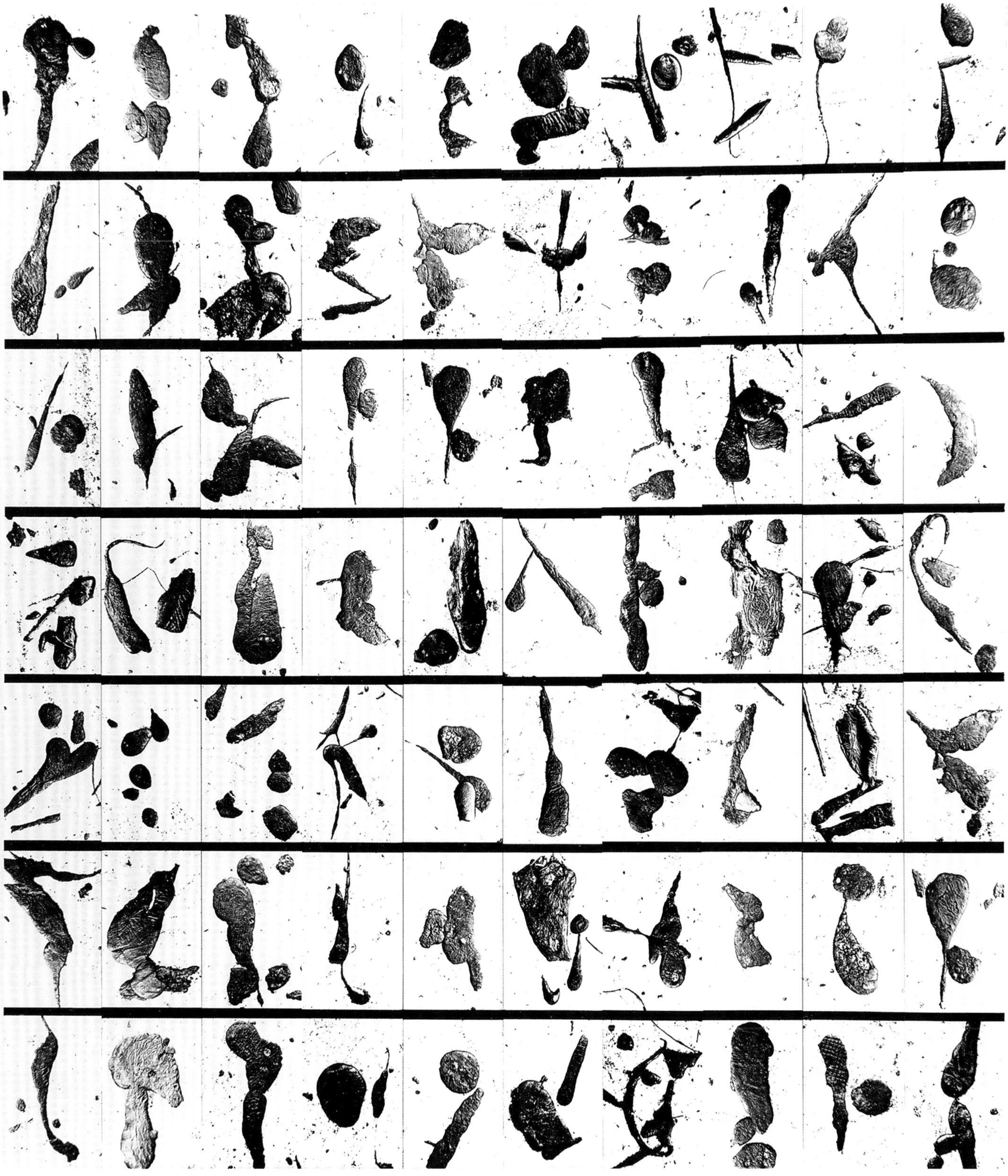

FROM THE INSTITUTE OF DESIGN TO THE ART INSTITUTE OF CHICAGO: PHOTOGRAPHY, THE SCHOOL, AND THE MUSEUM

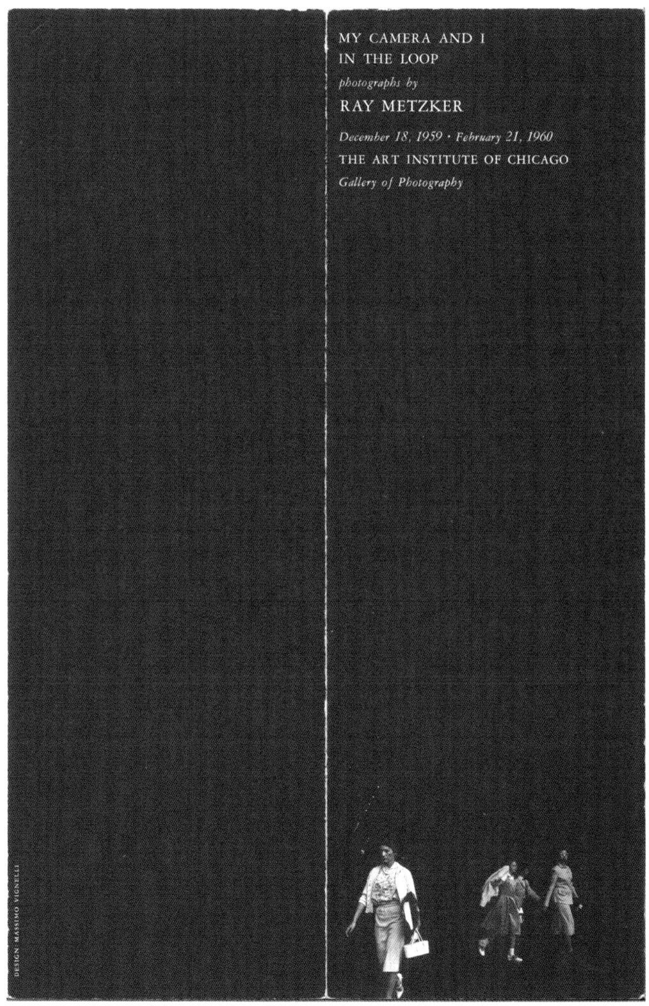

My Camera and I in the Loop: Ray K. Metzker
Art Institute of Chicago, 1959
exhibition brochure, cover

Elizabeth Siegel

"Yearly a few arrive at the threshold of camera work. But only in Chicago does the city art museum celebrate 'arrival' with a public exhibition."—Minor White, 1961[1]

In a special issue of *Aperture* dedicated to five students at the Institute of Design (ID), Minor White noted the unusual encouragement demonstrated by the Art Institute of Chicago to its local recent graduates. Ray K. Metzker had just completed the program at the ID with a thesis called "My Camera and I in the Loop," and the Art Institute mounted an exhibition that same year, 1959 (→ 170). But the "only in Chicago" practice White admired was a new phenomenon for photography at the Art Institute. Prior to that exhibition, the museum did not celebrate "arrival," but rather the careers of those who had already earned a place in the national or international discourse. The ways the Art Institute positioned itself vis-à-vis the ID reflects an understandable cultural difference between the two kinds of institutions. Whereas the ID emphasized experimental education, with workshops designed for exploration, tinkering, and even failure as part of the process for learning, the Art Institute was a civic, encyclopedic museum promising a transcendent experience from the culmination of an artist's career.[2] Changes over the course of both the museum's and school's trajectories, however, reveal how each institution was inevitably transforming as photography, during the second half of the twentieth century, claimed a more central place within artistic production and reception.

During László Moholy-Nagy's short decade in Chicago (1937–1946), he was arguably the most internationally renowned and versatile artist in the city. Moholy-Nagy who was already well known in Europe and the United States for his work at the German Bauhaus along with his prolific output of painting, photography, design, film, and writing—had come to Chicago at the behest of the Association of Arts and Industries, a group of local businessmen who hoped to revitalize industry by training designers in Bauhaus principles. He led the New Bauhaus (later the School of Design in Chicago and the Institute of Design), focusing on an ever-expanding curriculum and conducting a raft of administrative activities associated with the school, all while continuing

1 *ID 5* 1961, unpag. The five students were Joseph D. Jachna, Kenneth Josephson, Ray K. Metzker, Joseph Sterling, and Charles Swedlund.
2 It should be noted, of course, that the museum was already associated with a school, the School of the Art Institute of Chicago, with a relationship of more than four decades at the time of the New Bauhaus's founding.

his impressive output of photograms, paintings, and sculpture with industrial materials like Plexiglas. Moholy-Nagy's work was exhibited over three dozen times in the United States before his untimely death in 1946, including four solo presentations.[3] Compared to New York, where his work was regularly shown and collected by the Museum of Modern Art and the Museum of Non-Objective Painting (later the Solomon R. Guggenheim Museum), in his adopted hometown of Chicago the local museum was slower to act.[4] The Art Institute included Moholy-Nagy in several group annuals, but during his lifetime he received more individual attention at the Renaissance Society, the Arts Club, and the Katharine Kuh Gallery, which were focused on contemporary art and perhaps could be more nimble and responsive to trends in Chicago and elsewhere.

Moholy-Nagy only received a one-person survey exhibition at the Art Institute after his death. A memorial exhibition, *L. Moholy-Nagy, 1895–1946,* was hastily organized by the Society for Contemporary Art for September 1947, with a catalogue featuring essays by Katharine Kuh (she had closed her gallery and became a curator of modern art at the museum) and prints and drawings curator Carl O. Schniewind.[5] The show included paintings, constructions, collages, prints, drawings, and one photogram (but no straight photography), most produced while Moholy-Nagy was in Chicago. Whereas he had evinced a preference for more didactic displays (the museum as an offshoot of the classroom), at the Art Institute the museum's tendency toward the finished masterpiece surely won out.[6] The press release for the exhibition noted his pedagogical accomplishments but quickly veered to Moholy-Nagy's artistic credentials: "Though Moholy-Nagy, in our city, gained recognition for his efforts as an art educator, director of the New Bauhaus which he founded as director of the Institute of Design, which still flourishes, he is considered a pioneer Modernist, noted internationally as an industrial designer, photographer, painter, graphic artist, author and lecturer."[7]

In the subsequent decades, as the ID transitioned from a school of design with a general Bauhaus education to a postwar school with a highly regarded and specialized photography program, the Art Institute followed suit.[8] Regular exhibitions of photography had begun in the 1940s under the direction of Schniewind, in the Department of Prints and Drawings, and then Peter Pollack, who was operating out of the museum's publicity office. Solo exhibitions were mounted of some of the most important photographers of the day, including Berenice Abbott, Ansel Adams, Brassaï, Henri Cartier-Bresson, and Edward Weston. When Pollack turned his attention to the innovative work that was coming out of the ID in the 1950s, he logically focused on the teachers; in quick succession, exhibitions of work by Harry Callahan, Aaron Siskind, and Arthur Siegel filled the exhibition calendar, and acquisitions of photographs followed each of the exhibitions.[9]

The Art Institute opened new galleries for photography in 1951, and Pollack inaugurated them with an exhibition of Callahan's work. Callahan, whom Moholy-Nagy had hired at the suggestion of Siegel in 1946, had helped transition the ID's photography program from a light-based exploration to a curriculum positioning photography as a means of personal expression. At the moment of his first one-man museum exhibition, he was on the verge of gaining national attention for work that was both refined and experimental, exploring the technical possibilities of photography while investigating what he would modestly refer to as "nature, buildings, and people."[10] The exhibition

3 For information on Moholy-Nagy's exhibitions in the United States, see Vail 2016.
4 See also contribution Daiter.
5 *L. Moholy-Nagy, 1895–1946* 1947.
6 For example, the exhibitions of student work Moholy-Nagy mounted after the first year at the New Bauhaus, or the Museum of Modern Art–circulated exhibition *How to Make a Photogram*. Both are discussed in Siegel 2016.
7 Press release for *L. Moholy-Nagy, 1895–1946* 1947, Art Institute of Chicago archives.
8 For more on the ID and photography, see *Taken by Design* 2002.
9 It should be noted that the museum also mounted an exhibition of another important teacher at the then–School of Design, photograms by György Kepes in the summer of 1943.
10 Salvesen 2006, p. 16.

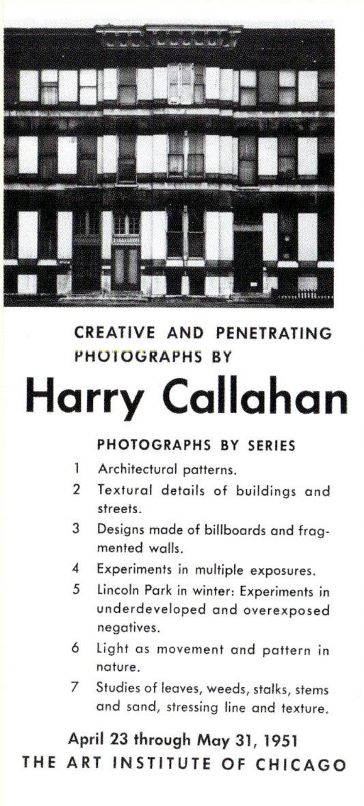

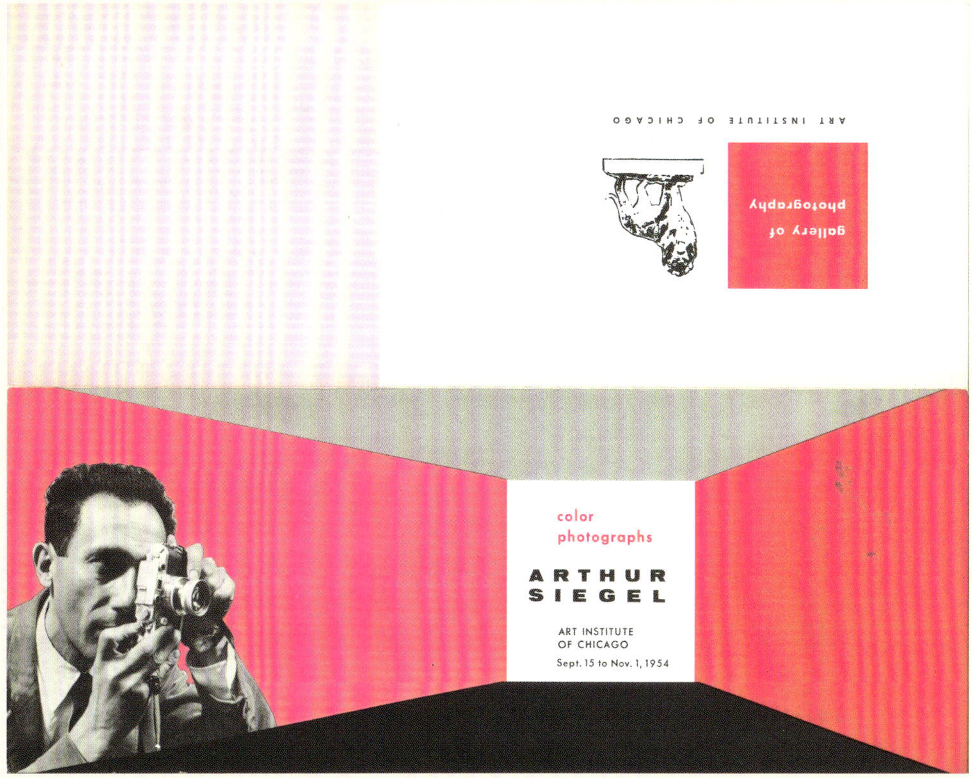

Creative and Penetrating Photographs by Harry Callahan
Art Institute of Chicago, 1951
exhibition brochure, cover

Color Photographs, Arthur Siegel
Art Institute of Chicago, 1954
leaflet

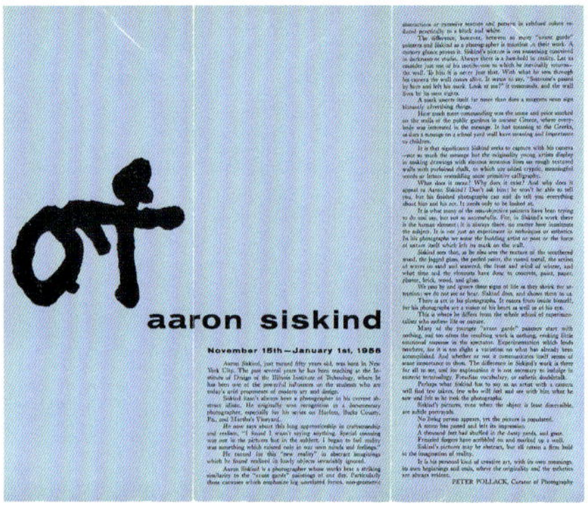

Aaron Siskind
Art Institute of Chicago, 1955/56
exhibition brochure, cover

brochure touted the "Creative and Penetrating Photographs by Harry Callahan," dividing them into seven groups that included architectural patterns, textural details, abstracted walls, multiple exposures, high-contrast winter scenes, light as movement and pattern, and studies of natural forms emphasizing line (→ 173).[11] The press responded enthusiastically, calling Callahan a "seeing artist with the camera," and praising his technical skills.[12]

Three years later, Pollack curated an exhibition of color photographs by Siegel (→ 173). Siegel had been involved with the ID from its earliest days as the New Bauhaus, when he attended one semester as a student; at Moholy-Nagy's request, he returned in 1946 to head the new photography program, which he led through 1949. His career then alternated between commercial and creative photography and stints teaching at the school. By the time of his 1954 exhibition, Siegel had begun a project inflected by Freudian analysis called "In Search of Myself": color photographs depicting State Street shoppers, storefronts, and reflections in an effort to explore the complex relationship between identity and consumerism. The exhibition brochure announced that it was the first exhibition entirely of dye-transfer prints at the museum, explaining that color itself could be the subject of the photographs (→ 180, 181). As Pollack wrote, "The subject is secondary; it is the color and what it says emotionally to him that Siegel explores."[13] It also included a list of photographic dos and don'ts that formed "Arthur Siegel's credo"—instructions his students would come to know intimately.[14]

The last of Pollack's exhibitions on ID teachers, in 1955, focused on Aaron Siskind, who had joined the faculty in 1951 and was one of the most well-known artists working in Chicago at the time (→ 174). Siskind began as a documentary photographer in his native New York, but by the 1940s had embraced a radical abstraction, making images that increasingly, as he put it, accepted "the flat plane of the picture surface as a primary frame of reference of the picture."[15] Socially and professionally close with many of the Abstract Expressionist painters, Siskind created photographs in dialogue with painting, attempting to find a new language for photographic depiction that could transform an object into an image; his work was exhibited most notably at the Charles Egan Gallery, a contemporary New York gallery that also showed Franz Kline and Willem de Kooning. Pollack's exhibition highlighted photography's "foothold in reality" as a counterpoint to the abstract-expressionist paintings his photographs resembled. The curator argued that Siskind's attention to the material details of the world showed viewers what they might normally overlook. "Siskind [...] sees the texture of the weathered wood, the jagged glass, the peeled paint, the rusted metal, the action of waves on sand and seaweed, the frost and wind of winter, and what time and the elements have done to concrete, paint, paper, plaster, brick, wood, and glass. We pass by and ignore these signs of life as they shriek for attention; we do not see or hear. Siskind does, and shows them to us."[16]

Pollack left the museum in 1957, and the position of curator of photography passed in 1959 to Hugh Edwards, a curator of prints and drawings with a curious mind and a long-standing interest in photography.[17] Edwards initiated a jam-packed exhibition program, mounting nearly eighty shows in twelve years, and added some 3,000 works to the collection. Although he understood the wide range of photographic history and programmed accordingly—he was the first to add nineteenth-century work to the

11 *Harry Callahan* 1951.
12 "Creative Photography Show," in: *This Week in Chicago / The Magazine of Chicago*, May 19, 1951, p. 17.
13 *Arthur Siegel* 1954, unpag.
14 For example, "I never give titles to pictures. They are meant to be visual experiences, not literary illustrations" and "I am not a frustrated painter who has taken up photography; I started with the camera and I will stick with it, for the camera is a means of making images, it seems to me, more suitable to this modern age than the methods of a painter.", in: ibid.
15 Siskind 1956, p. 27–28.
16 *Aaron Siskind* 1955, unpag.
17 See the website media.artic.edu/edwards for a comprehensive look at Edwards's career, including information on every acquisition he made and exhibitions he curated.

collection, and he regularly showcased the acknowledged masters in the field—his special interest was emerging photographers. He nurtured the careers of dozens of young artists, mounting the first one-person museum shows of Robert Frank, Danny Lyon, and many others, and gave particular encouragement to those in his city of Chicago. Whereas Pollack displayed the photographs of the ID's teachers, who already had or were building national reputations, Edwards chose to focus on the students, often giving them their first one-person exhibitions and adding their works to the growing collection.

The first monographic exhibition that Edwards organized was that of Ray Metzker in 1959. He selected seventy photographs from the 119 that comprised *My Camera and I in the Loop*, declaring by sheer size the value of an artist's vision in a single project. Metzker's student thesis, more an investigation of photographic form than a strictly documentary project, took the Loop as a starting point to explore light and shadow, human and architectural shapes, and the urban dramas of the street (→ 170). In an essay written for the exhibition's brochure, Edwards argued that the photographs took on a new existence once presented to the public. "One need neither to have seen the Chicago Loop nor have operated a camera to look at them with insight and understanding," he maintained. "Their honesty and refusal of compromise free them of the insecurities of art fashions and fads and somehow, in keeping their individual principles, they are able to communicate with everyone."[18] As Callahan and Siskind's reputation as a legendary teaching team at the ID grew, they attracted a new generation of talented students eager to understand how, as the instructors put it in a 1956 *Aperture* article, "from within the framework of a broad professional education to open an individual way."[19] In a departure from Moholy-Nagy's original project of interdisciplinary education in which light played a central role in a variety of endeavors, under Callahan and Siskind photography became a focus in and of itself; students in the master's program would additionally produce a thesis, a complete body of work with a particular theme or subject matter. Accordingly, as the museum began a new program for photography, Edwards focused on monographic exhibitions and included many of the recent graduates of the program who were just beginning to build their careers. Metzker was first among them, but Edwards also organized shows of Yasuhiro Ishimoto (1960); Rodney Galarneau, Thomas Knudtson, David Rowinski, and Joseph Sterling (group show, 1961); Joseph D. Jachna (1961); Charles Swedlund (1963); and Art Sinsabaugh (1963). He also exhibited the teachers, showing recent work by Frederick Sommer (1963), Aaron Siskind (1964), and Arthur Siegel (1967).

Edwards retired from the Art Institute in 1970, the year before Siskind left the ID. By that time, photography had become well assimilated in both the museum and the academy. In the coming decades, most major museums would initiate departments of photography (or separate them from prints and drawings, where photography activities were most often housed), and a new crop of photography professors—many of them educated at the ID—would fan out across the country to teach photography and satisfy the increasing demand for courses among students. It would be photography itself, not the work of an individual student, that in the end "arrived."

18 Edwards 1959, unpag.
19 Siskind/Callahan 1956, unpag.

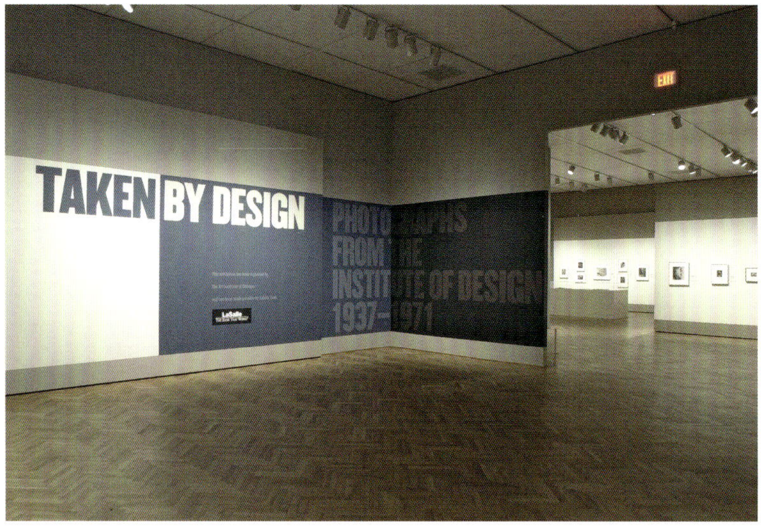

Anonymous
View of the exhibition *Taken by Design*,
Art Institute of Chicago, 2002

ID 5 1961
cover

POSTSCRIPT: *TAKEN BY DESIGN*

David Travis, Hugh Edwards's successor as curator of photography, continued the wide-ranging program of photography implemented by his predecessors for over three decades. As part of an encyclopedic museum, the Art Institute collected and exhibited photographs from the medium's beginnings on, made in Chicago but also increasingly worldwide. For years, however, Travis thought that a comprehensive exhibition ought to be mounted on the contributions—both artistic and pedagogical—of the ID. This idea culminated in the 2002 exhibition and catalogue, *Taken by Design: Photographs from the Institute of Design, 1937–1971* (→ 176).[20]

The time was right: With the exception of an important 1982 *Aperture* book, there had been no serious study of photography at the ID, and information was in danger of disappearing as earlier generations of students and teachers at the school were aging or dying.[21] I was fortunate enough to be hired by the museum, while still a graduate student, as a researcher for the project. My research took me into archives throughout the city and across the country, and I conducted one-on-one interviews with over twenty former students and teachers and another half dozen group interviews. Through the generosity of museum donors, we were able to add new works—often by relatively unknown artists—to the collection.

When the exhibition opened in March 2002, it felt like a family reunion, attended by numerous living former students and teachers. With over two hundred works by more than seventy photographers, *Taken by Design* carefully detailed the aesthetic and historical impact and continuing influence of the ID. Indeed, the *Chicago Tribune*'s art critic, Alan Artner, contended that the exhibition decisively demonstrated photography's rightful place in Chicago's contribution to the arts: "It cannot be said too often: In the last 65 years, Chicago made its strongest and most lasting impression in the art arena worldwide not with painting or sculpture but with photography."[22]

20 The exhibition traveled to the San Francisco Museum of Modern Art and the Philadelphia Museum of Art.
21 *The New Vision* 1982.
22 Artner 2002.

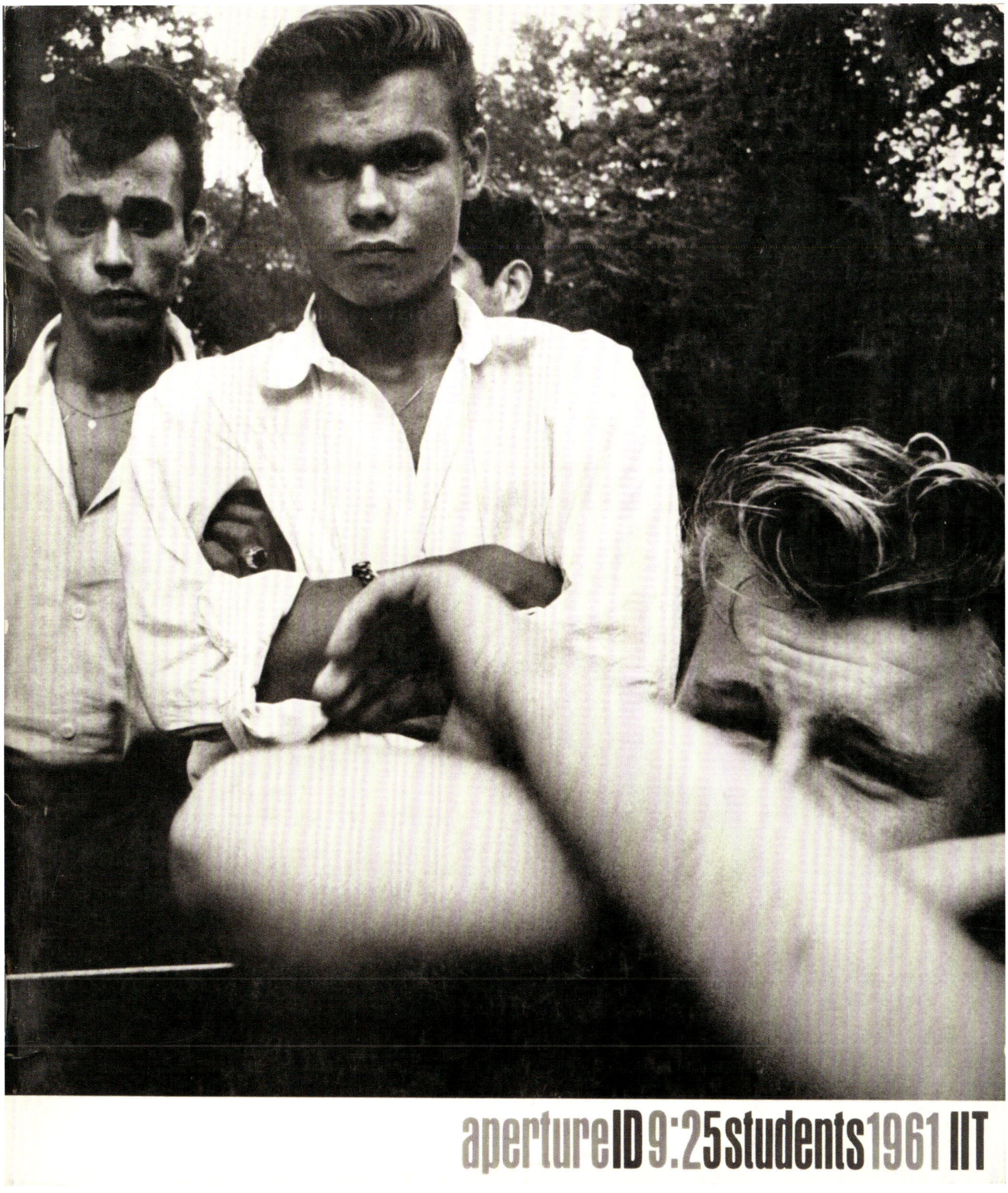
apertureID 9:25students1961 IIT

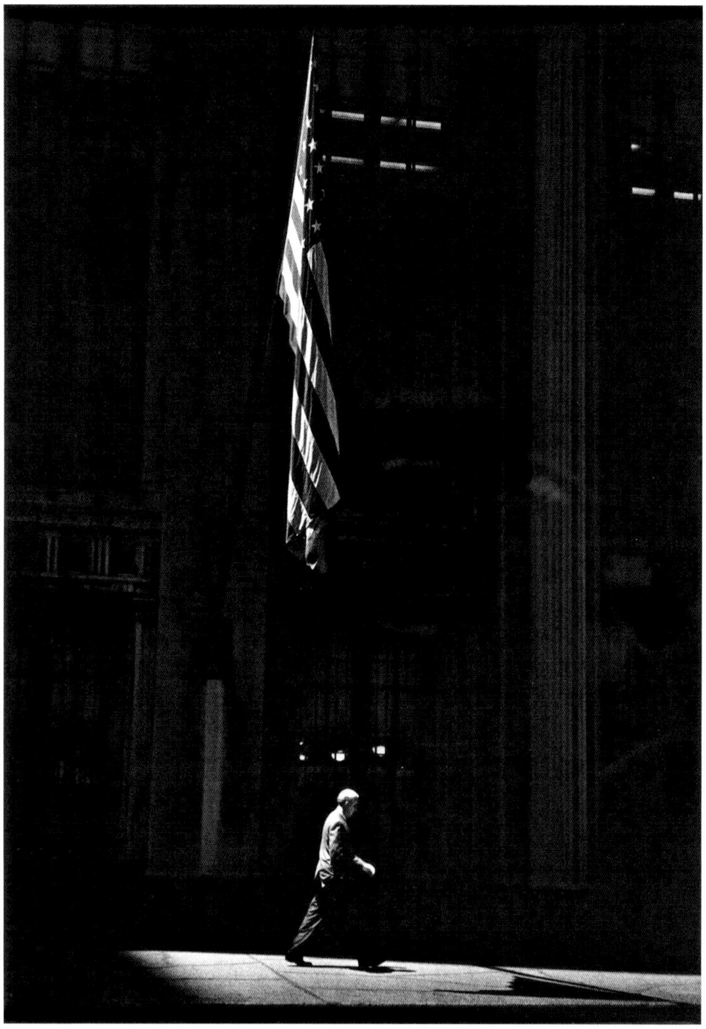

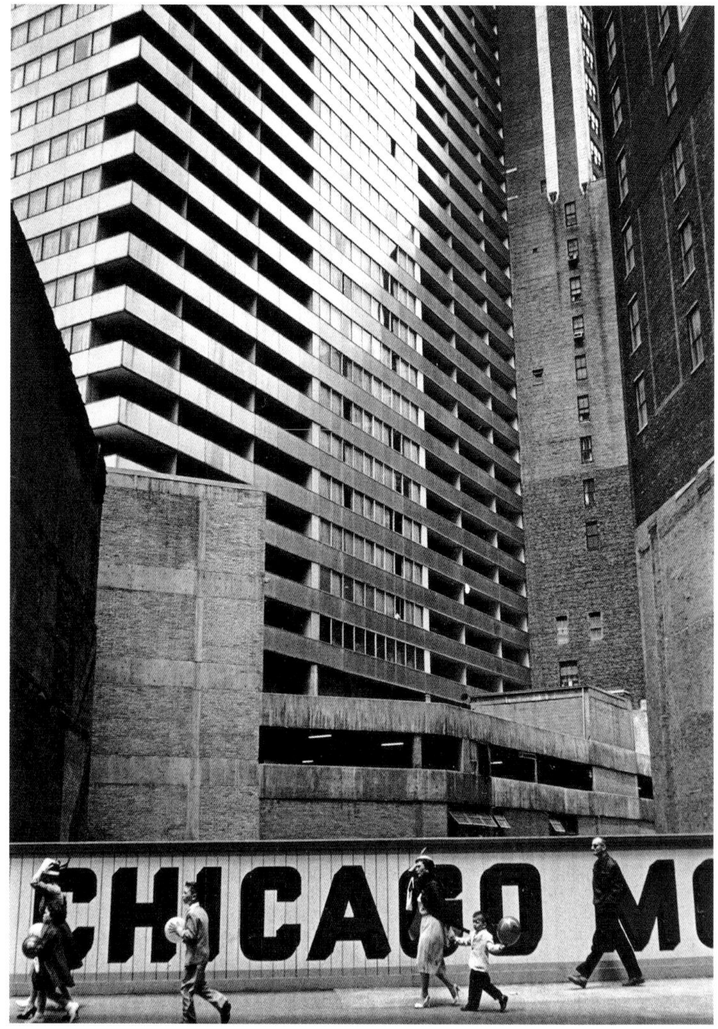

Yasuhiro Ishimoto
Untitled, from the series *Chicago, Chicago*, ca. 1960
gelatin silver, 35.6 x 27.9 cm each

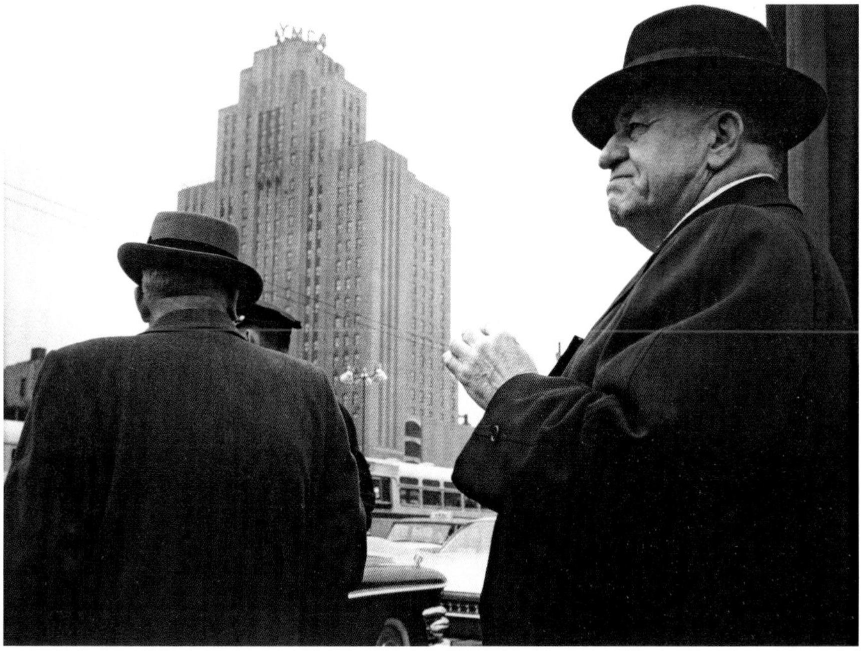

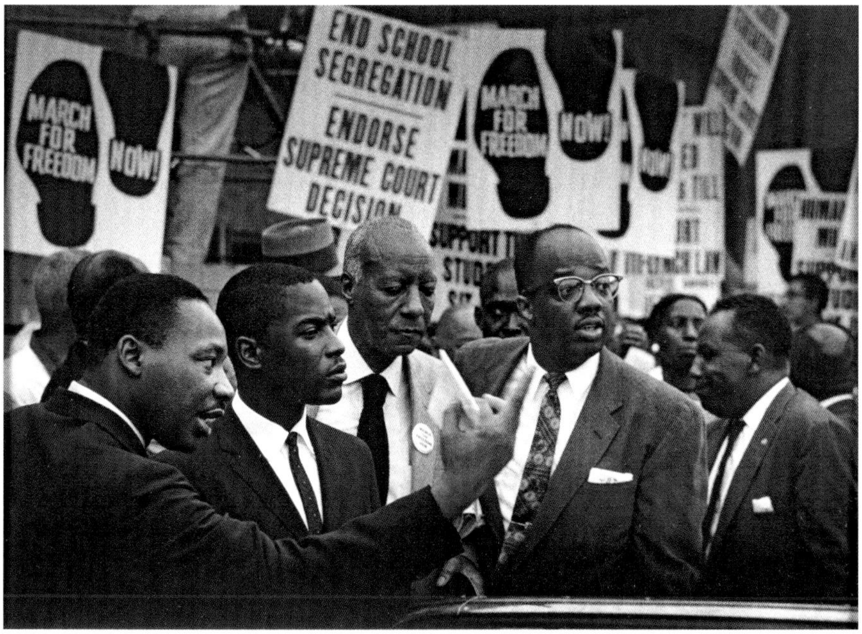

Yasuhiro Ishimoto
Untitled (b.: Martin Luther King jr.),
from the series *Chicago, Chicago*, ca. 1960
gelatin silver, 27.9 x 35.6 cm each

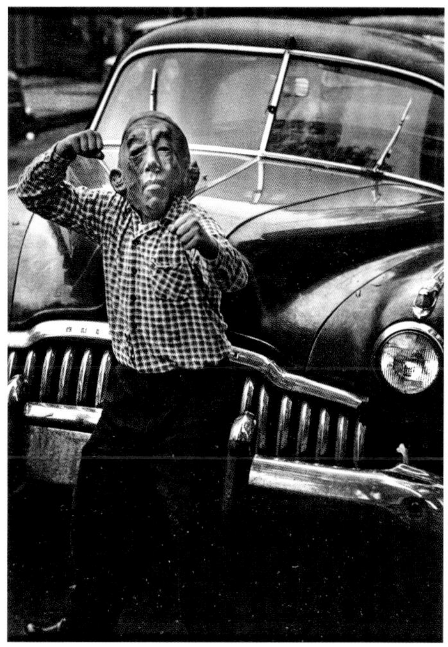

Yasuhiro Ishimoto
Untitled, from the series *Chicago, Chicago*, ca. 1960
gelatin silver, 35.6 x 27.9 cm

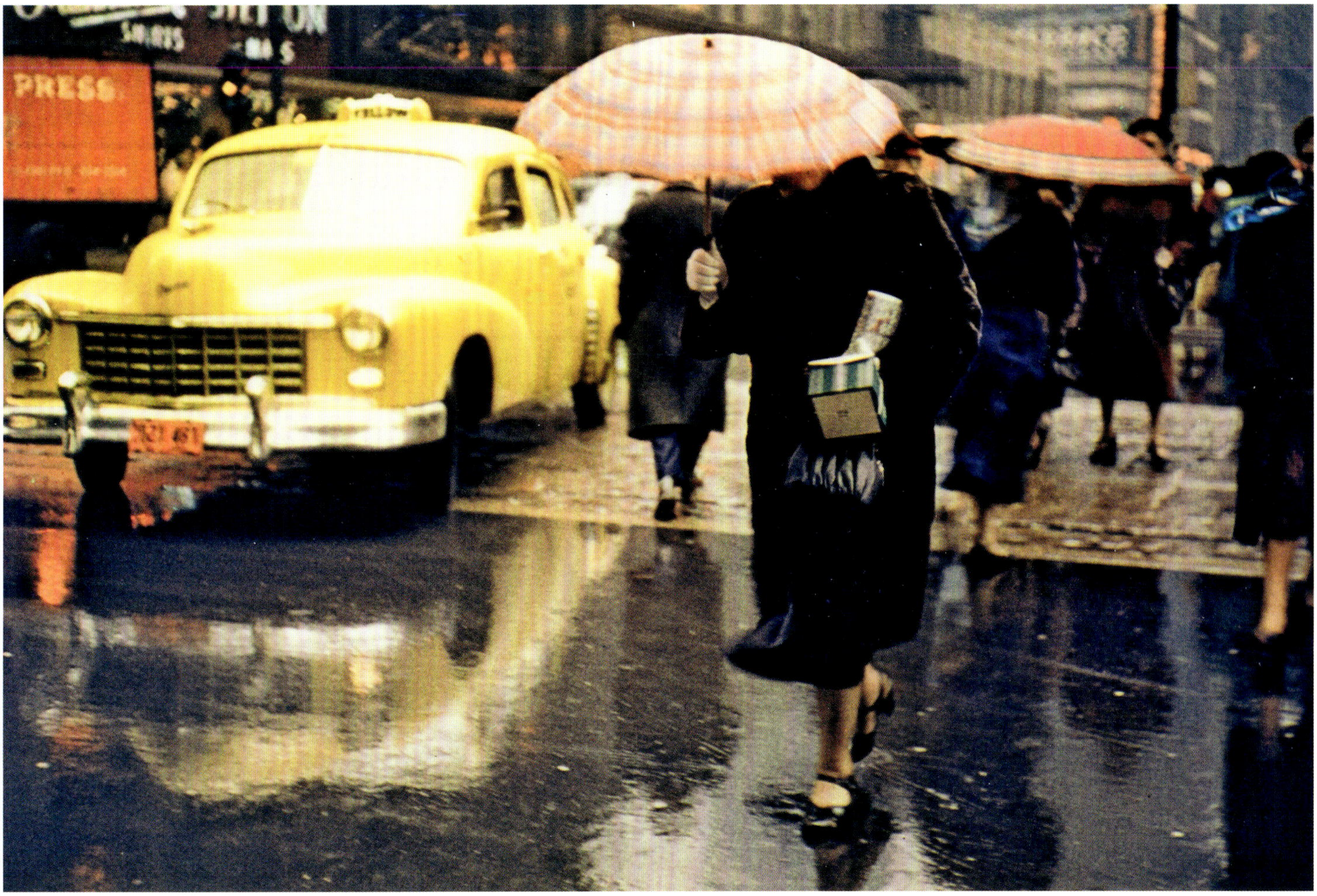

Arthur Siegel
Yellow Cabs, from the series *State Street*
1951–54
dye imbibition, 25.4 x 16.8 cm

Arthur Siegel
Rainy Day, from the series *State Street*, 1952
dye imbibition, 17.1 x 26 cm

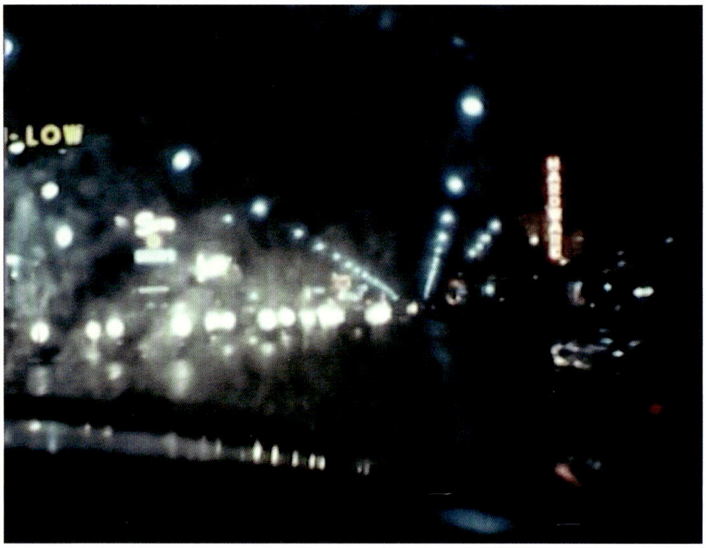
LOW

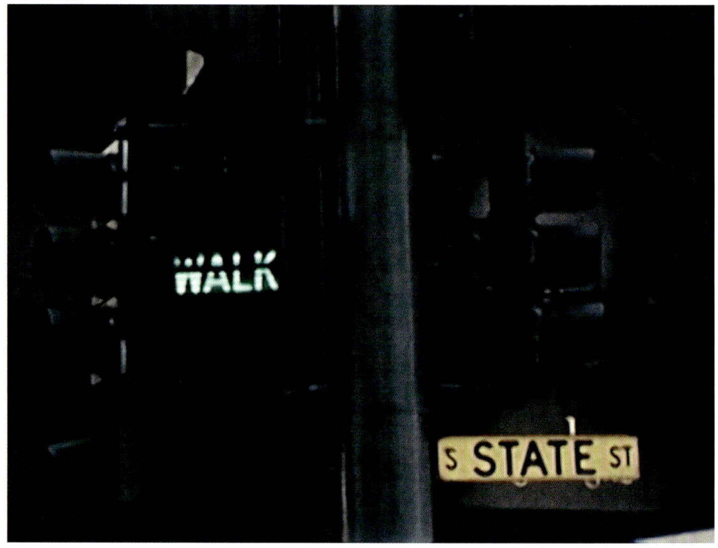
WALK
S STATE ST

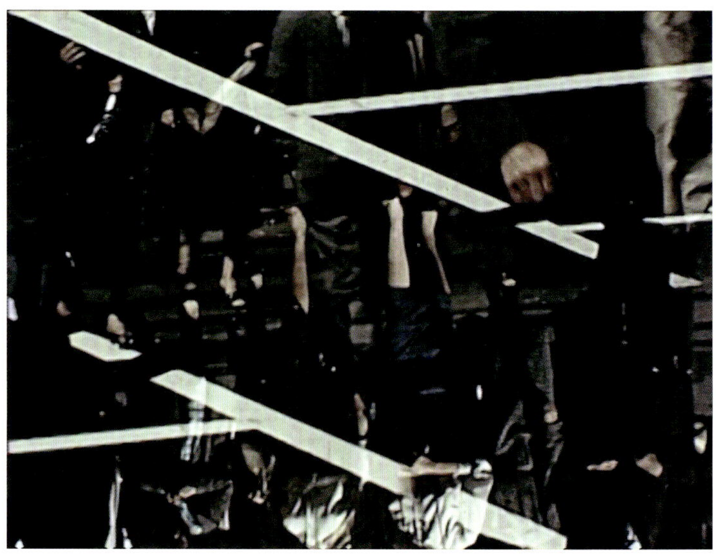

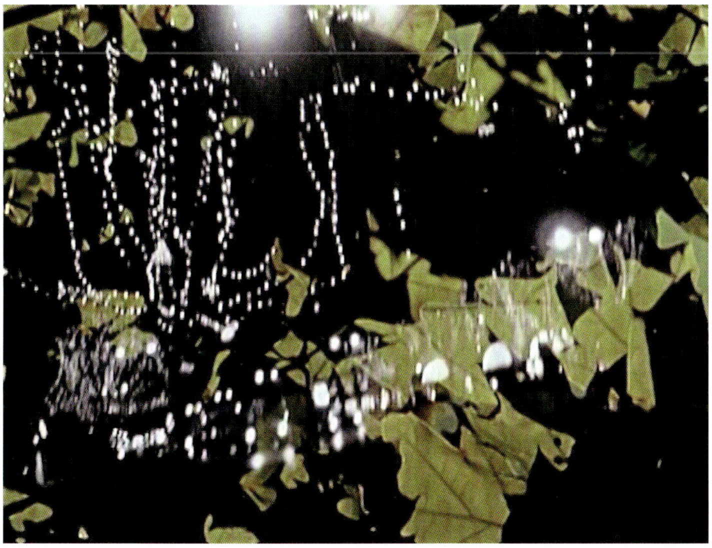

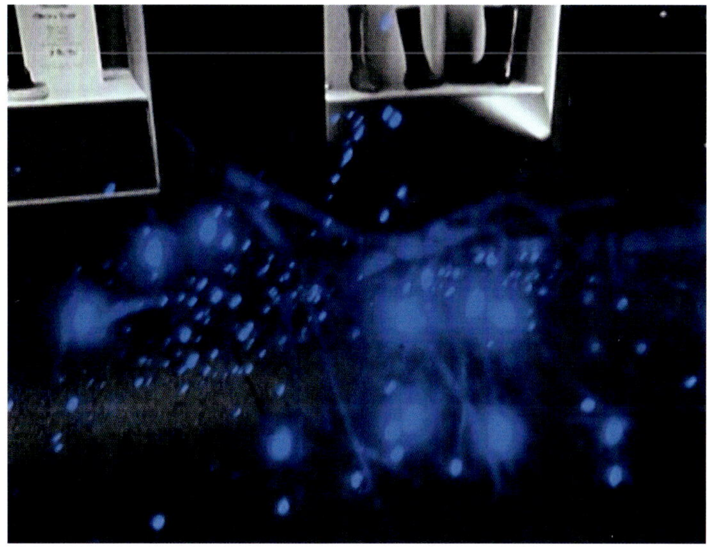

Robert Stiegler
Traffic, 1958
images from the digitized film

Larry Janiak
Adam's Film, 1963
images from the digitized film

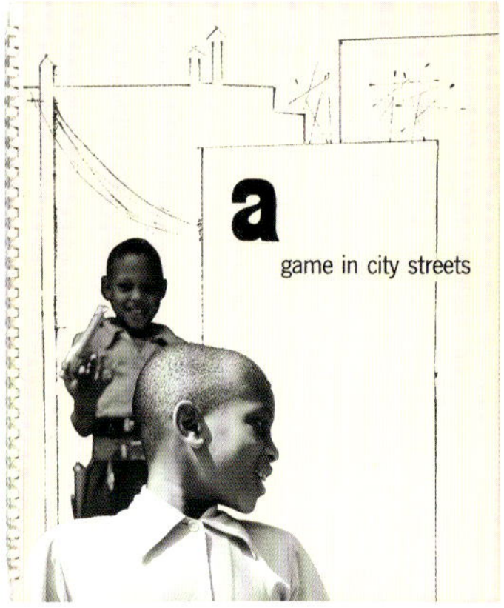

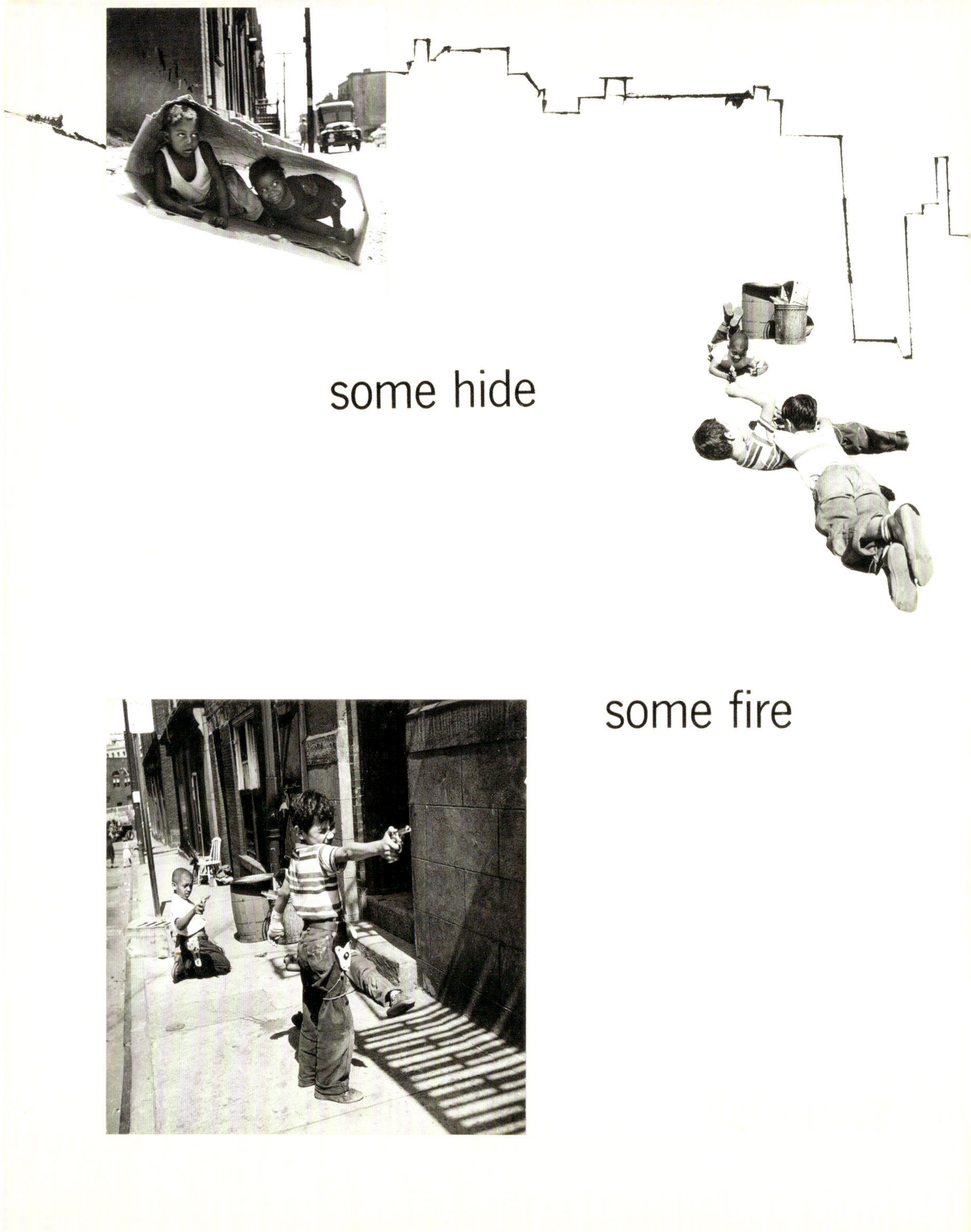

Else Tholstrup
A Game in City Streets, 1952
book maquette with six pages,
gelatin silver prints and ink on cardboard,
42.6 x 36 cm, cover and interior pages

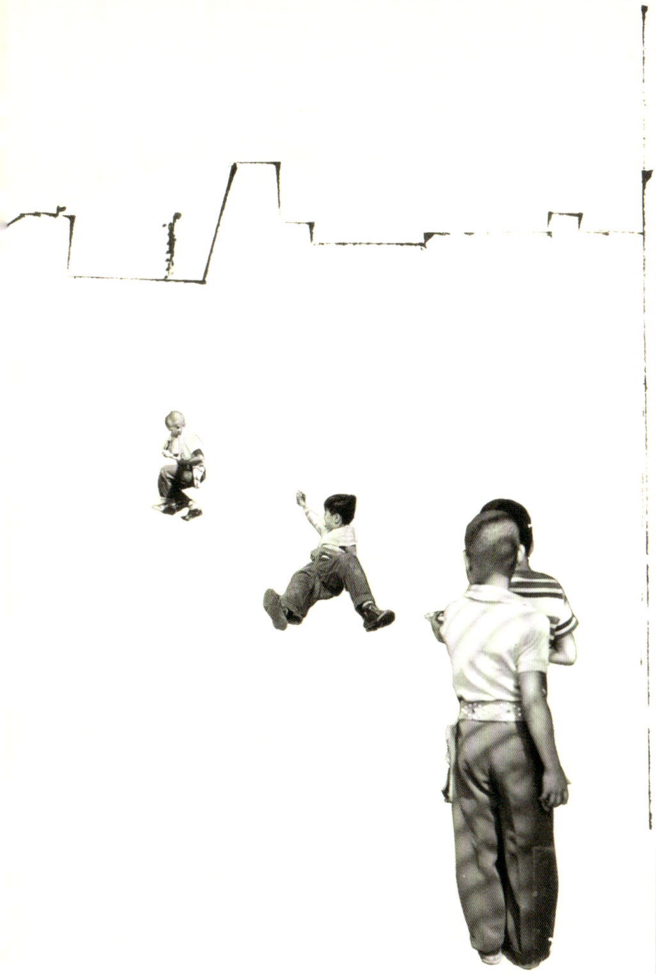

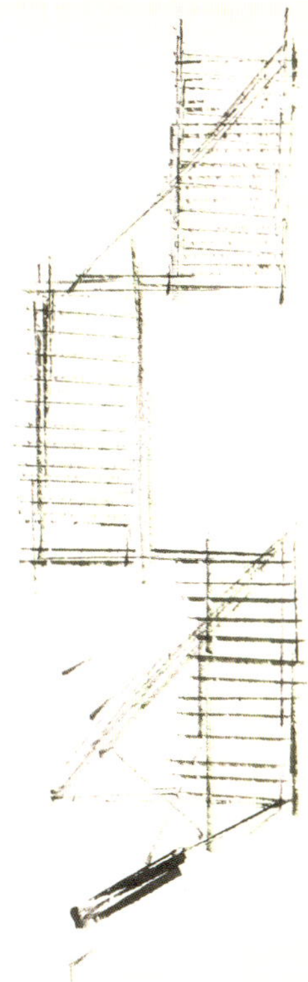

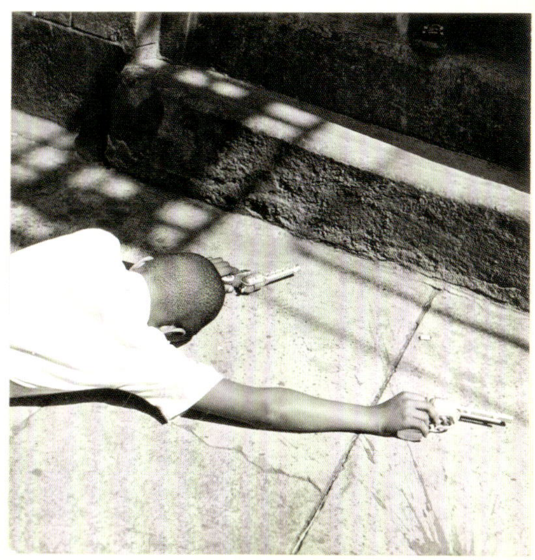

some fall

NEW PICTURES FROM CHICAGO

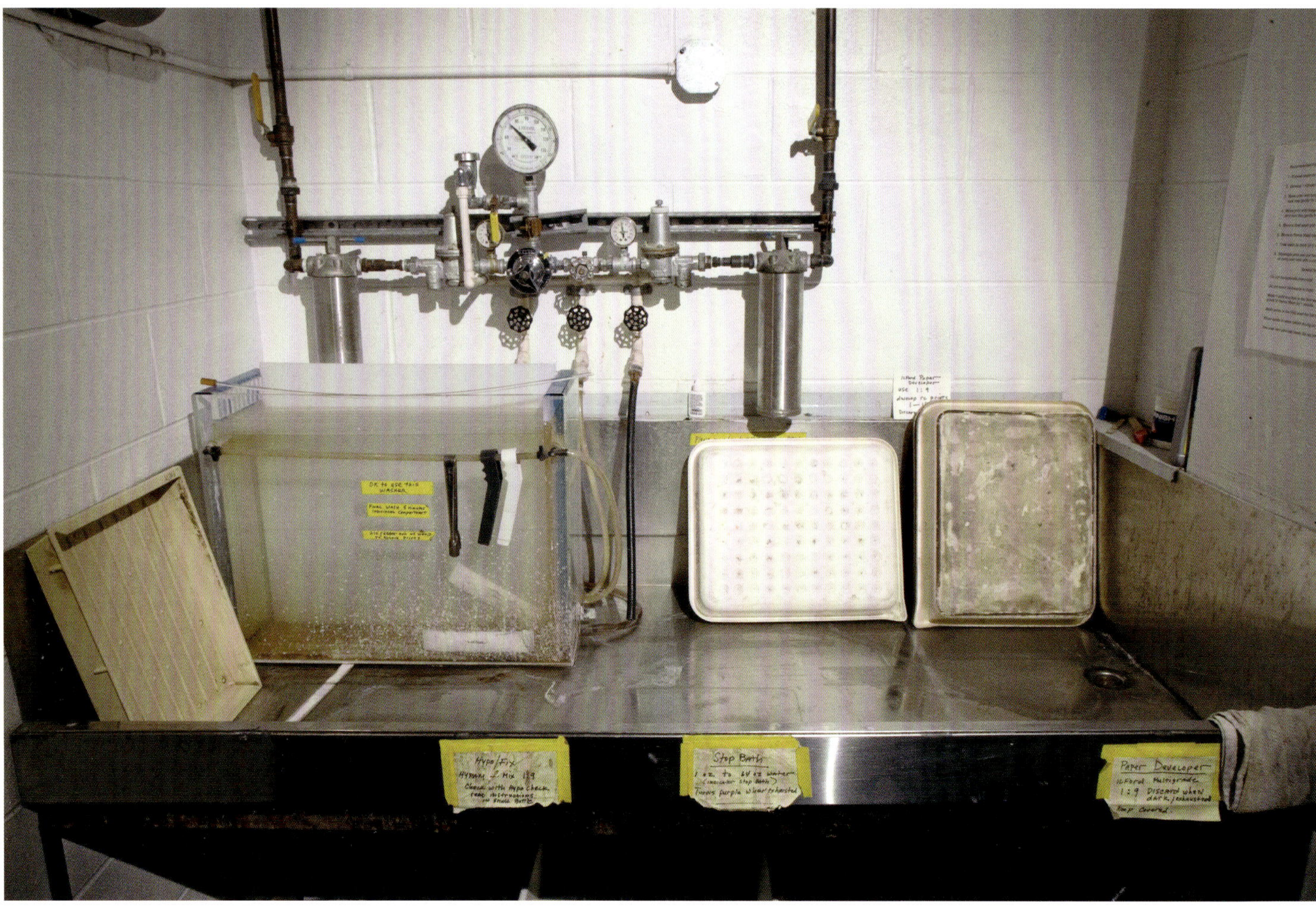

Kristina Lowis

Doug Fogelson
IIT's dark room shortly before its demolition, 2014
archival ink-jet print, 29.1 x 45 cm

Setting out from the premise that the *New Vision*[1] has become a *Lasting Vision*[2] over the last eighty years, the question of potential links to contemporary photography arises. Are there any characteristic aspects of the photography program at the New Bauhaus and Institute of Design that can be identified today? Freedom and naturalness in the photographic production of images, the recognition of individual inquiries and formal elements, the pleasure taken in pursuing a creative idea and in the concept? Do the phenomenology of light and the particularities of the photographic medium still play a role? Are technical and material experiments still being done at all in the digital era? Are relationships to forms and spaces being constructed photographically?

Attempts to establish connections between historical impulses and a specific contemporary work often harbor the risk of arbitrariness. The photography of artists working in the lineage of graduates from the Institute of Design, many of whom became instructors, is also thoroughly diverse,[3] widely dispersed, and can no longer be associated solely with this school. The following selection has been geographically limited to Chicago: the city where everything began. These six aesthetically independent positions are to be understood as examples offering conceivable parallels, retrospective references, and reformulations related to several of the photographic approaches presented in this catalogue.[4]

1 The often cited title of László Moholy-Nagy's final book and of the first major photo event at the ID was adopted from the European New Vision; see the first essay in this book.
2 The thesis providing the title of the exhibition *A Lasting Vision: Photographs from the Institute of Design 1970–2001*, shown at the IIT in the summer of 2015 with mostly works by graduates and instructors of the 1970s and 1980s.
3 We can also call to mind a number of artists who have dealt with the legacy of Moholy-Nagy by way of concrete appropriation, for example, Liz Deschenes, Jan Tichy, Barbara Kasten, and Floris Neusüss.
4 The selection was subject to the criterion that the photographers must currently be working in Chicago. It was based on the 2016 exhibition *Workshop in Light and Color: The Legacy of the New Bauhaus in Chicago* as well as the collection and expertise of the Museum of Contemporary Photography in Chicago. I would thus like to express my immense gratitude to the two curators Ashley Lumb, from the Hemera Collective, and Karen Irvine, from the Museum of Contemporary Photography in Chicago, for their advice and support.

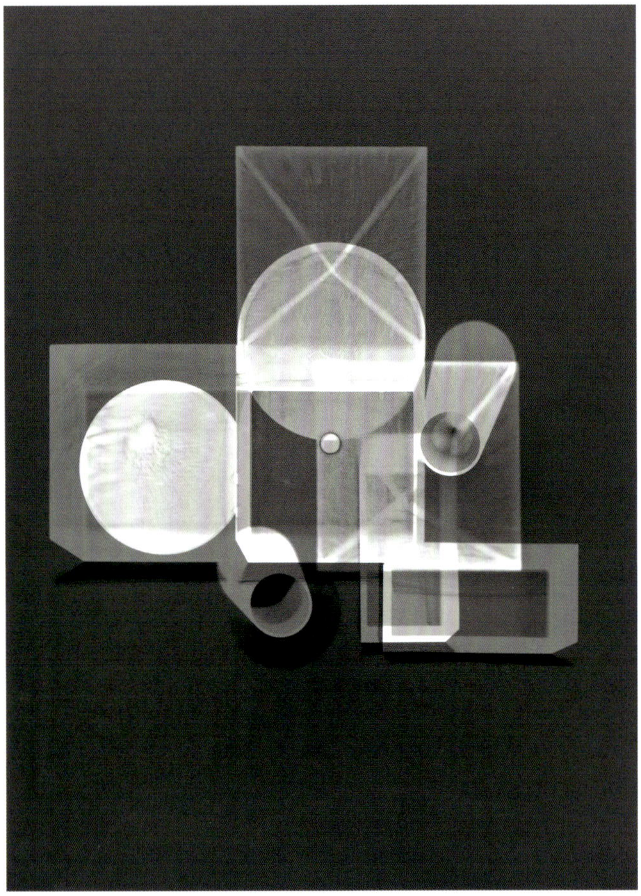

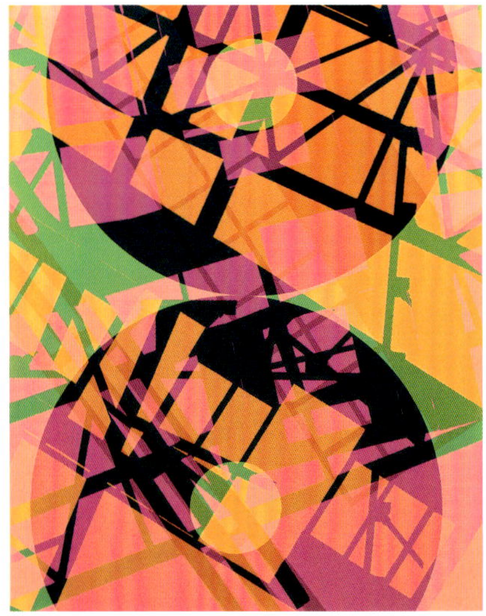

Doug Fogelson
Forms and Records No. 8, 2014
photogram, gelatin silver, 50.8 x 40.6 cm

Doug Fogelson
Forms and Records No. 8, 2014
photogram, color transparency, 25.4 x 20.3 cm

Doug Fogelson (*1970)
took a closer look at the physical historicity of the ID in 2014, when he photographically documented the photo school's soon-to-be-destroyed darkroom in the IIT campus's Crown Hall. It was also here that he used an analog technique to create color and black-and-white photograms dealing with the theme of storage media's obsolescence: He employed architectural models disposed of at the IIT, record singles, film and audio reels from the 1950s, and the support material itself as the subjects of his images. With the title *Forms and Records*, he points to concepts of recording, forming, documenting, and impermanence. Deliberately commenting from a position of historical distance, he recurs back to the foundations of light composition.

Raquel Ladensack Voakes (*1979)
fixes her attention on light itself, in a minimalist manner. In her work, which corresponds to a processual inching forward, she forms and then repeatedly photographs paper volumes until she recognizes the almost immaterial landscape she had been imagining. She experiments with a high-tech material designed for research into the refraction of light (*Aero Glow*): Enlarged many times over and standing in the tradition of research into light and color, it becomes the richly historically allusive subject of a photograph. She describes her approach as a learning process. Often she makes use of extremely diverse dimensions and materials, and she creates a controlled environment for her photos, like an experimental apparatus or a specially created "light box".

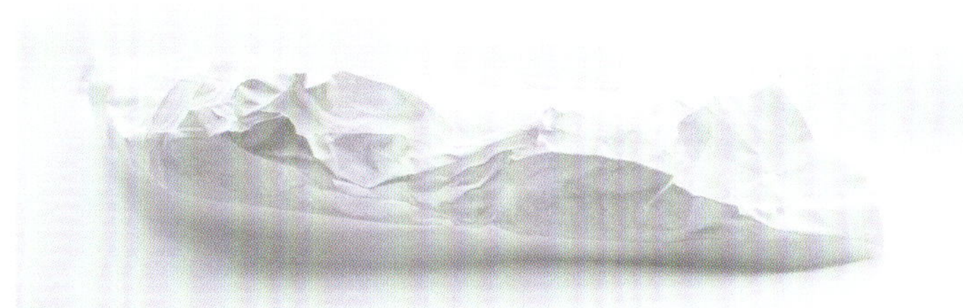

Raquel Ladensack Voakes
Paper Wave, 2010
archival ink-jet print, 33 x 50.8 cm

Raquel Ladensack Voakes
Aero Glow, 2016
archival ink-jet print, 70.5 x 50.8 cm

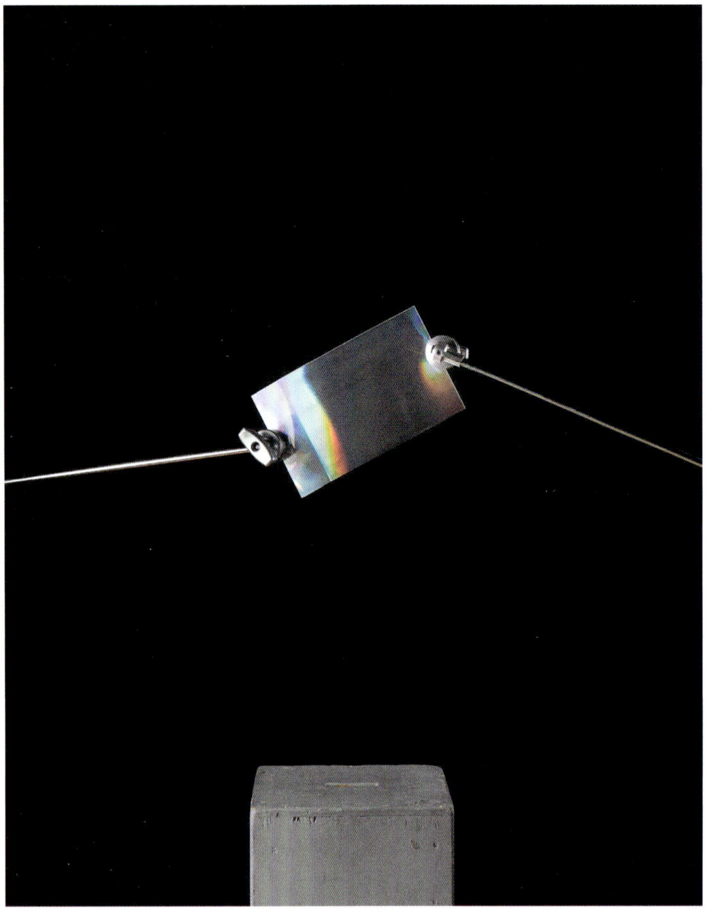

Sonja Thomsen
Construct, 2013
archival ink-jet print, 106.9 x 86.4 cm

Sonja Thomsen
Opticks 123, 2015
archival ink-jet print, 16.5 x 22.9 cm

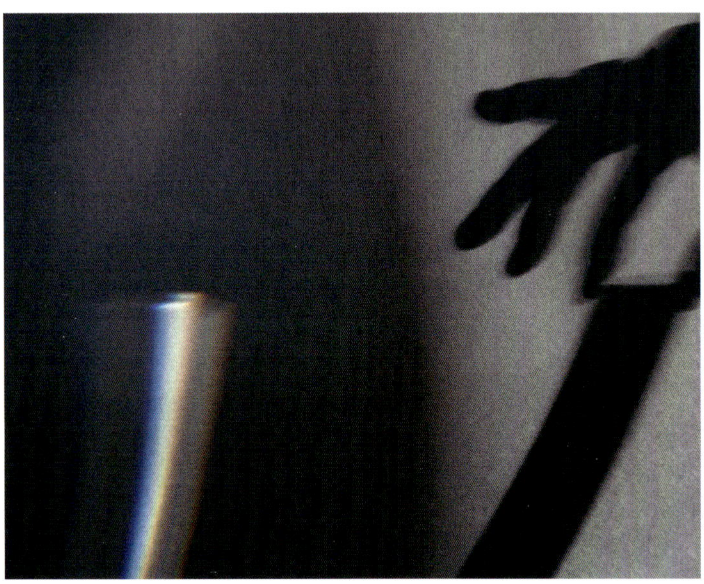

Sonja Thomsen (*1978)
prefers to utilize photography as a conduit for additional sequences of works in other media, such as prints, books, objects, and installations, which she sometimes once again captures with the camera, thus inscribing them within a cycle. She is committed to a generative process. In a number of works, she seeks to literally get hold of light: In seemingly scientific views she explores refracted light, sharp focus, and blurriness, while the repeatedly represented gesture stands for a literal desire to grasp. Mirrors, shadows, and transparencies simultaneously merge the layers of the images together. In her artist's book *You'll Find It Where It Is*, whose title also heralds a search, she additionally appropriates a passage from *Vision in Motion*—Moholy-Nagy's textbook, which she still makes use of today in her work as a photography instructor.

Clarissa Bonet (*1986)
carries on the tradition of the photographic experience of urban space (particularly in the work of Ray K. Metzker) in a decidedly contemporary manner. Her images present a meta level of the encounter between light, built environment, and passersby, because her striking photographs are meticulously reconstructed on the basis of her own observations. Light effects reveal an additional dimension here: as shimmering, blazing, palely overwhelming volumes, they provide the interpretive key. Upon closer inspection, Bonet's sparkling, nocturnal, window-filled landscapes reveal themselves to be composites of multiple buildings, frustrating any voyeuristic urge. As artifacts, they point to the photographer's complete control and the marginality of the documentary aspect.

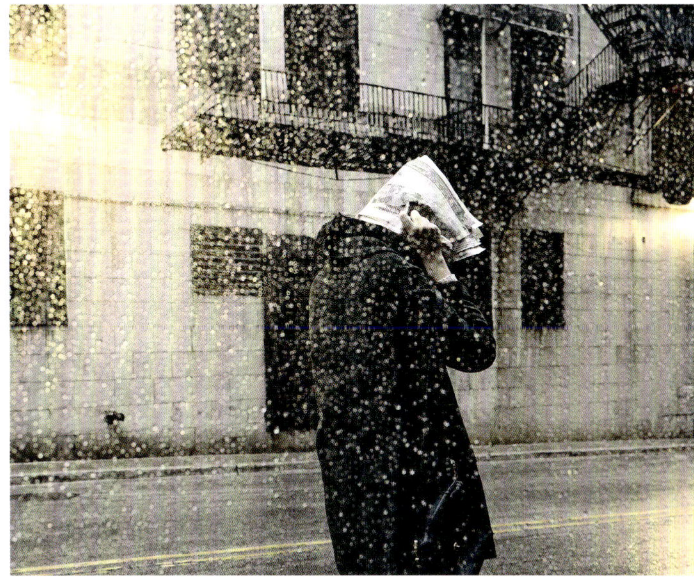

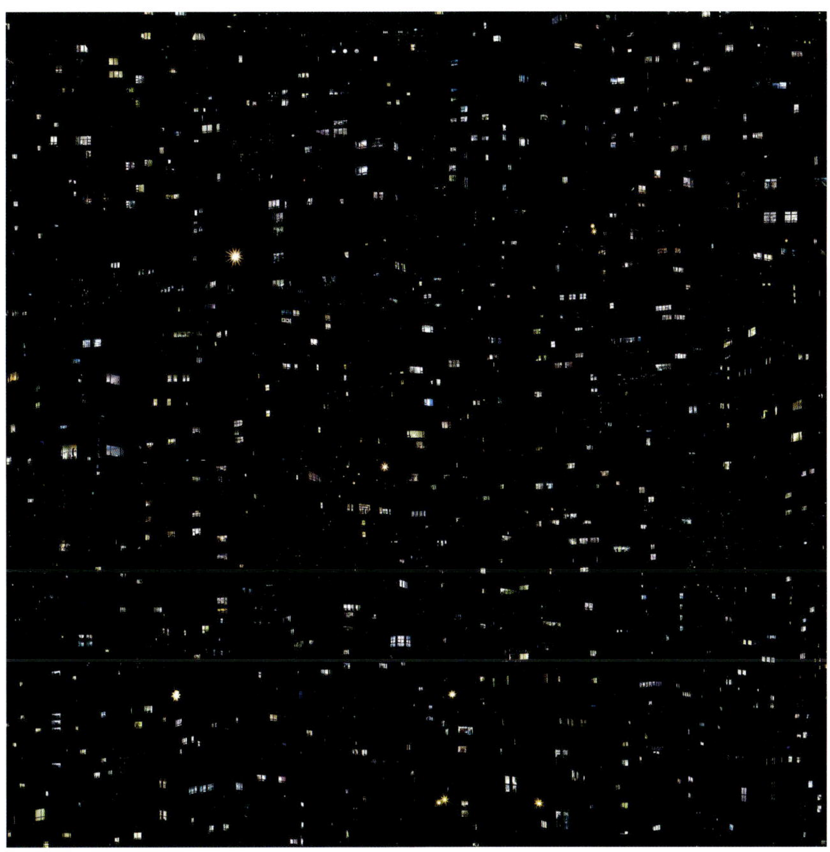

Clarissa Bonet
Caught in the Storm,
from the series *City Space*, 2011
pigment print, 61 x 76 cm

Clarissa Bonet
SL.2015.0608 Chicago,
from the series *Stray Light*, 2015
pigment print, 100 x 100 cm

Assaf Evron (*1977)
uses an infrared camera to record the beams emitted by a device that provides spatial orientation while playing computer games ("X-Box Kinect"). The subjects of his images include mirrors and glass volumes—favorite motifs among classic modern photographers. The new technology probes invisible processes' potential for depiction. Who or what perceives the objects in the purple glow of his works? The zeros and ones in the brain of the computer? The hand of a player within the virtual reality? The eye of the beholder, who is unable to recognize the views as photographs? What materiality, what level of reality allows itself to be recognized in them? At any rate, the depicted objects certainly no longer correspond to the representational images of traditional photographs.

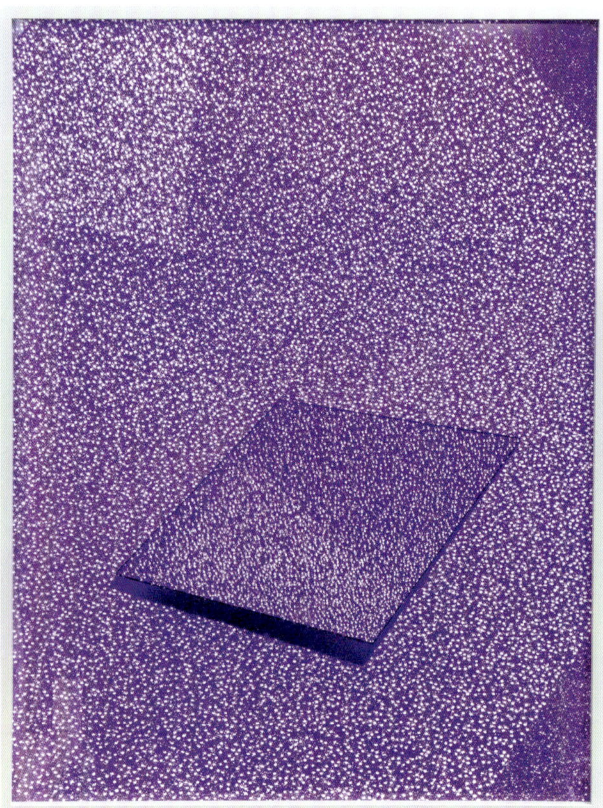

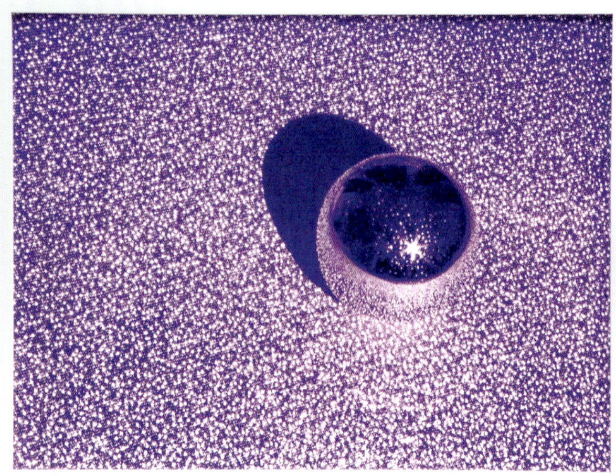

Assaf Evron
CRW-0335, 2015
archival ink-jet print, 114.3 x 86.4 cm

Assaf Evron
CRW-0135-1, 2015
archival ink-jet print, 48 x 63.5 cm

Amy Yoes (*1959)
likes to convey cooperative working methods as an art instructor, and she realized her animated film *Raft* in a team. It plays with our visual experience of abstract geometrical forms: She filmed the multicolored shadows of a Plexiglas-and-wood sculpture installed in a field, shooting the projected shapes at regular intervals over several days. Through the effects of sunlight, wind and weather, the completed version of the film undermines our expectations of a clinically sterile, abstract form and about the dimensions of the model, which could have been produced digitally on a computer. The simplicity of the material and the enjoyment of analog surprises in the only ostensibly digital image reveal an intentional departure from familiar forms of design.

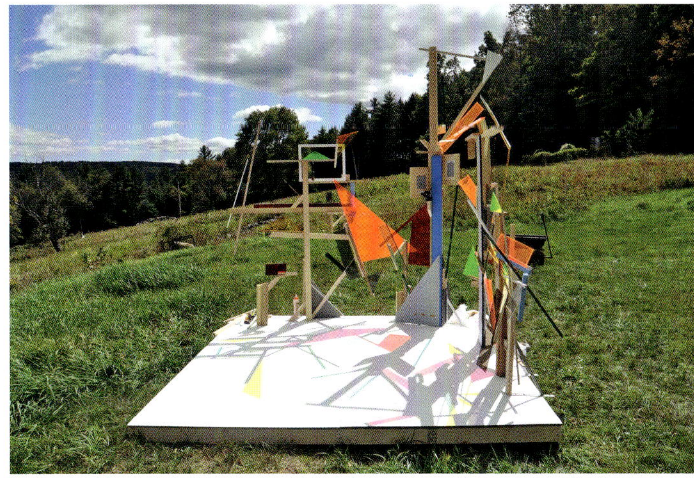

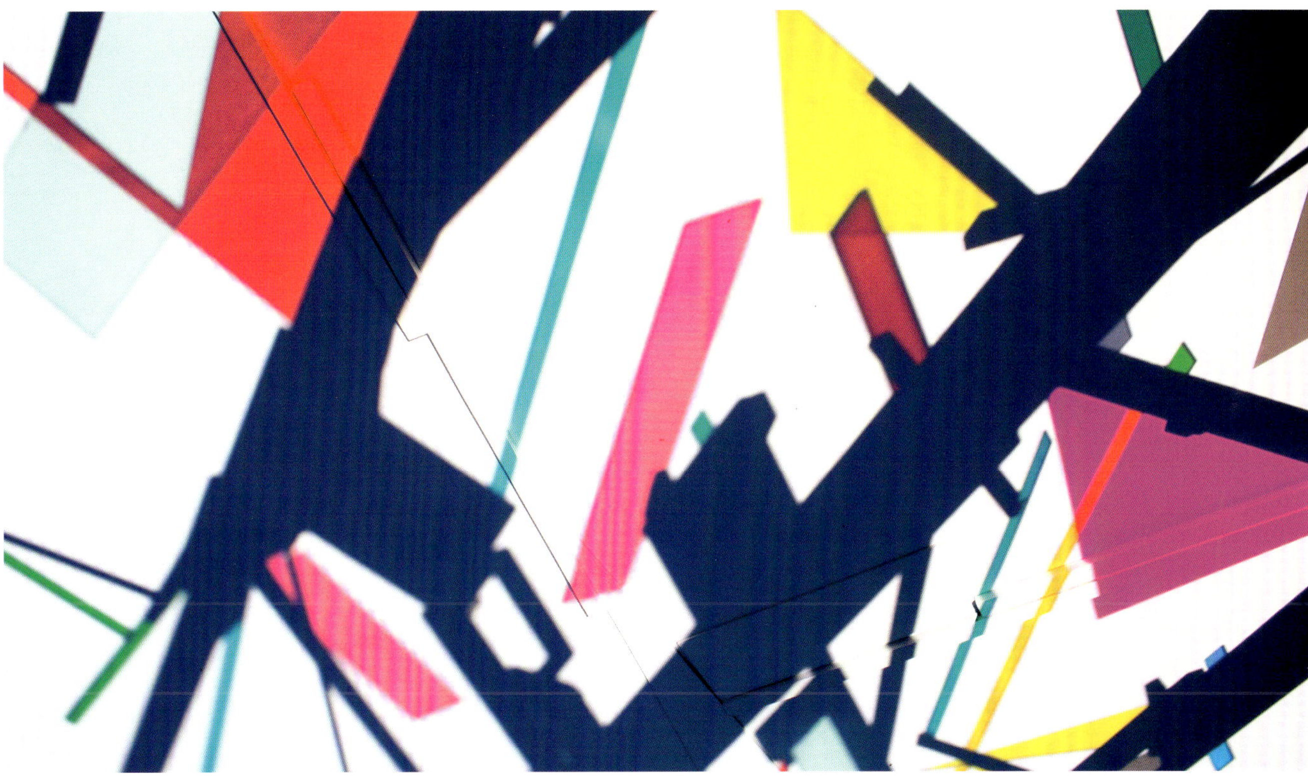

Amy Yoes
Plexiglas-and-wood sculpture for *Raft*, 2012

Amy Yoes
image from the animated film *Raft*, 2012

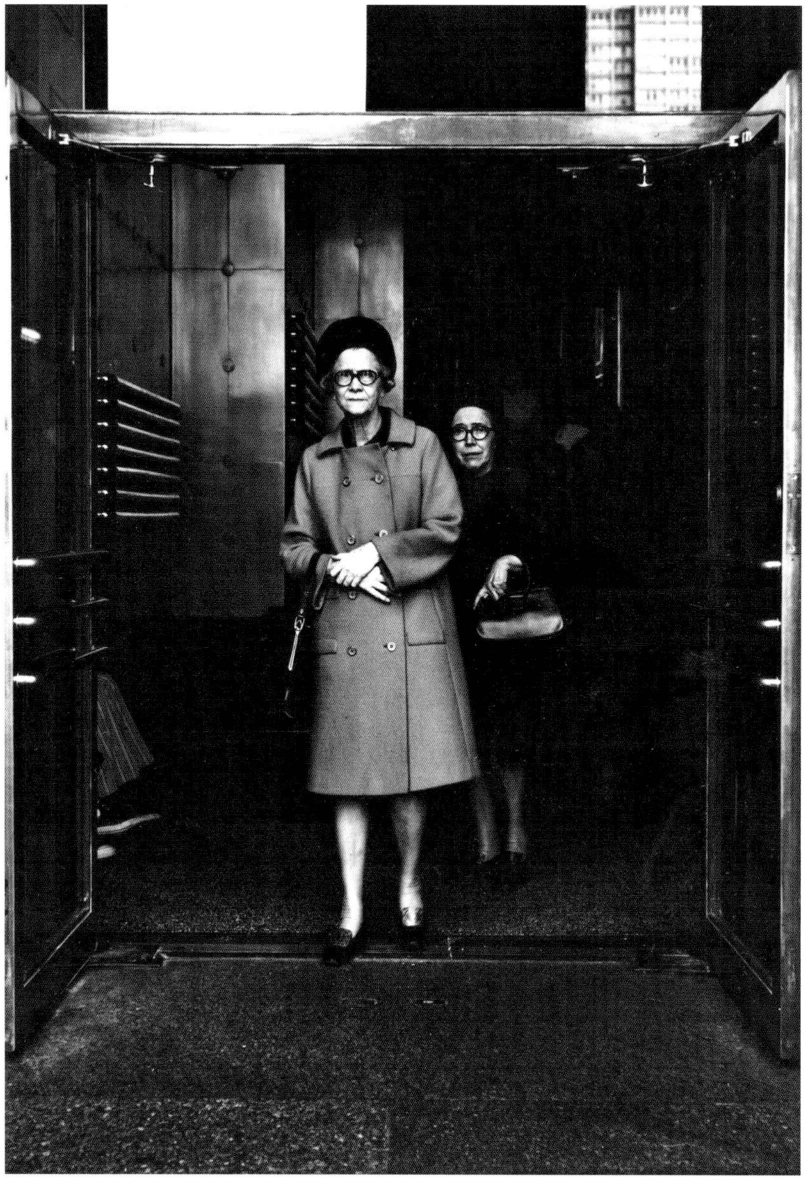

Barbara Crane
People of the North Portal, 1970
gelatin silver, 34.9 x 27.3 cm each

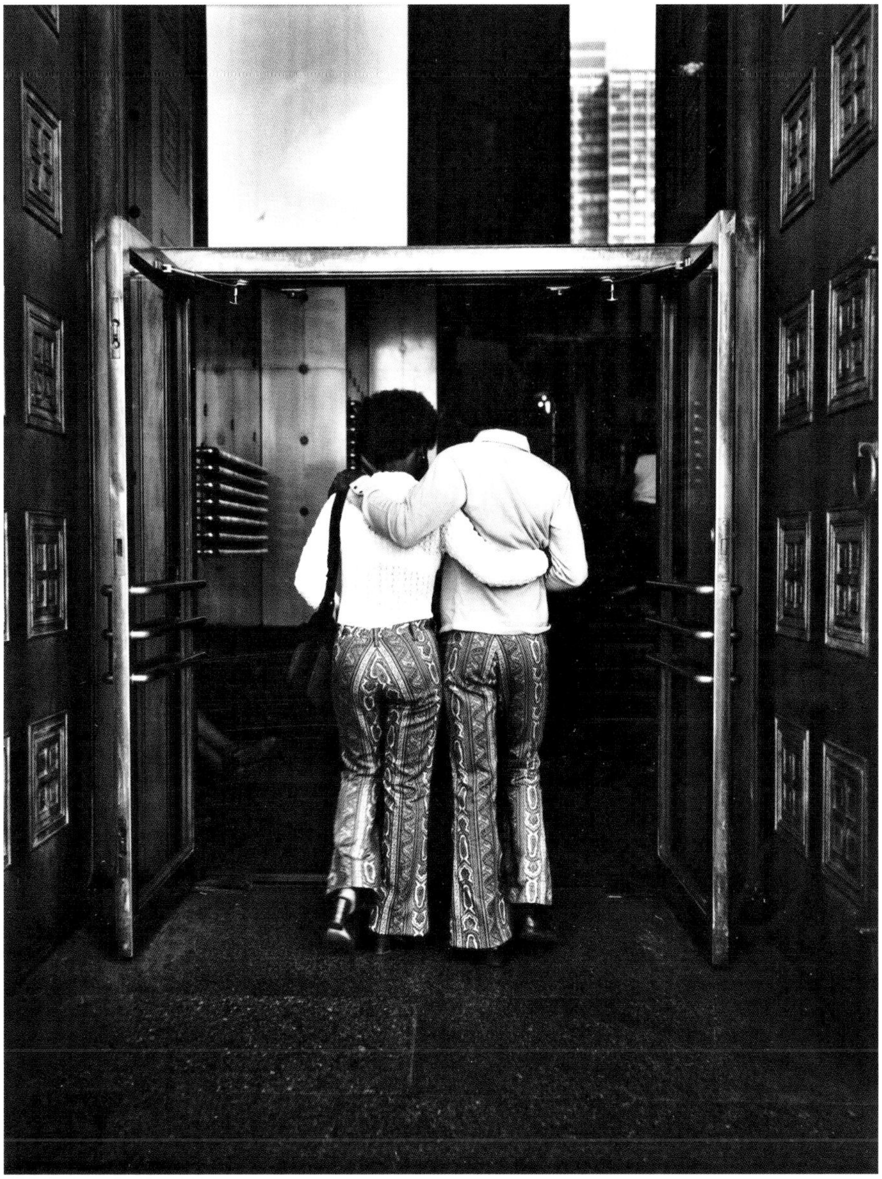

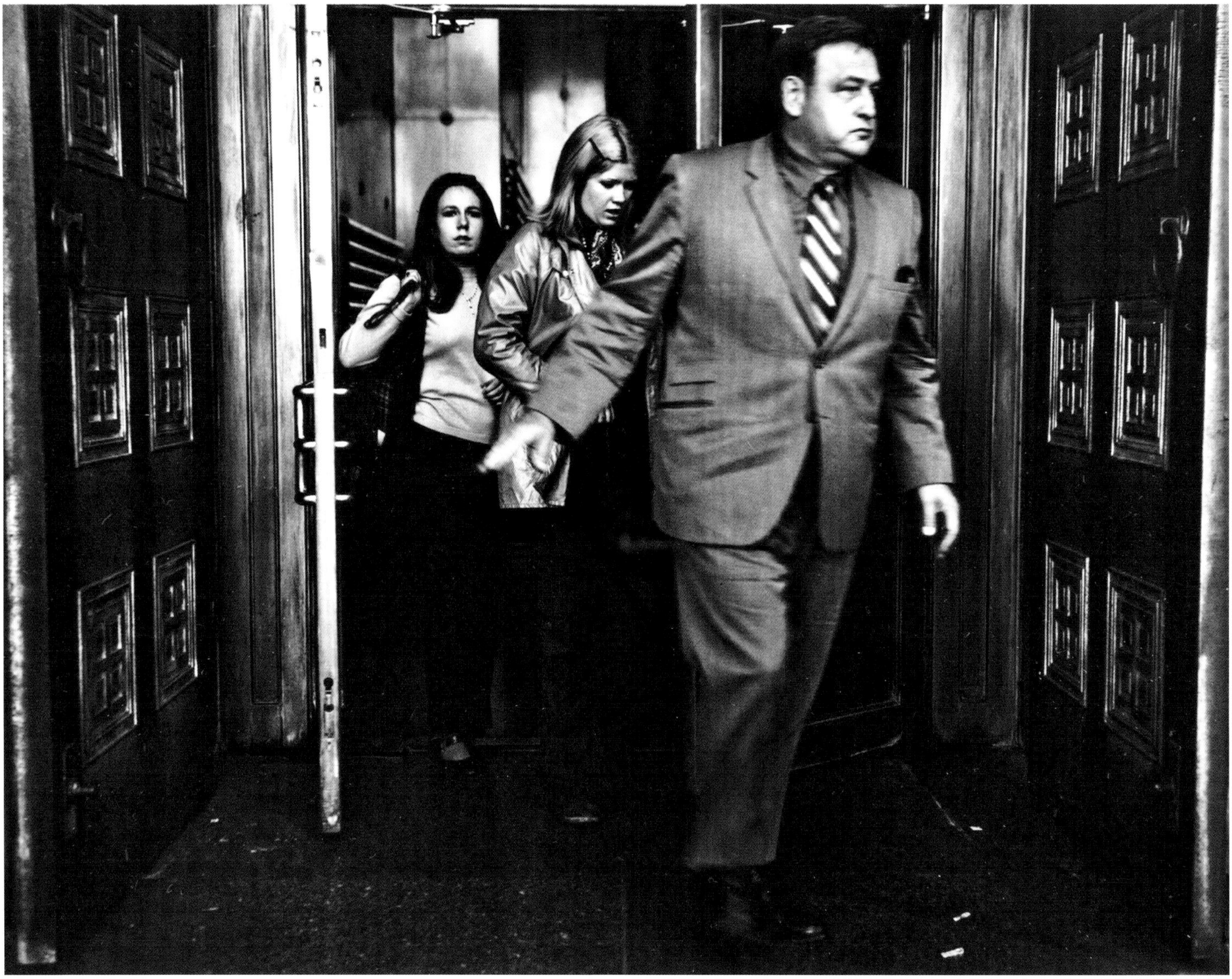

Barbara Crane
People of the North Portal, 1970
gelatin silver, l.: 27.3 x 34.9 cm, r.: 27.9 x 35.5 cm

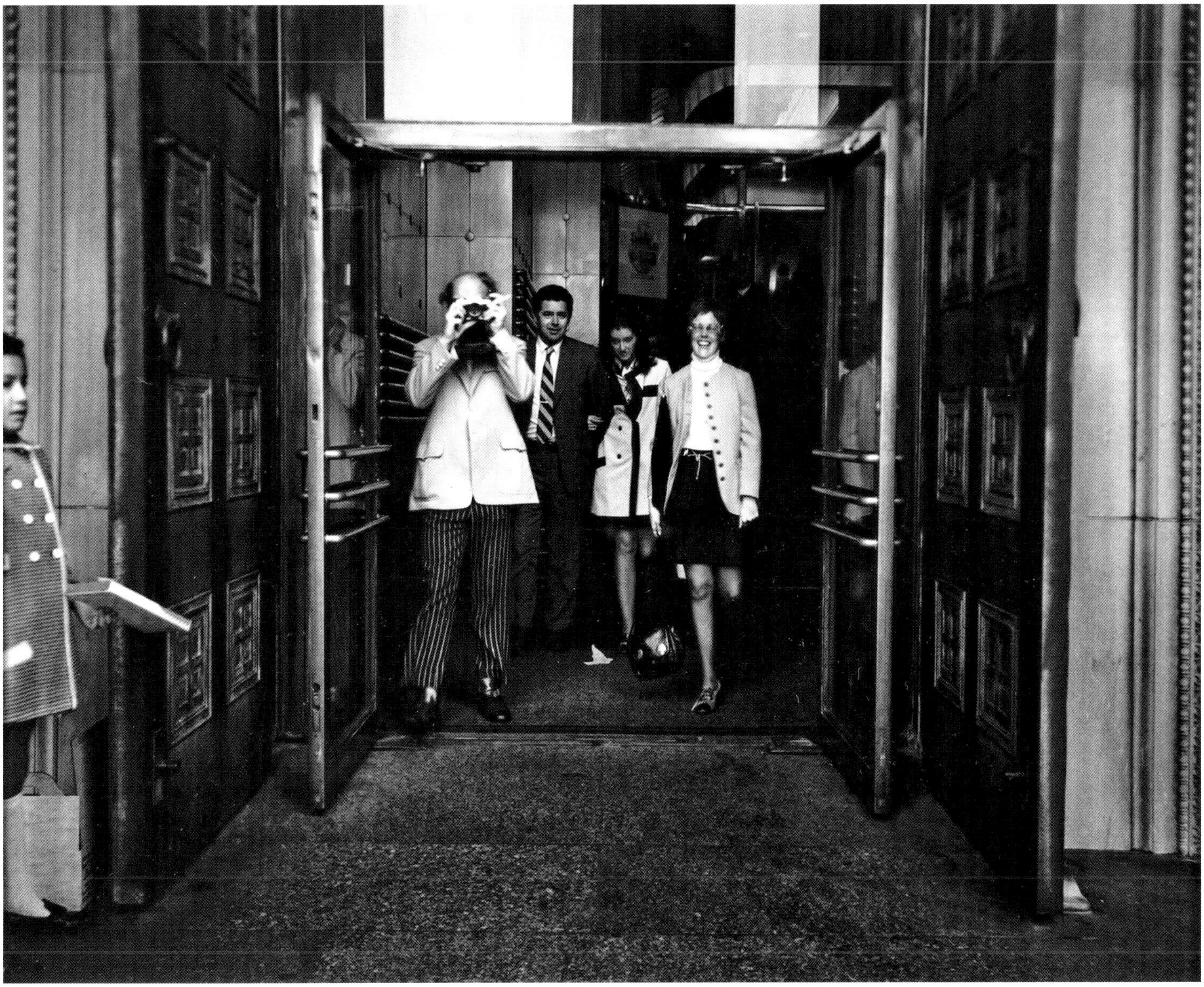

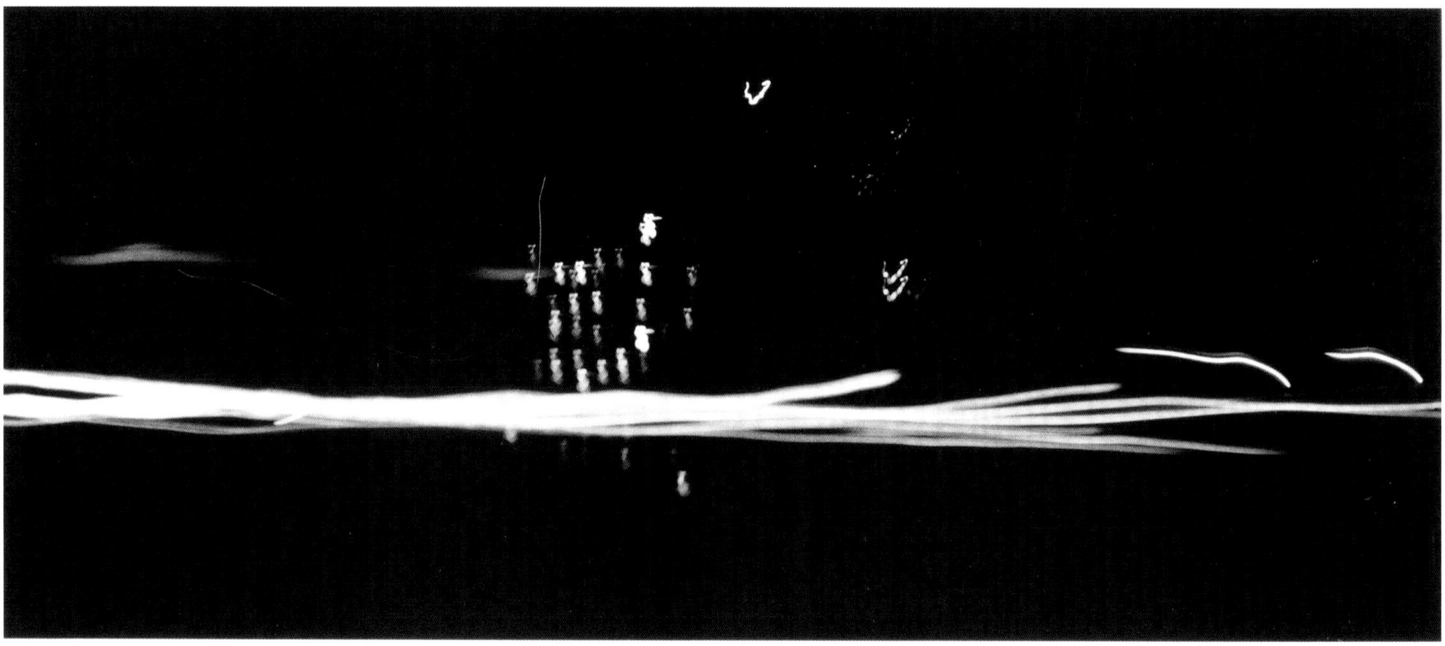

Nathan Lerner
Light Landscape, 1938, later print
gelatin silver, 18.7 x 43.5 cm

INDIVIDUALS MENTIONED IN CATALOGUE

The following overview lists the names and dates of birth and death of teachers and alumni related to photography at the New Bauhaus and Institute of Design mentioned in this catalogue.

BIBLIOGRAPHY

50 Jahre New Bauhaus 1987
Hahn, Peter, and Lloyd C. Engelbrecht, eds. *50 Jahre New Bauhaus: Bauhaus-Nachfolge in Chicago*. Exh. cat.: Bauhaus-Archiv / Museum für Gestaltung, Berlin. Berlin: Argon, 1987.

A

A Lasting Vision 2015
Kostiner, Anne Neri, ed. *A Lasting Vision*: Photographs from the Institute of Design 1970–2001. Exh. cat.: Illinois Institute of Technology Chicago. Chicago, 2015.

Aaron Siskind 1955
Pollack, Peter. *Aaron Siskind*. Exh. brochure: Art Institute of Chicago. Chicago, 1955.

Aaron Siskind 1965
Siskind, Aaron. *Aaron Siskind, Photographer*. Exh. cat.: George Eastman House. Rochester: Horizon Press, 1965.

Abstrakte Fotografie 2000
Kellein, Thomas, and Angela Lampe, eds. *Abstrakte Fotografie*. Exh. cat.: Kunsthalle Bielefeld. Ostfildern: Hatje Cantz, 2000.

Accordion book ca. 1989
Institute of Design. Chicago, n.d. [ca. 1989].

Albers and Moholy-Nagy 2006
Borchardt-Hume, Achim, ed. *Albers and Moholy-Nagy: From the Bauhaus to the New World*. Exh. cat.: Tate Modern London / Kunsthalle Bielefeld / Whitney Museum of American Art, New York. London: Tate Publishing, 2006.

Allen 1983
Allen, James Sloan. *The Romance of Commerce and Culture: Capitalism, Modernism, and the Chicago-Aspen Crusade for Cultural Reform*. Chicago: University of Chicago Press, 1983.

American Horizons 2004
Keith, David F. *American Horizons: The Photographs of Art Sinsabaugh*. Exh. cat.: The Art Institute of Chicago / Columbus Museum of Art / Krannert Art Museum, Champaign / Indiana University Art Museum, Bloomington. New York: Hudson Hills Press, 2004.

Aperture Magazine Anthology 2012
Aperture Magazine Anthology – The Minor White Years, 1952–1976. ed. by Peter C. Bunnell. New York: Aperture, 2012.

Arthur Siegel 1954
Peter Pollack. *Arthur Siegel: Color Photographs*. Exh. brochure: Art Institute of Chicago. Chicago, 1954.

Arthur Siegel 1978
Porter, Allan. "Arthur Siegel." *Camera* 57, no. 2 (1978): 14–23.

Artner 2002
Artner, Alan. "Show Has Designs on Attention for Photographers." *Chicago Tribune*, March 10, 2002: 7–8.

AutoMagic 2009
AutoMagic: Ray K. Metzker. Berlin: Only Photography, 2009.

B

Bahlmann 2007
Bahlmann, Katrin. "La perception d'images d'un corps: Human Forms, Barbara Crane." PhD diss., Paris 8 Saint Denis, 2007.

Banks 1981
Banks, Ann, ed. *Aaron Siskind: Harlem Document; Photographs 1932–1940*. Providence, RI: Matrix Publications, 1981.

Bauhäusler in Amerika 1976
Bauhäusler in Amerika: Das Werk der Emigranten seit 1933. Exh. cat.: Bauhaus-Archiv Berlin. Berlin, 1974.

Bauhaus 1919–1938
Gropius, Walter, Ise Gropius, and Herbert Bayer, eds. *Bauhaus 1919–28*. Exh. cat.: Museum of Modern Art New York. New York: Graphic Society, 1938.

Bauhaus Dessau Chicago New York 2000
Költzsch, Georg-W., and Margarita Tupitsyn, eds. *Bauhaus Dessau Chicago New York*. Exh. cat.: Museum Folkwang Essen. Cologne: DuMont, 2000.

Bell/Traub 2015
Bell, Adam, and Charles Traub. *Vision Anew: The Lens and Screen Arts*. Oakland: University of California Press, 2015.

Bergdoll 2016
Bergdoll, Barry. "Memento mori or eternal modernism? The Bauhaus at MoMA, 1938." In *Tributes to Jean Michel Massing*, ed. by Mark Stocker and Phillip Lindley, 15–32. London: Turnhout, 2016.

Beste 2012
Beste, Amy. "Designers in Film: Goldsholl Associates, the Avant-Garde, and Midcentury Advertising Films." In *Chicago Makes Modern: How Creative Minds Changed Society*. Exh. cat.: School of the Art Institute of Chicago, 59–75. Chicago: University of Chicago Press, 2012.

Bielefelder Schule 2014
Bielefelder Schule: Fotokunst im Kontext. Exh. cat.: Alte Stadtbibliothek Bielefeld. Ed. by Gottfried Jäger and Enno Kaufhold. Heidelberg: Kehrer, 2014.

Black Mountain 2015
Blume, Eugen, Matilda Felix, Gabriele Knapstein, and Catherine Nichols, eds. *Black Mountain: An Interdisciplinary Experiment, 1933–1957*. Exh. cat.: Hamburger Bahnhof Berlin. Leipzig: Spector Books, 2015.

Bossen 1983
Bossen, Howard. *Henry Holmes Smith, Man of Light*. PhD diss. Ann Arbor: UMI Research Press, 1983.

Botar 2014
Botar, Oliver A. I. *Sensing the Future: Moholy-Nagy, die Medien und die Künste*. Exh. cat.: PlugIn ICA, Winnipeg / Bauhaus-Archiv / Museum für Gestaltung, Berlin. Zurich: Lars Müller Publishers, 2014.

Breuer 2012
Breuer, Gerda, ed. *Lehre und Lehrer an der Folkwangschule für Gestaltung in Essen: von den Anfängen bis 1972*. Tübingen: Wasmuth, 2012.

Brochure for Summer School 1940
Summer Session for Men and Women: Mills College, June 23 – August 3 1940. Chicago, 1940.

Brown 2005
Brown, Elspeth. *The Corporate Eye: Photography and the Rationalization of American Commercial Culture*. Baltimore and London: Johns Hopkins University Press, 2005.

C

Cahan 1994
Cahan, Richard. *They All Fall Down: Richard Nickel's Struggle to Save America's Architecture*, Washington DC: Preservation Press, National Trust for Historic Preservation, 1994.

Callahan 1961
Callahan, Harry. *The Multiple Image*. Ed. by Institute of Design, Chicago. Chicago: Press of the Institute of Design, 1961.

Callahan 1976
Szarkowski, John, ed. *Callahan*. Exh. cat.: Museum of Modern Art New York. New York: Aperture, 1976.

Callahan 1980
Callahan, Harry M., and A. R. Ammons. *Water's Edge*. New York: Lyme Callaway Ed., 1980.

Cancellieri 2015
Cancellieri, Agathe. "Traditions et nouvelles visions américaines: 'New Vision in Photography,' le premier séminaire photographique à l'Institute of Design de Chicago en 1946." *Etudes photographiques* 33 (2015): 78–103.

Chancellor 1955
Chancellor, John. "The Rocky Road from the Bauhaus." *Chicago Magazine*, July 1955: 28–35.

Chiarenza 1978
Chiarenza, Carl. *Aaron Siskind and His Critics, 1946–1966*. Exh. cat.: Center for Creative Photography, Tucson. Tucson: University of Arizona, 1978.

Chiarenza 1982
Chiarenza, Carl. *Aaron Siskind: Pleasures and Terrors*. Boston, Little, Brown and Company / Center for Creative Photography, New York. New York, 1982.

Chicago Makes Modern 2012
Jacob, Mary Jane, and Jacquelynn Baas, eds. *Chicago Makes Modern: How Creative Minds Changed Society*. Exh. cat.: School of the Art Institute of Chicago. Chicago: Chicago University Press, 2012.

Chicago's Bauhaus Legacy 2013
Chicago's Bauhaus Legacy: The New Bauhaus School of Design – Institute of Design (Volume Two). Exh. cat.: Ukrainian Institute of Modern Art / Bauhaus Chicago Committee. Chicago, 2013.

Color in Transparency 2006
Fiedler, Jeannine, and Hattula Moholy-Nagy, eds. *László Moholy-Nagy: Color in Transparency. Fotografische Experimente in Farbe 1934–1946*. Exh. cat.: Bauhaus-Archiv / Museum für Gestaltung. Göttingen: Steidl, 2006.

Color Rush 2013
Bussard, Katherine A., et al., eds. *Color Rush: American Color Photography from Stieglitz to Sherman*. Exh. cat.: Milwaukee Art Museum. New York: Aperture, 2013.

Comer/Klochko/Gunderson 2006
Comer, Stephanie, Deborah Klochko, and Jeff Gunderson, eds. *The Moment of Seeing – Minor White at the California School of Fine Arts*. San Francisco: Chronicle Books, 2006.

Crane 1981
Barbara Crane: Photographs 1948–1980. Exh. cat.: Center for Creative Photography, Tucson. Tucson: University of Arizona, 1981.

Crane 2009
Barbara Crane: Challenging Vision. Exh. cat.: Amon Carter Museum, Chicago Cultural Center. Chicago, 2009.

Crane 2010
Barbara Crane: Chicago Loop. Exh. cat.: Museum of Contemporary Photography, Chicago. Chicago, 2002.

Crane 2014
Crane, Barbara. "Some of My Beliefs about Photography and Teaching." In *The Photographer's Playbook*, ed. by Jason Fulford and Gregory Halpern. New York: Aperture, 2014.

D
Dartevelle/Poivert 2009
Dartevelle, Raymond, and Michel Poivert. "Élites économiques et création photographique." *Etudes photographiques* 24 (2009): 2–9.

Das Bauhaus 2005
Das Bauhaus: Weimar, Dessau, Berlin und The New Bauhaus Chicago: Meister-Schüler, Theoretiker und Künstler der Bauhaus-Mappen. Exh. cat.: Galerie Orlando. Zurich, 2005.

Davis 2002
Davis, Keith F. "To Open an Individual Way: Photography at the Institute of Design, 1946–61." In *Taken by Design* 2002, 68–91.

Davis 2012
Davis, Keith F. *The Photographs of Ray K. Metzker*. Exh. cat.: Nelson Atkins Museum of Art, Kansas City / J. Paul Getty Museum, Los Angeles / The Henry Art Gallery, University of Washington, Seattle. New Haven: Yale University Press, 2012.

DeLillo 1998
DeLillo, Don. *Underworld*. New York: Picador, 1998. (1997)

E
Edwards 1959
Edwards, Hugh. *My Camera and I in the Loop: Photographs by Ray Metzker*. Exh. brochure: Art Institute of Chicago. Chicago, 1960.

Edwards/Lien 2004
Edwards, Elizabeth, and Sigrid Lien, eds. *Uncertain images: Museums and the Work of Photographs*. Farnham: Ashgate, 2004.

Ehlers 2004
Ehlers, Carol, et al. *Chicago Photographs*. La Salle Bank Photography Collection. Chicago, 2004.

Elemental Landscapes 2001
Ware, Katherine, ed. *Elemental Landscapes: Photographs by Harry Callahan*. Exh. cat.: Philadelphia Museum of Art. New York: Art Book, 2001.

Engelbrecht 1973
Engelbrecht, Lloyd C. "The Association of Arts and Industries: Background and Origins of the Bauhaus Movement in Chicago." Typescript, PhD diss., University of Chicago, 1973.

Engelbrecht 2002
Engelbrecht, Lloyd C. "Educating the Eye: Photography and the Founding Generation at the Institute of Design, 1937–46." In *Taken by Design* 2002, 34–67.

Entin 2007
Entin, Joseph B. *Sensational Modernism: Experimental Fiction and Photography in Thirties America*. Chapel Hill: University of North Carolina Press, 2007.

Evening Course Brochure 1941/42
Evening Session: School of Design in Chicago. Chicago, 1941.

Evening Course Brochure 1943/44
School of Design in Chicago: Evening Photo Class. Chicago, 1943.

Experiment in Totality 1969
Moholy-Nagy, Sibyl, ed. *Experiment in Totality*. Boston, MIT Press, 1969 (1950).

F
Fay 2015
Fay, Brendan. "How to Hold a Camera: Harry Callahan's Early Abstractions." *History of Photography* 39, no. 2 (2015): 160–76.

G
Grawe 1994
Grawe, Gabriele Diana. "Von der Hochschule für Gestaltung zur Schule des Stils: Facetten der Bauhausrezeption in den USA." In *Bauhaus-Ideen 1919–1994: Bibliografie und Beiträge zur Rezeption des Bauhausgedanken*, ed. by Christina Biundo et al., 116–24. Berlin: Reimer, 1994.

Grawe 2002
Grawe, Gabriele Diana. *Call for action: Mitglieder des Bauhauses in Nordamerika*. Weimar: VDG, 2002.

Grimes 2002
Grimes, John. "Photography on Its Own: The ID in the 1960s." In *Taken by Design* 2002, 152–67.

György Kepes 1977
György Kepes: Malerei, Fotographie, Light Images (Fotogramme, Licht-Bilder), Druckgraphik, Abbildungen (Fotos von Lichtobjekten), Abbildungen von Objekten (Farbdias). Exh. cat.: Künstlerhaus, Gesellschaft bildender Künstler Wiens, Vienna / Bauhaus-Archiv / Museum für Gestaltung, Berlin. Vienna, 1977.

György Kepes 1984
Hoy, Anne H., ed. *György Kepes: Light Graphics*. Exh. cat.: International Center of Photography New York. New York, 1984.

H
Harry Callahan 1951
Pollack, Peter. *Harry Callahan*. Exh. brochure: The Art Institute of Chicago. Chicago, 1951.

Harry Callahan. Photographs in Color 1980
Stern, Sally. *Harry Callahan: Photographs in Color; The Years 1946–1978*. Exh. cat.: Center for Creative Photography, Tucson. Tucson: University of Arizona, 1980.

Harry Callahan 2000
Harry Callahan. Exh. cat.: Fundación La Caixa Barcelona. Barcelona, 2000.

Harry Callahan 2010
Harry Callahan Variations. Exh. cat.: Fondation Henri Cartier Bresson Paris. Göttingen: Steidl, 2010.

Harry Callahan 2013
Luckow, Dirk, and Sabine Schnakenberg, eds. *Harry Callahan – Retrospektive*. Exh. cat.: Haus der Photographie, Deichtorhallen Hamburg/Münchner Stadtmuseum, Sammlung Fotografie, Munich. Heidelberg: Kehrer, 2013.

Haus 1980
Haus, Andreas. *László, Moholy-Nagy: Fotos und Fotogramme*. Munich: Schirmer/Mosel, 1980.

Helmer-Petersen 1960
Helmer-Petersen, Keld. *Chicago: Fragments of a City*. Copenhagen: Hans Reitzel, 1960.

Helmer-Petersen 2007
Keld Helmer-Petersen: Photographs 1941–1995. Kopenhagen: Ejlers, 2007.

Hess 1976
Hess, Thomas B. *Places: Aaron Siskind Photographs*. Light Gallery New York. New York: Farrar, Straus and Giroux, 1976.

Heyne 2003
Heyne, Renate, ed. *Kunst und Fotografie: Floris Neusüss und die Kasseler Schule für Experimentelle Fotografie 1972–2002*. Marburg: Jonas, 2003.

Heyne/Neusüss 1990
Heyne, Renate, and Floris M. Neusüss. *Das Fotogramm in der Kunst des 20. Jahrhunderts: Die andere Seite der Bilder – Fotografie ohne Kamera*. Cologne: Du Mont, 1990.

Heyne/Neusüss 2009
Heyne, Renate, and Floris M. Neusüss. *Moholy-Nagy: The Photograms; Catalogue Raisonné*. Ostfildern: Hatje Cantz, 2009.

I
ID 5 1961
Five Photography Students from the Institute of Design, Illinois Institute of Technology. Special edition: *Aperture* 9, no. 2 (1961). Rochester: Aperture, 1961.

Interior drama 2003
Interior Drama: Aaron Siskind's Photographs of the 1940s. Exh. cat.: Museum of Art, Rhode Island School of Design. Providence, 2003.

Ishimoto 1999
Yasuhiro Ishimoto: A Tale of Two Cities. Exh. cat.: The Art Institute of Chicago. Chicago, 1999.

J
Jäger 2016
Jäger, Gottfried. *Abstrakte, konkrete und generative Fotografie: Gesammelte Schriften*. Ed. by Bernd Stiegler. Paderborn: Wilhelm Fink, 2016.

Jäger/Wessing 1997
Jäger, Gottfried, and Gudrun Wessing, eds. *Über Moholy-Nagy: Ergebnisse aus dem Internationalen Lázló Moholy-Nagy Symposium*. Bielefeld: Kerber, 1997.

Jones 2006
Jones, Julie. "Un art publicitaire? György Kepes au New Bauhaus 1937–1943." *Etudes photographiques* 19 (2006): 46–67.

Jones 2009
Jones, Julie. "L'avant-garde européenne au service du capitalisme: Walter P. Paepcke et le couple art. Commerce aux États-Unis (1930–1950)." *Etudes photographiques* 24 (2009): 42–71.

K
Katsura 2010
Katsura: Picturing Modernism in Japanese Architecture; Photographs by Ishimoto Yasuhiro. Exh. cat.: Museum of Fine Arts Houston. Houston, 2010.

Kenneth Josephson 1983
Kenneth Josephson. Exh. cat.: Museum of Contemporary Art, Chicago. Chicago, 1983.

Kenneth Josephson 2008
Kenneth Josephson: The First Fifty Years. Exh. cat.: Stephen Daiter Gallery. Chicago, 2008.

Kenneth Josephson 2012
Kenneth Josephson: Matthew. Exh. cat.: Stephen Daiter Gallery. Chicago, 2012.

Kenneth Josephson 2014
Kenneth Josephson: Selected Photographs. Berlin: Only Photography, 2014.

Kenneth Josephson 2016
Kenneth Josephson: The Light of Coincidence. Austin: University of Texas Press, 2016.

Kentgens-Craig 1993
Kentgens-Craig, Margret. *Bauhaus-Architektur: Die Rezeption in Amerika, 1919–1936*. Ed. by Stiftung Bauhaus Dessau. Frankfurt am Main: Lang, 1993.

Kentgens-Craig 2003
Kentgens-Craig, Margret. "Transformation einer Idee: Das Bauhaus und Amerika." In *Architektur und Exil: Kulturtransfer und architektonische Emigration, 1930 bis 1950*, ed. by Bernd Nicolai, 115–32. Trier: Porta-Alba, 2003.

Kepes 1960
Kepes, György. *The Visual Arts Today.* Middletown: Wesleyan University Press, 1960.

Kepes 1964
Kepes, György. *Language of Vision.* Chicago: Paul Theobald and Co., 1964.

Kepes 1965a
Kepes, György. *Education of Vision.* New York: G. Braziller, 1965.

Kepes 1965b
Kepes, György, ed. *Light as a Creative Medium*. Exh. cat.: Carpenter Center for the Visual Arts, Cambridge. Cambridge, 1965.

Koenig 1988a
Koenig, Thilo. *Otto Steinerts Konzept 'Subjektive Fotografie' (1951–1958).* Munich: tuduv Verlag, 1988.

Koenig 1988b
Koenig, Thilo. *Subjektive Fotografie in den 50er Jahren*. Stationen der Fotografie 3. Berlin: Nishen, 1988.

Kuhn 1948
Kuhn, Charles C., "America and the Bauhaus." *American-German Review*, December 1948.
Kunstschulreform 1900–1933 1977
Kunstschulreform 1900–1933: Dargestellt vom Bauhaus-Archiv Berlin an den Beispielen Bauhaus Weimar Dessau Berlin – Kunstschule Debschitz München – Frankfurter Kunstschule – Akademie für Kunst und Kunstgewerbe Breslau – Reimann-Schule Berlin. Ed. by Hans Maria Wingler. Berlin: Gebrüder Mann, 1977.

L

L. Moholy-Nagy, 1895–1946 1947
L. Moholy-Nagy, 1895–1946. Exh. cat.: Art Institute of Chicago. Chicago, 1947.

László Moholy-Nagy 2010
László Moholy-Nagy: Kunst des Lichts. Exh. cat.: Martin-Gropius-Bau, Berlin/Círculo de Bellas Artes, Madrid / Gemeentemuseum Den Haag, The Hague. Munich: Hirmer, 2010

Leaflet *ID + IIT* ca. 1956
ID + IIT, Chicago, n.d. [ca. 1956].

Lichtbilder 1987
Buhlmann, Britta E., ed. *Moholy-Nagy: Lichtbilder*. Exh. cat.: Museum Haus Lange Krefeld. Krefeld, 1987.

Light Abstractions 1980
Light Abstractions. Exh. cat.: University of Missouri St. Louis. St. Louis, 1980.

Light and Vision 1994
Daiter, Stephen, ed. *Light and Vision: Photography at the School of Design in Chicago, 1937–1952*. Exh. cat.: Stephen Daiter Gallery, Chicago. Chicago, 1994.

Light Years 2011
Witkovsky, Matthew S., ed. *Light Years: Conceptual Art and the Photograph 1964–1977*. Exh. cat.: The Art Institute of Chicago. Chicago, 2011.

LUMA 2012
LUMA: Modern Photography in the First Half of the 20th Century from the Collection of the Shpilman Institute for Photography. Exh. cat.: Tel Aviv, 2012.

M

Modernist Eye 2000
Modernist Eye: The Art and Design of Nathan Lerner. Exh. cat.: Gallery of Art & Design North Carolina State University, Raleigh / Illinois Art Gallery, James R. Thompson Center / Illinois State Museum. Chicago, 2000.

Moholy-Nagy 1938
Moholy-Nagy, László. *The New Vision.* New York, 1938 [1930].

Moholy-Nagy 1944
Moholy-Nagy, László. "Photography in the Study of Design." *American Annual of Photography* (1944): 158–164.

Moholy-Nagy 1946
Moholy-Nagy, László. "New Education – Organic Approach." *Art and Industry* 40 (1946): 66–77.

Moholy-Nagy 1947
Moholy-Nagy, László. *Vision in Motion*. Chicago: Theobald & Co., 1947.

Moholy-Nagy 1990
Moholy-Nagy: A New Vision for Chicago. Exh. cat.: Illinois State Museum. Chicago: University of Illinois Press, 1990.

Moholy-Nagy Future Present 2016
Witkovsky, Matthew S., Carol S. Eliel, and Karole P. B. Vail, eds. *Moholy-Nagy Future Present*. Exh. cat.: Guggenheim New York / Art Institute of Chicago / Los Angeles County Museum of Art. New Haven and London: Yale University Press, 2016.

Mora 2014
Mora, Gilles. *Aaron Siskind: Une autre réalité photographique.* Exh. cat.: Pavillon Populaire Montpellier. Paris: Hazan, 2014.

More Business 1938
More Business 11, no. 3 (1938) [special edition: New Bauhaus].

Morgan 1974
Morgan, William. *Aaron Siskind: Bucks County; Photographs of Early Architecture*. New York: Horizon Press for the Bucks County Historical Society, 1974.

N

Nathan Lerner 1974
Nathan Lerner: Fotografie am New Bauhaus 1937–1945. Exh. cat.: Bauhaus-Archiv Berlin. Berlin, 1974.

Nathan Lerner 1984
Nathan Lerner: Fifty years of Photographic Inquiry. Exh. cat.: Chicago Public Library. Chicago, 1984.

Nathan Lerner 2008
Nathan Lerner: L'héritage du Bauhaus à Chicago. Exh. cat.: Musée d'art et d'histoire du judaïsme Paris. Paris: Archibooks, 2008.

Neugass 1955
Neugass, Fritz. "Aaron Siskind." *Camera* 34, no. 1 (1955): 2–11.

New Vision 1946
New Vision in Photography: Six Week's Session from July 8 – August 16, 1946; Institute of Design. Chicago, 1946.

Nickel/Siskind 2010
Nickel, Richard, and Aaron Siskind. *The Complete Architecture of Adler & Sullivan.* Chicago: Richard Nickel Committee, 2010.

Objekt + Objektiv = Objektivität? 1991
Objekt + Objektiv = Objektivität? Fotografie an der HfG Ulm 1953–1968. Exh. cat.: HfG-Archiv-Ulm / Bauhaus-Archiv / Museum für Gestaltung, Berlin. Ulm, 1991.

O

Otti 2014
Otti, Margareth. "Vom Schutt zum Schatz: Architekturfotografie im Dienst urbaner Umdeutung am Beispiel von Louis H. Sullivan und Richard Nickel." *Fotogeschichte* 34, no. 131 (2014): 25–34.

P

Photography Handbook 1974
Swedlund, Charles. *Photography / Handbook of History, Materials and Processes.* New York: Holt, Rinehart and Winston, 1974.

Plummer 2002
Plummer, Ellen A. "Photography at the Institute of Design." *History of Photography* 26, no. 4 (2002): 372f.

Pohlad 2000
Pohlad, Mark B. "A Photographic Summit in the Windy City: The Institute of Design's 1946 'New Vision in Photography' Seminar." *History of Photography* 24, no. 2 (2000): 148–54.

Polte 2012
Polte, Maren. *Klasse Bilder: Die Fotografie-ästhetik der "Becher-Schule".* Berlin: Gebrüder Mann, 2012.

R

Raeburn 2006
Raeburn, John. *A Staggering Revolution: A Cultural History of Thirties Photography*. Chicago: University of Illinois Press, 2006.

Ray K. Metzker Light Lines 2008
Ewing, William, and Nathalie Herschdorfer. *Ray K. Metzker Light Lines.* Exh. cat.: Musée de l'Elysée Lausanne. Göttingen: Steidl, 2008

Reid 2015
Reid, Michael. "Convergence/Divergence: Exploring Black Mountain College and Chicago's New Bauhaus / Institute of Design." In *Black Mountain College*. Exh. cat.: Museum and Arts Center. Asheville, 2015.

Rexer 2009
Rexer, Lyle: *The Edge of Vision: The Rise of Abstraction in Photography.* New York: Aperture, 2009.

Rhem 2003
Rhem, James Louis. *Aaron Siskind.* London: Phaidon, 2003.

Rice/Steadman 1975
Rice, Leland, and David Steadman. *Photographs by Moholy-Nagy from the Collection of William Larson*. Claremont: Galleries of the Claremont Colleges, 1975.

Richter 2016
Richter, Gerhard. *Verwaiste Hinterlassenschaften: Formen gespentischen Erbens.* Berlin: Matthes & Seitz, 2016.

Rössler 2009
Bauhauskommunikation: Innovative Strategien im Umgang mit Medien, interner und externer Öffentlichkeit. Ed. by Patrick Rössler for the Bauhaus-Archiv Berlin. Berlin: Gebrüder Mann, 2009.

Rosenberg 1959
Rosenberg, Harold. *Aaron Siskind: Photographs*. New York: Horizon Press, 1959.

S

Saletnik/Schuldenfrei 2009
Saletnik, Jeffrey, and Robin Schuldenfrei, eds. *Bauhaus Construct: Fashioning Identity, Discourse and Modernism*. London: Routledge, 2009.

Salvesen 2006
Salvesen, Britt. *Harry Callahan: The Photographer at Work*. Exh. cat.: Center for Creative Photography, Tucson / The Art Institute of Chicago. New Haven: Yale University Press, 2006.

Sayag 1995
Sayag, Alain. *László Moholy-Nagy: Compositions Lumineuses, 1922–1943; Photogrammes des collections du Musée national d'art moderne –Centre de création industrielle*. Exh. cat.: Centre Georges Pompidou, Paris / Museum Folkwang, Essen. Paris: Centre Pompidou, 1995.

School Brochure 1937
The New Bauhaus: American School of Design, Chicago, 1937.

School Brochure 1938
The New Bauhaus: American School of Design [reprint with altered date of publication: 1938].

School Brochure 1939/40
School of Design. Chicago, 1939.

School Brochure 1940/41
School of Design in Chicago: L. Moholy-Nagy, Director. Chicago, 1940.

School Brochure 1944
Institute of Design formerly School of Design. Chicago, 1944.

School Brochure 1948
The Institute of Design Chicago. Chicago, 1948.

School Brochure 1950
Bulletin of Illinois Institute of Technology, Institute of Design, Chicago, 1950.

School Brochure *Your career in design* ca. 1956
Your career in design. Chicago, n.d. [ca. 1956].

School Brochure ca. 1956
Institute of Design of Illinois Institute of Technology. Chicago, n.d. [ca. 1956].

School Brochure after 1966
Institute of Design, Illinois Institute of Technology, Chicago, n.d. [after 1966].

School Brochure 1974
ID IIT. Chicago, 1974.

School Catalogue ca. 1950
id. Chicago, n.d. [ca. 1950].

Schuldenfrei 2012
Schuldenfrei, Robin. "Assimilating Unease: Moholy-Nagy and the Wartime / Postwar Bauhaus in Chicago." In *Atomic dwelling*, ed. by Robin Schuldenfrei, 87–126. London: Routledge, 2012.

Schuman 2010
Schuman, Aaron. "Mike Mandel: 'The Baseball Photographer Trading Cards,'" *Aperture* 200 (2010): 60–63.

Selz/Koppe 1954
Selz, Peter, and Richard Koppe. *The Education of the Art Teacher* [reprinted in: *School Arts*, 1954].

Shadow Catchers 2010
Shadow Catchers: Camera-less Photography. Ed. by Martin Barnes. Exh. cat.: Victoria and Albert Museum London. London, 2010.

Siegel 1965
Siegel, Arthur, ed. *Chicago's Famous Buildings: A Photographic Guide to the City's Architectural Landmarks and Other Notable Buildings.* Chicago: University of Chicago Press, 1965.

Siegel 2002
Siegel, Elizabeth. "Vision in Motion: Film and Photography at the Institute of Design." In *Taken by Design* 2002, 214–23.

Siegel 2016
Siegel, Elizabeth. "The Modern Artist's New Tools." In *Moholy-Nagy Future Present* 2016. 223–34.

Siskind 1956
Siskind, Aaron. "Credo" in "What is Modern Photography?" *Spectrum* 6, no. 2 (1956): 27–28

Siskind/Callahan 1956
Siskind, Aaron, and Harry Callahan. "Learning Photography at the Institute of Design." *Aperture* 4 (1956): 147.

Solomon-Godeau 1983
Solomon-Godeau, Abigail. "The Armed Vision Disarmed: Radical Formalism from Weapon to Style." *Afterimage* 11, no. 6 (1983) [reprinted in *The Contest of Meaning: Critical Histories of Photography*. Ed. by Richard Bolton. Boston: MIT Press, 1989, 83–107].

Starburst 2010
Starburst: Color Photography in America 1970–1980. Exh. cat.: Cincinnati Art Museum. Ostfildern: Hatje Cantz, 2010.

Stein 2014
Stein, Emma. "László Moholy-Nagy and Chicago's War Industry: Photographic Pedagogy at the New Bauhaus." *History of Photography* 38, no. 4 (2014): 398–417.

Subjektive Fotografie 1951
Subjektive Fotografie. Exh. cat.: Staatliche Schule für Kunst und Handwerk Saarbrücken. Saarbrücken, 1951.

Subjektive Photographie 1984
Eskildsen, Ute. *Subjektive Photographie: Bilder der 50er Jahre*. Exh. cat.: Museum of Modern Art San Francisco, Sarah Campbell Blaffer Gallery, Museum Folkwang. Essen: Fotografische Sammlung im Museum Folkwang, 1984.

Swedlund 1973
Swedlund, Charles A. *Photographs: Multiple Exposures with the Figure*. Cobden: Anna Press, 1973.

Swedlund 2010
Charles Swedlund. Circa 1955. Exh. cat.: Stephen Daiter Gallery. Chicago, 2010.

T

Taken by Design 2002
Travis, David, and Elizabeth Siegel, eds. *Taken by Design: Photographs from the Institute of Design 1937–1971*. Exh. cat.: Art Institute of Chicago / San Francisco Museum of Modern Art / Philadelphia Museum of Art. Chicago: University of Chicago Press, 2002.

The City Lost and Found 2014
The City Lost and Found: Capturing New York, Chicago, and Los Angeles, 1960–1980. Exh. cat.: The Art Institute of Chicago / Princeton University Art Museum. Princeton, 2014.

The Golden Decade 2016
Ball, Ken, and Victoria Whyte Ball. *The Golden Decade: Photography at the California School of Fine Arts, 1945–1955.* Göttingen: Steidl, 2016.
The New Bauhaus School of Design in Chicago 1993

The New Bauhaus School 1993
Boxer, Adam J., ed. *The New Bauhaus School of Design in Chicago: Photographs 1937–1944*. Exh. cat.: Banning & Associates, New York / Illinois Art Gallery, Chicago / Ansel Adams Center for Photography, San Francisco. New York: Distributed Art Publishers, 1993.

The New Spirit in American Photography 1985
The New Spirit in American Photography. Gyorgy Kepes, Henry Holmes Smith, Harry Callahan, Art Sinsabaugh, Nathan Lerner, Arthur Siegel, Aaron Siskind. Exh. cat.: Krannert Art Museum, Champaign / Bowdoin College Museum of Art, Brunswick. Brunswick, 1985.

The New Vision 1982
Grimes, John, and Charles Traub. *The New Vision: Forty Years of Photography at the Institute of Design*. Exh. cat.: Millerton. New York: Aperture, 1982.

The People's America 1997
Cookman, Claude Hubert, ed. *The People's America: Farm Security Administration Photographs (1935–1943); Selections from the Henry Holmes Smith Archive*. Exh. cat.: Indiana University Art Museum. Bloomington, 1997.

This Was the Photo League 2001
Tucker, Ann Wilkes, Stephen Daiter, and Claire Cass. *This Was the Photo League: Compassion and the Camera from the Depression to the Cold War*. Exh. cat.: Stephen Daiter Gallery. Chicago, 2001.

Together Again 1996
Together Again: Ishimoto, Jachna, Josephson, Metzker, Sterling, Swedlund. Exh. cat.: Gallery312, Chicago. Chicago, 1996.

Traub 1982
Traub, Charles. "Photographic Education comes of Age." In *The New Vision* 1982, 23–72.

Turner 2013
Turner, Fred. *The Democratic Surround: Multimedia and American Liberalism from World War II to the Psychedelic Sixties*. Chicago and London: University of Chicago Press, 2013.

V

Vail 2016
Vail, Karole P. B. "Bridging the Atlantic: Moholy-Nagy at Exhibition in the United States." In *Moholy-Nagy Future Present* 2016, 255–66.

W

Warren 2006
Warren, Lynne. *Encyclopedia of Twentieth Century Photography.* New York, 2006.

Wingler 1975
Wingler, Hans Maria. *Das Bauhaus 1919–1933: Weimar, Dessau, Berlin und die Nachfolge in Chicago seit 1937*. Cologne: DuMont, 1975.

Witkovsky 2009
Witkovsky, Matthew. "Circa 1930: Art History and the New Photography." *Etudes photographiques* 23 (2009): 116–38.

Z

Zelluloid 2010
Hollein, Max, and Esther Schlicht, eds. *Zelluloid: Film ohne Kamera*. Exh. cat.: Schirn-Kunsthalle Frankfurt. Bielefeld: Kerber, 2010.

CREDITS

Bauhaus-Archiv Berlin
(Reproductions: Markus Hawlik, Felix Jork and Norbert Schropp) pp. 1-5 (2016/24.9); 10–11 (2013/160, 2013/161/Rebecca Dyer Szabo); 12 (2013/194.1); 18 (8456); 19 l. (1187 Archiv Moholy-Nagy M 8); 19 r. (891); 20-21 (Rara BC Chicago 10); 25 (2015/105); 26 (3872); 28 (2018/4); 38 (t.: Selz, b.: 2016/1550); 43 t. (2018/17.5); 44 (7689); 45 (5689); 46 (8219); 47 (8220); 49 (3863); 50-53 (F5034; 5737; 7094; 7095; 3866/1); 55 (3866/2); 56 (F8578/25); 57 (F8587/26); 58 (8213); 59 (2016/1566); 60 (F8587/23); 61 (3425/29); 62 (7414/2), 63 (5744); 64 (5738); 66 (Obj. Id. 113273); 70 (Obj. Id. 118109); 78 (6526/10); 79 (l.: 2016/1525, r.: 7812/14); 80 (7812/24); 81 (2016/1532); 82 (7414/3); 83 (2016/1523); 84 (2018/2); 85 (t.l: 2018/8, t.r.: 2018/9, b.l.: 2018/7); 86 (F8538/42); 87 (F8538/43); 88 (2016/1554); 89 (2016/1544); 90 (2016/1548); 91 (8252); 92 (2016/1502); 93 (2015/51.2); 94 (9717); 95 (9713); 96 (9715); 97 (9716); 98; 99 b.; 100-109; 110 (t.: 6708/2, m.: 1999/27.1, b. F8541/20); 121 (Obj. Id. 118110); 126 (9712); 127 (3861); 128 (9718); 129 (9719), 130 (2015/54); 131 (Obj. Id. 118111); 134; 136-144; 145 (Koppe); 146 (9707); 148 (9708); 151 (9706); 152 (2005/4.12); 153 (2005/4.8); 154 (7414/1); 158 (5408/2); 159 (5408/3); 160 (8564/1); 161 (3873); 163 (Obj. Id. 118112); 177; 184 (2015/104); 199 (2016/1537).
–The Albert Szabo and Brenda Dyer Szabo Collection: pp. 18 (2016/1217); 99 t. (2016/1187.1); 105 (2016/1336); 133 r. (2016/1228.4), 149 (2016/1266); 150 (l.: 2016/1228.2, r.: 2016/1228.6); 155 (2016/1333); 156; 177 (t.l.: 2016/1228.8, t.r.: 2016/1228.9, b.l.: 2016/1228.5, b.r.: 2016/1228.7).

Bauhaus Chicago Foundation: pp. 24, 48, 65, 69, 162.

Chicago History Museum: pp. 31 (1980.0024-18.8), 156 (NK1160 .S7).

University Archives and Special Collections, Paul V. Galvin Library, Illinois Institute of Technology: pp. 36, 41, 65, 69.

Museum of Contemporary Photography, Columbia College: pp. 123 (2003:55.6 Gift of Manny and Skippy Gerard); 164 (EL2003:206 Extended loan of the Baum Family Collection); 165 (1982:73); 166-167 (t.: 1982:58, b.: 2001:133.5 / both Gift of Jack A. Jaffe); 169 (1980:22); 178 (r.: 1981:118, l.: 1981:104 / both Gift of Roberta and Jack A. Jaffe); 179 (t.: 1981:116, b.: 1981:114, r.: 1981:106 / all three Gift of Roberta and Jack A. Jaffe); 194 - 197 (1986:232.70, 1986:232.79, 1986:232.36, 1986:232.28 / all four Gift of Jeanne L. and Richard S. Press).

Stephen Daiter Gallery: pp. 31 t., 48 t., 76, 111, 112, 117, 118, 122, 124, 125, 133 l..

The Art Institute of Chicago: pp. 54 (The Art Institute of Chicago, Restricted gift of Bernard M. and Caryl H. Susman, 2001.193 / image: bpk / The Art Institute of Chicago / Art Resource, NY); 157 (The Art Institute of Chicago, Gift of Richard L. Menschel, 1977.665 / image: Aaron Siskind Foundation, NY); 180 and 181 (The Art Institute of Chicago, Gift of Arthur Siegel, 1956.1073 and 1956.1074 / images: bpk / The Art Institute of Chicago / Art Resource, NY / Arthur S. Siegel); pp. 170, 173, 174 and 176.

Special Collections and University Archives Department Richard J. Daley Library, University of Illinois at Chicago: p. 48 b.r. (ID papers 3.78).

COPYRIGHT

THANKS

WE THANK OUR LENDERS

in Chicago:
Bauhaus Chicago Foundation: T. Paul Young
Chicago Film Archives: Brian Belak, Nancy Watrous
Chicago History Museum: Julie Katz, Ellen Keith
Museum of Contemporary Photography, Columbia College: Karen Irvine, Kristin Taylor
Special Collections and University Archives Department, Richard J. Daley Library, University of Illinois at Chicago: Valerie A. Harris
Stephen Daiter Gallery: Agathe Cancellieri, Stephen Daiter
The Art Institute of Chicago: Natasha Derrickson, Barbara Diener, Elizabeth Siegel, Matthew S. Witkovsky
University Archives and Special Collections, Paul V. Galvin Library, Illinois Institute of Technology: Greer Martin, Ralph Pugh, Adam Strohm

and also
Kunstbibliothek, Staatliche Museen zu Berlin: Joachim Brand, Katrin Käding

IMPRINT

This book was published on the occasion of the exhibition *New Bauhaus Chicago: Experiment Photography and Film*, presented from 15 November 2017 to 5 March 2018 at the Bauhaus-Archiv/Museum für Gestaltung in Berlin.

CATALOGUE
Editor: Kristina Lowis for the Bauhaus-Archiv/Museum für Gestaltung, Berlin
Project editors: Kristina Lowis and Sibylle Hoiman
Copyediting (Germ.): Kristina Lowis, Sibylle Hoiman and Astrid Bähr
Copyediting (Engl.): Michael Wetzel
Translation: Sonja Knecht (into German)
Michael Wetzel (into English)
Design: Birgit Schlegel, gewerkdesign, Berlin
Project management: Rainer Arnold, Hirmer
Production: Hannes Halder, Hirmer
Lithography: mediateam GmbH, Munich
Printing and binding: medialis Offsetdruck GmbH, Berlin
Paper: 170 g/m² Condat matt Périgord
Printed in Germany

Bibliographic information published by the Deutsche Nationalbibliothek: The Deutsche Nationalbibliothek lists this publication in the Deutsche Nationalbibliografie; detailed bibliographic data are available on the Internet at https://portal.dnb.de.

ISBN: 978-3-7774-2937-3

Published by
Hirmer Verlag GmbH
Nymphenburger Straße 84
80636 Munich (Germany)
www.hirmerverlag.de

EXHIBITION

Idea and project management: Annemarie Jaeggi and Sibylle Hoiman
Concept, coordination, texts: Kristina Lowis
Design and production management: Jens Imig, Birgit Schlegel, Bianca Mohr and Marie Uhle, gewerkdesign
Translation: Michael Wetzel
Registrar: Monika Tritschler
Exhibition installation: Falko Riepe
Preparator: Kruse AT
Print production: Atelier Köbbert
Lighting design: Leif Christensen
Conservation: Antje Möller-Holzhauser
Building technician: Carsten Klezath
Media technician: GATE and Filmkunsttechnik FKT16
Technical support: Berthold Eberhard
Photo archive: Sabine Hartmann
Office: Sulaine Herbig
Public relations: Dina Blauhorn, Ulrich Weigand
Education program: Jugend im Museum e. V. Programm Bauhaus Agenten

This exhibition project is part of the preparations for the 100th anniversary of the Bauhaus in 2019 and is supported by the Kulturstiftung des Bundes and the Federal State of Berlin.

www.bauhaus100.de

Senatsverwaltung
für Kultur und Europa

(→ 208)
Robert Stiegler
Full Circle, 1968
image from the digitized film

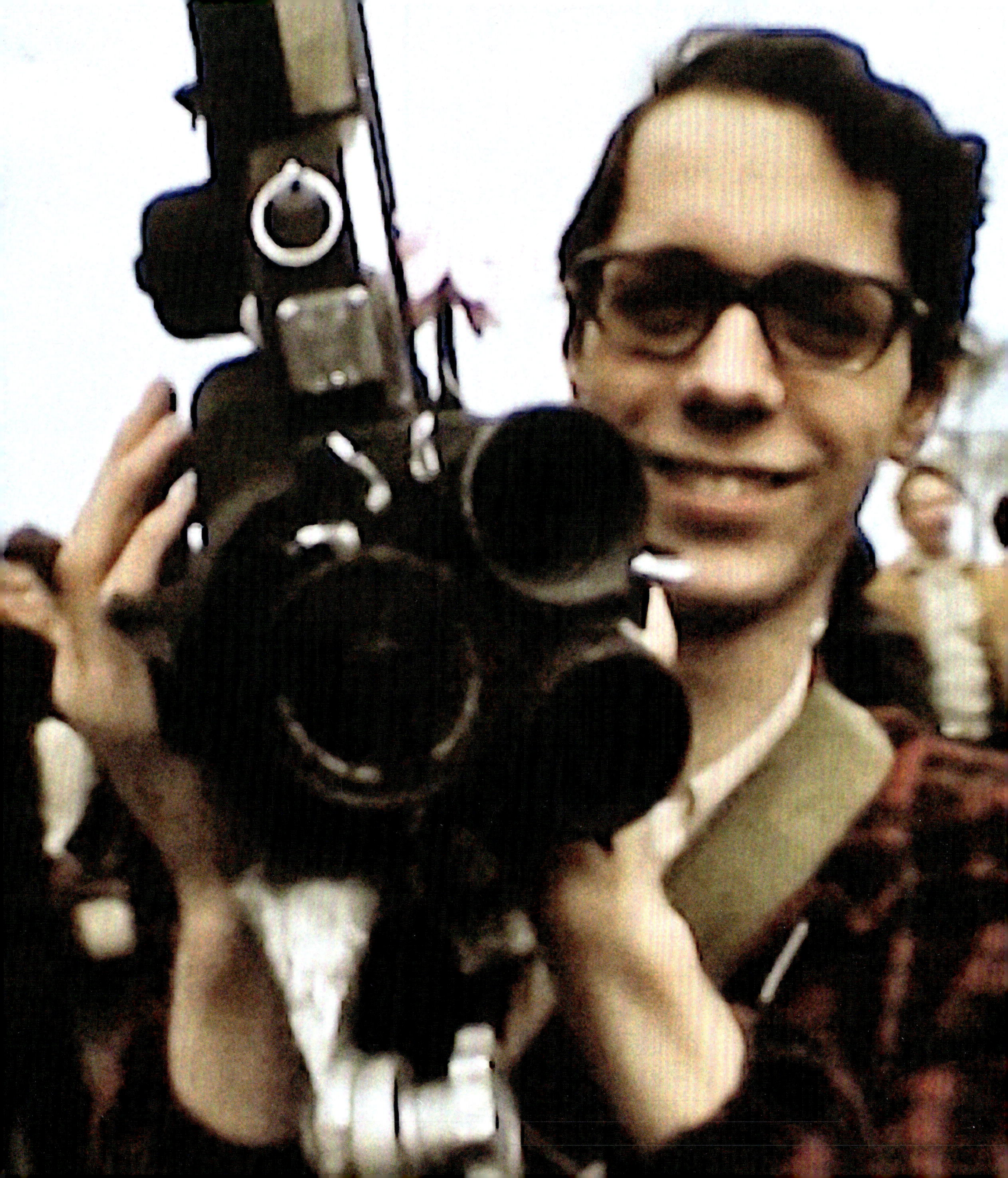